INTRODUCTION

How many lives is a movie star allowed?

The face on the poster has been following us around for four years now. Though thickening out it's still recognisable from the blue eyes, butterfly lips and dimple-bisected chin of yesterday. It's a face that shares its meanings with the public more readily than almost any other modern star's. And it's a face we lingered on less than we might the last time round, since in the seventies all the arrows of the era were pointing at other parts of that amazing box-office machinery called John Travolta.

At his legs, which were dancing. At his clothes, which were high disco fashion (or dictated it). At his hair, restyled for each movie. Even finally his physique, re-tooled from neck to ankle in a prodigal Pygmalion madness by director Sylvester Stallone for the *Saturday Night Fever* sequel *Staying Alive*.

Could such a star – such a seventies-specific heavenly body – come back if fashion ever chased him away? If so, in what shape?

Like many westerners I was taught that great F Scott Fitzgerald dictum, 'There are no second acts in American lives.' When *Pulp Fiction* came along, it seemed to scoff. No second acts? – then how come the curtain had risen on a new instalment of a nearly forgotten life? We knew it *had* risen because we were sitting right there in the front stalls, circa 1994, watching a scene destined to become a classic.

Two gangsters are driving through Los Angeles. One says to the other, 'You know what they call a quarter pounder with cheese in France?' The other, after some banter, says no. The first man

says, with grin drawn back like a bowstring and voice spreading in lazy, tickled delight, 'A Roy-ale with Chee-ese.' 'Royale with Cheese,' murmurs the other, reverencing the louche and luminous mystery.

This scene provoked euphoric giggles across the movie world, for the perfect match between the Dadaist inconsequence of its dialogue and the cool grandeur of its delivery.

John Travolta was back, doing more with less (once again) than almost any other actor around. Since *Pulp Fiction* he has tackled every role a demon casting agent could dream up, from heroin-addicted gangster to missile-stealing Major, from angel to President, and he still hasn't had a serious stumble. Instead moviehouses are filling with new converts – people who have barely heard of *Saturday Night Fever* or *Grease* – slipping in to watch this spry fortysomething give acting lessons to whippersnappers like Christian Slater and Nicolas Cage.

Fitzgerald's saying hasn't really been disproved at all, though. What makes Travolta's comeback special is that it isn't a second act. It's a third. He missed the middle one completely. For ten years he was out-for-the-count in Hollywood, an ex-wonderboy wondering why his fee had fallen from $4 million per film to $150,000 and why he was making films about dogs, orphans and talking babies.

Director Quentin Tarantino, who reintroduced Travolta to grown-ups, thinks the actor's talent never wavered. His curse was to have been the talisman of an epoch.

'The whole teenybopper-slash-disco stigma weighed John's career down tremendously. Even if you did like him, at a certain point in the eighties you couldn't admit to it. Because you weren't just talking about an actor, you were talking about a figurehead for something that was despised, disco.'

That gap in the career, however, is as fascinating as the career itself. Fame's stories are often seamless, characterless trajectories: they have no second act because they are one interminable first act. The spotlit hero seldom excites any seditious speculation over what might happen if the lights were switched off and the audience left him in mid-speech. This book tries not just to fill the gap in Travolta's story but to suggest that the gap was essential. If he

wasn't earning, he was learning. If he wasn't making good films, he was recharging for the good films that might yet come.

Though Travolta bounced back, however, he has suffered ever since from the downside of a second coming. It starts to seem the *only* significant talking point. The biographer comes to dread the word 'comeback': it lies in ambush in every press cutting, is scrambled into action by every interviewee. But the star of *Grease, Urban Cowboy, Blow Out, Face/Off* and *Primary Colors* is a man of many comebacks: almost no other leading actor brings such fresh quirkiness to his films. Re-tuning the Travolta essentials – that soothing but jaunty street slur, those looks of throwaway wonder or caustic appraisal, the loping walk that can be jived up for *Grease* or grunged down for *Pulp Fiction* – his characters combine the high definition of caricature with a textured humanity.

Writing about Travolta, I found myself following directions exactly opposite to those dictated by my last biographical subject Arnold Schwarzenegger. The Austrian hulk planned his movie career and chiselled his image with the monomania of the muscle sculptor he had been. He became a commodity star who sold one commodity, the implacable body.

Travolta is a more subtle phenomenon: a pliant actor and human being with unaccountable mystical trimmings – air and fire to Arnie's earth and heavy water. He gathers heat and light from diverse sources: flying, acting, mimicry, writing, healing. He also devotes himself to Scientology, a faith about as attractive (and accessible) to the ignorant outsider as Symbionese Liberationism.

An early question for the book was: Can a sane or intelligent person believe in this creed? John Travolta left school at sixteen and may have left it mentally and spiritually even before that. His own perspective on culture and learning is summed up by his Huck Finn-ish statement in 1983, 'Both those things are easily handled – just pick up some books and read a dictionary.'

Huck Finn, though, is no bad model for an aspiring movie star. A limber naivety and mental wanderlust, eager to raft down any river of the imagination including the tributaries of religious cultism, can be actorly assets. The ideal movie star may be entirely formed of negative capability, open to all the right influences

at the right time. Indeed Travolta has referred to himself as a 'sponge'.

If an actor is open to whims, crazes and mystical influences *off*screen, all the better for his onscreen talent. It should be part of the natural order that Jane Fonda mutates from a leftwing campaigner to a First Lady of media capitalism; that Marlon Brando vacillates between being an Indian Rights activist and a student of advanced inactivity in Tahiti; that Shirley MacLaine incarnates a witty, hard-nosed attitude to life and Hollywood one moment and reports back from the outer limits the next.

Never mind Fitzgerald: the movie performer's text should come from another American bard, Walt Whitman. 'Do I contradict myself? Very well then, I contradict myself. I am large, I contain multitudes.'

The actor's gift and mission are not to prescribe or inscribe, but to be inscribed upon. Like a handful of stars who first became famous by playing exposed-nerve youngsters – James Dean, Montgomery Clift, Brando – Travolta gives the impression of having wandered straight from his life onto the movie set. The osmosis between life and art is apparent in his first major role, in *Saturday Night Fever*, where you virtually *see* the crisis he was going through after the death of his real-life lover Diana Hyland.

Defencelessness and directness are his yin and yang. The baby who thinks aloud in *Look Who's Talking* is no bad symbol for the unformed innocence Travolta displayed in his early films and to a degree still radiates today, even when playing showy anti-heroes. Mixed Irish and Italian ancestry may also have helped in forming a gypsy sensibility that combines the sensitive and scatterbrained, and that seems permanently *depaysé*.

The only snag with this mobility and transparency is that almost anyone can shine a light through you as you move about: from friends or acquaintances who inspire you with characteristics for a role, to the director filling you with his vision, to the religionists using you to radiate their propaganda.

Finding world fame at twenty-three can induce a kind of schizophrenia. People treat you, the star, as a demigod or prophet and want to hear your wisdom. So you in turn defer to a higher authority like Scientology, first to get these new disciples off your back and onto someone else's, then because human beings cannot long endure being gods, especially if they have to exercise childlike qualities during working hours.

Something else is born of this dialectic between innocence and the burdens or impostures of fame. A sense of 'camp'.

Travolta has a gift for bringing life to 'retro' heroes, from his Brooklyn teenager blissed out on the Bee Gees (who in 1977 were already dangerously close to cultural extinction) to the scrapbook gangsters of *Pulp Fiction* and *Get Shorty*. Combine that with his readiness to plunge into cornball movies, at least in his early and middle careers – no less than four Travolta films feature in one leading concordance of bad-movies-we-love – and the whiff of kitsch is never far off. *Saturday Night Fever* itself passed swiftly into camp immortality, helped by the spoof disco sequence in *Airplane!* And what other top star could claim that five of his first ten films were made by gay directors?

The spirit of camp is nourished by the contradiction we sense between Travolta's kid-next-door naturalism and the *outré* characters he is increasingly hired to play. His performances in *Pulp Fiction*, *Broken Arrow* or *Face/Off* have something of the small boy dressing up, which Travolta did as the son of a drama-teaching mother and the brother of acting-mad siblings.

The perpetual child in Travolta makes his years in the movie wilderness even more intriguing. How *did* he react when his vocational costume trunk was taken away? Did he cleave more closely to support systems and surrogate parents, like Scientology. Did he spend more time in escapist toyrooms – flying aeroplanes, eating chocolate ice-creams? Or did he dimly discern that in the hands of the public he had been too long yoyo-ing between infantilism and near-godhead, and that he ought to start maturing?

I came to wonder if I was looking not so much at Huck Finn as at cinema's Peter Pan.

He flies (count the private planes).

He fights for good against evil (albeit in that strange ethical universe founded by L. Ron Hubbard).

And he came back, in a way no other actor has before or possibly will again, from the Neverneverland of the Hollywood waste tip.

PART ONE

PRELUDE

LOST IN NEW JERSEY

New Jersey is a terrifying state. It was clearly designed as an oubliette for the biographer. All the way from Newark Airport where you can drive around in circles for hapless hours until being rescued by police interception, to John Travolta's home town of Englewood, near the bluffs of the Palisades that frown majestically across the Hudson at Manhattan, there are possibilities for getting lost.

Dishevelled industrial vistas: maniac turnpikes; trucks driven by registered road-ragers; and to your right as you swing closer to the Big Apple, those mosquito-haunted reedfields that Woody Allen tramped through in *Broadway Danny Rose*, rightly comparing them to Vietnam.

Then you turn sharp right just before the George Washington Bridge, that double-decker span that would kthunk-kthunk you into New York, and find yourself in a sylvan town where every alternate street should have been named after Rip Van Winkle. The other street names could have been shared beween Norman Rockwell and Frank Capra.

The main street itself, Palisades Avenue, dives gently out of beech woods like a ski slope – one that has become flanked by bookstores, cafes and antique shops over the gentrifying years. Since the avenue runs roughly east to west it is also perfectly made for metaphors about ski-jumping towards Hollywood.

But metaphors don't put food on the table. My arrival in Englewood fired the starting gun to what biographers know as *IRS*: Initial Research Stress.

What to do?

Where to go?

Whom to accost?

Every biography in its first research stages stares at its author and taunts, 'How will you start? You have used up half your advance just to get here. Night is closing in. Get on.'

I began by tracking my way to the house where Travolta grew up, down a side street near Palisades Avenue. I had planned to get to 135 Morse Place in daylight but at five on a November afternoon it was dusking up in the broad, maple-lined street flanked by weatherworn frame houses. The Travolta home, long since abandoned by the Travoltas, is now a three-storey sub-Gothic pile in a state of scenic decrepitude.

That first evening I stared at it trying to imagine how anyone born there could have leaped up, flown to Hollywood, danced and sung people off the map, and then, after an intermission for career collapse, come back to *act* people off the map.

I wasn't allowed to meditate long. A man's face came to the door and peered through the storm netting at my car parked on the other side of the street. I could see only his head and shoulders, but the carriage of those shoulders suggested he might be carrying a shotgun.

I decided it was time to check into the hotel I had booked in New York.

When I returned to 135 Morse Place the next morning it had changed. In daylight you saw – more clearly, less mythopoeically – the peeling paint, dingy woodwork and faded chocolate-brown trim. I knocked at the house and received no answer. But I noted the National Rifle Association sticker on the door and the distressed furniture on the porch. This was a house clearly owned by a Gary Larson character. I imagined elk antlers on the wall inside, or more sinister trophies in bone and cartilage.

My courage was up by now. So I knocked, on a what-the-hell principle, at the next-door neighbour's house.

This proved the starting rap to three days of shameless but not fruitless doorstepping. The neighbour proved welcoming beyond my dreams. An elderly, large-built motormouth of Polish-Romanian origin, he showed me the Travolta family photographs

he kept and nattered about 'Johnny.' He had been the guardian of 135 Morse Place during the untenanted years between the Travolta family's departure for California in the late seventies and the house's requisition by 'Larson Man'.

During those years Eddie Costenuic (pronounced Kostenik) shooed away overzealous fans who picked at the gingerbread house and processed J.T.'s fanmail: 'about 6,000 letters a week.'

When not chatting to Costenuic on his porch, I visited Travolta's schools, quizzed shopkeepers and telephoned his relatives. I was impressed most of all by Joanne Calabro, the Board of Education supervisor. Apart from helping me, in a husky New Jersey twang, with dates and details of Travolta's schooling, she looked as if she should be in a movie herself. Skintight black velvet blouse, shiny black hair-brace, jewelled wristwatch wrapped round an extended black sleeve: every suburban man's illicit dream of Spiderwoman.

Shopkeepers I met had all known the Travoltas. Even when I buried myself in the microfilm section of the Engelwood newspaper library, the man handing me the spools said: 'I knew the Travoltas. I used to run a liquor store. The parents used to come in and show me photos of their kids. They showed *everyone* photos of their kids.'

The only wall of defence was presented to me by the relatives. John should be proud of them. Man, woman and child, they held fast against talking. Travolta's cousin Maryann declined to come to the phone, even though her policeman husband had rashly given me their home number when I cornered him in the Englewood precinct. John's aunt Evelyn reluctantly agreed to my telephone request to visit her, then refused to come to the door when I rang the bell. John's other aunt Mildred said over the telephone, in a frail but declarative voice, 'I don't give out any information about the children. That's why they love me. John's a wonderful, wonderful boy. That's all I can say.'

I soon realised that this loving solidarity stretched even beyond the film star's family.

'You're not really going to write this book about Travolta?' Pauline Kael asked me a few days later. I had driven to Massachusetts to interview the famed ex-critic of the *New*

Yorker on a parallel mission for my newspaper. We were sitting in her rambling woodframe home over two cups of coffee. Though frail now with Parkinson's Disease – the hands flutter a little, the astringent Berkeley twang guards its energy – she was for years the intelligentsia's top cheerleader for a star she first lauded in *Saturday Night Fever*.

Randomly, I gabbled to her of the fascination for the film critic of taking on a reporter's role and exchanging, however briefly, the lofty judgment for the salesman's foot in the door. I also said the advantage of an unauthorised biography, which to judge by the Travolta clan's response the book would be, was that a writer did not have to be sycophantic about his subject.

'Oh, but you wouldn't be negative about Travolta, would you?' she said, with every appearance of alarm.

At that moment I sensed what would be the true difficulty with a Travolta book. Everyone, including the acerbic Kael, is in love with him.

I realised this more with every person I spoke to and every magazine or newspaper article I scanned. Even the hardboiled men and women of counterculture rags like *Rolling Stone* seemed to succumb. The interviewer begins by coming on strong, launching at Travolta the required provocations about Scientology, sex or whatever, then gradually backs away, finally melting into a goo of warm feeling.

Has John Travolta always been lovable? Did he arrange things this way or can't he help it?

It seemed best to begin at the beginning.

1

ENGLEWOOD TALES

Gene-blending is a strange science, like that of a blindfolded man mixing cocktails. No set of ancestral ingredients could seem less calculable than John Travolta's. His Irish mother Helen, born Burke, set a record for swimming the Hudson River in 1932, performed on radio with a singing group called the Sunshine Sisters and later acted, taught acting and produced plays. These included no less than seven stagings of Thornton Wilder's *Our Town*, for one of which she wrote to Wilder asking where to put the chorus. The playwright, wrote back helpfully and signed himself 'Thornton'.

John's father Salvatore, nicknamed Sal or Sam, was burly and athletic, the son of Sicilian-Neapolitan immigrants. Once a semiprofessional football quarterback, he had helped coach the New York Yankees under famed trainer Vince Lombardo. Helen always said he looked like Cary Grant. Photographs suggest he looked like Aldo Ray with a touch of Ernest Borgnine.

In their romance they played tag with American economic history. They met in the year of the Wall Street crash, 1929, courted for eight years during the Depression, then married in 1937 with the blessing of Roosevelt's New Deal. It was not quite upward mobility to station themselves in Englewood – ten miles from New York's Times Square and the same in the other direction from Sam's job running the Travolta Tyre Exchange in verdant Hillsdale – but it was a decent bid for midstate self-esteem.

Englewood in the fifties had a population of 25,000. It had spread outwards into middle- and working-class residential belts from a

core of rich estate owners. The wealthy Lindberghs had settled there after a life of chequered celebrity, ranging from solo Atlantic flights to being victims of America's most famous babynapping case. And Lindbergh's father-in-law Senator Dwight H. Morrow, ambassador and millionaire, founded and gave his name to the local high school, a gaunt handsome *alma mater* resembling a British public school. (It can be seen, with fictionalised name, in the film *Running on Empty* where River Phoenix plays a pupil). Sports stars and even movie stars, like Eddie Murphy, have made homes in Englewood.

Back then 135 Morse Place belonged to a houseproud family. It was a modest suburban dream of sky-blue exterior panelling set off by a dark blue awning that sheltered the large porch. The porch in turn sheltered a neat wicker table, a window-box with red geraniums and a wooden white-painted rocking chair. Ripple-dissolving into the house's interior, we can tour the Travolta family's paintings and antiques: an 18th-century hunting print, a still life of roses painted by Helen's father, a framed reproduction of Andrew Wyeth's 'Christine's World', and the 19th-century carved Czech chest that would be so grievously gnawed in later years by Bootsie the mongrel.

By 1952 there were two sons and three daughters. Helen Travolta at forty-three was thought too old to have another child, so in the spirit of a woman who swam rivers and badgered famous playwrights she did bear one. The arrival of John Joseph Travolta was announced in the *Englewood Press-Journal* on February 18th 1954.

Being the late-born addition to a large family is a good and bad thing. Everyone spoils you, from your parents for whom you are a miraculous postscript, to your brothers and sisters who see anything small, live and anatomically similar as a living doll or as *their* substitute offspring.

'He was my mother's last child,' says Margaret Travolta, the eldest sister, 'and she knew she wasn't going to have any more. So to her this was a little blessing in disguise. We all kowtowed to John pretty much. He was a little bratty but no more so than any other kid.'

His mother declared later, setting a hindsight seal on future stardom, 'He danced in my womb.'

For Travolta, though, there was a sombre side to being a late baby.

'I started looking at life through [my parents'] eyes, but life through fifty-year-old eyes may not be as chipper as a kid deserves to see it. What I observed was fifty-year-old parents and their anxieties, their blues, their sensing the third chapter of their lives.' He would later see this as a shaping factor in his personality: 'I have always had an older person's point of view on life. In other words I sense the end. I get blue more easily because I'm not always appreciating the youth I have.' (His father, asked his son's age in the early days of John's fame, said, 'He's twenty-four, going on forty.')

Travolta the tot enjoyed enacting his own Toytown manias; high spirits and mock dismay, or real dismay theatricalised, came easily. If his mother raised her voice, he'd run upstairs and yell, 'I'm throwing myself out the window.' She would dash up to find him hiding in a dresser.

Later he specialised in contrary-minded cross talk. When his mother didn't make a chocolate pudding he wanted, he threatened to cut off his 'weeny'. Or he'd ask her which shirt he should wear to school. He: 'The blue one?' She: 'I think the green one.' He: 'Thank you. I think I'll wear the pink one.'

'I was a brat from five to fifteen,' he says. 'My family expected a lot from me. When I acted like a baby they told me to act like an adult. When I acted like an adult they didn't like that either.'

Life was already characterised as acting, for which he had every encouragement from his sisters. They used him as a human Barbie or Ken doll. Sticking him in a living-room chair, they would make him up and dress him, often in female clothes. Sometimes they allowed him to jump up and take part in their brothers' plays and skits. For these Sam built a little theatre complete with curtain in the basement. (Here too his mother earned extra money for the family by giving acting lessons.)

Jumping up from that chair may have been a formative moment. Once John took the initiative in the family acting gigs, goodbye Barbie doll. He had a hunger for observing and copying people: his own family and friends, finally and prophetically James Cagney. 'He was the only one outside my family who was a main source of inspiration,' says Travolta. Aged six, the boy is said to have danced

in front of the TV when Cagney performed his 'Yankee Doodle Dandy' number: that bottom-jutting, tippy-toed, angle-shouldered dance solo that destroyed whole traditions of movie choreography much as Travolta would later jut strange body parts – hip, arm, finger – to rewrite the musical for the seventies.

His mother seized on the Cagney obsession as a disciplinary aid. Pretending to be on the end of a telephone conversation, she would say, 'Mr Cagney is calling. He wants you to brush your teeth [and/or] tidy your room.' 'Okay,' John would stammer. 'Does he – does he *like* me?'

There was another linkup, of a kind, with a living Hollywood legend. Gene Kelly's brother Fred ran a dance school in New York, to which the pre-teen John was packed off for willing lessons.

Dancing was better than sitting in a chair at his sisters' mercy. And singing and performing all the roles from *Gypsy*, with help from mom's costume trunk, was better than playing the record over and over until it lost its grooves. These frenzies were witnessed by John's sister Ellen, a budding actress who had debuted at seven on a TV talent show singing 'If I knew you were comin', I'd have baked a cake.' Later she appeared in a roadshow production of the Styne-Sondheim musical, which John briefly accompanied her on and never forgot. His father recalled, 'He even did the *Gypsy* striptease number, "Let me entertain you".'

The boy's first showbiz appearance in public was in a Fourth of July pageant in 1960. He did the Twist, the new dance sensation, in front of what he recalls as 30,000 people. 'I wouldn't stop even when my mother said, "It's over. Get down off the stage." '

'The poor kid looked so trapped and exhausted,' Helen Travolta remembered. 'I kept gesturing to him, "Johnny, it's okay, you can walk off." '

This was at a church social, which even in devout midstate New Jersey seems unlikely to have attracted 30,000 people. The Travoltas themselves, though attending mass each week, were not fanatical Catholics. The parents did not din the doctrines overzealously into John. 'Although I was brought up a Catholic, I wasn't sure I understood it,' he says. 'I thought the confession aspects of it were good, but I didn't know you were actually supposed to confess things you did. I thought you were

supposed to make up things you didn't do, just to get through confession!'

Churchgoing seemed mundane, anyway, compared to other flights of the mind and soul. In John Travolta's case it was hard to tether him to terra firma. Even physically he was thin enough to have been blown into the air like pollen: you can see it in the photos – the gangling kid offering a yawny grin to the camera as he stands by a lake, or the boy sacristan engulfed in his robe. His brothers teased him with the nickname 'Bones'. Joey, the next youngest to John, would say to his father, 'Dad, when you take a chicken and take all the meat off, what do you have left?' 'Bones,' said Dad. John would go 'Aaaah!' and start screaming.

The pleasures of eating, which later dealt havoc to the Travolta physique, came to him slowly if at all in childhood. If he liked Mars bars, it was mainly because of the TV commercials. 'They were the best. They'd fly you right through the Milky Way.' Flying not feeding was the stuff of rapture.

He developed an obsession with Peter Pan from age three. After seeing the flying boy on television, in the musical version starring Mary Martin, he began using the third step of the hall stairs as a launching pad. Flapping his arms in a bid to fly, he would jump off and fall on his face. Before his bemused parents, he would do it again. Then again.

'As a child I was always playing Peter Pan. I would make my father lift me up and fly me around the room. I was so angry that I couldn't fly on my own.'

As if inspired by the sky-blue house he lived in, Travolta spent much of his imaginary life 30,000 feet above Englewood. As well as asking his father about the colour of the sky so often that Sam Travolta called him the 'Why-is-the-sky-blue kid', John shifted his whole fantasy life up into the New York air corridors.

'Both flying and acting meant being out of the crowd for me. When I was a kid in bed late at night I'd hear the drone of a plane coming out of La Guardia. That sound was very romantic to me. I'd wish my bed were in the plane and I could look out the window and see the stars.'

Each plane had its own character and magic. 'I'd dream what each of them would be like to fly, and I would dream of one day

owning my own plane, so I could just climb up there in the sky like I wanted and be free, really free.'

'He was a little tiny baby when he became fixated with planes, and no one in our family had even flown yet,' says sister Ellen. Later, says Margaret, 'Whenever I had to go anywhere, he made the flight reservations. He was, like, this little midget who would call the travel agency.'

His father built him a 'real' plane in the back yard: a thing of plywood and wooden planks with car batteries for power. It could roar even if it couldn't fly.

Unlike his Hudson-swimming mother he never took to water: he may have been deterred by a near-accident. Visiting Aunt Mildred and Uncle Joe who lived upstate, the five-year-old John fell asleep during an outing to Culver Lake. Waking, he saw his brothers far out in the water and wanted to join them. When he couldn't find a life-preserver that wasn't waterlogged he jumped in anyway – and sank like a rock. Pushing back to the surface, he screamed and sank again. Uncle Joe called out to John's father and amid flurry and fluster they pulled him out.

So the swimming pool his father built in their back garden, as a leisure oasis for barbecue parties as well as place to splash in high summer, was less of a passion for John than the idea of taking his first flight. His bedroom was already an aerial sculpture park berserk with model planes and mobiles, surveyed by Audi the black teddy bear. John read magazines about flying, comics about flying. And he collected air travel souvenirs, including anyone's used tickets.

'He still has them,' says Ellen. 'If asked him tomorrow, "When did I do this? What did I do?" he would give me the date, the time, what plane I took, where I took off and where I landed.'

So in 1962 when Ellen gave John two air tickets wrapped up in ribbons for his eight birthday, he looked at them and said, 'Where did you go?'

'Nowhere,' she said.

He looked again. They were two real tickets, for a flight booked with her from New York to Philadelphia.

He ran around the house screaming and yelling: 'When do we go?'

'In two weeks.'

Decades later he still remembered walking across the sunstruck airport tarmac, then 'climbing the steps into a four-engine, probably a DC6', then climbing still further: above the airport, the city, the state. 'There's never been anything like it in the world. "I'm flying, I'm flying!" '

Touchdown was feted with a grilled cheese sandwich in Philadelphia. Then came the return flight: except that there was no return, at least to the pre-rapture Travolta. He had put eight years of New Jersey gravity behind him to become a fully-fledged aeromaniac.

What did he like about flying? 'I think it's the aesthetics of it. I always thought that [aeroplanes] were beautiful pieces of art to be interpreted.'

At high school the only recorded club he would join, commemorated in the single photograph of him in any year book, was the flying club. John stands in the back row, a toothy grin under a mop of black hair, his slouch-shouldered body sheathed in a worn flying-ace-style leather jacket outside a gleaming white turtleneck sweater.

This could be the film star that almost got away. Only the sharpest-eyed Svengali, with questionable designs on the New Jersey youth, might have spotted the scatty ape-grin glamour of this teenager. Or noticed there was a already a scene-stealing sense of style – the whites of teeth and sweater are *so* white, the black of hair and jacket *so* black – in this kid who has agreed for one small minute to shuffle sideways into the spotlight.

Gazing back at an even earlier photo of himself at fourteen, John Travolta muses aloud: 'I always had pretty eyes. I was an adorable child, from the day I was born until about ten. Then from about ten on, my face was real small and I had a big nose and big lips. My eyes were always blue, very pretty, but it didn't seem to co-ordinate till about twenty.'

Neither did life. He is not remembered as a model pupil even by himself. 'I was a bit of a clown in school, only an average student.' In Englewood today his name brings a wry smile. 'Oh, yes, the talented drop-out' says the head of one of his four schools. This head never taught him but knows the legend; knows enough too

not to show me Travolta's grades. He says, 'We're not supposed to show anyone's.' But a record-keeper at his first school, the Catholic St Cecilia's, where he enrolled aged five on September 21st 1959, says that Travolta's mother came in soon after her son became famous and issued instructions that his grades were not to be revealed to any reporter.

'He was, let's say, "average",' she tells me.

'He was a devil,' says the schoolmistress who was in charge of the cub scouts when Travolta joined at age six. 'You know, a devil as kids are then. Very restless. Very mischievous.' 'He was gorgeous too,' she adds in mitigation.

'He was very goodlooking,' remembers ex-schoolmate Donna, who works in the school kitchens today. 'But he wasn't as outgoing as his brother Joey.' Joey became president of the Catholic Youth Organisation. Donna remembers dancing with him but can't lay claim – no one can – to having been the first to dance with John. 'They'd both come to proms at St Cecilia's High dressed in their best suits. Joey was very charming, very talkative. John was shy but better looking.'

Dances came later. Between five and ten he was more busy vanishing from the school record books. Here and at his next educational stopover, Liberty School, which he entered as a fifth grade pupil after leaving St Cecilia's in the fourth grade in September 1964, John Travolta left no photographic trace and barely a ripple in contemporaries' memories. Almost no one can even remember that he *went* to Liberty. The fact had to be teased from the mind of Travolta neighbour Eddie Costenuic who says his children went there with John. 'But they don't really remember what he was like.'

Travolta may already have been busy not 'being' at school – spiritually absent even if present in person. In class he got into trouble regularly, he says, for talking, fidgeting or 'telling a neighbour something stupid or funny.' He was more interested in following his mother around as she taught drama or put on shows, sometimes at St Cecilia's church hall. He was happier helping his father build things at weekends: a go-kart, a new attic, a fence, even a bowling alley in the capacious basement where Sam Snr would disburse beer and hot dogs to the boys from the neighbourhood

and to Bootsie the mongrel, a choosy beast who disliked tinned food. Later John and his brother would help dad at his Hillsdale tyre shop, with musical interludes when Sam Snr would bash away at the honky-tonk piano he kept for leisure occasions. In imitative tribute to his Dad, John would sometimes dabble theatrically with a cigar.

He hated the politics-and-protest culture sweeping through sixties America. 'When I was in high school, all they ever seemed to talk about was the Vietnam war. I didn't have much interest in the Vietnam war. I had more interest in why it felt so bad to be in school.'

He never joined the drug culture either. Marijuana made him feel sick and cocaine 'didn't take'. He conformed with hip times, though, in his dress. The greaser era demanded tight black trousers, pointed black shoes and white shirts with the sleeves rolled up. Later, when the Beatles ruled, it was a McCartney-style silver sharkskin suit.

John also hung out with black pupils rather than white. 'It started in the fifth grade, when I transferred from a Catholic school to a public school that was predominantly black. Right away I loved the black people and they loved me because I could dance and was funny to them. The white kids never laughed at me, only the black kids.' When football jocks on the school bus broke into the James Brown song. 'Say it loud, I'm black and proud.' Travolta sang back, 'Say it light, I'm white and outasight.'

Englewood in the sixties, like much of America, was busy trying to harmonise the races. A town with an elite educational system, thanks to millionaire endowments, also boasted a degree of racial harmony scarcely believable a mere bus-ride away from Harlem. In the school yearbooks black faces jostle freely with white, a sea of gleaming youths clutching their books and flaunting their gowns.

Travolta, though, responded to the *differences* between races not the harmonies. He found blacks more sympathetic both at Liberty and at his later schools Janis Dismus and Dwight Morrow High.

'I sensed their strong sexuality and it made me feel comfortable. They'd always say, "Hey, Travolta, get your fine ass over here. You wanna fuck me?" It was always real open. And when you danced with a black girl, you could grind and get down without

necessarily meaning you were gonna have sex with her. It simply meant you could move seductively and enjoy it.'

He liked talking with black friends about sex, vividly and frankly. 'I loved it because it satisfied my voyeurism. I find I always edit myself around white people.'

Talking was easier than doing, though. Gossiping about girls or sizing them up from afar was simpler than being pushed towards them. Travolta never forgot one incident even though the hurt that came to him was through another's pain.

'In the seventh grade there was this girl Mary Jo. And all my friends kept teasing me that this girl liked me. She was a strange-looking girl that everyone made fun of. And they kept on saying, "John, Mary likes you" and they made up all kinds of stuff. Finally I saw her at an assembly and I said, "Look, I don't like you. Just stop talking to everyone about me."

'This girl was totally innocent. And the look on her face was so devastating that I'm still not over that. Because that was the cruellest thing that I had ever done. And it had all been fabricated by my friends.'

According to Travolta, the first girl he ever kissed was black. He was twelve, she was sixteen and she offered him a reefer. 'Do you soul-kiss?' she asked. 'No, I don't think so,' he mumbled. So they tried it.

He claims to have had sex for the first time with a white girl, though, when he was thirteen. She remains nameless, as does his soul-kisser.

Travolta's only fully identified girlfriend in his teens was Denise Wurms. She looked, he says, like Ali McGraw. 'She was kind of an earth girl, brunette. Tall girl, five feet eight inches.' Height and looks were nothing, though, compared to 'the way she danced with me to "Tighten Up" by Archie Bell and the Drells. She was a good dancer.'

An ex-schoolfriend of Travolta claims that this prom night *coup de foudre* almost blew up in Travolta's face. John had gone out shopping to look his best for the high-school dance. 'He wore wheat-coloured bell-bottoms with a policeman-blue shirt and brown boots,' says the friend. But while dancing, Travolta 'said something to Denise and she kicked him in the seat of the pants.'

The desecration of the new trousers caused Travolta more distress than the girl's emotion. 'He went wild – he said later he felt like he'd been shot. "Do you know how much these cost?" he screamed at her. "Eleven dollars." '

Denise reportedly burst into tears. But by evening's end she had handed John a note indicating forgiveness and they ended up going back to her house for a pizza. 'It was the start of his first romance.'

Possibly. Yet it remains odd that Denise features in almost none of Travolta's later reminiscings about his adolescence. And though John's sisters have alleged that she was a constant feature at 135 Morse Place throughout his middle teens, nestling with him over records, magazines or homework, neighbour Eddie Costenuic does not remember her. Nor can he identify her in any of the copious photographs he has of the Travoltas at play.

If Denise *was* John's girlfriend she was hardly his muse or inspiration. His references to her are outnumbered by his bardic monologues about flying, his ravings about black culture, his besotted memories of family life – not least the conjugal bliss of his own Ma and Pa.

Nothing ever said by John about Denise, or indeed any girlfriend save the later, tragic and older Diana Hyland, comes near to the sensual affection and delight he seems to have felt in his own parents' love.

'Even after they'd been married twenty-seven years, you could walk into their bedroom in the morning – like I sometimes did as a kid – and there they'd be, nestled in each other's arms, their bodies totally locked together.'

It was an emotional event for the boy to wait up for his mother to come home. He even attributes his eccentric sleeping hours in later life – seldom in bed before three – to this habit. But his love of her seems never to have detracted from his feelings for his father. Sam Travolta was like an older brother, never holding John back from ambitions which might have sent the usual shockwaves through other parents: 'No, it's too dangerous' (flying) or 'No, it's too risky' (acting).

The first of these dreams began with that flight to Philadelphia and continued in his teens with flying lessons at nearby Teterboro

Airport. Sam paid towards them, but John helped out by working for a furniture repair shop, aged twelve, and later by bagging groceries at a supermarket. He also joined that flying club immortalised in the 1968 Dwight Morrow High School yearbook. Ken Sarfin, who was president recalls its brief – very brief – glory.

'I think we went up once. That was with a schoolmistress who had flying experience called Miss Patton. To be honest I remember John, who was a nice, rather untidy kid with hippy-style hair, but until you reminded me I had completely forgotten the flying club. It was one of those great ideas kids think up and then forget about the next week.'

The second dream, slower to find fulfilment, was acting. He had been doing this in effect all his childhood: not just in the basement theatre at Morse Place but also in his habit of playacting his emotions. There were other childhood dry runs for acting. Aged seven, he had accompanied his sister Ellen on her *Gypsy* tour. Aged twelve, he had joined an Actors Studio workshop in Englewood, playing the title role – three lines – in *Who'll Save the Ploughboy*. Mingling with the beautiful and bohemian intensified his dislike of academia. 'How do you go back to school and make anybody understand how it was to be with those theatre people, watching the sun come up over cigarettes and wine.'

His first outbreak of movie mania occurred at age fourteen. Infected by *Bonnie and Clyde* fever, he bought a double-breasted black suit, black shirt and white tie for $18 at a local store. With sister Margaret dressed as Bonnie and himself dandling a toy machine-gun, he had their picture taken in Dunaway/Beatty style.

It wasn't the historical gangster and moll he cared about so much as the way they had been transmuted into movie legend – and the show-business wonderland the stars must inhabit. 'If I had thought while watching *Bonnie and Clyde* that Warren Beatty and Faye Dunaway didn't jet around and dress up and have fine things, it would have killed me.'

The lives he had tasted himself during childhood – jetting around and dressing up – came together in this reverie of life in Tinseltown. So did another idea: that of leaving his handprint on history. 'When I was a teenager, I remember thinking that I did not want to leave this world without its being

marked by my presence in some fashion. That was a compulsion for me.'

By 1970 he had a decision to make. He had won a small summer acting role in the musical *Bye Bye Birdie* at a club theatre in nearby Fort Lee. Rather than return to school in September to graduate, he wanted to stay out and act. When he took his dilemma to his parents, his father was more hesitant than his mother. 'He wanted me to finish school,' Travolta recalls. 'My mother, who was very liberal, told him, "I think what he wants to do isn't going to interfere with any of that." So she let me go.' Neighbour Eddie Costenuic, who used to chat from porch to porch with John's father, remembers that he quickly became resigned. 'His dad said, "He's made up his mind." As far as Sam was concerned, that was it.'

It was. That summer a New York agent called Bob Le Mond got in his car and kthunk-kthunked across the George Washington Bridge to see a young actor he had heard about who was playing a bit role in a smalltown supper theatre. He liked what he saw.

2

BOILING SPRINGS AND GREASED LIGHTNING

Today the resort is plagued by horrifying incidents. One evening recently, in the dining room of this old-world hotel *cum* country club set off by woods from the corn-bright plains of central Pennsylvania, guests were shocked to see a trap open in the ceiling and a body drop down at the end of a rope. It was not the only fright that weekend. A waiter was shot dead while serving drinks outside. Another body, slain by methods unknown, was brutally suspended over a stream.

The young John Travolta had been to Allenberry in Boiling Springs a quarter century earlier. Back in 1971 it was an exclusive golfing, fishing and weekending resort ten miles from Harrisburg, the state capital. Today owner John Heinze, a ruddy man with a country squire cap fixed almost surgically to his head, stages Agatha Christie-style murder weekends. But when Travolta came to earn his Equity card back in his seventeenth summer the Allenberry Playhouse – still playing today, between murders – was the heart, soul and cash-earner of the Heinze operation.

Though no other major Hollywood star was ever shot out of its genteel canon of production choices, mostly musicals and well-behaved Broadway comedies, medium-powered celebrities like Roy *Jaws* Scheider and Eileen *Private Benjamin* Brennan were launched here, and Broadway luminaries like Shirley Jones and Shelley Berman occasionally touched down for a sparkle.

When Allenberry hired Travolta, he was an unknown actor with little in his resumé save a few weeks' singing and hoofing

at the obscure Club Bene in New Jersey. Travolta told Heinze he was getting calls for TV commercials, which explained the boy's weekend trips to New York. All Heinze knew, as he drilled his players for back-to-back productions of *The Boy Friend* and *She Loves Me*, was that the young actor was nice-looking, willing and could dance.

'He was an honest-to-goodness gypsy. They say he learned to dance for *Saturday Night Fever*, but it isn't true. He didn't have a principal role for us, he was in the chorus. But he was good enough for us to give him one special dance number.'

That was a 'tango tragique', danced with one Marjorie Horne. It was almost certainly the first high-style step Travolta took towards the disco-Valentino deliriums of *Fever*.

By now he had a manager. Bob Le Mond, a New York agent and talent-spotter, had caught Travolta in *Bye Bye Birdie* on a friend's recommendation. 'I was dragged out to this club theatre in Fort Lee yelling and complaining,' he recalled. 'Then once I saw him I couldn't take my eyes off him. This kid, there was such a reality about him, a commitment that was riveting. He made all the others look as if they were acting while he was "being." '

Le Mond went backstage to offer his services. Travolta hesitated for three weeks before deciding it was a good idea. One: he could share a coldwater flat in Hell's Kitchen with his actress sister Ellen as soon as he got steady work on stage and in TV commercials, as he was assured he would be by Le Mond (whom his clients affectionately called 'old silver tongue'). Two: Travolta said, 'I have a Kabuki actor face and that was good for the stage.' Three: he could grow up and start to look after his parents, one of whom was beginning to need extra care.

That fall Helen Travolta, after being diagnosed with cancer, had surgery on her legs. John took on nurse duties at home, changing bandages and applying salve to the open wounds, while his weekdays were spent being nursed by Le Mond through the probing ordeal of auditions.

From her recovery bed Helen pitched advice. 'Don't make an entrance by running into a room. You let people look at you as you walk in.' An actor nourishes his craft by observing people, she said, but please remember that *everyone* is worth observing. 'My

mother thought people were attractive even if they weren't,' says John. 'We [children] all kind of inherited that, to see the beauty in people.'

The next year, at Allenberry, Travolta had to see the beauty in appearing on stage in a one-cow town in remotest Pennsylvania. Resort manager Rogene remembers the seventeen-year-old with the beautiful blue eyes. 'He was very shy and soft-spoken. In rehearsals he stood out 'cos he had so much energy. But he wasn't as outgoing offstage. At the end of a show, rather than joining the other actors in the Carriage Room for a drink, he'd go back to Carlisle [the nearest small town] with Katie Coutts the costumer, whom he was lodging with. And he was always gone at weekends, for auditions.'

'He was absolutely the junior member of the company,' states John Heinze. So junior that his name is mis-spelled on one page of the playbill as John 'Fravolta'. 'He would have been paid around $100 a week, of which $25 would have gone on lodging. But he didn't come here for fame and money, he came to earn his union membership. My one claim to fame is that I signed the contract that got John Travolta his Equity card.'

Soon after leaving Allenberry, he was waving it around the country's capital of live acting. Broadway then, as now, did not encourage seekers after overnight fame. Most of those wanting to excel had to do a little off-Broadway first, while painfully aware that the two theatre worlds barely interconnected. Broadway is about famous plays by famous writers or hit musicals. Off-Broadway is about art, innovation and the quest to be recognised, or even reviewed.

Travolta won small roles in brief runs. He was in a workshop production for the New Dramatists Guild called *Metaphors*, a one-act play by Martin Duberman in which he played a disturbed youngster. He then attracted the same amount of critical attention – none – as Private Griggs in a Greenwich Village staging of Somerset Maugham's *Rain*. *Rain* opened in late March 1972 and closed a few days later. (One cast member, Joan Prather, would go on to play a longer, more impactful role in Travolta's life).

The unpromising start could have led to depression and sometimes did. Travolta made friends with a fellow client of

Bob Le Mond, a young actor with a showier line in volatility called Jeff Conaway. Conaway was addicted to almost anything that rattled in a bottle, especially vitamin pills. As a vocational hypochondriac he was a perfect sounding-board for other people's anxieties. If he and Travolta were to be lost and confused in a big city, they might as well be so together. Conaway remembers giving his friend a sixteenth birthday card, 'It was these two puppies entangled together and he said, "This reminds me of us." '

'John and I had a lot in common,' he says. 'We both had show business mums, we were both young and searching for ourselves. And we both had a youthful angst, an anxiety about making it. "Were we good enough or were we kidding ourselves?" I remember walking down Broadway with him one day and we were both kind of miserable, and we looked at each other and said, "Why are we so upset? We're young guys, on Broadway, we should be ecstatic." But we're not 'cos there's more we wanted.'

Le Mond kept pushing Travolta towards TV, where there were well-paid bits in soaps or commercials. While the going pay for summer stock was $50 a week and for off-Broadway $112, a single commercial could net you $8–10.

Le Mond began lining up the customers, starting with a spot for 'h.i.s. Slacks' and then a Mutual of New York commercial that first drew attention to Travolta's ease and magnetism on screen. The sixty-second ad featured him as a young man who had planned to go to college but whose father died without taking out life insurance.

British writer and journalist Nik Cohn, later to transform Travolta's life by providing the source story for *Saturday Night Fever*, remembers the commercial. 'It was very affecting. It just showed John Travolta going to open up some shop as a lowly assistant when he could have gone to college. But it made an impression because he had this enormously appealing, hangdog look that he was so good at.'

After a failed tryout for the film *Panic in Needle Park*, with Travolta losing the lead to a short lisping, unknown Italian called Al Pacino, Le Mond reckoned it was time for a long reconnaissance trip to Hollywood, especially since a leading film-maker – the late Hal Ashby – and a top casting director, Lynn Stalmaster, had

both noticed Travolta in the Mutual ad. They wanted him to audition for the role of the young sailor hauled across America towards a disciplinary hearing in the Jack Nicholson movie *The Last Detail*.

'I'd read a number of contenders and John was very impressive,' remembers Stalmaster. 'He was one of the last three or four we had whittled down from thirty or forty. We wanted a very sympathetic, sweet lost soul and the first quality I recognized in John was that genuine warmth and honesty. Then I discovered he had instinct and timing too. He didn't learn it formally, like all those actors who study at the Actors Studio. He was born with it.'

Travolta lost the role to Randy Quaid. 'It was a narrow decision, but Hal decided Randy was a more offbeat way to go,' Stalmaster.

Barren weeks turned to barren months. Small roles in Tinseltown soaps or medical sagas (*Owen Marshall M.D., Emergency*) highlighted the emptiness all around. And even when Travolta tested for a touring production of the new musical *Grease*, the omens didn't seemed favourable.

'He was all over the place,' remembers the show's director Tom Moore, who held the auditions in a room behind the open-air Greek theatre in L.A. 'Some of our group were ready to dismiss him. His singing was better than his acting but neither was focused. He was nervous and he knew he hadn't done well.'

Another invigilator at the auditions was *Grease's* co-author Jim Jacobs. 'I wrote "Eighty-six" on my notes. That's shorthand for "Forget it, get rid of him." He was very unprepared.'

Moore championed Travolta's casting, though. 'He was very young and though it was a bad audition there was something magical about him. I know everyone says this when someone becomes a star, but Pat Birch [the choreographer] and I had got pretty good in recognising it. We fought his casting through.'

Le Mond and Travolta also fought with each other, when manager told client that he didn't want him to do the show, due to begin rehearsals in New York. 'Bob said, "I would rather you stay in California and become a film star,"' Travolta remembers. 'But I was going to go back and do what I knew best. The stage.'

*   *   *

In the late sixties Jim Jacobs had a day job as an advertising copywriter but spent evenings and weekends acting in amateur theatre in Chicago. His friend Warren Casey also acted when not nine-to-fiving for a chain of retail shops. One night at a party Jacobs pulled out some old fifties records – 'loud guitar and doo-wop,' he recalls – and said to Casey,

'Wouldn't it be great if one could have a hit on Broadway with this kind of stuff instead of *My Fair Lady* and *Oklahoma*? It would be about all the people we grew up with at high school: the greasers, rock-n-rollers, leather-jacket guys, the tough broads.'

'What did they ever do that was interesting?' Casey asked him.

'That's the challenge!' responded Jacobs.

When Casey was fired from his job by happenstance a week later, he bought a typewriter to console himself. 'I want to get into ad writing like you,' he told Jacobs, 'but I don't know how to type.' So he practised by banging out a scene from that airily proposed pastiche-fifties musical.

'A couple of weeks later he said, "I've got that first scene." ' Jacobs recalls. 'I said, "What first scene?" He said, "That show we were going to do." He had written a pyjama party scene with all these tough chicks. I said, "You mean, we're really going to *do* this?" '

They wondered what to call the play. 'I said, "We'll call it *Grease*," ' Jacobs recalls. 'It'll be about the greasy hair, greasy food, under-the-hood-of-the-car with all the sludge and grease. It was a very greasy way of life in the fifties – girls spraying it on their hair from all those cans . . .'

Once written, *Grease* had one of those baptisms that authors dream of, or believe happen only in old Judy Garland-Mickey Rooney films. Scheduled to play for four nights in a barn-like former tram shed, *Grease* ran for eight months and was reviewed by top newspapers from New York, Washington and San Francisco.

'Audiences were crying "Author! Author!" and all that cliche stuff,' says Jacobs, 'it was quite astounding.' Agents and impresarios descended on the 'Kingston Mines' theatre, turning it into Chicago's answer to the Beatles' Liverpool Cavern. By 1972 the

show was ready for Broadway and a national tour and casting auditions began.

In the fall of that year an unknown actor called Jerry Zaks, today a stage and movie director best known for the Meryl Streep-Diane Keaton weepie *Marvin's Room,* had just won the second male lead role of Kenickie for the national tour. He bought a standing ticket to check out the Broadway production. 'There was a young man next to me, and in the intermission I remarked to him something like, 'Great show, isn't it?' I was feeling full of myself, so I added, "I'm going to be in it" He said, "Oh really? Me too." It was John Travolta.'

Zaks remembers him as a 'wide-eyed kid, very sweet, very innocent.' So does Jim Jacobs, who some weeks after eighty-sixing Travolta in L.A. visited the rehearsals conducted in an icy Manhattan hotel during November 1972.

'It was a cold and sloppy day outside and John had bought these new lumberjack-boot-type shoes in bright orange. And Tom Moore happened to look over and said, "Oh John, I see you got new shoes." He said, "Yeah, they're brand new. You know, my other ones, they're still perfectly good. There's nothing wrong with them. Would you be interested in *buying* them?"

'For some young actor to say this to an older director! Tom just howled. I laughed till I had tears. But this was so like John. He was an open book, so honest.'

'He was like a puppy, very funny and enthusiastic,' says Judy Kaye, who was cast as the butch gang leader Rizzo. 'He was constantly doing impressions, he locked into people's idiosyncrasies. He would do each of us, he got us down very quickly.'

Travolta was not cast as Danny Zuko, the lead role he would play five years later on screen and that a rival unknown called Richard Gere was then grooming himself to play in the London stage production (prefiguring a bizarrely overlapping future for the two actors).

Travolta played Danny's gauche, sweet-natured sidekick Doody while the main role went to his friend Jeff Conaway. 'As I was two years older,' Conaway says, 'the Danny-Doody relationship – Danny always keeping an eye out for Doody – kind of mirrored ours.'

Conaway had already done a six-week stint in the main Broadway production. 'Grease was a phenomenon. It had opened to mixed reviews in a medium-size New York theatre, the Eden. Then by midsummer it was booked out on Broadway and all the critics who had turned up their noses came to rave. It cost $125,000 and became the first show to top a hundred grand. And it was perfect for the fifties nostalgia craze of the time.'

Choreographer Pat Birch saw Grease as more than just nostalgia. 'I felt we were doing a documentary of our lives. We approached it that seriously. We had terrific fights about the colour of the cereal bowls in the cafeteria. We did endless improvs on how you felt at the high-school dance. It was faithful to the fifties, which was America's last innocent moment: the time when all you worried about was whether you got the record, or the car, or the girl. But even today you can go in any class in any school in the country and find a Danny, a Doody, or a Rizzo.'

The tour production limbered up in its own limbo. 'It was freezing cold,' remembers Judy Kaye. 'Then when the day came to go to Boston for the opening, we were put on a cold leaky bus with the rain coming in. We all got 'flu and were sick as dogs.'

All except John Travolta, who helped to keep spirits up. When bored with amusing audiences, the Grease cast amused each other. When a character on stage was supposed to take a tuna fish sandwich out of a paper bag, he might find a lobster had been substituted. Travolta cracked the company up one night by slicking his hair with a giant Disneyland comb. Another time he brought a teddy bear on stage, using it as a comic prop.

'We got into a fight about that,' says Jerry Zaks. 'I, being the elder statesman, lectured him in a way that was excessive. But it was typical. John would do silly ad-lib things on stage, he was totally unafraid.'

Zaks credits Travolta's family with creating that self-confidence. 'He was close to his folks, particularly his sister Annie, who was on the Grease tour with us as a general understudy for the female roles, and his mother. I don't recall meeting his dad. But his mom treated him like God. It can't have hurt him growing up to feel that special.'

One relationship failed to survive the tour. Travolta broke up

with Denise, or she with him. Tired of no longer being a priority in his life, if she ever had been, she crackled out the end of the affair on a state-to-state telephone from New Jersey to Chicago. 'He was devastated,' remembers sister Ellen. Travolta is said to have flown straight home to Englewood to plead with Denise, without avail.

Was there another man in Denise's life? Evidently. The next time she and Travolta saw each other was when the *Grease* tour touched down in San Francisco and Denise visited John backstage to say she was engaged.

Was there another girl in Travolta's life? Possibly. Attractive redhead Marilu Henner, the daughter of a Chicago dancing teacher, was a fellow *Grease*-er, playing like John a down-the-cast buddy role, that of Rizzo's friend Marty. She and he were the cast's youngest members. Judy Kaye remembers her as a bubbly, off-the-wall trouper and a universal problem-solver: a junior den mother with a sideline in shtick. Henner went on to medium fame as a film actress (*The Man Who Loved Women, Johnny Dangerously*) and larger fame on TV, both in sitcoms (*Taxi, Evening Shade*) and on talk shows. Watch her gabble with self-possessed effervescence on the Jay Leno or David Letterman shows, and you see why Travolta might have fallen for this mix of scatterbrain and earth matriarch.

Jim Jacobs remembers her from early days. 'She was in the original Chicago show. She was very gregarious and outgoing. Relentless, you know, but you couldn't help loving her. She's very smart and blessed with this extraordinary memory. She can recite dates – birthdays, anniversaries – that you'd never imagine anyone could remember.'

True to form, Henner records in her autobiography that she and John 'met on November 28th 1972 and became lovers on July 15th 1973.' This was at the Golden Gate Bridge TraveLodge in San Francisco.

'It was absolutely incredible, tender, open, passionate. It wasn't some big now-it's-the-time-for-me-to-seduce-you thing. Our slide into intimacy didn't have a dramatic movie-score montage feel to it. But it was hardly disappointing. It was natural and effortless, more like: Oh, we're going to sleep over like we used to but now

we get to play doctor too. There was a comfortable, exploratory feel to it . . .'

Nice, but evidently no earth movement. This seems to be par for the course in Travolta's recorded love life, now and in future years. One reason for the constant press inquisition over his sexual persuasion may be that he seldom seems to have been involved in a straight relationship where one senses the tang of passion or compulsion. From his childhood sweetheart Denise he segues to playing doctor with the den mother. Later he will have an enigmatic affair with an older woman. Still later he will marry a pretty girl whom he never talks about, only about the joy he finds in their baby child.

Travolta and Henner were the best of friends pre-sex and post-sex. She saw in him 'soulmate potential. He was sweet wonderful, beautiful, and like me, insanely curious.' She counted up the things they had in common: Catholic families, showbiz mothers, automobile-connected fathers (Henner's dad sold cars while Travolta's sold tyres). 'It was like rediscovering a long-lost sibling.'

Even earlier on the tour, before John's breakup with Denise, they had flown off on platonic away-trips – weekend here, night there – staying in adjoining hotel rooms. When neither could sleep, one would knock on the other's door at 2 am and they would stay up all night chatting. The subject, if not yet the practice, was sex. 'I'd never known anyone I could talk to until sunrise without a break,' writes Henner. 'More than an urge for seduction, there was profound comfort and exhilaration in knowing we would be in each other's lives forever.'

After the TraveLodge night, their relationship 'blossomed from friendship to genuine couplehood. He and I were never ones to miss our cue for passion.' These included quickie lovemakings in the Los Angeles Schubert Theatre's backstage first-aid room (conveniently provided with cot and key) during the intervals between acts one and two of *Grease*.

After the tour, from which John was plucked away for a brief run in the Broadway production, he and Marilu moved into an 85th Street apartment lent by Jeff Conaway. Then they co-auditioned successfully for another musical, *Over Here!*, written by the

Sherman brothers and starring the Andrews Sisters: or two of that singing legend, the third having died.

This sibling-powered delirium, set on a train with a plot about spies and *femmes fatales* during America's World War 2 mobilisation, proved a hit on Broadway and might have gone on a national tour itself. But one Andrews sister complained that she was too frail in health to sing and dance across America, though her agent said her health problems could be cured with a higher salary. It was not offered, so John and Marilu had to stay content with the New York revenue and reviews.

As in *Grease*, Tom Moore and Patricia Birch were director and choreographer, this time guiding Travolta through a larger, more eye-catching role, that of a maladroit serviceman called Misfit.

'He pulled off some of the funniest comedic bits in the show,' says Birch. 'One moment I'll never forget. We had this vampy spy singing a song. "Wait for me, Marlene," and crossing and uncrossing her legs while sitting on the bar counter of the train. And these four soldiers were standing there melting with lust. And suddenly – this was one night during previews in Philadelphia – John dropped to his knees, crawled around and putting his arms carefully behind him looked up her skirts. It got *huge* laughs. He repeated it each night. People credited it to me, but it was John's idea.'

Other ad libs were born from despair rather than inspiration. Tom Moore remembers the night the treadmills failed to work at the climax of Travolta's big song 'Dream Drummer'. His character's fantasy of himself as a band leader was supposed to be crowned by the entry of an orchestra rolling on in glory from rear stage. No orchestra appeared. Travolta invented bits of business, added lines of song, in a frantic search to find a way out of the number.

The evening ended without further mishap. But later that night Moore remembers being woken by a telephone call from Bob Le Mond.

'Bob said, "Tom, I just want you to know there is a little bit of a problem. John is at the airport and he's leaving." I said, "What?" He said, "I think I can talk him back, but I want you to know he's *very* discouraged. You must take this very seriously."'

Travolta did return to the show and the subject was never mentioned again by either the actor or Tom Moore. It's the first

recorded instance, though, of Travolta going to the wall, and all but taking a project with him, over a matter of professional self-esteem. Years later, directors from John Badham to Roman Polanski would experience that unnerving phenomenon, the Protest Exit.

The actor's old employer John Heinze made the journey one day from Boiling Springs to Broadway and caught the show. As in the stage production of *Grease*, the cinema's future king of cool was playing an endearing stumblebum whose comic acting and dancing suggested to Heinze a performer to whom Travolta had, and still has, a little-sung resemblance.

'He reminded me of Jerry Lewis,' Heinze says. 'He played this goofball, disjointed kind of guy, a soldier on the way to his ship going to Europe. It was a comedy-dancing role and he did it with a lot of charm and skill.'

Heinze didn't go backstage to see and congratulate Travolta. When I ask him why not, he brushes it aside: 'I didn't really know him that well.'

This spotlights one of the mysteries in Travolta's early life. To some he is outgoing and vivacious, a cartoon blur of lovable fun. 'Oh, there's John bouncing off the wall again!' was the *Grease* cast's view of their resident youngster, says Judy Kaye. To others he could be reticent, unreachable.

Grease director Tom Moore knew Travolta well in both New York and Los Angeles. The knockabout John was always on standby in group occasions. When Moore and he, with Bob Le Mond, actress Katherine Helmond and other West Coast friends, took trips to Disneyland, they used to eat at the themed restaurant inside the 'Pirates of the Caribbean' fun ride. Travolta's party piece was to stand up imitating one of the animatronic dummies: he did it so convincingly that people passing in boats thought he *was* one of the 'pirates'.

At other times Moore sensed another Travolta.

'I suspect that anyone who's funny has a strong melancholy side, otherwise the humour never develops. I think John felt an outsider. He was very close to his family, he was the youngest of the cast in both our shows, and he hadn't the others' schooling. You'd see this side of him when he was "off", when the curtain had come down or he was no longer in the middle of the arena. There was

a loneliness there. He expected a great deal from friendships, and he wouldn't form them unless he thought the person would really be there for him.'

Also, who knew – friend, foe, acquaintance – where John Travolta's head was for much of the time? It might have been cooking up dreams of stage or movie success. 'He was very ambitious,' says Tom Moore, 'much more than people think. He had a real hunger and a need for success.' Or it might have been up in the clouds while his feet walked, tapped or kicked on Broadway. That dream of flying was still with him. He had begun regular lessons at Teterboro Airport on which he spent large portions of his performing pay.

Was flying a form of exultation, an extension of dance that took that form's gravity-defying impulses higher and higher, from three to thirty thousand feet? Or was it a form of fugitive solitude: a way to be alone, adrift, far above the crowd pressures and career worries, nearer the stars?

Jerry Zaks remembers the flying obsession, since Travolta carried it round with him, literally. 'He used to travel with the airline schedule. This big book like a phone directory with all the timetables of the different airlines. He just loved anything to do with planes. He'd talk about it constantly.'

Judy Kaye became so familiar with Travolta's aero-mania that when she looked for a nineteenth-birthday gift for him on the *Grease* tour, she recognised it as soon as she saw it. The signed autobiography by famed aviator Amelia Earhart came complete with Earhart's written log of an early flight and a 45 rpm record of her transmissions to the tower.

Two other friends gave him a copy of Antoine De Saint-Exupéry's *The Little Prince*. Saint-Exupéry was not just a writer, he was a famous airman. Years later Travolta would use *The Little Prince* and the French author's bestknown flying memoir *Vol De Nuit* as joint models for his own first venture into book-writing.

3

THE DEVIL'S REIGN

In the summer of 1974, in the desert around Durango, Mexico, John Travolta encountered another kind of flying. His spirit flew out of his body.

On location for *The Devil's Rain*, a shlock-horror movie starring Ernest Borgnine and Ida Lupino, he was reunited with actress Joan Prather two years after working with her on the other, off-Broadway *Rain*. Prather was a practising Scientologist and Travolta was a barely practising actor. His debut movie was a 'piece of shit' – his words – about devil worship. His main acting challenge was to wear a mask and melt into a puddle of goo while crying 'Blasphemer! Blasphemer!' He was ripe for Scientology.

'I was on a thin line for survival. Every job I got was like my last hope that I'd survive. This girl was really decent and she said I can help you, read this Dianetics book.'

He had been in analysis for seven months in what he later called the 'self-destructive time' of his life. His career was in limbo; his friends and family were 1500 miles away; his insomnia was worse than ever. And in Mexico he came down with the 'flu. Prather talked to him, comforted him and performed what Scientologists call a 'process'.

'I went outside my body,' remembers Travolta. 'It was like the body was sort of on its own and I was outside walking round it. I got real frightened, and she said, "Oh my goodness, you've gone exterior."' She produced another process that put Travolta back in his body. The whole happening lasted about five minutes.

Part of an actor's business is to open himself up to experience, to

try on different existential clothing. But Scientology and its ungainly patchwork of religion and psychotherapy might not have seemed so comfortable a fit for Travolta if he wasn't already bent out of shape, at this time, by his low feelings.

There had been stresses too in his relationship with manager Bob Le Mond. Back in 1972 Le Mond wanted Travolta to stay in Hollywood when the actor insisted on touring with *Grease*. And when in 1974 Travolta was offered $750 a week – 'the most money I'd ever heard of' – to play on Broadway in the comedy *The Ritz*, Le Mond reversed his priorities and advised him to take the live theatre payday. But for Travolta staying in New York treading the same old boards was 'horizontal movement'. So he uprooted himself to Los Angeles, sharing a sock-strewn apartment with an old friend who had become a new business adviser, Jerry Wurms (brother of Denise). 'We were like the odd couple,' Wurms says. 'I was the neat one. John was the slob.'

The only thing worse than all the films Travolta failed to get into, as he tramped between tests, was the film he did get into. *The Devil's Rain*, unavailable today at all respectable video stores, melted into the same gooey oblivion as Travolta's character. 'I was just a make-up dummy really.' And then he met or re-met Prather. One shudders at the vortex this tender soul from New Jersey had fallen into, where Z-movie career humiliations were combined with a friendship that forced on him exophysical raptures and the *primum opus* of L. Ron Hubbard.

Travolta would surely not have ploughed through the whole of this Scientologist's bible at that time? Or perhaps he would. Since he was acting in a film about the Devil he might have been drawn to Hubbard's observations on the subject. Says the guru, science fiction author, former explorer, war invalid and nuclear physics student – the man who wrote *Dianetics: The Modern Science of Mental Health* for that unique period of American alarmism, the early fifties (Cold War, the Bomb, *Attack of the Fifty Feet Women*, Korea) when almost any new creed was welcomed into the fold – 'If there was ever was a devil, he designed the reactive mind.'

The reactive mind, explains Hubbard, is that part of the human brain where messages are scrambled and 'engrams' – malicious tracings of past bad experiences that literally incise the brain

(Hubbard's sci-fi version of the trauma) – run riot. The reactive mind 'shuts off hearing recall . . . places vocal circuits in the mind . . . makes people tone-deaf . . . makes them stutter'. Worse still, it 'can give a man arthritis, bursitis, asthma, allergies, sinusitis, coronary trouble, high blood pressure and so on.' (The 'and so on' is par for the book's scientific rigour).

We shall come back to Hubbard's tome later. For now, just imagine the impact such booming, all-encompassing salvationism might have on a young man with a butterfly mind and bruisable heart. Neither of these is protected even by the armour of a completed education. Travolta picked that book up with an innocence that is touching even as he recalls it, still with apparent innocence, years later, 'The title alone means "through the mind" and it deals with physical and emotional pain which is what I had.'

That simple. Here is the pain, here the 500-page apothecary.

Prather plied him with other Scientology literature. 'I was so impressed with these works,' he says, 'that I suddenly had a sense that I wasn't just a body, that I was actually a spirit in the body, and my life changed from that moment. I knew I was going to live forever.'

The drop-out high-school student may also have thought of Scientology at some deep level – his deep level, not Scientology's – as a *substitute* for education. For Hubbard has a wonderful flair for downscaling or contextualising 6,000 years of human learning. 'The work of Louis Pasteur formulated the germ theory of disease [he writes]. With Dianetics is gained the non-theory of disease. These two, with biochemistry, complement each other to form the whole field of pathology at this time.'

So farewell, 'flu and depression, along with bursitis, sinusitis and coronary trouble. Helped by Prather, with whom Travolta may or may not have had a romance – the love annals, are foggy – he could survive *The Devil's Rain* and stride back to Hollywood, to search more determinedly for his career and kismet.

Jeff Conaway says that in their years of friendship in L.A., Travolta would try to explain what Scientology was all about. 'He said, "It's getting to zero." "Getting to zero?" I said, 'that's where I am all the time. I'm trying to get *above* zero." I was doing drugs, therapy, taking pills to get to sleep. John was

never into drugs really, he seemed to have his head together.'

Travolta took Conaway to one or two Scientology meetings
as well as bringing him cut-price vitamin tablets from the cult's
Celebrity Center. But he failed to make a convert. 'I didn't really
want to connect,' Conaway says. 'But I was supportive of John.
If that's what he wanted, fine. And he seemed more centred with
it as a person.'

So much more so that he won the role that would transform his
life, ensuring him nationwide fame and the beginning of that lasting
tracing on America's brain that has been the Travolta career.

The show was an ABC Television sitcom about school life
called *Welcome Back Kotter*, based at several removes on British
TV's *Please, Sir!* series starring John Alderton. ABC's Senior
Vice-President in charge of talent and special projects at that time
was Gary Pudney. 'I had to approve all casting,' says Pudney, a
cherubic fiftysomething with a Gore Vidal drawl. 'In essence I gave
Travolta his job, though the producer Jimmy Komack picked him
and presented him to me.'

Komack himself had been tipped off about Travolta by casting
supremo Lynn Stalmaster, still championing the actor after his
near-miss with *The Last Detail*. 'There were other contenders,'
Stalmaster says, 'but I knew John would be the answer, particularly
in a role where he could use his body language which is a major
part of his acting and *re*acting.'

Travolta's appeal as a performer and sitcom character was soon
clear. As leader of the Sweathogs, the dumbskulled school rowdies
who operated in *Kotter* much as the Fonz did in the rival youth
sitcom *Happy Days*, this blend of pin-up and goofball was two
icons for the price of one. He was a discount Presley combined
with a sexier Jerry Lewis. And if his luxury black locks and
melting blue eyes – the gossip columns would supply the colour
even if black-and-white TV didn't – seemed inappropriate to this
young classroom Attila, they were also irresistible. This was a
delinquent every woman could swoon over: such as his co-star
Marcia Strassman, a telegenic brunette who played schoolteacher
Kotter's wife.

'When we were casting, Jimmy Komack had me over to his

house to show me tests of the Sweathogs. I looked at Travolta and went "Oh my God. That's a star. That's another David Cassidy." (Cassidy was the seventies heart-throb who starred in TV's squeaky-clean *The Partridge Family*.)

'What they had to do for their auditions was, someone asked questions off-camera and they had to answer in character. John was brilliant at this and it set a pattern. You couldn't script for the Sweathogs, they spent their whole time ad-libbing. It was like the Marx Brothers.'

Designedly so, says ex-Sweathog Ron Palillo. Playing Horshack to Travolta's Barbarino, he and the cast's other paid hellions Ron Hegyes and Lawrence Hilton-Jacobs helped to turn the whole programme around, if not upside down.

'It started off very gritty and documentary, like *The Blackboard Jungle*,' says Palillo. 'But when the pilot episode was banned in Boston, and other cities like St Louis, we were told we had to change the show drastically. We became less tough, more lovable and entertaining. We'd improvise everything from spoof musical numbers to rip-offs of *The Godfather* or *Mean Streets*. Usually a sitcom script comes in at forty-five pages; ours were long at thirty because the Sweathogs were supposed to come up with six to eight minutes of comic business. John was very good at this. He was crazy, silly, childish. He could mimic anything, anyone. If he was not intellectually stimulating' – faint sound like a half-suppressed chuckle – 'he was instinctual down to his fingertips.'

Not intellectually stimulating?

'He was not the brightest person in the world. John was very sweet but he was a little slower than everyone else. Having never finished high school, he was aware that other people were one step ahead of him. It made him feel intellectually inferior, which probably compounded the problem.'

So did being one of four fame-dazed youngsters prey to new paranoias. Says Palillo, 'We all went through this large crisis of having been New York actors on not much money to being big TV stars. We went into rehearsal one morning and learned that Freddie Prinze, who was the hottest star on television at that time, had committed suicide.' (Prinze was a pin-up Puerto Rican who starred in the long-running sitcom *Chico and the Man*). 'The four

of us got together and made a pact with each other that we would never do that whatever the pressure or anxiety we might feel. If one of us felt that low, he would call one of the others.'

One way for the Sweathogs to relieve pressure was to go out to dinner every week on Tuesdays after blocking rehearsals. Marcia Strassman went too. 'We hated those days in the studio. It was walk two feet, stand, walk two feet, stand, just to lock in your positions for camera. So we and the boys would go to the Palm Restaurant and eat lobster, steak, more food than you've seen in your lives. You could put anything in front of John and he'd eat it. It was frightening.'

Travolta and his cronies set a standard for social nonchalance on and off screen. 'I blame the breakdown of my marriage on John,' Strassman half-jokes. 'When it comes to drinking, he is like me. One glass and we're happy, two and we have lampshades on our heads. When I got married I insisted that the only people sitting at my table at the lunch were my husband and the Sweathogs. We'd hardly started eating when John leans across and says to my husband, "You know, I wouldn't have missed this for anything. I had to see who she married, 'cos she's been with all the best men." I thought that's it. The divorce papers. Let's go.

'Yet it was quite innocent. He didn't think he was saying anything harmful. He is just a completely silly person.'

Strassman also remembers an early instance of Dianetics at work. It happened in her dressing room. 'I had a headache, I wasn't feeling good and John came in and told me to relax. He put his hand over different parts of my body, slowly, gently. This went on for about half an hour. I said, "What are you doing?" He said finally, "Are you feeling better?" I said, "No." I didn't feel better at all, I found it rather annoying. But I learned later that this is what Scientologists call a "contact assist".'

By this point Travolta had become virtually part of the Strassman family. He moved from a chaotic, model-plane-strewn two-roomer in Hollywood's Crescent Heights to an upscale Doheny Drive apartment soon, also strewn with model planes. He lived on the floor below the actress's parents. Strassman would drop by to see her folks and the first sight would be Travolta, who had himself dropped by to gaze at their open fridge door.

'He was always eating. No one back then was into dieting or jogging or fitness. The nearest John came was when he was in our house once with my sister. We were trying out one of those metal traction things for the arms that they advertise in muscle mags and we'd attached it to the door and were pulling at this ridiculous thing and becoming more hysterical. Then there was a knock on the door and the pizzas arrived.'

While no one was looking, *Welcome Back Kotter* and its young star became national phenomena. Travolta's weekly fan mail went from three figures to four, later to five. Back in New Jersey, Helen and Sam Travolta shooed fans away from the house, where anything was a hostage to adoration from the clothes hanging in the backyard to bits of the building. Helen was at pains to point out that all resemblances between Vinnie Barbarino and Johnny were coincidental. 'He is not a Sweathog. And when people think he is, I say, "I once acted Mary Magdalene in a high-school play – what do you want to make of that?" '

'The public went crazy about John,' says Gary Pudney. 'He was an original.' He was also, Pudney points out, a 'triple hitter'. He could act sing and dance and occasionally did all three at once.

Says Travolta, 'By about December [of the series' first year] I started doing all the Elvis shit. I added all that.' He also added the touches of childlike vulnerability that separated Vinnie from the Fonz. 'He's a fifties character and I'm a seventies Brooklyn character,' said the actor. 'You wouldn't be surprised if Vinnie cried, but you would if Fonzie did.'

The singing Travolta and crying Travolta would both have major workouts in 1976. A hit record and a made-for-television weepie added cubits to his fame and charisma.

After hearing one of his *Kotter* songbursts, a take-off on a Beach Boys' hit with Travolta substituting 'Barbarino' for 'Barbara Ann,' record manager Bob Reno of the RCA-distributed Midtown International label signed him up in February 1976 to record an album. (Legend claims that Reno's small daughter was watching the TV show and twittered with amusement over the name Barbarino, which sounded like Bob Reno: so she summoned dad to the television).

It was not Reno's first association with Travolta. He had already

studio-taped some songs with him back in pre-*Kotter* 1974, on strength of the small sample of Travolta's singing at large in the *Over Here*! album. Combining the unreleased tapes with newer songs, the *John Travolta* album came out in March 1976 along with a first single, 'Let Her In'. The croony love ballads, delivered in a crushed-hormones voice somewhere between Johnnie Ray and Donny Osmond, sold 800,000 copies and reached number five on the bestseller charts. A second album followed, *Can't Let Her Go*, which despite *Time* magazine's dismissal – 'bland rock album tailored to subteens' – proved another hit.

Realising he had a prodigy on his client list, Bob Le Mond prepared some Ciceronian dicta for the press.

'Within the realm of stardom,' he said, 'you have people operating on three different levels: the sex symbol, the actor, the personality. When you have all three in combination you have a potentially important film star who changes the course of American film and the very nature of acting that will go into film from here on.'

Le Mond pushed his client from pillar to pedestal on promotours, then on up to roofs. At Cleveland 5,000 fans clamoured to touch John Travolta. There were more devotees in Chicago and New Jersey. And in a Long Island Shopping Centre, after obliging 10,000 screaming teensters by gyrating on a roof, he had to be disguised as a policeman to make his getaway.

Even quiet Englewood caught the infection. Dwight Morrow High proposed a John Travolta Day, to the horror of the school early-leaver turned performing star.

His mother comforted him with, 'That's what you bargained for, Johnny. That's just part of making it.'

But surely there were ways to retreat from a fame as virulent as this? In 1976 Travolta decided to reject a concert tour that might have bought him a decade of comfortable retirement: 'There was the potential of making an enormous amount like $25,000 for personal appearances. Just to go on and sign autographs. They didn't want my ability, they wanted my presence . . . It was based on heat at the moment.'

Instead he chose to act in a two-city stage production of *Bus Stop*. Even here, hopes that the art of acting could be displayed to a quiet gathering of William Inge fans were dashed as soon

as he loped onstage. Travolta wore skintight jeans and a white sombrero. 'Mah name is Bo Decker and ah'm twenty-one years old. Everywhere ah go, ah got all the women.' All the women in the audience clutched their faces and screamed, 'Vinnie!'

Adoration brings its own horror and perhaps its own counter-kismet. If the Devil was still tailing Travolta from Durango, we cannot be surprised that the actor failed to make the film *Days of Heaven*, although he was passionate to play the offered lead in this elegiac prairie epic by director Terrence Malick. ABC would not release him from *Kotter*, so the part went to Richard Gere. Gere, who had already headed the London production of *Grease*, would go on, after *Days of Heaven*, to haunt Travolta in the strangest instance of long-running *doppelgangerkeit* in modern Hollywood history.

The Devil's consolation role for Travolta was a Stephen King story being directed by suspense stylist Brian De Palma. *Carrie* offered the actor, in a small role, a satanic variant on Vinnie Barbarino. High-school boy Billy batters a pig to death to provide the bucketful of blood with which virginal Carrie (Sissy Spacek) will be splattered and deflowered at the school prom. Billy's girlfriend and ally was played by another movie newcomer Nancy Allen. The two actors lived near each other and car-pooled to the set each day.

'He had two cars, a Mercedes convertible and a wonderful classic Thunderbird,' says Allen. 'But the car we spent all our time in on the film was an old boneshaker. It was not the nicest start to a movie career. For one scene we had to drive up down, up down Vermont Avenue with John – who's not a heavy drinker – popping these beer cans and drinking and spilling them until the car reeked with beer. It was horrible.'

There were also the Travolta-boppers. 'When we drove out to the location for our last scene together, where Carrie blows up the car, they had to barricade the road because of fans. Even though it was the middle of nowhere, there were hundreds of them screaming "John, John!" '

Travolta made the most of minimal acting opportunities. He brings to *Carrie* that elasticity of response which would be acclaimed in the neon light of *Saturday Night Fever's* success

but which is already discernible under the dim street lights here. Bickering and backchatting with Nancy Allen's character in their car-cruising scene, Travolta plays his emotions like a master cardsharp. When a remark of hers causes him to spill his beer and she cries 'Stupid shit!,' he gives her a deadpan, moment-registering look; then turns back and erupts in a split-second giggle, then turns again scowling and gives her a no-ceremony slap across the face. Three different emotions in three seconds, dealt from one capriciously credible mind.

Later this character – the only one in the movie who keeps riffing freely on different personas – is lit with blaring pallor by De Palma as he crouches atop a ladder fixing the blood bucket. With his shoulder-long black hair and aquiline features, Travolta looks like a delinquent Richard III. With this actor, though, even that mask is up for exchange. When he teases Allen, who is busy giving directions from below, he slips into Stepan Fetchit – 'Yis, ma'am, we's doin' the best we can, we really are, boss' – and as easily out again.

Carrie's closest relative in the Travolta canon is not his second De Palma collaboration, *Blow Out*, where he plays a virtuously motivated amateur sleuth, but the 1994 *Pulp Fiction*. It would take Quentin Tarantino to re-endow the actor with the draggled black locks, cheesy pallor and lucent amorality. *Carrie*, though, is fiercer even than that in showing Travolta's un-cuddly side. (You almost *could* cuddle Vincent Vega, between murders and heroin sessions.) De Palma's film broadens at a brushstroke the Travolta range. The pact that its plot makes with the Devil, in a story that ends by skewing almost every main character's life towards the vengeful or paranormal, streaks darker colours across the persona of an actor whose main risk of perishability in the mid seventies lay in his clean-teen, anodyne lovability.

The Devil never restricts his missions, though. On *Carrie* he didn't just bring the best acting tunes, he brought his favourite newspaper reporters. The tabloid tittle-tattlers.

'There were these constant rumours that John and I were having a romance,' remembers Allen. 'We got a kind of kick out of it at first and giggled at them. "Oh really? Wonder where they got that from?" Because I was living with someone else at the

time. John thought it was fun: "Did you see? We're in the papers again?" '

Sometimes, though, entire interviews were made up. One tabloid reported a conversation with Allen, full of direct quotes about Travolta and romance, that she says never took place. 'I never even spoke to their reporter.'

No newshound bothered to snoop out the actual Nancy Allen romance that began during the film. After the blowing up of the car, Travolta sat down to chat with De Palma and her and when De Palma rose to return to work Allen's co-star said to her, 'He really likes you, you know.' She said, 'Whaddyou talking about?' Travolta said, 'I mean it. You'll see. I know what I'm talking about.'

Three months later Nancy Allen and Brian De Palma were married.

Travolta the gypsy, Travolta the clairvoyant. The multi-talent mystic left his magic touch on another of the film's lead actresses. 'He used Scientology to get my headaches away,' said Amy Irving, later Mrs Steven Spielberg. 'He learned this trick about concentration and it worked. He really is one of the sweetest guys on earth.'

He was rehearsing, without knowing, it for a longer encounter with pain and compassion: one whose memory would last a whole lifetime.

4

LOVE AND DEATH

Travolta moved almost straight from *Carrie* to another movie, this time for television. ABC stretched their sitcom idol by casting him in a tears-and-message drama based on a true story about a boy born with no immune system. The title teenager of *The Boy in the Plastic Bubble* lives in a transparent indoor tent made to deter germs and filter air. His real-life younger prototype lived likewise, though only to age twelve; a news item about his birth inspired the original story treatment by writer Joe Morgenstern, later film critic for the *Wall Street Journal*.

'It was a boy in Texas,' he recounts. 'I just picked up the paper one day and read about this kid who had just come out of the womb and into the bubble. I called my agent, wrote a six-page treatment, sent it on an Adirondack Trailways bus – no faxes then – and a couple of days later had a script deal with Aaron Spelling.'

Morgenstern was attracted to what he now wryly calls the 'bullshit existentialism' of the story – 'someone who has to choose between confinement on the one hand and freedom with death on the other.'

ABC were attracted to a nice juicy tearjerker. They hired as director a down-the-corridor talent called Randal Kleiser. His past lay in commercials and sentimental documentaries (*Dawn: Portrait of a Teenaged Runaway*): his future would lie in directing large-screen, high-earning kitsch (*Grease, The Blue Lagoon*). He had also enjoyed a colourful if non-stellar career in front of the camera, from chorus work in big movie musicals (*Camelot, Hello Dolly*) to understudying Ryan O'Neal on TV's *Peyton Place*.

Meanwhile young Glynis O'Connor was cast as the girl next-door who inspires the boy's first love, in the syruping-up of the script entrusted to veteran Douglas Day Stewart. Morgenstern, while hating the maudlin twists given his story, later went to Writers Guild arbitration to contest Stewart's solo screenwriting credit.

The most important cast member, from a crystal-balling Travolta viewpoint, was the actress playing the boy's mother. Diana Hyland was a pretty forty-year-old with looks that could be classed 'ethereal'. She resembled Tippi Hedren with a touch of Susan Strasberg. On TV she had swanned through *Young Dr Malone* and *Peyton Place*. She had a small role in the film *The Chase* and a larger one on Broadway in *Sweet Bird of Youth*, opposite Paul Newman and Geraldine Page. She had even stretched downwards in age to play the Fonz's girlfriend in a *Happy Days* episode.

'You don't look like you could be my mother at all!' exclaimed Travolta when they met on set. And some noticed that between takes the young heart-throb and the career starlet fallen on parent roles would retreat into deep chat sessions. Glynis O'Connor recalls that their relationship 'sort of grew. I became aware of them being together and I remember thinking, "Oh, of course." It was almost like an equation, two plus two equals four. The age gap didn't really occur to me. Because there was something ageless about John which I think came from his being a late child, and there was such youthfulness about Diana. She didn't feel like the "parent", even though she was was playing one. Their two personalities were so strong, it made a bigger impression than what point they were each at in their lives.'

But it made no impression at all on Randal Kleiser.

'I had no idea there was a romance until I saw them arm in arm, much later, at the premiere of *Carrie*. I was shocked. I said, "What are you two doing here together?" It turned out the affair had been going on for months. It never occurred to me he'd be dating the woman playing his mother.'

John's sister Ellen, stirring further ironies into the plot, claims that she tried for the mother's role in *Bubble* but her agent, who also represented Hyland, went to bat for the older actress. 'I never said anything to John,' says Ellen. 'And about a month later he called me and said, "I'm in love with Diana Hyland." '

Nothing could be suspected from the film, where Hyland and Travolta barely interact and even then from either side of a polythene wall. *The Boy in the Plastic Bubble* is poignant neither for its offscreen heart-flutterings nor for its onscreen sentimentality and symbolism. (The boy's name is Todd, German for death.) It is intriguing for the glimpse of an early Travolta stretching his talent. His incandescent naturalism is the movie's strongest suit. Though Kleiser turns this debutant star into a *liebestod* pin-up – boyish-sultry in T-shirts, shorts and luxuriant hair – he also gives Travolta a licence to act. And the face is so transparent that you can see thoughts dart and turn in it like fish in water.

Travolta had only one weakness as a performer, Kleiser says. Strong emotion did not come easily. 'He had a scene with the girl where he is supposed to become upset and tearful about his situation in the bubble. He wasn't getting it and I didn't know what to do. Then Joel Thurman the producer said to me, "Why not make him play angry?" John did that and it triggered the grief.'

Glynis O'Connor remembers, 'There were a lot of takes in that scene because John wasn't happy. And as an actor if you don't get something in the first two or three takes, it becomes more difficult the further along you get. It's very rare you can find the feeling or rhythm by the eighth or ninth take. But he did, and I remember being really impressed.'

One Travolta trait that became apparent on *Bubble* was his retro-active style in designing a performance. 'I never noticed him do anything as preparation for a scene, but afterwards he'd be meticulous about which take to use,' says Kleiser. 'He knew when he was good and when he wasn't "on". He'd keep calling me late at night and say, "On scene thirty-two are you gonna use take one or two? 'Cos I prefer one." I said, "John, I want to get some sleep!" '

In the film's final scene Morgenstern's 'bullshit existentialism' is delivered gift-wrapped in maudlin triumphalism. The sequence begins promisingly. Travolta clearly saw the point of this true-story-as-drama and its happy/tragic denouement – 'I thought that if you had to be confined in a cage your whole life it would be better to live shorter moments out in the real world, breathing real air and touching and holding, than being confined in that bubble' –

and he has a beautifully inventive moment poised in the doorway, when he gulps air like a swimmer storing breath before plunging into the fatal summer day.

But then we have the tritely smiling girl, the long-awaited kiss and the Paul Williams song on the soundtrack. As the girl's horse carries two united hearts, plus owners, off into the horizon, we forget about death altogether in the gallop to a romantic finale.

Many critics swallowed it without grimace. 'An immensely affecting, carefully documented story'; 'exquisitely nuanced performances from Travolta and O'Connor.' As well as good reviews the actor had another memento to treasure, a photograph of astronaut Buzz Aldrin, who after straying through the film in a bizarre guest role gave Travolta this framed gift inscribed, 'To John – Enjoyed our ball in the bubble.'

Travolta's personal romance was going its sweet slow way. On the set of *Kotter*, to which he returned after weepie duty, Marcia Strassman noted that Hyland was becoming a fixture.

'The relationship with Diana became really beautiful. She'd come in and sit at tapings for hour after hour. They worshipped each other. I really think – I shouldn't say this, because he's married now – but I really think she was the love of his life.'

It was a late love for Diana. She was technically still married to writer-producer Joseph Goodson; the divorce proceedings never reached final dissolution. With Goodson, after losing premature twins who died twenty hours after delivery, she had had one child, born in July 1973, a son, Zachary.

Neither her history nor her age bothered Travolta. 'The age thing, because it was awkward in society's eyes, only made the relationship more titillating to me. I like older women. Ladies like Angie Dickinson and Dinah Shore are terrific.

'Besides,' he adds with classic Travolta logic, 'when you're twenty-two most women are older.'

During the first weeks of their romance, and not just because of the romance, the world was opening up around him. He was a national television idol. He had shaken off typecasting by playing a sensitive, tragic teenager after the high-school hellraisers of *Kotter* and *Carrie*. He was a bestselling record artist. He had even – worthy of celebration by *his* lights at least – completed his initial

Scientology course. He purred up to the graduation ceremony in his Thunderbird and right there outside the church, before the gathered Hubbardites, he pranced and sang 'in character' as Vinnie Barbarino.

In the best or worst tradition of TV drama, though, all this happiness had arrived at the moment when it could not last. There was something about Diana that John Travolta didn't know.

Years before, she had detected a lump on her breast. Although she had confided in her father Ted Gentner she waited a year, against his advice, before having a mastectomy. The operation seemed successful and silicon reconstruction followed. Hyland's bedtime disrobing scene in *The Boy in The Plastic Bubble* is carried off as gracefully as by any nymphet.

By then, though, she had learned that the cancer had spread and might prove inoperable. This was the main reason the agent she shared with Ellen Travolta pushed for the *Bubble* role to go to Hyland.

'I never said anything to John [about the illness],' says Ellen. 'Diana and I started to become friends and she said to me, "I don't know how to tell Johnny about what's going on with me." And I said, "Well, I think you should tell him." '

But how would someone so young and vulnerable take it? Or was John Travolta, at twenty-two, so young? 'Sometimes I feel like an old spirit in a young body,' he mused. And the media sensed in him these weird, anguished, unstarry, depths. 'His early start for him without a true adolescence,' cerebrated *Time* magazine, 'and emotionally Travolta is an odd combination, half boy, half man.' He was pressed by interviewers about this odd May–December passion with Hyland. The woman is old enough to be your mother, someone said. 'I don't know about that,' replied Travolta. 'My mother's sixty-five.'

For him Diana 'was a real woman. Her femininity knocked me out, yet she was so bright and ironic! She could be a tease, you know. Her humour was both funky and very elegant and it was always there.'

'John is probably the most mature man I've ever met,' Diana said in turn. A born father too: 'He's wonderful with children,

really. He's able to get right down to their level and knows where they're coming from.'

So were there nestmaking plans? Travolta later claimed that he had picked out a house for them to move into. And Diana, who lived with her only son and a housekeeper Margarita, was a manic decorator; she kept her hand in by stripping and bleaching the floors in her own Westwood home to make them match the white walls. She created a living *House and Garden* photospread for the couple.

In late 1976 Diana, keeping her illness a professional secret, won the lead role in a new TV sitcom called *Eight is Enough*. She was cast as the mother of a large family, with light comedy actor Dick Van Patten as the father. Around the same time Travolta himself, still not knowing of Diana's true condition, signed a deal for his career to go stratospheric.

Robert Stigwood is a multimillionaire music entrepreneur. His ruddy, sunswept Australian face goes, or doesn't quite, with a voice whose rotund vowels and discombobulated consonants suggests a 'strine Alfred Hitchcock. He may be the most important single human being in John Travolta's career. He also, as a sideline, helped to midwife the Beatles, the Bee Gees and Andrew Lloyd Webber.

He almost let the Travolta legend slip through his grasp. In the early seventies he auditioned him for the Broadway production of *Jesus Christ Superstar*. 'I made a note of the audition because I was very impressed,' he says. 'But I thought he was too young against the other apostles.'

Some years later Stigwood watched him on TV and heard the records. 'At least they showed he could sing.' And with the gesture of a man who can move mountains, or turn foothills into mountains with a view to doing so, Stigwood signed Travolta in 1976 to a $1 million three-picture contract. All he will say today to explain this prophetic brainstorm is, 'I thought he was perfect.'

Travolta was not so sure. He might not have agreed to make the first film in the deal at all without Diana. She encouraged him to read the script based on a feature in *New York* magazine by English reporter Nik Cohn. The film's provisional title

was the same as the article's, 'Tribal Rights of a Saturday Night'.

Cohn fanfared, at least at the time, the sociocultural authenticity of his essay. 'Disco is not just a camp fad,' he told an interviewer. 'It's been going on for years and there's a whole lost generation out there, dancing and doing the things they used to do. And no one will mention them except in a patronising way.' But he had actually based his story on a ragbag of American and English street lore. He came to New York after studying disco life firsthand at the Locarno, Stevenage, and drawing a mental identikit of roughs and toughs he knew on London's Goldhawk Road.

'My knowledge of street kids was basically mods in Shepherds Bush who went up to the West End at weekends,' he says today. 'When I went off to Brooklyn I was totally out of my depth. I'd just arrived in the States. I couldn't begin to get to terms with the reality, except that it was obviously the same thing with a different accent, so I used my novelist's imagination.'

His summons to movie fame came when his wife said he'd had a telephone call from one 'Rabbi Stigfeldt'. This was finally interpreted as Robert Stigwood, who offered Cohn money for the rights and a chance to write the first script.

'It was incompetent,' Cohan says of that effort. 'I couldn't do the Brooklyn accent. I ended up producing an extended sketch that I talked through with the American screenwriter Stigwood hired, Norman Wexler. Then Wexler wrote the script which was more based on my original article.'

This was the script John Travolta read. But he thought the hero Tony Manero, a Brooklyn paint-seller who devotes his Saturday nights to the promiscuous glitter of a Bay Ridge discotheque, was too close to Vinnie Barbarino. Diana took the script into the bedroom to read. She came out saying he had to make it.

'Baby, he's got all the colours! He's miles from what you've played. He's furious because he feels the excitement of the whole world when he dances. Staying in Brooklyn is torture for him. Baby, he cares. Catholicism has mixed this boy up; he tries on his brother the priest's collar in front of the mirror. What a moment for an actor. And he grows, he gets out of Brooklyn.'

She saw his sceptical expression, 'Okay maybe all that isn't in the script. But you'll know how to put it there!'

'Diana, he's also king of the disco,' said Travolta. 'I'm not that good a dancer.'

'Baby, you'll learn!'

Spoken like a command. So Travolta began exhaustive dance lessons with teacher-choreographer Deney Terrio. 'I told him he should think of himself as Valentino from the waist up and Elvis from the waist down,' recalls Terrio, who says Travolta was 'physically out of shape and a fairly mediocre mover [and] came in wearing clothes you couldn't dance in.' 'Jeans don't give and sneakers stick,' Terrio barked at him.

He ran the actor through dozens of different steps in front of a mirror. 'The ones he'd pick up naturally we'd keep. The awkward ones we threw away.' Then he taught him to articulate the individual moves. 'If you study him closely in the movie, you'll notice that for every step he takes he moves three or four parts of his body. We spent weeks teaching each part of the body to move separately. That's what makes him so sensuous, so sexy.'

It was a struggle, though, 'John's what I call a sleeper. He doesn't act very sharp until he's talking to the right people, or into the right situation, and then he's dynamite. I taught him that disco movement must be bold and macho and aggressive. The trouble was that John is naturally quiet and fairly timid.'

The bullying and discipline were shock treatment for an actor used to goofing up weekly in *Welcome Back Kotter*, with occasional breaks to play pig-murderers or immune-deficients. Marcia Strassman remembers Travolta would arrive dazed at the *Kotter* studio, his brain bleary with dance movements that he would then gamely demonstrate to her and the Sweathogs.

Peace and privacy came with Diana, who could soothe his stresses and anxieties. She told him not to be so sensitive: he had to 'put a shield around himself.' One such shield was their own love. The need to be together and close out the world sometimes extended to closing out Diana's son Zachary. Though the boy was often a member of the idyll – Travolta's surrogate-fatherly delight in him can be seen from a photograph in which, one arm around Diana, he gazes down at the kid with an inward, fathomless bliss – at

other times, when John visited Diana at her house, Zachary was farmed out with next-door neighbour Bobbie Boschan.

Another shield was geographical distance from Tinseltown. John and Diana spent weekends together in Palm Springs. Two hours out of Los Angeles, past the valley of the windmills, the palm trees were a miraculous shade of unsmogged green and the journalists kept away; few could afford the price of a Palm Springs drink.

The couple stayed with Ellen Travolta's parents-in-law Harry and Ann Fridley, who bunked in a double mobile home on their eighty-acre ranch, leaving the main house to the youngsters. John never saddled up a horse, says Harry, but liked walking. Ann Fridley read about Dianetics to keep up with John's *dernière chose*. (Later, Diana's mother discovered that John had inducted Diana into the cause. Mrs Genther found cheque stubs made out by her daughter to the Church of Scientology).

The lovers also spent nights at the nearby Ingleside Inn, a high-security celebrity hangout with lovenests designed in a range of kitsch luxuriousness. And in preparation for Christmas John rented a house in the mountain retreat of Big Bear, where he, Diana and all the family – or families – could join up.

In L.A. Deney Terrio continued to tutor Travolta in his dance antics, with their Presley-Valentino dual coordination. And if that seemed a bizarre, centaur-like combination, events surrounding *Saturday Night Fever*'s script development on the east coast more suggested pantomime horse. Stigwood's first choice as director was John Avildsen, who brought in the writer who had penned Avildsen's feature debut, an acclaimed, low-budget urban stress drama called *Joe*.

Norman Wexler, who won an Oscar nomination for that film as well as the later *Serpico*, had a history of depressive illness. He took Lithium and his occasional paranoia could take the form of circling a block several times before a meeting to make sure he was not being followed.

To meet him today, he is immensely likable: a man insatiably curious, kindly-mannered and possessed of a mournful, funny candour about the processes of filmmaking. Back in 1976, as he told me one night in 1996 in the large, borderline-Gothic

house where he lives in Greenwich, Connecticut – to go with the Munsters-style home Wexler bears a startling resemblance to the actor (pre-make-up) who played Fred Munster, the lantern-jawed, baggy-eyed Fred Gwynne – he began writing what he thought the best script of his life.

'I wrote *Saturday Night Fever* purely, organically, scene by scene, trying to imagine this boy's life. I thought there ought to be a bit of message: that with a little bit of luck and guts you can break out of your social and family programming. I also put in devious, sinister cultural things like showing the repression in a Catholic family! I wrote in the moment where Tony takes his priest brother's dog collar and mimes a noose motion with it like that.' Wexler mimes an alarmingly vivid self-hanging gesture.

'When these things are embedded organically, symbolically in the narrative, they add to the power of the story because the whole point is it's a catharsis, a purging. When I got to the final period of writing I got that "glow" I'd barely ever had in my life and that I only get when I look at a few things in this life like a Vermeer or a Magritte or I hear Tebaldi singing *Vissi d'Arte*.'

Saturday Night Fever's executive producer Kevin McCormick witnessed the script's birthpangs: 'Norman lived in an apartment in the Chelsea area of New York that was empty save for a bed and the table he wrote on. He'd stay up all night writing.'

'I handed the script to John Avildsen,' describes Wexler, 'saying, "I don't know what we've got here, but if it's good as it feels, it's terrific." '

Avildsen, who had been busy jetting between Manhattan and Hollywood prepping the release of his forthcoming film, a then unfanfared little boxing tale called *Rocky*, took one read and handed it back to Wexler.

'No,' he said. 'It's not my vision.'

Wexler's face mimes his stupefaction. He digresses to curse directors: 'The only writers who like directors are film critics!' (forgetting he is in the presence of one). And he bewails the writer's place in a world run by auteurs and their shock troops: 'You know the old joke. "The starlet was so dumb she fucked the writer!" Everybody hates the writer because they're dependent on him. Until somebody has a script nobody makes

a buck. Nobody has a swimming pool, nobody has a Range Rover.'

Back to the story. To Wexler's dismay Avildsen offered new, unwelcome suggestions. 'He said, "Shall we have Tony working in a clothes shop, not a paint store?" I said, no, that would feminise his image. "Why don't we have him get mad and raid a disco?" Avildsen said. I said, no, that's another film.'

Mainly, though, the director wanted to punch some of *Rocky*'s folksy triumphalism into this downbeat story. So on the advice of friend and *Rocky* star Sylvester Stallone, he hired another scribe, Louis La Russo, to start rewriting. Wexler became depressed. Rumours of disorder and panic spread to Robert Stigwood, resident in Bermuda.

The parties were summoned by the producer. They were questioned, lectured, dismissed to do better. Wexler had Stigwood's personal assurance that he preferred his (Wexler's) script but the producer had to be loyal the director he had hired.

The crunch soon came. Kevin McCormick, Stigwood's chief assistant as well as *Fever*'s executive producer, remembers the moment. 'The Bee Gees delivered rough tracks of five brand new songs and Avildsen said he didn't want to use them, they were too passé.'

Stigwood imploded. In New York McCormick fetched the impresario from the airport. By now weeks had gone by. *Rocky* had opened to world-boggling acclaim and *Saturday Night Fever* was a collection of tattered script pages looking for an owner and an order. Stigwood invited Avildsen to his New York apartment.

'I told him that Norman Wexler's script was so brilliant that I just wanted ten minutes cut. I told him there would be no new script he had to shoot Wexler's. He refused and so I said, 'I'm afraid you'll have to go.

'At that point my office called me, because they knew about the meeting, and said, "Perhaps you should know that John Avildsen's been nominated for the Best Director Oscar for *Rocky*." I had to stop and congratulate Avildsen. He said, "I suppose this'll make a difference?" I said, "No. You shoot the Wexler screenplay or you go." '

Avildsen went. His departure ushered in John Badham, who had

made one modest feature, *The Bingo Long All Stars and Travelling Motor Kings*. He was talented, young and, above all, available. He was promised the *Fever* job if he could cut those vexed ten minutes from the script. Stigwood was worried about waffle – scenes like that between Tony and his lapsed-priest brother Frank in their bedroom: 'You could do it in two minutes, not five' – and there had to be lots of room for those Bee Gees songs he had signed up at vast expense.

Norman Wexler and John Badham got on like soul twins. To the screenwriter's delight Badham junked all the Avildsen-commanded rewrites – never even read them – and excised the required ten minutes. The director also decided it was time for Travolta to come into frame. If the film was to explore the Serious Social Phenomenon of Brooklyn disco-dancing, then Badham, Wexler and their star must visit the real places.

Wexler and Travolta had already enacted one Brooklyn field trip. 'John and I walked all over Bay Ridge when I began the script,' Wexler recalls, 'and everyone shouted out at him because they recognised him from *Kotter*.' In later trips to discos in New York and L.A., crowd adulation did not stop at the vocal. 'These girls would come straight up to John and say, "Hi", and start pawing his crotch.'

Wexler also looked for colourful or characteristic non-disco venues to take his hero through. 'We saw a pizza shop and I thought, let's have Tony eat a pizza at one point. And I said to John, let's go in.' John takes up the story, as rendered in a later newspaper interview, 'We were talking in a pizza parlour, and I just swallowed a whole slice and immediately got another one and ate it without chewing. I didn't realise he was taking all this down.' Wexler wasn't. The writer says that 'all this' never happened; John didn't eat the pizza the way he came to remember. 'When writing, I wondered how to transform the pizza scene,' Wexler says, 'and I thought that some multi-layered method was how Tony should eat. After that John thought that's how he really did eat. It's what an actor's sensibility's about. They don't have psychic boundaries; they become whatever they're playing.'

If they 'are' their roles, they also 'are' their fame. After Badham found the real Brooklyn discotheque the film would use, the 2001

Odyssey. Travolta went along by himself one night disguised in dark glasses and sat in a corner. He wanted to check the place out and do an anthropological study of the natives.

Five minutes went by, then – 'Hey, man! It's fucking Travolta!' Soon the patrons were all coming over to him, at which point the idol resignedly removed his shades. The private observation session turned into a seminar, though for males only.

'A couple of guys would be talking to me,' Travolta says; 'their girlfriends would come up and they'd say, "Hey, stay away from me, don't bug Travolta. Don't bother me, I'm talking to the Man." And they'd actually push the girls away. Tony Manero's whole male chauvinist thing I got from watching those guys in the disco.'

More mob madness is recalled by the film's costume designer Patrizia Von Brandenstein, later production designer on films such as *Amadeus* and *Sneakers*. She and Travolta went on a hunt for what would become the movie's key icon.

'On the first occasion we went shopping for the white suit I remember being in this store for twenty, thirty minutes and having an *enormous* crowd suddenly materialise outside. The police had to come and hustle us back to the car.'

The white suit was to become not just an emblem for the film but a talisman for John. The choice of that blinding three-piece began, says Brandenstein, as an aesthetic one. 'When we went to clubs, particularly the 2001, we loved the strobing effect the big block lights had on white. Also someone casually said at a meeting that John was at, "But heroes wear white." Exactly.'

Brandenstein finally picked an off-the-rack polyester number that she and Travolta saw in a Greenwich Village store. 'The whole point had to be that it wasn't a designer suit, it was worn by a Brooklyn kid who could barely afford to go out on a Saturday night but spent eighty percent of his income on clothes.' Once the suit was bought Brandestein took it apart and remodelled it since it had to 'hang in a certain way' for Travolta.

But there was another white suit in his life, or the dream of one, in which even more meaning was invested. He and Diana had planned a trip to Rio, via London, for the late spring/early summer of 1977, when *Saturday Night Fever* would be finished. They would fly on Concorde to Britain, then travel on to Brazil.

It was a way of denying or defying Diana's present illness, which he now knew about, by holding up a future treat. And they were set on buying John a white suit for the trip. For what else does a handsome westerner wear in the exotic tropics?

Diana Hyland had begun work on her TV series with all the determined optimism Travolta brought to *Saturday Night Fever*. But early in the run, illness caught up.

'After the third show of *Eight is Enough* she told me she had cancer and had only a few weeks to live,' recalls her co-star Dick Van Patten. 'We all went into shock. One thing that amazes me is: before you do a TV series you get a medical test to see if you're fit. And she had passed. She said she knew she was ill but wanted the part so badly.'

She went into hospital, pretending to the other actors that it was merely a back pain. Van Patten visited her and watched the shows they had recorded together. Her character was put on long-distance hold rather than written out. In ensuing episodes her voice could be heard talking to other characters down telephone lines.

This was the year in which the self-confidence of the man she loved was supposed to be at full throttle. *Saturday Night Fever* was due to start filming on St Valentine's Day 1977. But now, all Travolta knew about hearts and arrows was that the first were freshly pierced by the second every day. And what was he to do about that newly urgent film star ego which demanded that *he* come first, everything and everyone else second? When he voiced sympathy pains with Diana one day – 'I felt my scalp and said to her, "Oh, what if this is tumour, what if I have cancer too?"' – was that a touching attempt to deflect her from suffering by seeming to share it? Or was he worried about damage to his own star machinery?

Diana returned home for a while, but remained largely bedridden. In February 1977 her condition worsened. Having lost her hair through chemotherapy and barely eating, she went back to hospital. Tumours had travelled down her spine. She put a traction machine in her room so that visitors would believe her back injury story.

With Diana ill, John had already left for New York. The first day's shooting ended with a Valentine's Day party, to cap the ad-lib

party enjoyed by the 10,000 fans mobbing the location. Not for the first time Jeff Zinn, Travolta's stand-in, was togged up in the star's clothes to do a Pied Piper routine, leading the teenyboppers off in other directions.

Four days later another party celebrated John's twenty-third birthday. Crew members remember him sitting in a corner drinking fruit juice.

But the show did go on. Travolta started creating a performance that matched Wexler's script. Perhaps the underswell of grief helped, or perhaps it was put out of mind at each call of 'Action!' The film's cinematographer Ralf Bode is amazed when I tell him the Diana crisis was going on at this point. 'Surely not. Surely that was all over before the film?'

For him Travolta was on the mark every day, without fail or falter. Bode even remembers the day they began shooting the famous walk that kicks off the opening credits. 'Stayin' Alive' thumping away on the soundtrack, Tony Manero jouncing along the street, a paint can hip-hopping in his hand, a discotheque-dandy spring in his walk.

'We had the camera down low on a wheeled platform and I kept telling John, "Kick the lens, kick the lens!" I wanted it to seem as if those feet were really kicking up off the ground in rhythm to the music.'

Travolta never completed the sequence. Just before the weekend of March 26th he heard that Diana was going home from hospital, this time almost certainly to die.

When after the long flight he walked into her room at home he said, 'My angel, you are just as beautiful was ever.' She was well enough to talk, even to take a short walk in the garden, his arm around her waist, her head on his shoulder. At one point she whispered gently, 'I'm going now. But you are going to have this work.'

She could still eat a little. The last conversation John recalled was about what they would have for dinner. He went out for Japanese food; when he returned, she was no longer conscious. Diana's mother, who was staying with her daughter, remembers his reaction. 'He was shocked to learn that she was unconscious and how close to death she was. That it had come on her so quickly.'

Dick Van Patten and his wife visited Diana on what would prove her last day. Van Patten found a Travolta different – more human, more bewildered – than the nobly suffering idol celebrated in later, fanzine versions of the Diana Hyland tragedy. 'I went round on the Sunday with my wife and John opened the door and said, "Come in, I'm here with the nurse, and Diana's dying. I don't know what to do." Diana's mother was there, but she wasn't talking, she seemed to be in shock. I went into the bedroom, Diana was almost in a coma. John was all upset and didn't know what action to take.'

Van Patten asked if he had called a priest. No, said Travolta. Van Patten said that as a Catholic Diana should have the last rites: he would take care of it. So he and his wife drove to their nearby Catholic church, St Paul's, where they knew the priest Father Robert Curtis.

'They came to me after Mass as I was cleaning up and asked me to go over to Diana's little house,' recalls Curtis, a former actor and movie producer who had met Diana on visits to the *Eight is Enough* set. 'So I went over to perform what I call the "sacrament of health", or the last rites. When I arrived she had, I believe, just entered a coma.'

Travolta had been calmed by Van Patten's taking over the practicalities. He sat by Diana's bedside. He communed with her even though she was no longer conscious.

'John was there holding her and he kept holding her all the time I did the sacrament,' Curtis says. 'He talked to her as if there were no change, as if the bridge was still there between the two of them. It was a very sweet thing. He was very tender and gentle, and it was obviously quite solid what was between them. I had a very strong sense of the presence of love.'

'The priest said to us all, "You can talk to her",' remembers Van Patten. 'She knows you're here. She knows everything that's going on." And when he said that, Diana actually made a noise, a little "Unhhh". Like letting us know the priest was right.'

Father Curtis left after giving the rites. A little over an hour later, Diana Hyland died.

Travolta took it with a numbed, undemonstrative sense of shock. He seemed overcome by disbelief as much as by grief. Says Van

Patten, 'Here was this forty-year-old girl he was in love with and suddenly it was all over.'

Ellen Travolta saw her brother later that day. 'He looked about twelve in his crewcut and khakis. And I remember him saying to me, "Ellen, it's very easy to die. And I've had so much in my life. I've had so much success, and I've loved someone. I've had a full life." He couldn't believe she was gone. And he was a baby.'

The world was not about to draw back and allow him space for grief. The proposed strewing of Diana's ashes on Santa Monica Beach on the following morning, Monday March 28th, was abandoned when the beach filled up with rumour-alerted Travolta-boppers. In mobbing this innocent stretch of sand, they came close to having a preview of *Saturday Night Fever*. For their idol had gone out that very morning to purchase a white suit like the one in the movie. Only this was the suit he and Diana had dreamed of for their vacation.

He wore it at the memorial service re-arranged for Diana's home and attended by friends, relatives and fellow actors. Those who questioned the suit in a muffled whispers were told, during Travolta's address, his reasons for wearing it. 'John and I were doing the service together,' recalls Father Curtis. 'Without any pre-consultation we were taking turns saying words, and I remember him talking about the white suit and what it meant in his and Diana's plans for the future.'

Soon it was over. The weekend had come and gone; the day had come and gone; leaving only a twenty-three-year-old man who had lost a forty-one-year-old lover in a relationship no one could quite fathom. Most of the magazine-reading world had been caught up in it though, as well as all those who went on to read 'John and Diana', a romanticised chronicle by Mary Ann Norbum written, published and widely sold, some months later, in the teeth of Travolta's objections.

On that March 28th the actor headed for the airport to return to *Saturday Night Fever*. A widower in all but title, he would now have to resume playing a teenager whose emotional world stopped at the four walls of a New York disco.

Seated in the first-class section of the plane, he wept quietly, to the puzzled concern of the passenger just behind, one Andy

Warhol. Watching the famous TV star buffeted by grief, Warhol recorded the occasion in his *Diaries*.

'John Travolta kept going to the bathroom, coming out with his eyes bright red, drinking orange juice and liquor in a paper cup, and he put his head in a pillow and started crying. I saw him reading a script too, so I thought he was acting . . .

'I asked the stewardess why he was crying and she said, "Death in the family," so I thought it was a mother or father, until I picked up the paper at home and found out that it was Diana Hyland, who died of cancer at forty-one, soap-opera queen, his steady date.'

Travolta remembers only someone with odd hair who kept craning over the back of his seat. 'I couldn't control it. I'm thinking, "I don't want to be watched while this is happening." '

That very night – no rest for the famous – he would have to go on set and act.

5

SATURDAY NIGHT

After the quizzical in-flight surveillance conducted by Andy Warhol, John Travolta had a more sympathetic support group back in New York. For the *Saturday Night Fever* shoot he had moved into a Central Park West apartment that had once housed Mick Jagger and was now being specially vacated for him by a famous singing couple.

'I love your TV show so much, I can recite the last soliloquy of *Welcome Back Kotter*, James Taylor had exclaimed on opening the door the day John moved in. Travolta tested him and found him word-perfect. 'You've got me on the happiest day of my life,' Taylor added. 'My wife just gave birth to our son Ben.'

By the time John returned from his west coast bereavement Taylor's wife Carly Simon was back from hospital and installed in the couple's new apartment upstairs. Travolta visited them and they sang for him in their kitchen. Later, because he couldn't sleep, Carly wrote a lullaby for him and taped it, and James doodled a little song with a long title called 'My Name is Barbarino but My Good Friends Call Me John.'

'If someone had said, "What's your ultimate dream?" in the seventies,' Travolta mused, 'it would have been to be befriended by these two people, sung to by them, and have songs written for me by them. I could have died, joined Diana, and it would have been just fine.'

The most seventies thing about such a sentiment is its wistful mysticism. But loss brings out the otherworldly flakiness in us all, a desire to pass beyond the clouds into an impossible reunion.

With Travolta these flirtations with parallel worlds and weird ascensions, from aeronautics to Dianetics, may even have run in the family. In her last years his mother, who became ill again with cancer soon after Diana's death, had a dream after falling asleep on Travolta's plane.

'When I woke up [she dreamt], Johnny was gone and the two pilots were sitting in the cabin. I ran to the cockpit and there was Johnny flying that thing, and singing and looking so gorgeous in a white turtleneck and a scarf – it was just like a movie. "Johnny," I said, "You can't fly this." "Come on, Ma," he said, "I'll give you a lesson." I took the wheel – Johnny can make me do anything – and the plane shot up in the air. Everybody thought the world had ended.'

Even if we put this dream off-limits to Freudians, who could swarm all over it like ants at a picnic, it has a wondrous *liebestod* delirium. Ecstasy and Armageddon are mysteriously linked. (Why did everyone think the world had ended?) And the vision of a sparkly white Travolta acting as high-speed escort to the heavens is as close to throbbingly angelic as a mother's dream image of her son can decently get.

This blend of the mundane and the metaphysical was already at work – honed no doubt by grief – in Travolta's performance in *Saturday Night Fever*. The character as written by Norman Wexler is already a cut above his context, more richly imagined, especially in his family and religious background (close to the actor's own Catholic upbringing), than the club-crawling dandy of Nik Cohn's original story. Travolta took it further still. Instead of a disco-dancing dimwit whose brain cells have been scorched to extinction by his hair-dryer, the actor suggests deeper preoccupations and an elusive, haunting sadness. James Dean with touches of Hamlet and Vinnie Barbarino.

None of his *Saturday Night Fever* co-workers understands, even today, what triggered his performance in one scene. His character Tony is sitting on a bench by the Verrazano Bridge with girlfriend Stephanie, played by Karen Lynn Gorney. As he recites the bridge's measurements and statistics for her, the scene's almost comical study in useless information as romantic sweet talk – the stuff of dating everywhere – is winched

into poignancy by the sudden welling of tears in Travolta's eyes.

'It was quite unexpected; the scene does not call for him to cry, nothing in the script says it,' says director John Badham. Nor were the tears coaxed by glycerine. 'There's no reason in the world in that scene why I'd send make-up over to him with their little box of tricks. It was just John who came up with it.'

'I remember distinctly the moment he started crying,' says cinematographer Ralf Bode. 'I thought, "Ohh, this interesting." It was a poignant moment very sweet. None of us knew where it came from.'

It came in part from Travolta's talent for erasing the line between being and pretending. 'When the girl suddenly turned and kissed me, it really touched me,' he says. 'I was really living that moment. It's a very relaxed way of acting and the most fun way of acting – to be able to live on the screen.'

It also made days or hours of rehearsal redundant. Travolta, at the peak of his instinct, simply segues from life into fiction. With *Saturday Night Fever*'s schedule he almost had to. Karen Lynn Gorney remembers that although the filming was preceded, for her at least, by exhausting days of tests – 'Did I look right? Could I do the dialect? Could I dance with higher and higher heels?' – after that 'we did everything very quickly. There was no money. We had two weeks of rehearsal, when we did improvs and worked on our parts, and then we just shot the sucker.'

So the leading man never asked for time out to mourn.

'When he came back from California he was very distraught, almost like a zombie,' Badham recalls. 'He'd sit over in a corner not speaking. Everyone was respectful and gave him his space. But when I shouted "Ready" he'd get up and pull the life out of I don't know where. When we filmed the scene round the dinner table in the parents' house he was emotionally in a mess. But he'd do it with everything he had and then go sit in a corner.'

'I remember thinking how extraordinary it was not just to carry on with the calibre of work he was doing but to remain professional, friendly, open, sweet,' says co-star Donna Pescow, who played Annette, the girlfriend and dance partner rejected by Tony in favour of Stephanie. She is convinced, though, that the

Verrazano bridge scene revealed the *actor's* emotions as much as the character's. 'It dealt with what he was going through after Diana. He was "in the scene", but I think it became emotional because of what was happening in his life.'

'They drove him inward,' says executive producer Kevin McCormick about Travolta's feelings. 'They made him focus on his performance in a very basic way.'

That performance, to complicate matters, had to be two in one. *Saturday Night Fever* was, first, a social drama about Brooklyn teenagers: their attitudes and mating rituals, their daily battle with overbearing parents and under-achieving lives. 'Watching Tony, I saw loneliness, frustration. I saw everything people deal with in real life,' Travolta said. His hero was also based in part on one of the character sketches he improvised and stockpiled in his early New York days with Marilu Henner, an endearing street slob called 'Strip' (who also ancestored Vinnie Barbarino). 'I always stored things up about people and when I had a character to create I found I had this whole reserve of behaviour and mannerisms to draw on. The last thing you do, you add your own emotions to the script. That part's the most important of all: it's like, inside a character's facade *I* live.'

But *Saturday Night Fever* was not just psycho-social potraiture. It was also a musical, with a cargo of Bee Gees' songs to be pushed perspiringly towards popularity.

It was easy to mix and match the two movies stylistically, Ralf Bode says. 'I thought the film should be hard-edged and realistic outside, but dreamlike in the discotheque. All the colours in the outside world – the Budweiser sign, the garish neon – should be in the disco scenes as well, but romanticised and fogged with star filters and the like.' So he turned the 2001 club into a Brooklyn Valhalla and even tore down a brick wall to bring in a Nike crane for whirly, soaring shots. Badham himself suggested the coloured glass floor, having seen one like it in a dance club in Birmingham, Alabama, where he grew up. A specialist New York firm provided the two four-by-eight-foot sections costing $15,000. Badham too encouraged the swirls of smoke, despite sceptical rumblings from Norman Wexler. 'There's no disco in the world that has smoke on the floor,' grumbled the writer, as

he watched the trial fumigations. Badham replied, 'Well, Norman, after this maybe there will be.'

The visual mechanics were one thing. But what of the human factor? How could any one performer be expected to be James Dean or Marlon Brando one minute, then Gene Kelly or at least George Chakiris another?

Travolta saw his dance solo as his true bid for stardom, a showpiece for his versatility. Yet the most memorable musical scene in the movie might never have happened, at least in the shape it finally achieved. Ralf Bode claims the dance was originally planned as a few moments of virtuosic gyration seen behind the dramatically more important scene in which one of the hero's friends asks Tony's ex-priest brother about absolution for an abortion. 'I remember Badham telling John Travolta that it was basically a background piece,' says Bode, adding, 'it wasn't the best thing to tell him at all.'

For by then Travolta had trained for it, strained for it, even had a Damascene moment of revelation for it. He never forgot the night he and Deney Terrio visited an L.A. disco and Terrio performed a solo in the middle of the floor that froze the clientele in wonder. Travolta had two conflicting reactions to the occasion. First he was so frightened he would not be able to perform Terrio's big Russian leaps and other flourishes that he telephoned Robert Stigwood to suggest calling off the solo. Then he realised he wanted to appropriate Terrio's feat to himself, translating it into movie myth.

He already had the public – or the young public – on his side. There were a lot of screaming Barbarino-boppers out there who wanted to watch Travolta strut, smirk, sing and dance; never mind anything subtler or more inward. They might not mind a glimpse of him with no clothes on either, so the script included a scene of the hero emerging from bed naked. When Travolta said he wouldn't do it (though he had already cooperated in some heavy-duty crotch shots when a stripped-to-the-briefs Tony preens in the mirror), Badham found a compromise. 'We agreed he'd wear a pair of skimpy black underpants and "adjust" himself, so to speak, as he sat up.'

This was the first sign that not *all* would be plain sailing with

this seemingly obliging star. Like any film director negotiating the seas of actorly temperament. Badham could not see every hazard at once. So knowing little of Travolta's anxieties regarding the dance solo, he was startled when at the end of the rapturously received dailies of this sequence – which in deference to the star, had been promoted to a full set piece with a tracking, craning camera – Travolta came quietly to sit next to him and said, with ominous finality, 'My legs are too short.'

'What?,' Badham said.

'My legs are too short' said Travolta.

The director recalls his bafflement. 'I couldn't figure out what he was talking about. Then I looked at the film again and I saw that because the big wide master-shot was on a crane and higher than eye level, there was a very slight foreshortening effect on his legs. Now nobody had complained when I put the camera at Travolta's feet in the mirror scene and he looked like the Colossus of Rhodes. So I kind of ground my teeth a little, because I didn't think he was seeing the whole picture.

'Then a whole chain of unfortunate circumstances happened. There were a number of close-ups during the dance when the camera had run out of film and because of the loud music we hadn't heard the warning "flick-flick" noise. So John sees these, gets panicked and says, "What are we gonna do?" And since I was so annoyed by the legs-too-short remark I turned to him and made one of the stupidest remarks of my life. I said, Well, John, I guess there's only one solution. I guess we're gonna have to cut the whole dance out of the movie.'

Badham meant it as a smart-aleck joke, but regretted it as soon as it left his mouth. 'John gave me a look of such hate I'll never forget it. Don't ever tell me he is not an expressive actor. He communicated such loathing that I've never forgotten it.'

Badham received a phone call the next morning from Robert Stigwood's office, saying that Travolta had left town and would not return until the director had been fired. The weekend crawled by, with attempts at mediation by Stigwood, and finally Badham was woken by the producer's telephone call in the middle of Sunday night. Stigwood told him to go to Travolta's apartment and eat large helpings of humble pie. By 2.30 am Badham and Travolta

had hugged and made up. By 6.30 they were on the disco floor preparing to reshoot the dance.

Pampering the star, or polishing his character's iconic radiance, became a major mandate. Outside the disco Tony Manero might be a sexist lunkhead raised to undeserving humanity by Travolta's skill and translucency as an actor. Inside, he was that phenomenon every neighbourhood knows: a local god made good. During dancing scenes the two identical white suits supplied by Patrizia von Brandenstein performed shift work. While one adorned the strutting, sweating body, its perspiration-drenched companion would be dried off behind the camera with a hairblower. By the end of the each day, Badham recalls, the suits 'were so funky they could have walked out on their own.'

All around, as with any great enterprise, there were blessed and not-so-blessed accidents. One day the crewman who was crouched on the floor dropping chunks of dry ice into a bucket of boiling water, to create the disco's mist-swirl effects, passed out through lack of oxygen. Another day Travolta nearly had a trailer disaster when his mobile home was rocked by fans trying to coax him out.

Happier surprises included Travolta's extemporisations on camera. Asked by Stephanie whether he invented a new dance step he has just put into their routine, he ad-libbed the beautifully cuckoo line, 'I saw it on TV, then I invented it.' Badham also says the actor came up with the cheerful brutalism delivered to the lovelorn Annette, who won't 'go the whole way' in the back of the car. Sitting up straight Travolta-Manero says to her with brisk, cold abstraction, 'Okay, so just give me a blowjob.'

Saturday Night Fever was the first popular feature film to sprinkle its dialogue freely with 'Fuck' and other obscenities, and to offer an exposé of boneheaded Brooklyn machismo so exact (and funny) that it probably prepared the way, through satire to sermonising, for political correctness. At the film's climax Badham was determined to reflect the chauvinism, verging on racism, that resulted in Tony and Stephanie being awarded a prize that rightly belonged to the Puerto Rican couple who danced them off the stage.

'They win the prize because Brooklyn is as racist and prejudiced as any community,' Badham says. 'We could have reincarnated Fred

and Ginger and they'd have given the prize to two neighbourhood paraplegics.' He drew for the scene on actual conversations with the Bay Ridge extras, who told him that if two strangers came and outdanced the local talent they – the watchers – would walk off the floor too, in contempt. 'I grew up in Alabama in a supposed hotbed of racism,' says Badham, 'yet this was as bad as anything I'd encountered.' So it was the director's idea to have a Tony disgusted with the crowd hand the prize to the Puerto Ricans. 'All the anger in subsequent scenes came out of that upset,' Badham says.

It was redemption of a sort for a hero who could have been a horrorshow on legs: a narcissist who mirror-checks his hair and physique each evening before climbing into the flared trousers and tight shirt and who then unfeelingly casts off the besotted dance partner (Pescow) for the ballet-trained snob with 'claaass' (Gorney).

But Travolta added a dreaminess to Tony as he had to Vinnie. We warm to him as a scapegrace escape artist; a boy-man using his dancing and daydreaming to break free from his background, but in whom even the spirit of rebellion is bewildered and half-formed. 'The character's underwater most of the time,' says Travolta. 'When he comes up for air he sees everything very clearly. Then he'll go underwater again and get confused.'

When Tony takes to the disco floor, it is not just a piece of time-out virtuosity, a mechanical frenzy of footwork, armwork and blinding white body-upholstery. The dance redeems all the character's inarticulacy elsewhere. Compared to almost any previous dance solo in a movie, even the funkier excesses of Gene Kelly or Buddy Ebsen or James Cagney, it is a *berserker* ballet. Foot stompings, Russian knee-bends, arm-jives, splay-foot leaps – but all done with a rapt demotic seamlessness. It is as if a young Italian waiter has decided to clear the floor and astonish the customers of a flash eatery.

Neither this dance nor the later one with Karen Lynn Gorney ends with, or even features, the famous iconic moment of the jutting hip and pointing finger. That Badham explains, was a providential postscript. 'Robert Stigwood hired Martha Swope to come and take some publicity shots during two lunch hours on consecutive days. They worked that pose out between them.

There were a lot of attempts to get it right, as I realised later when I looked through the contacts. They finally picked a shot that had a little sparkle coming off John's finger from a star filter Swope had used. In retrospect it would have been nice to have choreographed that into the movie.'

Then again, what need? The press and public swarmed all over the film anyway, before, during and after its release.

The 'before' time involved a stream of tabloid gossip about the star's love life. The less the newspapers could work out Travolta's oxymoronic personal appeal – old-young, cool-goofy, smart-slowwitted, macho-feminine – the more they *tried* to work it out. They knew that for their better understanding and that of their readers, it was time the actor-idol was paired with a girl his own age after that mystifying Diana affair.

So they invented romances that never were. One was with Karen Lynn Gorney, who giggles when the rumour is re-submitted to her today. 'Romance? I don't *think* so! He was fun to dance with.' (Gorney, in any case, was amorously linked with John Badham at the time.) Another light-on-reality liaison was with Donna Pescow. 'If you're seen together more than once outside the actual making of the film, the newspapers go mad,' she says. 'I'm surprised they didn't have us married with several children.'

Travolta was just a generous-hearted fellow professional, she says. 'He looks out for you. He never approaches a scene in terms of what he needs but what the film needs. If he feels you're unhappy, he'll go for another take. The sex scenes in the back seat of the car – my claim to fame! – were tremendously difficult. I was scared to death and John was very supportive. He'd say, "Take your time, if you don't feel ready then we'll stop, take a break."'

Saturday Night Fever finally premiered on December 12th 1977. Marcia Strassman remembers that Travolta and the rest of the *Welcome Back Kotter* gang had been up all night taping a show, since he was still contractually bound to the series. 'I remember John saying at 4am, "Tomorrow is the biggest day of my life and I'm going to miss it!"'

He missed neither the premiere nor the party afterwards, a 2,000-guest champagne and caviare thrash on a Paramount

soundstage that had been tranformed into a disco. His parents were there too, Helen in an expensive hairdo, Sam in a rented tux.

Life was never the same again for any of them. 'Literally, that movie opened,' Strassman says, 'and the next day he was the biggest star in America. We had to start wearing backstage passes on taping night for *Kotter*. And they wouldn't let anyone under fifteen into the audience. It was like having the Beatles working with you. And it happened literally overnight.'

Reviewers praised the star and the movie, usually in that order. 'John Travolta is a revelation,' said *Time*. 'His dancing is electric, his comic timing acute. In the timeless manner of movie sex symbols, his carnal presence can make even a safe Hollywood package seem like dangerous goods.' Echoed critic Stanley Kauffman, 'John Travolta is – the exact word for this performance – terrific . . . When he hits that dance floor on Saturday night after six days of obeying his boss, he sheds his chains and becomes a king. When the girls rave about him, we believe it.'

His Bacchic influence soon caused the Arthur Murray dance studios to be besieged by new clients. Business rose thirty percent, with wannabe Travoltas or Gorneys demanding to be taught the tango hustle. The same fans bought the tie-in records in their millions. 'Staying Alive,' that thumping hit forever linked to the image of Travolta moving through Brooklyn to the motor of his own machismo reached the singles charts in the week of *Saturday Night Fever's* opening, becoming the second number one from the movie songtrack. ('How Deep Is Your Love' reached the top spot in September). The album would become the largest seller in record history, peaking at over twenty-five million.

'To this day we can't figure out why [the film] was so phenomenally successful,' says the Bee Gees' Maurice Gibb. 'We just figured it was gonna be a little story about this New Jersey guy who worked in a paintshop and blew his wage every Saturday night in a club across the bridge in New York.'

Everything Travolta touched turned to fashion, though as he pointed out, 'The look I created [in *Saturday Night Fever*] was three to four years behind the times.' (Flared trousers and torso-hugging shirts had peaked in the early-middle seventies.) So when a publicity shot of the new star showed him wearing accidentally mismatched

cuff buttons, Bob Le Mond's niece told Le Mond that all her friends in Junior High were flaunting mismatched cuff buttons.

Soon too, the fan letters to the star himself, which had reached 10,000 a day even under, *Kotter*, had to be put in storage since there was no economical way to answer them. There were some he wouldn't answer anyway, like the letter from a supermarket tycoon who offered Travolta 'anything in the world' if he turned up at his daughter's birthday party. 'What does the guy think I am – a prostitute? And what kind of values is he teaching his daughter?'

At bay from adulation and mobbed wherever he walked in teenager-intensive Los Angeles, Travolta began looking for an out-of-town address: somewhere well back from Fame Boulevard, preferably with tall walls and a landing strip. His only other chance of repose was at his parents' home, assuming he could sneak into Englewood unobserved, which for the most part he couldn't, especially when *Saturday Night Fever* had its box-office life extended by being released in a PG version without bad language or oral sex.

Travolta said to his father, 'Pa, please don't sell the house. I need a place to come home to.' He liked sitting on Sam's lap in the forty-year-old rocking chair, with his arms draped around the sixty-year-old neck, saying, 'What do you think, Dad? Am I doing good? Do you think I'm making the right decisions.' Sam took time off, to rock him, from counting the missing shingles in the roof and the plastic flowers stolen by fans from the porch planters. 'If we had auctioned the house off bit by bit,' he cracked, 'we'd probably have made a million.'

To neighbour Eddie Costenuic, in the days of mild Travolta fame before *Saturday Night Fever*, Sam Snr used to say of his son, 'He walks around here with sneakers with holes in them and then goes over to New York to buy a $300 suit.' Now his son was an epiphany in a limousine. Or he was a brief detour in busy schedules that had John's private plane landing at Teterboro and his motorcade proceeding to Manhattan, if possible via Morse Avenue

So many mobs, so many street maps.

At least John Travolta could still fly. At least his spirit above

a certain altitude, was solo-powered. With the earnings from *Kotter* plus *Carrie*, plus his records and the Stigwood contract, the new millionaire had bought a secondhand AirCoupe and Cessna Constellation. As more money flowed in, he would buy a twin-engined Rockwell 114, replacing the Coupe, for cosy local flights and a DC3 for longer hauls.

'I get very nostalgic and romantic on airplanes,' he says. And at the end of a long interview in *Playgirl* in March 1977, with a journalist who ironically will turn into a filmmaker, *Jerry Maguire*'s Cameron Crowe, he makes a late conversational lunge to ensure the priority topics are in place.

Crowe: I'll let you go. Thanks a lot.

Travolta: Did you want to know what I do, like I fly an airplane and all that? Do you have all that information?

Crowe: Yes.

Travolta: Great. Thanks a lot.

After *Saturday Night Fever* ended shooting, Travolta had a mere four-day turnaround between his first picture in the Robert Stigwood deal, and the start of work on the second, a film of the musical in which he had made his Broadway debut, *Grease*. Bob Le Mond whisked Travolta and Jeff Conaway, with others in tow, to the Virgin Islands. The manager wanted a three-way heart-to-heart. Travolta was concerned, it seems, about taking from Conaway the lead role that his friend had had in the stage musical. Conaway was cast in the movie, but down the billing as Danny's gang croney Kenickie.

Conaway was touched that Travolta was troubled by this. For him it was just one of the ironies of fame. 'John was very sweet and said, "You were like my idol as Danny, I don't know if I can do it." I said he'd be wonderful as Danny and he shouldn't feel selfconscious. I was perfectly okay about it. We're friends, I said. I had no ego problem. I said, if you want it you've got it. I said, "I'll always be here for you. I love you, man."'

Conaway, like the rest of the world, was giving Travolta no respite from love.

6

PARTYING ON

Record impresario and budding film producer Allan Carr saw *Grease* the stage play in the seventies and never forgot it.

'It was considered the bastard child of Broadway, because it didn't get good reviews but kept running, running, running, till it became the longest-running musical ever. I went with Michael Bennett the choreographer and Marvin Hamlisch the composer [later the co-creators of *A Chorus Line*] and we were like three teenage boys at a party. We just adored it so!'

Carr put out a Mayday call for the movie rights. But they had been acquired by filmmaker-cartoonist Ralph Bakshi (of *Fritz the Cat*). Carr gave *Grease* up for dead, or worse, animated. Then three years later he met the play's producers at an opening night party for Bette Midler. They told him the rights were free again, whereupon Carr pounced. 'I bought them for about $225,000, which in the mid seventies was a lot of money.'

He contacted Robert Stigwood, with whom he had made a small killing with a Mexican movie of *Alive!*, the Andes air-crash story. Stigwood joined him as investor and they began paying off the *Grease* rights by instalments of $25,000 a year.

'Funnily enough,' says Carr, 'a girl agent in New York at that time called Ronnie Chasen sent me over an eight-by-ten photograph and said, "When you do the movie of *Grease*, this boy's gonna play the lead." I said, "Sure, of course", and tucked it away in a drawer in my office. Sure enough, it was John Travolta, and it was the first time I'd heard of him.'

By the time *Grease* the movie became a reality, Carr had both

heard of him and seen him: 'I liked him in *Kotter* and thought he was terrific in *The Boy in the Plastic Bubble*.' But Travolta was not first in line to play Danny Zuko. The main contender was his television sitcom rival, Henry 'Fonz' Winkler of *Happy Days*.

'Henry turned it down, saying he didn't want to play another high-school part,' says Carr. 'It was a huge mistake, happily for us; because John's name came up as the next number one.'

Carr met Travolta for the first time in a recording studio – 'So I heard him sing. He always behaved like a star, though not in a bad way. You just knew he was a star. Even then he had the car, the driver, all the amenities of a big star. And no one even knew yet that *Saturday Night Fever* would be a hit. They were freaked out at Paramount because they thought the film would bomb. I was nervous too.'

No nerves were allowed on the set. Nor were any doubts about Travolta's pending stardom. *Grease* was not just a screen musical. It was – or would become – two hours of shameless legend-enhancing as a cast of dancer-singers wielding the mimetic equivalent of mops and chamois leathers pranced around that overweening charisma vehicle known as John Travolta.

Allan Carr, who also wrote the screenplay, says he deliberately removed the harshness and realism from the original musical. 'The authors were a little mad at me because it was my vision to suburbanise it for a wider audience. I didn't want the characters grabbing their crotch and using vulgar language. I wanted to make it very much like how I grew up in a suburban town where there were regular kids and hoodlum kids, mischief-makers. We weren't making *West Side Story*.'

But were they making *Grease*? The film's choreographer Patricia Birch, who with Tom Moore had masterminded the Broadway and national tour productions, had increasing doubts.

'I wanted to hang onto the show for dear life, because I was scared to death we would lose all the roughness. The play was about these gritty kids from the raw side of Chicago. Though Tom Moore was from Yale and I was from the Martha Graham company and there wasn't a greaser in the cast, we had played it documentary-real.' For Birch, part of the softening going on in the movie was due to Travolta. 'He never had the

toughness one associates with Danny, though he grew into the part.'

Randal Kleiser, picked for director after his double-strike past associations with Travolta (*The Boy in the Plastic Bubble*), and co-producer Robert Stigwood, for whom he had made the TV documentary *All Together Now*, refereed the conflicting views about what kind of film *Grease* should be.

'The writer of the screenplay [Carr] had tried to improve everything from the play,' he says. 'So I got together with the actors and we read both texts to see which versions of each scene we preferred. Then we cut and pasted, going back to the play as much as possible, because a lot of the cast had been in the play and knew where to get laughs and so on. There was no conscious effort to clean it up.'

But Kleiser's version of keeping faith with the fifties consisted less of laying down grit more in spreading nostalgia straight from the fifties freezer.

'We hired a lot of actors famous to TV audiences in the baby-boom generation. Sid Caesar, Eve Arden, Edd Byrnes from the 77 *Sunset Strip* series. Frankie Avalon for a singing cameo. The film was filled with fifties references, it was a campy look at the decade.'

And it starred an actor who would soon be subjected to an idolatry as airheaded as anyone from America's previous culture-reign. *Saturday Night Fever* had not opened – had barely finished shooting – when the first clapperboard sounded on *Grease*. So Travolta was still this unguessable quadruple hyphenate: an actor-singer-dancer-pinup whose career could jump in any direction. Dazed by the adoration he already had and bemused by the possibilities in front of him, Travolta was now offered the push-pull bewilderment of a 'new' musical he had already performed, presented as a 'modern' movie set in the decade he was born in.

No wonder Kleiser found him dazed. 'He was tired when he started *Grease*, really exhausted. Every day he'd go dance and work out with our choreographer Pat Birch. Jack Nicholson was preparing his Western *Goin' South* in an office right above the stage and he'd keep shouting, "Turn off that music!" '

On one occasion the ghost of Diana Hyland stole onto the set, courtesy of the tabloid press. Kleiser remembers the day Travolta found a copy of *People* magazine. Rehashing the John-Diana romance, it used and abused quotes that had been trustingly given by Travolta. Or *he* thought it abused them: to anyone reading the piece today, it seems anodyne to the point of sycophancy. 'Kotter's co-star tries to forget his lady's death,' proclaims the headline, after which it itemises such scandalous matters as the fact that John doesn't drink or smoke and wraps special gifts for fellow cast or crew members.

But Travolta was so distraught by the piece, says Kleiser, that when they rehearsed that day's big number, 'Greased Lightning', he kept mispronouncing one of the lines.

'He kept singing "Heap-lap trials" instead of "Heat-lap trials". Even though we were miming to playback, we had to have the right lip movements. So just before each take I'd stand by the camera and say, "Heat! Heat! Heat!" He'd still do it.'

He was a trouper, though: which means the sun sets on anger or distress and rises on 'Show me my chalkmark'. Travolta refined and accessorised his performance, ensuring that Danny Zuko was distinct from Tony Manero; that they were not just two Italian punks convoying through successive music-movies. 'I put a walk in that was sort of "black bop," ' he says. 'I made the character a little more *black* fifties, because I think the cool side of the fifties was based more on a black undertone.' His Danny 'was really a white person imitating black jive'.

At the same time, 'There had to be an innocence that nobody was really aware of. *Grease* is stylised, it's a musical, a *parody* of the fifties almost.'

It traded an another familiarity too. 'Everyone knew and liked the music,' Kleiser points out. 'A lot of the songs were hits already and playing regularly on radio.' And though four new songs were written for the movie, the original ones were given fresh treatment and lavish production values. Too lavish for Patricia Birch.

'They turned "Greased Lightning" into a fantasy number, which they should never have done,' she says. 'It's set in a garage. They gave it silver costumes and glitzy lighting. I lost my battle on that one.'

Jeff Conaway lost his too. In the play this thumping, tuneful serenade to a souped-up car is sung by Kenickie, but in thrall to Travoltaphilia, Carr and Kleiser gave the song to Danny Zuko.

Conaway protested. 'I said to them, "Wait, I gotta sing *something*. This is my car and he's singing about it? That's like, I get married but he goes to bed with my wife!"'

He rebounded by inventing for a later scene the single wittiest moment in the picture. When Danny and Kenickie, in a sudden surge of unprotected buddyism, hug each in view of their cronies, the two men instantly realise their lapse from machismo. They turn away from each other and whip combs through their greased hair while chatting of ball games and other 'guy's things'.

Recalls Conaway, 'I had the idea that it's really a love scene. I was staying in the same apartment building as John, because I'd had a fire in mine, and I went up to see him and said, "I think we should hug!" He gave me a look, then saw what I was talking about. "We should hug," I said, "and then realise, What the hell are we doing!" And what do guys do in the fifties when they want to be cool? Comb their hair!

'We rehearsed it and shot it the next day. Randal Kleiser congratulated John, and John said, "No, no, Jeff thought of it." For me, there's something personal in that moment, to do with the years John and I had known each other.'

Travolta was good at waiving praise due to another. But there were also, claims Kleiser, the first stirrings of star vanity. An actor who according to *Saturday Night Fever* cameraman Ralf Bode hadn't cared *how* he was photographed in his starring debut – at least above the million-dollar dancing legs – fell victim to that deadliest star foible, the preferred profile.

'He had ideas about blocking,' says Kleiser. 'He was a much bigger star since I had last worked with him, and maybe people had told him how he should look and what side of his face looked good. In the first scene with him and the boys, when they call out "Danny" and he goes over to them, instead of standing on the left which is the direction he came from, he insisted on circling all around so he stood on the right.'

Kleiser says it was through vanity. But watching the manoeuvre today, you wonder if Travolta wasn't right dramatically. The long

walk around gives his character a bolder entrance. It implants the idea of a leader since his minions must stand there, looking foolish, while they wait for him.

To complicate matters though Allan Carr says the movement was *his* idea, not Travolta's. 'I asked the director to reshoot. I got up and went to the building to show Randal what I wanted. I don't do that often, I don't meddle. But I said, "This is a *star*, the scene has to have a star's impact." I don't think John cared anything about which side of his face looked better.'

In Kleiser's defence there is a bizarre preponderance of left profile shots in Travolta's *Grease* appearances. Yet actorly vanity scarcely impeded his inventive risk-taking, or his satiric take on Danny's *own* vanity. Travolta makes him a punk peacock: foolish, endearing, posturing, almost effeminate in the calculations of his self-conceit.

When Olivia Newton-John's Sandy accuses him of being embarrassed to show his feelings in front of his gang, he says, 'Embarrassed? Don't make me laugh.' And lifting and turning his head, he executes a slow, gauche, campy 'Ha! Ha! Ha!' like someone mimicking from a phonetics book on laughter. Few actors could do it with a lither comic skill; no other actor, one suspects, would have thought of it.

Kleiser credits Travolta with finding moments of emotional subtext that were never there in the stage show. 'For instance, what we got in the movie was the "look" he gives Sandy, after pretending to be cool towards her for his buddies. That half-second look that suggests "I'm sorry". That was John.'

It's a deft touch. But maybe in *Grease* the film, with its *idée fixe* about innocence, there are too many such lovable moments of 'I'm sorry' or 'I'm really sweet after all'.

Travolta's co-star Olivia Newton-John, stuck with playing Sandy, the Sandra Dee clone, suffers worst from the general bland-out. She is not helped by an Australian accent that has to be explained by dialogue about exchange studentships. This was the singer's own idea.

'If I was to play the part I said it had to be Australian,' she says. 'I was really concerned whether I could pull off an American accent. So they rewrote the part making it a different Sandy from the original play.'

The English-born rose with the Bondi Beach hair – a singer forever immortalised by the unsourced quip, 'If white bread could sing, it would sound like Olivia Newton-John' – was offered the movie role after meeting Allan Carr at a dinner party. Carr remembers, 'I went to [singer] Helen Reddy's house in Florida and Olivia was there, and she was so adorably fresh and cute. I said, "My God! You should be in my movie."'

'Apparently Allan remembers me making funny faces at the table,' says Newton-John. 'When he offered me the part I had just made a terrible movie in London called *Tomorrow* and I was very afraid of making another film. I said I'd love to play Sandy but I want to make a screen test first to be sure I can do it.'

So she auditioned by playing the drive-in scene with Travolta and won the role over rival contenders Marie Osmond and Susan Dey (of TV's *The Partridge Family*).

'We had real good chemistry from the start,' Newton-John says of Travolta. 'He was so sweet. When we filmed the scene where I'm in a pom-pom outfit at the drive-in, we were doing my close-up – he'd already done his – and in the middle of speaking his off-camera lines he suddenly blew it and said, "Oh sorry, we'll have to do it over." At that moment he came over to me and I said, "What happened?" And he whispered, "*I think you could do it better!*" Which was really generous.'

Travolta, she says, kept a party spirit going on the production with comedy routines between takes. He would improvise mock chat shows, interviewing the extras; he would impersonate everyone. 'He got us all down. He did Randal, he did an impression of me singing. And he did his own characters. I remember he had a black guy, a very funny "old man" and half a dozen others.'

Once cast, Newton-John walked straight into the tabloid love trap awaiting any leading lady of Travolta's. The newspapers, casting their real-life novelette, decided she was his latest sweetheart. Here were two heart-throbs and fellow songbirds, thrown together in a movie all *about* throbbing hearts and trilling tonsils. 'The growing, glowing love between John Travolta and Olivia Newton-John ignited on the first day they met' drooled *Modern Screen* magazine. The press forgot yesterday's Travolta gossip, which included a supposed flutter between John and Cher's sister

Georgeanne La Pierre. (They were seen dancing in a disco some time after Diana's demise.) And they back-burnered rumours about John and Marilu Henner; those could be reheated any time. For there was something about John and Olivia that had True Romance written all through it.

Newton-John was separated from her steady boyfriend at that time. But she denies there was a romance with Travolta. Like Nancy Allen, she sees gossip as the price of fame, or at least the tax on it. 'For years when I wasn't married gossip was reported with people I didn't even know. I was "having a baby with Burt Reynolds" when I hadn't even met him. Even when I got married, they made up a story about another guy. It can destroy the trust in a relationship. But I don't think they ever said anything about me and John, did they?'

They did. And even he said enough. In 1979 Newton-John reportedly went ballistic after Travolta answered a British journalist's enquiry about love between the two stars with a vague but injudicious 'There was something, yes.' When Travolta next stepped into London in 1983 the same reporter who had scooped this kiss-and-tell admission, plus the diva's reaction, re-mentioned the incident. 'Oh my God,' Travolta said. 'Yes, I do remember something about that. I suppose that's what the journalists hit her with when she came straight off the plane at the time, so she would be angry. The thing is, when you know the truth, you've no reason to be upset.'

This fabulously meaningless response – does it indicate yes or no? – protects everyone's reputation, except that of Travolta for speaking lucid English.

But what is a star to do when mobbed by what seems the entire planet and its chroniclers? By the time Travolta was catechised in London, he was the new miracle child of show business: with the dangerous progression that goes from Bethlehem to Bedlam.

For between *Grease* the production and *Grease* the release came *Saturday Night Fever* the madness. This did not stop at the initial rapture of good reviews and cash-register noises, or even bestselling albums and besieged dance studios. It crept across America, then the world, like a benign pandemic. The film was the perfect climax to what Tom Wolfe christened the 'Me Decade'. It had no values

beyond its hero's self-fulfilment but there was something driven and infectious about that character's pursuit of idiot hedonism and skin-deep, or suit-deep, self-esteem. Tony Manero was an Everyman in whose shallowness Travolta found something deep, quirky, even pop-tragic.

Discotheques graduated from a fad to a frenzy. These palaces of loud music, jutting bodies and strafing chiaroscuro appeared on every high street. Twenty new ones opened each week in America. Vampirically, they operated only at night. Vampirically, they rejoiced in ornate gesticulation and a sacrificial energy at once solemn and wild. (George Hamilton's Dracula spoof *Love at First Bite* was one of the first films to incorporate a Travolta parody, though not as witty as *Airplane!*'s jacket-twirling, hand-jiving, medallion-flying scene of disco shtick.)

Donna Pescow, Travolta's co-star, believes *Saturday Night Fever* defined an age. 'It was a statement of the decade. People think of the fifties as being *Rebel Without a Cause*. The seventies was *Saturday Night Fever*, disco, and the lost generation going into the Me generation.'

And what better way to shrug off the Vietnam/Watergate age of conflict and corruption, and the answering solemnity of counter-culture protest? No more folk singers offering reedy ballads to peace and freedom. Just the chunky blast of a disco system accompanied by twirling coloured lights. And at the centre of the lightstorm, the perfect apolitical pin-up: an Irish-Italian street youth with his arm raised not in war or protest but in iconic exultation, a showbiz *acte gratuit*.

Even *Time* magazine pondered the phenomenon. Its April 3rd 1978 cover featured a dancing, grinning J.T. in a lime-coloured suit. Sash-headlined 'Travolta Fever', the image dwarfed the tiny top-corner announcement of the issue's subsidiary story, 'Hard choices for Israel', with a stamp-size photo of Menachem Begin.

Three weeks later, the magazine surrendered its letters page to Travoltamania. 'He is an electrifying, sumptuous boy-man,' breathed one correspondent, 'who exudes a magical aura-on-screen that could cause volcanic eruptions.' 'When cloning is perfected, would you please send me a copy of John Travolta, please?' wrote another, cloning even her words of entreaty.

Fan worship took every form known to man, woman and teenager. In one part of the United States of Travolta, the idol's fan club offered a 45 rpm record of the singer plus 'Yours free! A personal message from John to you!' The complete Fan Membership Kit also included full-colour signed photos, an exclusive biography, and 'fantastic savings' on John Travolta jewelry, T-shirts and stickers.

Fever fever, and its dandyish manifestations, infected the entire education system. After sending inspectors to the city's high schools the *New York Times* reported, 'Mirrors have gone back up on locker-room doors and there's often a dryer and as many as five brushes on the shelf.' Johnny Lorenzo, a Bronx schoolboy, the newspaper adds, gets up at five to do his hair and carries three brushes in his briefcase. He hates windy days because it messes up his hair. Another Bronx student has a dryer, five brushes and hair conditioner.

Across the land there were Travolta lookalike dance contests, with pompadoured youths pushed to glory by their girlfriends, boyfriends or mothers. When Roger Blaha, a Baltimore auto parts salesman, won his contest his mother said to the newspapers, 'I guess we'll have to put a bandage around Roger's head so it doesn't swell up.' His Pa's comment was, 'He didn't lose my gold medallion, did he?'

Travoltabilia collectors got serious, Even today, twenty years on, Danna Black, formerly of New Jersey, cherishes her *Saturday Night Fever* trashcan, her 'John Travolta's Firebird Fever' model car, her Official John Travolta Picture Postcard Book ('twenty-three gorgeous photos in full colour'), her *Welcome Back Kotter* boardgame and her John Travolta dolls including the 'Superstar' dressed in a sky-blue turtleneck and flared jeans.

As with any outburst of idolatry, though, there were naysayers. 'Is John Travolta queer for older women?' wrote a troublemaker to *Walter Scott* magazine, rewinding to the Diana Hyland episode. Amid the fusillade of fanmail printed by *Time* one dissident declared, '*Saturday Night Fever* is a racist, sexist and offensive film. It has a Neanderthal mentality with 1970s vulgarity.' And outside the States, in countries the movie reached later, there were more determined demurrals.

From South America came a prolix appraisal of *Saturday Night Fever* in the January 1979 issue of *Young Cinema and Theatre*, the bilingual journal of the International Union of Students.

Fever is a musical-cum-youth-movie? No: it is a capitalist tractatus. The film, says writer Fernando Reyes Matta, is about 'the legitimacy of the transnational ideology in a world conceived as a retail store. Ever since synthetic fibres became a substitute for wool and cotton (raw materials which are, after all, from the Third World) . . . the chemical industry has tried to impose the convenience of clothing made of polyester and nylon. And then we see that Tony Manero adores those loud shirts of artificial fibres . . . The film places in circulation an ideological apparatus which undermines the national norms and local conducts of these non-industrial countries in which it is shown.'

Finally and biblically, 'Must we then expect in this International Year of the Child, the arrival of a small Travolta who will offer the marvel of a new mode of child life in which the roots of the transnationals shall be firmly set?'

As the debates multiplied around what began as a simple Hollywood movie (though semiologists will tell you there is no such thing), can we be surprised that its young star, pinballed around the philosophical universe by his film's commentators, sought help from a 'philosophy' every bit as strange as the rest?

At least Scientology, unlike South American agitpolitics, had a personal help policy. So when in the summer of 1978 *Grease* followed *Saturday Night Fever* into the record books, becoming the most profitable movie musical of all time, John Travolta could put his head and heart in order by spending ten hours a week being 'audited.' (One newspaper says the hourly fee was $30). And after he felt sated with fame and love and spiritual bookkeeping, he could give back some of what he had received. He could give people 'assists'.

In the last week of filming on *Grease* Randal Kleiser got the Dianetics treatment. 'While shooting the car chase in the river bed I stubbed my foot and got water in it and came down with an infection. I was so sick they decided to close the company down till I was better. I was lying in my dressing room and John came in and said, "I think I can help you."

'He spent an hour moving his finger all over my body, saying "Feel my finger?" Finally he said, "Feeling any better?" I said, "I don't know." I realised later it was a Scientology curing session. The next day I was a little better, but I have no idea if it was because of this treatment.'

Travolta loves ministering to people. Almost everyone I spoke to during research for this book had some story about a moment of help or care, with or without Dianetics, that had been dispensed by the star.

Was the Messiah effect of fame stealing into his braincells and re-programming them during these bewildering late seventies? Was his mind saying, 'John, you now have the power to *give* miraculously, in return for all this miraculous receiving', or 'John, you who fly among the stars in your Cessna and your celebrity must also be an engine of goodness on the ground.'

Or perhaps he was taught to care simply by stern experience. Diana's death stayed with him even when he didn't want it to. Her mother remembers a visit from him a year after her death. 'He dropped by our apartment and caught me as I was weeping,' she says. 'I apologised. "I'm afraid my eyes are red, John. I don't like anyone to see me like this, but I cry every day." John looked at me and then said, "So do I." '

He cried not just about Diana, and the part of him lost with her, but about a world that was taking so much else away under the guise of giving. That world allowed John Travolta so little time to be John Travolta. His old friend from *Grease* the stage play, Jerry Zaks, remembers attending a wedding with him.

'It was shortly after *Saturday Night Fever* and *Grease* came out and he was sitting with me and my fiancée. I remember him trying to tell us something, a story. He'd begin and someone would come over and say "Oh you're John Travolta" and pester him for an autograph. Then he'd begin the story again and another fan would come over. And this went on over and over, until finally he started to cry. It was out of sheer frustration. He literally could not speak to us without being interrupted by people who'd fallen in love with him because of the movies he'd made.'

Jim Jacobs too encountered Travolta fever and its frightening effects. The *Grease* author had already been startled when the

airheaded gypsy who played Doody on the *Grease* national tour won his *Kotter* fame and began limbering up for *Saturday Night Fever*, 'Warren [Casey] and I were in Atlantic City in the summer of 1975, walking down the boardwalk, and we started seeing all these T-shirts with his name and picture on: "John Travolta for President" and so on. And we both turned and looked at each other and said, "*John Travolta*??" We were blown away.'

After *Fever* Jacobs had cause for more stupefaction. He and Travolta re-met in Chicago at a barbecue party in Marilu Henner's backyard. The event was literally crashed by fans, breaking through Henner's fence. She hid Travolta in her garage until mid-evening, when she decided they should all three go to a disco.

'It was a big club called Faces,' Jacobs recalls, 'and Marilu called them and said, "Can we come down?" And they said, "No, you need a reservation and you need to be a member." She said, "What if I have John Travolta with me?" They said, "If you have John Travolta you can come right in!" They thought she was kidding. I said to her, 'You're crazy, you can't take him to a place that, he'll be ripped apart!" Well, we went and I swear as soon as we were inside we saw about twenty guys who were wearing the Travolta white suit and black shirt and gold medallion.

'The waitress put us at a corner table in the dark and for ten minutes it was quiet. Then the first person spotted John and soon it was pandemonium. They had to lock him in the coatroom, with the Puerto Rican busboy, while I brought my car round to the kitchen entrance. He and Marilu jumped in. I just peeled out of there with the tyres burning. We ended up in the apartment of a friend of Marilu's, having pizzas.

'I thought I'm only privy to isolated moments like this. He has to go through it every day and night. I was a nervous wreck, shaking and gasping. What must it be like to *live* like this?'

Even Hollywood couldn't protect him. Nominated for the Best Actor Oscar for *Saturday Night Fever*, Travolta was yelled at by besotted fans as he entered the ceremony and one girl 'actually broke down the barriers and jumped my head. It was not only the feeling of the fingernails in my face but the pressure of feeling my neck snap backward. It was like a scene from *The Day of the Locust*.'

Inside, he lost the statuette to the star of *The Goodbye Girl*, to the loyal dismay of Andy Warhol, who had graduated from rubbernecking Travolta on aeroplanes to rooting for him at the Awards. 'Nobody good like John Travolta won,' the artist grumbled in his *Diaries*. 'I mean, Richard Dreyfuss? I mean, if he's a sex symbol, I don't know what the world is coming to.'

7

SUNDAY MORNING

During the Oscar ceremony Helen Travolta, diagnosed some time before with cancer, spent hours in pain massaging her knees. She refused John's offer to take her out. But though she got through the evening, painful months lay ahead. John probably knew that 1978 would be her last year.

In return for the love, support and panfuls of lasagne she had lavished on him during his years of struggle, Travolta did his best to spoil her and his father now he was rich. He had already bought Sam Snr a new car. Neighbour Eddie Costenuic remembers the day that John, visiting Englewood, shouted to his father to come out of 135 Morse Place and see the present he had brought. Sam emerged and set eyes on a brand new silver Cadillac. It was adorned with a red ribbon and, also in red fabric on top of the bonnet the word 'Love.' Sam drank in the sight, then turned to his next-door neighbour and gave him the keys to his old 1969 Pontiac.

Costenuic, whose wife fell ill with cancer at the same time as Helen, felt the touch of Travolta's caring nature at the wedding of John's sister Annie. 'I had stopped drinking for fifteen years before my wife got ill. John kept coming round to me at the wedding to make sure I wasn't drinking the hard stuff but still had plenty to keep me going.' Costanuic shows me a picture of the wedding. He is seated with his heavy-set, humbly-suited frame facing in one direction. Travolta, behind him, faces in the other, aglow with the bloom of celebrity. It could be a latter-day Poussin: 'Landscape in Arcady (N.J.): peasants visited by an angel.'

Soon Travolta's parents had been whisked from Englewood to

Hollywood, settling in California in a house bought by their son. It was pleasanter than living at an overfamous address in Morse Street, fending off John's worshippers or battling the daily avalanche of fanmail. Sons Joey and Sam also made plans to migrate westward, lured by their brother's success.

Helen was keener on making the move than her husband, whom Eddie Costanuic remembers heaving a sigh one day as they chatted from porch to porch in Englewood, saying, 'What am I going to do in California? All my friends are here.'

Helen found swift acting employment in *Saturday Night Fever*. She is the shrill, diminutive paintshop customer in the film's opening dialogue scene, asking Tony why he is late into the store. (John's sister Annie also has a cameo as the pizza waitress in the preceding credits sequence).

In the summer of 1978 John took his mother on trips to Bergdorf Goodman and other L.A. retail shrines, telling her to buy what she wanted. 'She kept looking at price tags when she thought I wasn't watching her,' he remembers, 'and she wouldn't buy a thing. She was sick, then, dying, and thinking it was wrong to spend my money.'

He also took his parents on the *Grease* promotional tour to Europe. They wouldn't order room service in hotels, nor eat big expensive breakfasts. Travolta was learning a lesson of stardom, that to give is harder than to receive. After Paris, tired of crowds, they decamped to the Cap d'Antibes, where he remembers his mother sitting proudly with *Time* magazine – his cover issue – on her lap on the hotel terrace. 'She watched me eat croissants in the sun,' he recalled, 'and we were intensely happy.'

She became worse in the fall and entered L.A.'s Valley Presbyterian Hospital. Though her left breast was removed in November, it failed to halt the spread of cancer. On December 3rd 1978 she died with John at her side. In the commemorative photograph of her, sitting with Sam and John, in the *Englewood Press-Journal* on the day after her death, she is wearing the same gold medallion – indeed the same of almost everything, including the black blouse and the centre parting in her hair that betrays the roots of a blissfully imprecise dye job – that she wore in *Saturday Night Fever*.

Funeral arrangements were kept secret in a successful attempt

to prevent fan hysteria. More public was the row Travolta had with his mother's surgeon. 'She should never have been opened up, and I feel I let them do it because the doctor made me feel it was okay,' he told a reporter. '[He] persuaded me to have the operation, and then, when it was over, he said, "Hey, man, we're only a practice." We had a big fight.'

Friends and family members say Travolta was hit hard by his mother's death. 'Really broken up' is how a nephew describes it. And neighbour Eddie Costenuic says he disappeared for days. No one could find or contact him.

Even the saddest loss, though, can have a gain. 'When my mother died I guess I grew up. My career didn't have the same significance or excitement. Until then it had always been about doing well for my family. Then something interesting and important happened. I started doing things for me.'

Emotionally, if not strategically, anyone scrutinising his career up to December 1978 would note that he had got by nicely with other people deciding what he should do. Robert Stigwood and Allan Carr had coaxed him into two high-performance vehicles that were passing every chequered flag on the track. And Stigwood, with *Grease* promising to outpace even *Saturday Night Fever* at the box office, would be no less shrewd, surely, in his third choice of movie.

This time Travolta did have an influence on that choice. A natural and irrepressible mimic, he had a passion for the work of comedienne Lily Tomlin. Marcia Strassman remembers him doing her routines during *Kotter* rehearsals. 'He worshipped her, he did all her characters. Like the switchboard lady and the cheerleader she used to do. He was crazy about her one-woman show in New York.'

His conveyed his craziness to Robert Stigwood, who was searching in 1977 for that elusive third movie in the Travolta deal.

'Lily was doing her show on Broadway for the first time and it was a smash hit,' Stigwood says. 'I brought her round to see some rushes of *Fever* and got her to agree to star with John in a comedy film.'

But there was the rub. 'After the success of *Fever* and *Grease*,' Stigwood goes on, 'Lily and John decided they wanted to do a

drama. Well, the whole world was bidding for this third project all the distributors. I didn't like the story that Jane came up with, but everyone wore me down.' Jane was Jane Wagner, Tomlin's longtime collaborator, who would write and direct the new film called *Moment by Moment*.

'Lily was coming off her stage show and there was that feeling, She can do anything,' says executive producer Kevin McCormick. 'And John had made it clear that he wanted to do something different, not a third musical. There was some friction between Robert and John at that moment. Robert wanted to do something bigger, but he had all these distribution deals sewn up, so he thought "If John doesn't want to commit to another musical, then fuck it, let's do it." '

'It' was not half as bad on the page, says McCormick, as it became on film. 'Jane said she had this tiny story that had been cooking in her mind and wrote a simple script that could have been something.'

The story was of a California matron of a certain age who falls for a handsome beachbum-cum-gigolo. It was a 'Malibu Spring of Mrs Stone', with Travolta playing a low-rent Warren Beatty. But the actor liked the story outline when he first read it. 'I was so excited I called at 2.30. am and woke Lily and Jane to talk about it.'

Lily liked the story too and the serious contours in her bored-wife character. 'With marriage she opted for all this stuff – the home in Beverly Hills, the house in Malibu. Suddenly she wakes up and things are a little different. She wouldn't marry that kind of person now and he's not the kind of person he was when she married him.'

Tomlin and Wagner, longtime partners on and off screen, worked away at the project all through the shooting of *Grease*. By the time cameras rolled, though, the story had not so much cooked as turned to mush. Essentially there *was* no story: just a lot of wistful attitudinising between two characters, and later two stars, who turned out to have no chemistry together. 'In retrospect Lily was the wrong person to play the role,' says McCormick. 'There was no fire between them.'

When things go wrong on a film there is a process of spontaneous

proliferation: *more* things go wrong. Every aspect of the John-Lily screen link-up started to seem ill conceived. Here was a lusty heterosexual passion played out by two actors whose own sexuality was either opaque (his) or confessedly gay (hers). And here was an 'opposites attract' romance whose parties boasted a peculiar, overpowering resemblance to each other. Equine features, large cupid-bow mouths, shaggy-luxuriant locks. Watching them kiss or clinch was like watching someone wrestle amorously with a looking-glass.

No one questioned Travolta's initial commitment to his role, though his perspective on it alternated between objective clarity and semi-autobographical confusion. On the one hand, 'Strip in *Moment by Moment* has none of the defence mechanisms that Tony had. There's a real purity to Strip all the time.' On the other, 'I think Strip is a little more innocent and pure than I am – or let's say than I was. I was looking for that romantic ideal and was crushed real easily. I think I'm very sensitive, but I think I've gotten over the stages of being as easily – God, I'm carrying on about this – maybe I haven't changed that much . . .'

An actor expounding his character who gets lost in abstracted self-revelation is a curious, treasurable beast in Hollywood. It is the blurry line between life and movies, though, between 'self and 'other,', that makes Travolta in his early stardom years so fascinating. He did go outside himself for inspiration, says Kevin McCormick, although not far. 'He based his character on a kid who worked on the film, a sort of hippy-dippy teamster, a beach guy. Unlike Tony Manero who was very New York, Travolta tried to make his character in *Moment* as West Coast as possible.'

The road to Hell is pot-holed with good intentions. Travolta tried to bring a rueful, quotidian reality to his role. But since the character was called Strip, there was an open invitation to audience uproar in scenes like the hot-tub get-together.

Travolta: I love you. I just thought you should know. Do you love me? I know you do. Just say it.

Tomlin: Strip . . .

Travolta: You don't love me . . .

Tomlin: Oh, Strip.

Travolta: Am I not good enough for you, is that it?

Tomlin: Oh no, Strip, that's just not true . . .

If the hero's name sounded like a tribute to the homonymous street hunk Travolta invented in his let's-create-characters days with Marilu Henner, it did not have the actor's blessing. 'I begged them to change the name. I begged them.'

Why change a name, though, when so much else points to disaster? Wagner, on her own admission, was floundering. She would wave at the movie equipment and say 'It's so elephantine.' Or she would demand more than twenty takes of a shot to the exhausted bemusement of Travolta. (Some beach scenes were shot with the stars dressed, then undressed, then semi-dressed, because Wagner couldn't make up her mind.) Or she would give soundbites about the movie that were more confusing than the movie itself. It was 'both a romance and something that might be seen as political: wealth and the Third World.' In a moment of honest surrender she told the *Los Angeles Times*, 'After this is all over I'll probably have a breakdown.'

According to Kevin McCormick, she asked to be taken off the film. So, later on, did Travolta; but his manager Bob Le Mond persuaded him it would be unprofessional. With mournful amusement Robert Stigwood remembers how the two stars began falling out.

'I'd never seen anything like it. They started off all sweetie-pie and great friends. And then it became a nightmare. They'd be bouncing off to their trailers on location in Malibu, over things like John objecting to Lily wearing gold bracelets when they first make love. Lily's response was that it was an automatic, spontaneous moment when they make love, so she wouldn't have taken them off. That's the kind of thing that held up filming. I'd have to go from trailer to trailer making peace.'

Stigwood decided to find someone else to do this. After two weeks' shooting he shut down production for what he calls a three-week 'cooling off'. He looked for a troubleshooter who could – if not exactly take over the film – be a 'technical adviser.' He brought in Ralf Bode, *Saturday Night Fever*'s cinematographer.

'I saw the dailies and understood what the problem was,' says Bode. 'The script was fine, it was gentle and sensitive, but the actors weren't following it. They were improvising. They'd improvise for

wide shots, then for close-ups, and no editor would have a chance to put the movie together that way.'

Bode advised Wagner to follow the script. He also appointed himself the film's 'R.V. shrink', taking over Stigwood's duties in padding between recreational vehicles sorting out the star's psyches. Bode had toughened up since his early days on *Saturday Night Fever*, when he contracted shingles through anxiety. But he still began to feel the stress.

He was in good company. 'It was like being on the Voyage of the Damned,' said a crew member. Others confirmed Stigwood's account of star tensions. Mutual glowering was the reported mode after each scene together, though the two players were later persuaded to pour the balm of PR over bad rumours. Tomlin declared that Travolta 'has every dichotomy in him – there's masculinity, feminity, refinement crudity. It's all there. He is everything. It's incredible.' Travolta in turn applauded Tomlin's 'talent and sensitivity'.

Were there any problems with the love scenes, they were asked by an interviewer. Travolta paused to think of something tactful. 'You have to watch out for the camera, so your head won't fall off the pillow and get out of camera range.'

The media love movie disasters as much as disaster movies. So the makers of *Moment by Moment* did their best to mitigate reality. Even today Ralf Bode proclaims that despite all his RV shrinkwork, there was only one serious rumpus involving John and Lily. That was about nudity and united rather divided the two stars. 'They didn't want anything to be explicit. They didn't want to show bums or breasts or anything.'

Moment by Moment retired to the quarantine area of the editing room, where for a few weeks at least it would fail to infect the Travolta career. This was in a state of health so extraordinary that normal mortals could only look on and marvel.

Grease, now released, was becoming the most successful movie musical in history. It had pop chart triumphs to match. 'You're the One I Want', a duet for Travolta and Olivia Newton-John added for the film, topped the US list for a month and became one of the longest number ones in British history. The soundtrack album, released in May, spent three months at the top in America and

Britain. And the singles 'Summer Nights,' 'Sandy' and 'Hopelessly Devoted to You' dominated the charts in late fall. No movie had ever exercised such a grip on western stereo systems.

Cultural commentators were bemused. Scarcely had *Saturday Night Fever* begun defining a new pop-culture epoch than here was *Grease* defining another. This epoch was just as large with hormonal drama: everyone danced, delivered chat-up dialogue and tried to make out inside cars. But we were in the fifties, or a wistful version, where everything was cleaner, from the clothes to the language.

So all the young adolescents who had been kept out of *Saturday Night Fever* by X-certificate dialogue could storm this new citadel of John Travolta. As Randal Kleiser points out they knew and loved the music already, and there was the bonus of new material from the Bee Gees' Barry Gibb (title theme) and Olivia Newton-John's songwriter John Farrar (Hopelessly Devoted to You, 'You're the One I Want'). And if they didn't know the musical and cinematic styles that *Grease* was satirising – you had to be over sixteen to have seen a peak-period Sandra Dee film – they could respond to the bubblegum innocence of it all: the picture of an America where grown actors playing at being high-school kids merely mirror-reversed all those teenyboppers in the audience who wanted to grow up, drive cars and fall in love.

What the critics thought about *Grease* – 'bogus', 'clumsy', 'flashy' and 'frantic' were favoured adjectives, and the *Washington Post* wrote, 'If it's true that *Grease* reflects producer Allan Carr's fondest dreams of what a movie musical should look and feel like, he should be put away' – mattered to the cash register no more than what the play's original creators thought.

'When Warren Casey and I went to the opening, we were both appalled,' says Jim Jacobs. 'They had promised us, "We're gonna keep it the way it is," and then later, "Oh we're only going to change it to make it better." Allan Carr had said to me, "Oh don't worry, there won't be any palm trees in the background," because my concern was that it would be Frankie and Annette and beach-blanket bingo or some crap.' (Meaning Frankie Avalon and Annette Funicello, sixties teen-dream idols; of course Avalon *does* make a guest appearance in *Grease*.) 'We wanted the picture to

have that integrity, that look of the industrial north in America. But they sanitised the whole thing. We couldn't believe our eyes. The whole nitty-gritty of these tough kids was gone.'

One or two commentators, especially in Britain, even dared to be rude about Travolta. 'A moronic, loose-lipped creep,' wrote the *Evening Standard*'s Val Hennessy. 'Singing "Sandy", he sounds like a rusty bicycle pump. With his haemorrhoidal gait he saunters across the screen, his capped teeth hanging out towards Olivia Newton-John, who has as much appeal as a dripping tap.' And years later Quentin Crisp, who liked the Phase Two star of *Michael* and *Face/Off*, recalled the *Grease* and *Fever* Travolta as 'a horrible, throbbing, stick-like creature'.

What did audiences care? These views were in a nanoscopic minority. *Grease* was a sensation all the way from Yugoslavia where it called itself *Briljantin* and starred 'Dzon Travolta' – and where a Wall Street journalist dropping into a Belgrade cinema noted the breathless fans intoning '*Tra-vol-ta*!' at the star's first appearance – to South America where it was named *Vaselina*. There was no escape even in the deepest Amazon. When Robert Stigwood retreated there for a weekend's rest during promotional exertions he remembers, 'I was woken by a phone call on my first morning and there was an on Oriental voice on the other and saying, '*Glease* velly big hit in the East!'

For Travolta as well as Stigwood, travel abroad gave him more of what he got at home. In London, despite Hennessy and Crisp, he was nearly dismembered by fans. 'I was frightened that the roof of the car was going to cave in under the crush,' he says of the *Grease* premiere at the Odeon Leicester Square.

'The fans were going nuts,' recalls Olivia Newton-John, 'they were literally climbing all over the car, looking through the glass, I thought my God, what's going on. I can still see it in my mind.' Director Randal Kleiser was in the same car: 'People were pushing it back and forth, there was a huge mob. When John got out they pushed him and pulled his hair. He was terrified. If he hadn't been protected by two lines of police he would have been torn apart When he finally got into his seat in the theatre, he just sat there shaking.' Then he sat in the manager's office with his sister, trying to calm down. Before the film ended, he left for his hotel,

absenting himself from the 1000-guest *Grease* party held after the show at the Strand Lyceum.

Vacations were only marginally safer. When Travolta took friends and family on a trip to Hawaii, borrowing producer Allan Carr's house, fame was lying in ambush. 'I was in a canoe going up this little ravine, and a native approached me and said, "John Travolta!" I said to myself, "It's over. There's no place in the world I can go to."'

Travolta stepped back from the madness whenever he could. He had just bought a $1.2-million mansion set in a fourteen-acre avocado ranch twenty-two miles west of Santa Barbara. Here at Rancho Tajiguas Adobe, previously owned by a Crocker Bank executive, the actor lived 'in a pair of baggy khakis – full of holes – that he couldn't bear to throw out' says his sister Ellen. It was a laidback *palacio* where he could stop being the king of cool and resume being a shambolic kid, even amid Xanadu trappings.

'He was still a baby,' Ellen says. 'He sat at the head of a long, long table with a buzzer at the foot [to summon servants]. We giggled so hard. This was not – repeat not – how we grew up in New Jersey.'

Every time he stepped outside, the spotlight went on again. His name was 'romantically linked' with Olivia Newton-John and Marisa Berenson. He was invited to the TV Academy ball by Fred Astaire and taken to dinner by Barbara Stanwyck. Even at home, famous film folk sometimes clogged up his pool. Danny DeVito remembers almost drowning at one end after hearing a joke from Robin Williams at the other.

It was not too much to expect an invitation to the White House. This came in October 1978, when President Carter's daughter Amy wanted John to come to dinner. He left the Rancho to the servants and flew his private DC-3 to Teterboro Airport, so that he could touch down in Englewood to see the folks. Neighbour Eddie Costenuic remembers the black limousine pulling up to 135 Morse Place, plus a two-car FBI escort. Limo-watching was now a neighbourhood sport. Costenuic had also been at home the evening Travolta and Newton-John were chauffeured up in a stretch Cadillac to fetch Sam and Helen Travolta for the New York premiere of *Grease*.

A famous man must have famous romances, even if they exist in print rather than reality. 'John and Olivia' was probably a tabloid figment. And 'John and Marisa [Berenson],' rumoured in all the fanzines, may or may not have been one. New Yorker film critic Pauline Kael remembers Travolta flying into Los Angeles to attend a dinner given in her honour. After changing from his pilot costume into a formal suit Travolta sat next to her and they talked 'for hours' about movies, his career and the directions his acting might take. Another guest sitting nearby noted, 'Marisa Berenson came and sat down on his other side and he kept trying to fight her off. Somehow or other she'd managed to leak a news item that they were a hot couple.'

Formal dinners are places for social masquerade. Kael, for instance, says the actor seemed better educated than his screen image. 'He's nothing like the guy he was in *Kotter*, more like the boy in the plastic bubble,' she says. 'I was surprised. He seemed very intelligent and spoke in this gentle, quite cultured voice.'

But *Kotter* friend Marcia Strassman giggles when I tell her this. 'That's John putting on his posh voice. Even now I'll watch him on TV being interviewed and I'll say, "Oh he's doing his grown-up voice." I remember one day coming out of my dressing room on *Kotter* and John was walking up and down the hall speaking with this swank voice. I said, "What are you doing?" "I'm practising speaking," he said. We had some benefit to go to, where he was going to get up on stage and say something. Because he never went to college, whenever he went out to "be a movie star" he thought things were expected of him, like speaking properly.'

Yet at some semi-public appearances, such as round-table interview sessions, nothing was expected except that he be John Travolta. That was more than enough, noted one reporter. 'The eyes are seriously blue. The teeth are white, the hair wavy. Several of the press people melted under the strain and were unable to regain their cynicism for several hours. It was pathetic.'

Interviews, benefits, White House do's – but over them all the impending spectre of *Moment by Moment*. As if manoeuvring himself into a defensive position before the film's opening, Travolta became prickly with the media. In December 1978 he banned TV and radio crews from a press conference, on the pretext that he did

not want to answer questions about his mother's death. 'There's no way to monitor revealing questions on tape. I prefer not to be in that vulnerable a situation.'

Sometimes – while there *was* still time – he sat back and pondered the spectacle of his own celebrity. He counted the blessings and curses. 'I wanted this fame and these things are part of it,' he tells a reporter shortly after having his fork plucked from his hand by a fan. But it is still hard for him to deal with the rapid alternation of public love and public (or media) malice. 'I was from a very protected background. I was like' – he opens his arms and gives a big goofy grin – ' "Here I am!" And then, bam, bam, the darts get thrown at my heart and my head.'

They were just target practice for *Moment by Moment*.

Every anxiety proved well-founded when the film opened. A reporter at the first press show noted, 'People laughed at the wrong time, giggled at the sex scenes and there was little applause at the end.' *Time* magazine's verdict was, 'An awful movie, but it may someday occupy a hallowed place in the pantheon of high camp.' *Time*'s Frank Rich gave Travolta a partial exculpation: 'It is reassuring to know there is at least one professional on screen' (he describes Tomlin as 'a somnambulant Elaine May'). But in Britain the critic and author Peter Ackroyd wrote in the *Spectator*, 'Travolta or Tomlin alone could rescue [the film] from both its plot and its dialogue. Together they are unbearable.'

'Every time I did an interview after *Moment by Moment* they went right for the negative things first,' Travolta said. 'I feel that the criticism after the film became abusive. It went beyond mere criticism.'

He resented the commentators who dragged up Diana Hyland to make a life-and-art comparison between one age-mismatched romance and another. And he struggled to make sense of a world that had taken one failure as the cue to ridicule or reverse previous judgments: 'It was the first time I heard the words, "Your career is over." ' Meanwhile critical derision was accompanied by audience desertion. Cinemas showing *Moment by Moment* emptied across the land.

What ever could Travolta have felt? Lathered with praise from his previous movies, he was expected to adjust to the jets of cold water

hosing him naked to public view. It was his personal psycho-drama, though as well as being in the shower he had apparently wielded the knife. 'You would have thought Lily and I had committed murder. I thought, my God, don't ever do a movie people don't like; they'll murder you.'

'None of us was prepared for the vicious attacks that followed,' says Lily Tomlin. 'It involved an enormous amount of pain. For a year I couldn't pick up a magazine without discovering some new dirt.'

Memories haunt the behind-camera participants too. Robert Stigwood says, 'I can still hear in my head those lines, "Oh Strip, oh Strip." And as for salad nicoise, after that scene that had to be shot thirty times or something, I can't bear to eat it ever again.' He adds, 'I have to take full responsibility. I could have shut the film down completely.'

For Jane Wagner the wounds cut deep. 'Sometimes I think people were expecting Lily to be funny and maybe John to be dancing. I'm not using that as an excuse or as a cop-out but I feel there was a great sense of overexpectation . . . Maybe there will be a day when the humiliation is forgotten, a time when I can forget it. I don't know.'

At least she did not have several million fans to pacify. If you are a twenty-four-year-old super-idol, what do you say to aggrieved admirers, even if you feel they should never have admired you so much in the first place? How do you satisfy a public that looks for the mythic in an ordinary mortal – you – and refuses to be persuaded that it isn't there? (At least until the first brutal crisis of disenchantment.) Travolta tried to explain: 'One's own life is not as colourful as a character that's created in a movie because, you see, they go through a million colours in a short period of time. In one's own life it may take four years to go through those colours.'

But no, people wanted those colours now and didn't mind how they looked for them. Even before *Moment by Moment*'s release, frustrated in their search for hard, saucy gossip about Travolta and women, the interviewers had moved on to the next offensive. He must be gay. And if not gay, he must admit that he *appeals* to gay men. Travolta is patient. 'If I'm creating that effect that's

more power to me in a sense. If I have that effect on everyone –
heterosexual, homosexual, whatever – then why be discriminating?
I'm not gonna say, "Gee, I wish these people weren't turned on
to me." '

The actor re-deployed his signature technique for interviews:
turn the inquisition lamp on the questioner. Ask him about his life.
Flatter or tease the hack about *his* or *her* mores or mannerisms. He
studies one reporter and says, 'I bet I could get a good imitation
of you down before the night is over.' Others he asks about their
lives, beliefs, problems; what cars they like, what food.

The dilemma facing any ambitious actor, who feeds his craft by
observing those around him, is that the more he fulfils his ambition
and becomes famous the less easy it becomes to observe people. (Or
to observe them unobserved. Recall Travolta's chaos-crowned trip
to the 2001 disco.) So, perversely, the reporters who helped to
rob you of your vocational nourishment by making you famous
now become the closest thing to a new nourishment. They are
the only fresh faces you regularly meet and study at close range.
On some days they are a necessary evil; on others they may
seem helpful prey for your scavenging instincts as an actor.
They can even be a one-person audience as you practise your
latest repertoire of characters. Interviewer Tom Burke remarks to
Travolta on how six different people have momentarily 'possessed
him' during the course of their lunch together. 'Different people
do "pass through", ' muses Travolta. 'An actor is . . . a constant
metamorphosis.'

So what happens when that media audience, attentive and polite
for so long, suddenly turns on you? *Moment by Moment* provided
not just the anguish of a bad movie poorly received. It ruptured
Travolta's faith in the media's limitless love for him – in its loyalty
to the avocation of making him famous. Compounded with the
loss of his mother, it was another withdrawal of unquestioned,
unquestioning emotional support.

Then, to the lubricious awe of a showbiz press that always
scents blood when a career is about to gore itself, Travolta became
indecisive about a major movie project. It was *American Gigolo*,
written and to be directed by Paul Schrader, the screenwriter of
Taxi Driver. Travolta was offered – indeed signed for – the role

of Julian Kaye, a high-society hustler in Schrader's Americanised homage to Stendhal's *Le Rouge et le Noir*. Then he backed out.

'After *Moment by Moment* I just didn't want to do anything that would make that kind of negative explosion again,' Travolta explained. He had looked at the script from all angles, weighed it, measured it. He had even been measured himself, by Giorgio Armani. The clothes maestro held a tape against the million-dollar body before devoting two months to styling twenty suits. Back in Hollywood, Paramount hired the veteran Czech-born actor Francis Lederer to coach Travolta in elocution and urbanity. 'He teaches me a certain manner and grace that the character should have,' explained Travolta.

But at the centre of the film's plot was a romance with an older woman, played by Lauren Hutton. That motif, so soon after his Tomlin screen fling and the reprise Hyland gossip it prompted, gave Travolta the tremors.

For professional purposes, he maintained that the minutiae of the script were unsatisfactory: 'The dialogue was stilted.' Then when Shrader refused to make changes, Travolta made his own. Sitting in his kitchen one day, he turned to his then assistant and said, 'Kay, I have a nauseous feeling in my stomach. I shouldn't be doing this, should I?' Kay said, 'No.' The next day Travolta told the producers he was out.

He invited Paramount chief Michael Eisner to his Hollywood penthouse to explain that with his mother's death and other adversities, he was too unhappy to make the film. Eisner said, 'How about you owe us one movie and you give us one?'

Paul Schrader thinks that Travolta backed out for a combination of reasons. 'He had had his first flop, which threw him for a loop. His mother died. And he suddenly became very anxious over whether he should be playing this kind of character.'

'Scientology played a role too,' he adds. 'In fact I first heard that he was going to drop out from someone in Scientology circles.' The Hubbardites might well have taken a dim view of their movie-star protege lending his charisma to a male prostitute.

The role of Julian Kaye passed to Christopher Reeve, who turned to it down, then to the actor fast becoming Travolta's stand-in apparent. 'Since I had a contract with Travolta,' Paul Schrader

says, 'I was able to force the studio to go forward with Richard Gere, though back then he was relatively unknown. That way they were able to get out of a lawsuit that would have been thrown at them over John's walking from the picture.'

Gere brought to the movie a lacquered grace and feline self-awareness. Since neither of these are Travolta attributes, the casting change illuminates the subtle way film history can be re-inflected by an accident of casting. Played by Travolta, Julian Kaye would have been more naif, more vulnerable: a man whose 'cool' was partly masquerade and whose romance with an older woman might indeed have seemed as fraught as Oedipal as in *Moment by Moment*. With Gere, an actor who bares his thoughts less readily than his body, we get more suave opacity and also more sense of a grown-up handling grown-up relationships.

Career mishaps, once they start, multiply: spontaneous proliferation, part two. In 1979 Travolta won the Hollywood Women's Press Club's annual Sour Apple award for 'the star who most believes his own press releases'. He was bitten in the face by his own dog in the grounds of Rancho Tajiguas. And in one infamous incident in Beverly Hills he proved his own worst enemy.

Outside Trader Vic's restaurant, a hangout for glitterati at the intersection of Wilshire and Santa Monica Boulevards, Travolta's limousine driver got out of the car to beat up an advancing photographer. It happened within a few yards of the star, nestling in the rear seat behind his tinted window. Witnesses saw the incident and one photographed it. The victim Todd Wallace, a slight-looking paparazzo with camera dangling off shoulder-strap, is seen being hauled and punched by a large bearded man who looks as if he could bounce contestants at a Mr Universe contest. Wallace sued Travolta for $500,000, claiming he had been punched in the mouth by the driver and had a tooth loosened before two more of Travolta's bodyguards joined in. (The suit was finally, settled out of court.)

Travolta distanced himself literally and morally. He vanished into seclusion, while taking time out to brief a British newspaper, 'It's been said that I did nothing to stop it, that I even asked someone to do it. Well, you have to believe me, never in a million years would I ask anyone else, I'm just not capable of it.'

This answers the question, 'Did he encourage the beating?' It does not answer the question(s), 'Did he try to stop the beating, and if not, why not?'

The incident could have been designed by a malign deity playing sarcastic riffs on Travolta's career. The last Todd in his life was the immune-deficient hero of *The Boy in the Plastic Bubble*. Now, artfully disguised as a shutterbug, here was another doom-bearing youth with death-like name, thrown up against the plastic bubble of the superstar's car. By another fanciful dramatic quirk. Travolta had been driving away from the Golden Globe Awards ceremony at the Beverly Hills Hilton, of which Trader Vic's is the in-house restaurant: an evening where his sole role was as presenter and which seemed designed to remind him that his harvest of prizes, in the year of *Moment by Moment*, consisted of one Sour Apple.

Fate does not actually go round shaping these moments. But there must have seemed a macabre unanimity in the hammer and chisel blows Travolta was receiving. From as far away as Russia the new iconoclasm was in full swing. Moscow's *Literary Gazette* gloated at the high flyer's downfall, 'Only one joy is left to him – the childish habit of glueing together brightly coloured model aeroplanes.'

The picture beside Travolta's kingsize bed at this time in Rancho Tajiguas is of a plane he used to own. Perhaps it reminds him that there is a happier world above the one he lives in. 'When I wake up,' he says, 'it's such a disappointment . . . almost like everything's been reversed. As if my realities are dreams and my deepest dreams aren't yet realities.'

Nor, when he gets out of bed, can he do as the rest of us do: carelessly put a slice of bread in the toaster and a coffee pot on the hob, then open the day's newspaper or tune in the news. 'I would be going along just fine, then I'd see an article about me or hear something bad on the radio; and then I'd be brought back down again.'

Free of work, he could be his own master. But flying his own plane is almost the only way he can leave the house. Terrestrial outings are none at all.

'I would like to be able to go to Disneyland one day,' he dreams, looking back on the days when acting consisted of nothing more

problematic than imitating plaster pirates. 'I make it sound sad, but it is just that sometimes it gets overbearing. I like [fame] and I want it but I just have to realise that if I don't feel like being recognised in the streets I have to stay in.' Meanwhile he receives phone calls from someone who has found out his telephone number and keeps ringing all night.

The better to brave the world, he grows a beard. (Also, perhaps, to disguise the nine-stitch surgery left by the dog-bite.) And he receives, among the dwindling mailbag of scripts, one called *Urban Cowboy*. It arouses a flicker of interest. It contains no disco scenes and no romance with an older woman. And it is to be shot a thousand miles from that Hell-disguised-as-Heaven known as Los Angeles. In Houston, Texas, where Travolta will be required to play that all-vindicating icon of American life and culture, the cowboy.

8

MECHANICAL BULL

John Travolta was not so forgotten, in those dark nights of the Santa Barbara soul, that important Hollywood projects passed him by completely. A prestige vampire story was dangled before him, fifteen years before it would be grasped by fellow Scientologist Tom Cruise. When author Anne Rice saw *Saturday Night Fever* she thought Travolta a natural for *Interview with the Vampire*. 'I was very surprised. He's a sensitive actor with extraordinary power on the screen. This material would be quite different for him, but I think he would be terrific in it.'

If Travolta was going to star in a blood opera, he preferred the sound of *The Godfather Part Three*. Everyone thought he would be good in this, except Mario Puzo. 'He's not going to dance, you can't have a dancing godfather; it would ruin everything,' complained the Mafia saga's originator. No one had taken Puzo gently aside to point out that Travolta had done some acting too.

He was not making life easy for his loyalists. Did movie-makers now have to write in a *beard* for any new role? The accessory had had a trial run in 1978 at the Golden Globe awards, the year of Todd Wallace's beating up. A furry-faced Travolta was seen linking arms with Fred Astaire and best actress winner Jane Fonda.

Beards look good on some stars, but on Travolta they are like putting a briar hedge in front of a panoramic view. Each inch of that sallow complexion, with its subtle tides of expression, is prime acting real estate. So journalist-turned-screenwriter Aaron Latham, author of *Urban Cowboy* and the *Esquire* article about

Western-style honkey tonk bars in Houston on which it was based, was mildly taken aback, in the late summer of 1979, to see an actor he envisaged as Tony Manero turn up for rehearsals resembling a worse-for-wear El Greco saint. Explained the actor, 'Because I'm so physically identifiable, I thought it would be a clever twist to get people into the new character for the first ten minutes. Throw away the *image* so they could believe in the new character.'

Yes: possibly. The character he was playing was Bud, a Texas oil worker newly arrived in Houston who catches the ersatz rodeo fever gripping a country and western hangout named Gilleys bar. Men compete with mechanical bulls; men compete for women; men do what men generally gotta do in the Wild West, though this was a designer west that came with beermats, jukeboxes and dance floors.

Director James Bridges (*The Paper Chase*, *The China Syndrome*) saw the role as a rite of passage. 'You have to play the cowboy, you know. It has certified all the major stars. McQueen, Newman, Brando – they all had to play that American hero to solidify their careers forever.'

Nor, on this cusp of Reaganite America, was the quest for pioneer values confined to movie stars. The read-through headline of Latham's article proclaimed, 'In these anxious days, some Americans have turned to God, others to gurus. But more and more turn to the cowboy hat.'

As the film geared up, a Texas University folklore professor was persuaded to put the same point differently to the *New York Times*: 'We have a need to recreate spurious forms of our cultural roots, but that doesn't mean the forms are harmful.'

This was reassuring. Before filming began, Travolta had spent three weeks risking spinal damage by practising on a $3000 mechanical bull installed in his Santa Barbara hacienda. It was as demanding as any training he had done. As with real rodeo riding, the secret is to make the opposite movement to the counteractive one you *want* to make. (It is like steering into a skid.) You push down when the animal's head goes down, rear back when it rears, and push your body against the centrifugal force when the bull goes into a spin, otherwise known as 'going into the wall'. Travolta's trainer turned the

beast's speed gauge up daily until the actor could ride full-out at 'twelve'.

Meanwhile, back at the beard. The only man deeply unhappy with this growth, when everyone met in Texas after Travolta and Bridges had train-travelled down in the luxury club car the star had asked the studio to hire for him, complete with bedrooms, kitchen and an exclusive chef, was Robert Evans. He was co-producing the movie with Irving Azar. A former head of Paramount and the man who greenlighted *The Godfather* and *Chinatown*, Evans still regarded himself as master of all he surveyed. He said, 'I'm making one Travolta film in my career and I'd like it without the beard.'

Everyone nodded and, according to Latham, did what they were going to do anyway. This was to give the hero a razor twenty minutes in. Evans consented to the compromise, seeing good box office in a blade-and-lather sequence in a steamy bathroom. For his star was still a coast-to-coast, nay continent-to-continent sex symbol even after *Moment by Moment*. He was still fawned on by female fans and as Travolta himself wryly observed, 'Ten million women can't be wrong.'

The beard was the first of many tests of wills. Warlike sounds were soon carrying all the way to Hollywood. Travolta was said to be behaving like a prima donna. He wouldn't talk to the press and his army of minders exasperated even the faithful Bridges: 'I cannot make this movie this way. When I want to talk to John, I cannot have to go through three secretaries!'

Meanwhile the equanimity with which the star had arrived in Houston, hoping for relative anonymity, was revealed as a cruel illusion. The scenario was the same here as in Hollywood: Night of the Living Fan. Travolta had to autograph cash-till receipts in the supermarket. A restaurant manager xeroxed and framed his credit card. Two garbagemen obliged a car full of passing Travoltaboppers by emptying his trash into their boot. And hordes of fans swept round his rented home or followed him to the the edge of the set which since it was Gilleys itself they fortunately couldn't enter.

Aaron Latham, who had found him 'incredibly charming' at first, meeting, now noted the under-pressure Travolta. For the star's sake a decision was made to close the set and impose a media blackout.

'He was still the biggest star in the world and every day would have been a press conference,' says Latham 'Also we thought he was in fragile shape. His last movie hadn't worked, his mother had died, and his girlfriend.' Only close friends or major celebrities, like Jane Fonda who interrupted a thirty-city anti-nuclear tour to pay a visit, were suffered anywhere near the shooting.

The publicity moratorium wasn't popular. 'I've never seen a location where they won't allow you to talk to the press,' said co-star Scott Glenn. 'Bruce Bahrenberg [the publicist] walks around feeling as useless as tits on a bull.'

Ironically, the one supposed insider who did keep gabbing to the press – Robert Evans – was not in constant attendance at the shoot. 'Evans and his co-producer hated each other and were always fighting,' Latham says. 'At some point James Bridges said to Michael Eisner [then Paramount president], "If these two are gonna stay in town and I'm gonna have to referee their fights every day, this movie's gonna cost half as much again to make." So Eisner told Evans and Azar to get out of town by sunset.'

While Evans raved from afar, taking his verbal kamikaze dives into his own movie ('The press relations on this film stink'), Travolta found space and freedom to throw himself into his work. With Houston choreographer Patsy Swayze, mother of Patrick, he learned the dances native to the Lone Star state: the Cotton Eye Joe, the country hustle, the hoedown and the bizarre Texan Two-step, resembling two tarantulas trying to get out of a broom cupboard. He also had a mechanical bull installed in his backyard, and he hung out with the bar's locals, picturesquely named Gilleyrats. 'You could see him gain in confidence day by day,' Latham says.

He had a head start on his co-stars. Debra Winger, playing the girlfriend he breaks up with to trigger the film's love-and-jealousy subplot, had less time to learn bull-riding, and so did Scott Glenn as her ex-convict lover. They did their own stuntwork, nonetheless. They ran greater danger than the Gilleyrats, since the mattresses surrounding the bull had to be removed to put the cameras in place. In one scene, with nothing to catch her fall but concrete, Debra Winger was almost thrown off: a moment you can still see in the film.

The most perilous incident, though, waited for their return to Los Angeles. Filming moved there in the last two weeks, with a trailer park in East L.A. standing in for its Houston equivalent. One day, with no warning, gunshots were fired into the location from a perimeter embankment. Said witness and ex-policeman Jerry Ray, employed as a security guard on the film, 'Six men came over a bank. They were armed with sawed-off rifles. I believe they were members of a street gang by the name of Pico Viejos.'

What had seemed exaggerated security in Houston, with six to ten guards on duty at $200 each a day, seemed less frivolous now. No one came near to being injured, says Aaron Latham, but Travolta was badly shaken. 'We all bundled into a jeep as fast as possible and got out of there. The rest of the trailer scene was shot on a soundstage.'

Urban Cowboy is remarkable for two things. It was the first time, apart from *Moment by Moment*, that the media's gossip machinery failed to trump up an offscreen romance. (It is not something one imagines Debra Winger lending herself to.) And it was the first time Travolta passes through a movie almost without being noticed.

For much of the film he looks as if he is in shock. The limpid blue eyes are lifeless as marbles; the jaw is slack: the face is a lambent pout canonised by sidelighting. The voice has Travolta's characteristic gentle slur but an uncharacteristic lack of life or variety. Throughout the film, the hero's responses lag behind the script instead of (as in *Fever* or *Grease*) detonating subtly all around it.

Either Travolta had failed to wake naturally from his soul's midnight or the script hadn't provided a loud enough alarm call. The great American stud-you-like is outshone by a stud you like more. Scott Glenn brings so much leathery authority to his skimpily-written part – while scarcely seeming to stir an eyelid – that you feel cheated by an ending in which this noble giant must live down to his baddie role by robbing the Gilleys till. Travolta goes off with the girl, who has also spent the whole movie outacting him. This was Debra Winger's first big role and she draws it in bold, raspy strokes like a charcoal artist.

What ever was going on inside Hollywood's favourite tortured

soul? Aaron Latham tells a story intended to praise Travolta's healthy detachment as an actor, but which can just as easily be construed as a reflection on his *unhealthy* detachment from *Urban Cowboy*.

'The whole time we shot the film, everybody, Debra Winger, me, James Bridges, all of us for some reason started wearing cowboy clothes, except John Travolta who never did. I think this was to keep straight what was the role and what was him. And as soon as we finished shooting he immediately started wearing nothing but cowboy clothes. So he was very clear about the fact that he was an actor, not a character.'

Fine. Except that he never becomes the character at all. And perhaps this more-*degagé*-than-thou attitude had something to do with it.

Another story of life on *Urban Cowboy* hints at Travolta's muddled mind-set as he tried to reconcile being an everyday mortal with being an – albeit endangered – messiah-superstar. A young extra was carried off to hospital after being hit by a car. Travolta went to see him and gave him on his return to the set the present of a stetson. Before the extra could try it on, the star tossed $1000 into it and said, 'Here, live on that till you feel better.'

This addled mixture of Christliness and condescension is par for this period. On the few occasions Travolta spoke to the press, he showed a preference for self-orienteering soliloquy over rousing movie pitches. 'I'm a person who likes to inspire and to be inspired: I like to exchange that flow. And I'm unsettled, anxious, compassionate, hungry, excited, disappointed. I go through the gamut of emotions a lot: I trust very easily and mistrust very easily.'

Trust and vulnerability are the themes of the season. As an actor, or at least a Travolta-style actor specialising in negative capability, he leaves the windows of his personality almost permanently open to other people's minds and mannerisms. 'I'll hold on strongly to what I believe, and then someone comes along and I want to understand him and duplicate him so that suddenly I let his viewpoint really affect me.'

In turn he wants to propound or practice his own viewpoints in a give-and-take spirit: 'If I can have a conversation with

someone who won't judge what I have to say, he has me as a friend.'

But friends are so hard to come by: especially when the motive for friendship is compromised by fame. Even one's own family – are they friends? Or are they newly cast as dependents?

Travolta's brothers and sisters had already piled into Hollywood looking for a piece of the action. 'Everyone wants a part of you and your own family hasn't adjusted to your success,' he said. 'They're wondering where they fit in – why they aren't stars too, or why they aren't making the money you're making.'

At least Ellen had been an actress from the start – indeed had had a six-year start on him. Now she was working in the ABC sitcom *Making It* and had her own Palm Springs chat show. And Sam at Paramount had strayed into non-encroaching areas of the movie biz, taking jobs in special effects and editing.

But Annie was picking the crumbs of tiny roles in *Grease* and *Urban Cowboy*. And Joey, who had majored in education, had given up his East Coast job as a teacher of special needs children to travel west and to doorstep Tinseltown. Having done a little nightclub singing in New Jersey, he now aspired to be a singer-actor. 'I got to Hollywood because I had a hit record,' he insisted, meaning the single 'I don't Wanna Go' which reached number forty-three in the charts. But although Paramount 'wanted to develop some television things for me,' there was nothing he liked. 'We couldn't agree on any material . . . I'm kind of holding back until I find the right vehicle.' Meanwhile, 'If I have something that's offered me because of John, I usually don't take it.'

How awful it must be to be the brother of a show business celebrity. You either stay well away from his nimbus of fame, or you hope that by sidling towards that radiance you might find a grow-light for your own lurking talent.

While researching this book I rang Joey in Hollywood, where he had just directed a microbudget feature. 'Hi, how ya doing?' said a friendly voice; he probably hoped that I wanted to talk about his film. When he realised I wanted to quiz him about his brother, the voice went dead. You could sense the disappointment even though he remained polite. I never heard from him again, though he vaguely promised to get back after talking to John.

Just at this time in Travolta's life – when friends were suspect and family were scanned for opportunism – a bizarre meeting of soulmates happened. As if summoned to revive a sea-fallen Icarus, James Cagney dove into Travolta's life. It was mutual adoration at first sight. The youngster had grown up capering before the older star's 'Yankee Doodle Dandy' number on TV. And the veteran from Hollywood was an excited convert to the boy from Englewood: 'When I saw *Urban Cowboy*, I said, that kid's got it all!'

They met at a Saint Patrick's Day party, where Travolta performed a hoedown for Cagney and then accepted an invitation to spend the night with him and his missus. When he returned the hospitality by having James up to Santa Barbara for a long weekend, the scene was set was for a get-together dazzling in its poetic congruity. Two part-Irish hoofers who changed the face of hoofing. Two actor-entertainers who alternated dancing pumps with gangsters' spats.

Not that *Pulp Fiction* or *Get Shorty* were glints in the Travolta agenda when Cagney checked in at Rancho Tajiguas. At his host's insistence the older man had the freedom of the mansion. No one had to get up for breakfast, which was helpful since Travolta had a hard time getting Cagney up for elevenses. 'Can we wake Jamesy now?' he would whisper to Marge Zimmerman, Jamesy's friend and assistant. Then they would gently rouse the older man and Travolta would lie on the guest room's adjoining bed, urging tea or coffee and making cheerful small talk.

Later there was the magazine photo-session.

'This way, buttercup, now smile,' the awakened eighty-year-old said to a Travolta beginning to weaken under the day's media pressure.

'My hair keeps getting in my eyes,' said Travolta.

'Then get rid of it' snapped Cagney.

And they hugged and smiled for *Life* magazine.

Cagney warmed up as the day went on. He spat out ebullient memories of music hall and movie career. 'Let me tell you, son, vaudeville was so cut-throat that after that the films were a piece of cake.' He gave Travolta personal career advice. 'Start with one thing: they need you. Without you, they have an empty screen. So

when you get on there, just do what you think is right and stay with it. If you listen to all the clowns around, you're just dead.' And he admired the Aztec-style pool, surrounded by majestic shaggy palms and strewn terracotta pots. He was welcome to take a dip, said Travolta, though he himself would stay out, explaining, 'I once broke my nose diving in a pool, so I don't swim. I hate the sun too.'

The two men discussed the possibility of John starring in a film about James's life. But nothing had gelled by the time James signed the guest book with the obscure text. 'For Johnnio. Young love.' 'Three of the nicest days of my life,' exclaimed the old man as they said goodbye. 'Truly, Mr Cagney?' asked Travolta. 'I wouldn't lie to you, son.'

Later Cagney summed up the sojourn for *Rolling Stone*, 'There's no furore to the boy, no fanfare,' he said. 'But in the time we spent together there was no great display of affection by him.'

Perhaps they should have met earlier or later. (Cagney did have Travolta over for a return weekend at his farm in Stansfordsville, New York.) But there is something touching in the absence of a thunderclap rapport. Anticlimaxes are the stuff of life – it doesn't form itself into neat patterns even for movie stars, nor their biographers.

Besides, there were times when Travolta had no quarrel with his own company. 'My favourite time, I got to spend three days by myself up there. I smoked cigars and watched movies. I took two days just to watch Bertolucci's *1900*. I had a ball. No one bothered me. I'd eat by myself, take a couple of cigars and go up to the screening room. I sat there and I said, "Oh this is the life!" '

Back in the bad world, *Urban Cowboy* was going through delivery pangs. Watching the rough cut, Travolta was torn between opposing impulses: self-effacement and vanity. He wielded his right of final cut to excise what he called 'glamour shots' of himself as well as snipping away at that shaving scene. Yet he insisted on his thighs being slimmed down with an airbrush for publicity shots.

Some reviewers liked the film; many thought it as synthetic as its setting. 'All packaging and no execution,' judged Richard Schickel in *Time*: 'If [Travolta] keeps on this way, he will turn out to be not the Brando of the eighties but the Troy Donahue of the

decade.' For Andrew Sarris in the *Village Voice*, 'Travolta gives the dreadful impression that he spends much of his time figuring out how to tease his fans without letting them get too far into his beautiful, sensitive soul.' And Pauline Kael switched from leading the Travolta hurrahs to conducting the catcalls, 'You get the feeling that if anybody slapped Bud he'd start crying . . . [Travolta] seems whipped, anxious, scared: he shows the sick bewilderment of an actor who can't get a fix on his character.'

The film moved smartly into overdrive at the box office, though, scattering exhaust fumes over America's consumer culture. Where *Saturday Night Fever* had encouraged sales in combs and hair oils, *Urban Cowboy* made millionaires of mechanical bull manufacturers. There were soon an estimated 4000 such machines across the States, not including bulls sent to Belgium, Sweden, South Africa and a US Navy aircraft carrier in the Pacific. *Variety* buttonholed one Bruce Lehrke, a Nashville rodeo manager, who reported a booming business in Western-style concession products, with cowboy boots and hats snatched as soon as they reached the shelves. And rodeo owners were reopening their businesses just when they had seemed poised for extinction.

Travolta looked on but exempted himself from the euphoria. He would later say, 'I created several themes for people to party on – *Saturday Night Fever, Grease, Urban Cowboy* – and people partied on those themes in a way I never did.'

So what *was* he partying on? His romance with Marilu Henner was on again, off again, on again. She had accompanied the *Grease* star on his promotional tour through Europe, staying with him at the Plaza Atheneé in Paris and sharing the horror of the London premiere, while realising that life with Travolta meant being involved with an entourage, not a man.

'I was starting to tire of getting sucked into the jet wash of exhaust behind Johnny's star-making engine, commanded by his imperious manager, Bob Lemond [sic]', she writes in her autobiography. Digressing briefly to slam her and Johnny's Svengali – 'For 15 percent off the top, he gave me the worst advice I ever got. I had business meetings at his home while he would be getting manicures and pedicures' – she compares the new, schmoozing, synthesised Travolta with the untidy, lovable sexbomb who

occasionally re-emerges: for instance when she stopped over in Texas during the *Urban Cowboy* shoot. Maybe it was all that work on the mechanical bull at Gilleys, she muses, but 'he was very sexy to be around'.

In December the couple visited Las Vegas, where they caught the Bette Midler film *The Rose* and Henner experienced an emotional lighting bolt. Up there on screen was the man who would chase away all romantic thoughts of Travolta, at least for the few years in which a temperamental, dynamic, opinionated, hard-drinking actor called Frederic Forrest seemed someone with whom Henner could share a home, or indeed a planet.

The new love rivalry climaxed in the new year. Travolta and Henner had planned a skiing trip to Mammoth in northern California. On departure day she received a call from her agent saying Francis Coppola wanted her to audition that afternoon for *Hammett*, an arthouse film noir to be directed by Coppola's new Euro-protegé Wim Wenders. Its star, already cast in the broody-romantic role of the forties detective novelist, was Frederic Forrest.

Henner handed her skis to Travolta. She would catch him up in Mammoth the next day: a day that never arrived. On the *Hammett* set she was caught up in a vortex of passion with Forrest which lasted through several years, one marriage and many rows, including an extended tiff about their Mulholland Drive mansion, which fell down the hill when Forrest said there was no need to reinforce the retaining wall.

Travolta might have been expected to slide downhill himself without the emotional retaining wall of Henner. Instead he did the opposite – began soaring. He had one love that thrived on emotional freedom, and unlike many of his other support systems it was disappointment-proof. It was his love of that big blue back-projection called the sky.

It was surely time to go to the limit and earn his jet pilot's licence. During *Urban Cowboy* he had bought a seven-seater Cessna A14, which could be parked next to his reconditioned DC3. Up there in smog-free Santa Barbara, where the jet fumes dispersed amid the fragrance of avocado groves, the definition of happiness and freedom was to climb aboard one of his throbbing, customised

kites and to say goodbye, for an hour or ten, to agents, managers and movie deals. Like Orson Welles in *The Third Man,* he could place himself where it no longer mattered if one of those 'dots' stopped moving.

One of them soon would. Bob Le Mond called Travolta up with the excited offer of the leading role in a film called *An Officer and a Gentleman.* Great script and story. Le Mond didn't envisage a refusal, nor did the movie's casting director and old Travolta loyalist Lynn Stalmaster. 'We were very excited about him playing the lead. Then John, to our amazement said he couldn't take the part. He wouldn't interrupt his twenty-one-day training course at jet pilot school to come and do the audition. If he had done the film, which was a huge success, who knows? His whole career might have been different.' Meaning, it might not have gone into the long tailspin awaiting him a few years hence. And Bob Le Mond might not have parted company with him, as he now did, after ten faithful years spent easing his path to stardom. Meanwhile, with a certitude bordering on the supernatural, the lead role in *An Officer and a Gentleman* went to Richard Gere.

9

BLOWING HOT, BLOWING COLD

John Travolta didn't just fly planes: he gazed at them, made models of them, hung photographs of them, obsessed about them. Down in Long Beach, California, in 1980, Howard Hughes's famous Spruce Goose, the giant wooden transport plane that never flew after its first bellyflopping trial, was attracting attention since it was being moved to another display site. At the same time Travolta was reading a suspense thriller about a man who tries to steal the Goose. He sent the book to director Brian De Palma, with whom he had kept in touch since *Carrie*, and suggested it would make a good and timely movie.

De Palma in turn sent Travolta the suspense script *he* was developing, about wicked deeds visited on a humbler mode of transport, the motor car. Swathed in shades of the JFK assassination and Chappaquiddick, *Personal Effects*, later called *Blow Out*, offers an ambitious political candidate whose car and career are shot from under him one night when a concealed rifleman blows out a tyre. The car skids into a lake, drowning the politician but sparing his girlfriend, who is rescued to face fresh dangers by the hero, a sound effects expert who had been out scouting for midnight noises.

The story evolves into a designer riff – detractors later said rip-off – on two earlier movies, Antonioni's *Blow Up* and Coppola's *The Conversation*. A crime is deconstructed and reconstructed through hi-fi technology and the protagonist finds his own life in danger as he tries to protect both his evidence – in *Blow Out* it is spools of minutely analysed sound and image – and the assassin-stalked girl.

When he finally gains mastery of the evidence and its meaning, it is too late to save the girl.

De Palma set the story in Philadelphia, the birthplace of American democracy. That way he could explode democracy, America and notions of heritage at one go. As he had shown in *Carrie*, and since then in *The Fury*, this director loved movie plots that were like dangerous laboratory experiments. He was the cinema's answer to a mad scientist: a grown-up version of the schoolboy who had won second prize in a National Science Fair with a project on 'The Application of Cybernetics to the Solution of Differential Equations' and also of the child-voyeur who used to watch his surgeon father perform operations.

Blow Out, though not the gothic extravaganza of *Carrie*, would still be a visceral change of direction for Travolta. De Palma initially wanted an older man for the main role of Jack Terry. The director's wife and Travolta's ex-*Carrie* colleague Nancy Allen, who would also be his *Blow Out* co-star, says her husband envisaged 'someone like Richard Dreyfuss or James Woods, more cerebral, less emotionally sensitive than John. The character was very cynical, over the hill, beaten down: very dark.' De Palma confirms, 'I didn't write the role for John, because I thought he was too young. But when we met again I saw he was no longer a boy but a grown man and quite right for it.' (*Blow Out*'s producer George Litto complicates the picture, though, by saying that two other young stars *were* considered: Harrison Ford and, inevitably, Richard Gere).

Allen is thankful Travolta came into the picture. 'He brought heart and soul to it and a warmth that didn't exist on the page. You didn't give a damn about the guy as written, he was very self-serving.'

Travolta made him a workaholic craftsman living in his own mental garret. '*Blow Out* is the first time that I'm playing a fully-fledged adult. In the picture I don't use an accent, a walk, any of the physical characteristics that we call "hooks".' The only specially chosen appearance details were designed *not* to draw attention. 'It was my idea to grease down my hair and go for that rumpled Ivy League look.

'The role [is] very different since I've always played characters

that go directly from the heart. Jack is so very analytical.' At least until the film's final scene when the horror the hero has known before only in fiction, finding perfect screams to attach to low-rent splatter movies, becomes all too real. He plays the last scream of his own murdered girlfriend over and over as he and his producer soundmix their latest shlocker. This bleak, lurid payoff, a nihilist flourish typical of the director of *Dressed to Kill* and *Body Double*, would have defeated most actors. But Travolta strove to find the reason behind the hero's unreason: '[Jack's] crazed and in that state of mind anything goes. Nothing's rational. . . . I played it like "What does it matter? It's all anarchy!" Also, if you want to see it as a positive gesture, it's a way of keeping Sally alive, the way he's continually listening to that tape at the end.'

It is typical of Travolta's search for an upbeat humanity in his characters, though, that even this scene did not write 'Finis' for him. 'He [Jack] feels responsible for two deaths. He's murdered someone. It's going to take some time – several years maybe – but I wouldn't like to think he's totally done in.'

It is equally typical of De Palma that he *did* see this scene as Finis. 'I think Jack's is a hopeless situation. I think when you have a truth that does not fit in with what people want to accept, you are an odd man out and you will be driven crazy or totally ignored and killed.'

De Palma constructed the film like a series of Chinese boxes: ones that fold in and crush or suffocate the characters. *Blow Out*'s themes were paranoia and runaway conspiracy. 'The most amazing result of the [JFK] assassination was that for the first time the American public realised it was being lied to,' says the filmmaker. Citing the film's deliberate references to Dallas and Chappaquiddick, he added, 'What I've gleaned from my reading is that a conspiracy sort of happens by accident. What I wanted to show in the film is how haphazard, as opposed to precisely worked out, a conspiracy is.'

He made a precisely engineered audiovisual machine to do so. *Blow Out*'s gifted cinematographer Vilmos Zsigmond had shot *Close Encounters of the Third Kind* and *The Deer Hunter*, and points out that the movie's whole colour palette was based on the reds, whites and blues of the American flag, in keeping with the

Liberty Day climax in which Travolta runs through Philadelphia's streets in a race to rescue Allen from a roving killer.

Though De Palma sketched his own precise storyboards for each shot, he gave the actors freedom within that framework to improvise, as he had in *Carrie*.

'The structure never changed, but the dialogue did,' says Allen. 'The scenes in the hospital and the railway bar, John and I made up our own. John would always do something that would take the movie by surprise. We shot the bar scene a million times, in which the hero Jack asks me to stay and help him investigate the crime. For instance, when I ask "Oh you're a sound engineer. How'd you get that job?" in the script John's character responded with a speech explaining how. But in one of the takes John just shrugged and said "I don't know" and gave a pause before going into the speech. You can see my look of "What? What's he up to now?" That's the take Brian kept. Then during another shot in the scene John suddenly leaned over without warning, when the camera was rolling, and whispered something in my ear.'

This provides one of the teasing mysteries in the finished movie. We are never told what Jack whispers to the Nancy Allen character; we only know that it is enough to make her giggle and win her to his side. So what *did* the actor actually whisper to her?

'We both love to eat and he said, "If you stay I'll buy you an ice cream." Which got me to laugh, since it was one of John and my secrets.'

Travolta had become friendly with both Nancy Allen and De Palma, on and off the set. During filming he helped Nancy through the tribulations of the underwater rescue sequence. 'I'm claustrophobic and I almost panicked. John was very reassuring, taught me how to buddy-breathe and insisted on seeing that all the stunt equipment was safe and in place.' The crew honoured him with the gift of a chaise longue garlanded with flowers and inscribed 'Esther (for swimming star Esther Williams) Travolta'.

'Now of course I'm curious to go out and discover that amazing world that exists under the sea,' Travolta told the press. Blarney no doubt; but at least it showed he was *trying* to flaunt that responsiveness to a role's colours that had been so lacking in *Urban Cowboy*, when he shunned the regalia of his character offscreen.

Travolta also became a frequent visitor to the De Palmas' home in the Hamptons, where Nancy and he pursued their covert mania for ice cream. She remembers the two of them more than once taking early leave of a game of Monopoly – they were usually the first to go bankrupt – and leaving Brian and a friend behind, still absorbed in shifting hotels around Park Avenue, while they went out to wolf quantities of pizza, hamburgers or ice cream.

This opens a whole new Pandora's box in the praxis and pathology of stardom. How *do* you feed a megastar with a mega-appetite? You either home-cook for him night after night, or give him a crash diet of takeaways, or disguise him in a raincoat and turned-up collar so he can go to the takeaway himself. Or you risk the full glare of a restaurant or nightclub with all the public-recognition mishaps that can entail.

'John was very polite, he handled fans well,' says Allen. 'But if one person came up for his autograph it was like permission for everyone else to do so. One night Brian, John and I went to the Ritz in New York, a big music club with different levels. They seated us upstairs where the lights were dark and we were set back. But one person looked up from below and spotted him and you could feel this whole *wave* start. Everyone started looking up and pointing, and people began to come towards us. We had to leave. It was phenomenal really – how did they spot him?'

Blow Out, a thriller layered like a lasagne, was on one level a movie in which art imitated its participants' life: a darkly flavoursome parable about fame and the vexations of living in a surveillance society. Everyone can run, but no one can hide. Everyone can enjoy what they think is a private life; no one can be sure that the techno-snoopers are not watching from the opposite window or lurking in the basement. De Palma used his repertoire of quirky camera angles and unsettling, metallic colours to make this city seem a place where the hold on reality constantly slips and slides; where people are always ready to give you that extra push towards destruction.

Persecution mania, though, can be self-fulfilling. 'Just because you're paranoid, it doesn't mean they're not out to get you,' goes the adage. Travolta was less its victim finally than De Palma. The director might have persuaded himself that he was only a

movie-maker making a movie. But a punitive karma lay in wait for him and *Blow Out*, as if the fates were determined to chastise a thriller that presumed to put pessimism above populism.

Late on the afternoon of Friday May 15th, 1981, a Graf Air Shipping truck carrying fifty cartons of unedited *Blow Out* footage, due to be shipped from New York to the Technicolor labs in Los Angeles, stopped to make a pick-up at 48th and 6th Avenues. Someone – never named or known – peered in, saw a brief window of opportunity and stole two of the cartons: ones that contained expensive and spectacular Liberty Parade footage. There were no copies except for an unusable rough cut and De Palma, in his words, 'went crazy'. He spent days searching the surrounding streets in hope that the 2000 feet of film, valueless to anyone else, had been discarded in a trashcan. Then finally he put out the bitter, unavoidable call – or recall – for 1000 extras, five cameras and two helicopters.

'We had to re-shoot at the cost of $750,000,' says the director. 'We had negative insurance, all companies carry it. Still it was just awful. I'd have been happy to ransom the film, but we were never contacted to do so.' Since Vilmos Zsigmond had left for another project, his Hungarian-born compatriot Laszlo Kovacs was brought in. De Palma was haunted by the incident for weeks. He saw it as confirmation of the rule proposed in his movie: that man's subtlest plans can be outsmarted by a greater, arbitrary malignity. 'It was like *Blow Out* – a totally haphazard accident out of nowhere.'

After this, he and his company could face anything, and soon had to. Against the director's judgment Paramount opened his dark, downbeat, fall-friendly movie in the summer. Producer George Litto realised it was a bad move and bitterly regrets not using the one piece of leverage he had.

'The film was committed to all those summer theatres, but when the footage was stolen we had the perfect cop-out. We could have said, we cannot complete on time. But we were too damned efficient.'

The film bombed. Good reviews from some, including Pauline Kael, made no impression on audiences who either could not unscramble the intricate conspiracy plot or did not try. They

were also confronted with a Travolta barely recognisable in his pale, Hamlet-like inwardness. Why didn't he sing? Why didn't he dance? Couldn't he even smile?

It was and still is a daring performance in a film worthy of it. Travolta invents a new physical reality for himself: the round-shouldered, cramped-rhythmed body language of a man absorbed in thought and staled by sleeplessness, in which gestures are at once abrupt and weary, and vitality has retreated behind the eyes. (Even Travolta's arms seem longer, as if lack of exercise has sent them into a simian-looking atrophy).

Yet playing a sound effects wizard, in key scenes he is all motionlessness on the *qui vive* for motion. The way he keeps cocking his head in the night scene in the park, as wind and owl-hoot and the first screech of tyre mesh into a macabre polyphony around him, is precise, subtle, bird-like. And he has a dazzling moment – dazzling because underplayed – when during an extended flashback to his police days he stumbles on the hanged body of an undercover colleague murdered by a mobster who had discovered his 'wire'. Pauline Kael annotated Travolta's simple virtuosity.

'He cries out, takes a few steps away, and then turns and looks again. He barely does anything – yet it's the kind of screen acting that made generations of filmgoers revere Brando in *On the Waterfront*: it's the willingness to go emotionally naked and the control to do it in character. (And, along with that, the understanding of desolation.)'

Travolta probably had a diploma in desolation. As if the underachievements of *Moment by Moment* and *Urban Cowboy* were not enough, *Blow Out*'s commercial performance was disastrous. Even among critics, scorn competed with praise, with some reviewers happy to bludgeon the film simply because it carried De Palma's signature. (Stanley Kaufman in the *New Republic*, '*Dressed to Kill*, De Palma's previous film, was odious. *Blow Out* is ludicrous. Onward!')

Then there was the anti-violence lobby. Science fiction writer Harlan Ellison, after walking out of a Writers Guild screening, wrote to the Guild urging 'restraint in showing films that consciously, gratuitously debase the human spirit.' The US Catholic

Conference spoke out against *Blow Out*'s 'nudity, violence and pervasive air of amorality'. And by the time the film was previewed in Britain, sense seemed finally to have surrendered to sensationalist overreaction. One wondered if some commentators had actually seen the film De Palma had made. Wrote William Marshall in the *Daily Mirror*, '*Blow Out* is doing stupendous business in the States' – it wasn't – 'and will no doubt do the same here with its naked savagery, scenes of female masturbation and straightforward, homespun fornication.' (Where?)

Even these imaginary attractions failed to draw audiences, as the $18 million film limped to recoup a mere $8 million in its native country.

Was Travolta down and out again emotionally? No: he clasped to his heart the portfolio of reviews, especially Kael's. 'The highbrow critics flipped and it was, for me, the first time I've felt one hundred percent approval for the role.' Also, he had ridden these turbulent thermals before and was learning that he could switch on the mental auto-pilot or climb to a higher altitude. There were other realities, other dimensions. He was happy to lay these before the British press, who quizzed him on matters eschatological as soon they realised they could not agree about the quality, or even the content, of *Blow Out*.

'I know I've lived before,' Travolta told the bemused Brits. 'And I know I've been born again. There's no doubt of it. I believe in life after death.'

What kind of life? Could those in this life, for example, communicate with the dead?

'I made no attempt to contact the loved ones who passed away,' says Travolta. But then he talks about how a dying person's spirit goes into a newborn baby and how you must not talk to a dying person because it would drain the energy they need to move on to the next life cycle. He also says that he believes he lived before as a silent star, possibly Valentino.

Travolta's reincarnation mysticism may come out of Scientology, or Travolta's interpetation of it. Or it may be a new metaphysical direction altogether, since for once in the long years since he became a convert the actor's interest in Hubbardism seemed in recess. Shortly after *Blow Out* he gave up regular counselling

sessions and in August 1983 told *Rolling Stone*, 'I haven't had any auditing for about a year and a half.'

Of the two great celestial obsessions in Travolta's life to date, aeronautics and Dianetics – those beyond-the-clouds cults giving him so much relief from fame's stress – flying was well in front now that he had earned his jet pilot licence. He tells a British reporter, 'I get up there in the moonlight, all alone, silver on the wings, and look down on the little houses way, way below and what problems I have suddenly move into perspective or fade away for a while. I guess I'm just a romantic.'

The prose sounds as if it has passed through the empurpling process of *Daily Mirror* sub-editing, but it still does justice to a Travolta whom friends portray as a total aeromane at this time. Nancy Allen remembers a flight to Chicago, where he was going to check out some *Blow Out* publicity pictures. He took Allen and two friends along.

'We drove to Butler airfield and they said there was a storm coming,' she recalls. 'I said, let's go eat until it blows over. But it didn't. So we got on the plane and John made all these pilot-style announcements. "Welcome on board. We hope your flight will be comfortable and we'll make sure you're served good food." And he served us personally, he played flight attendant as well as captain, and the plane was bouncing all over the sky since we had flown straight into the eye of the storm. John said afterwards he knew it was scary, but hadn't wanted to say anything to scare us further during the flight.'

Travolta is not the only movie star to have fallen in love with flying, though he may be the most passionate. The hobby almost goes with the job – or the need to escape the job. Down on the ground is the notional earthly heaven of fame, wealth and audience adoration. But it is a paradise where you can barely move without being pawed or ogled by the people strewn along the roads and rail-lines, or milling towards you in crowded restaurants or shopping malls. This may be fine when a well-upholstered black matron approaches you at a sidewalk cafe saying, 'I just want to tell you that I really enjoy your work. And you're just as beautiful in person!'; at which point you (Travolta) smile and kiss her and then tell your reporter companion, 'That's my favourite kind of

encounter. As long as it's genuine, I eat it up.' But what of the old lady who shrills out in a hotel lobby, right in the middle of a photoshoot, 'What's yer favourite position, love?' If you are as goodhumoured as Travolta you will go straight into 'Friends, Romans, countrymen,' as he did. But wouldn't you rather not *have* to?

Up in the sky you are invulnerable. Your capsule is fan-proof and no paparazzo can suddenly appear on the nosecone, exploding a flashbulb.

'It's almost as if you're not a part of society any more,' James Stewart once mused. 'All you can think about is what you're doing and you have a complete escape from your worldly problems. You have a real feeling of power up there – that we human beings aren't really that helpless, that we can be completely in command of an amazing machine, that we do have some control over our destiny. And of course, it's the only place where one can be really alone.'

'You get in and just declare your freedom,' Clint Eastwood agrees. 'All of a sudden you're just a number in the sky. Nobody knows who you are unless you happen to be flying by an airport that's familiar with you and they recognise your call number. But by and large you're out there, going where you want to go, and landing where you want to land.'

Born again by being airborne again.

Even on the ground, though, Travolta was finding multiple ways to be reborn or recharged. A friend introduced him to the music of Stéphane Grappelli, so he started learning the violin: three hour-long lessons per week plus neighbour-assailing practice. Since the next-doors in Santa Barbara were an agricultural Moony commune, deaf to all noises beyond their leader's call to till the ground and hoe the word, they barely registered Travolta's renditions of 'Ain't Misbehavin'' and 'Sunny Side o' the Street'.

Then there were the French lessons. These would help him converse with his new friend Gérard Depardieu. Having fallen for the beefy French actor's charisma eight years before, on seeing *Les Valseuses*, he got to know him and his wife and visited their home in Bougival near Paris. He would love to make a movie with Gérard, with Catherine Deneuve as co-star.

Then there is a third hobby: Brooke Shields. He is dating her

and the world's press is going demented. At last a romance! The twenty-seven-year-old *Grease* star going steady with the eleven years younger bombshell of *Pretty Baby*! And no hint of sleaze, or even sex. For this was still John Travolta the *preux chevalier*, who after meeting Brooke at the studio of photographer Patrick Demarchelier focused on her inner qualities. 'There are lots of women with physical beauty. But Brooke exudes goodness. She's untainted.'

If she was, it may not have been thanks to her mother. This lady was said to have been dismayed by the slow progress of the liaison. According to *People* magazine, she not only arranged that first 'chance' meeting between her daughter and Travolta, she also expressed dismay when, on the couple's first official date, John brought Brooke home in his chauffered limousine at 7.30pm.

'Brooke said they had a lovely Chinese dinner and she told him she had schoolwork, so he brought her home,' explained Mrs Shields.

Things developed slowly. John gave Brooke a Rolex on her sixteenth birthday and kissed her on the lips in a hotel car park the day after they saws *Superman* 2 (claimed a tabloid). The day after that, he flew her off to Santa Barbara in his Cessna plane, empty but for the two of them, the co-pilot, the personal assistant and the Travolta security entourage. At Rancho Tajiguas they picked artichokes and made plans to visit a Bruce Springsteen concert.

Brooke's father was full of approval. He assured the press of his daughter's eligibility for a platonic romance. 'The nuts and bolts are pretty good, but Brooke's been marinated properly.'

Yet no one was quite sure if there would eventually be, or was planned to be, an actual love match. All John would say months later was: 'We had something of a romance, yes. It depends on the degree you want to get involved.'

This being almost as gnomic as Mr Shields's utterance about marinaded nuts, the press shrugged the case off. All they knew was that the bright, beautiful, career-smart Brooke was the *kind* of girl Travolta would like, assuming he liked girls. He himself said he approved of the fair sex when it came out fighting. The women in his own family could combine careers with child care, why couldn't everyone else? 'I suppose that's the way I expect

women to be and if they aren't like that I feel there's a dimension missing.'

His ideal of the self-sufficient woman who retained her female allure was Jane Fonda, an actress he had once had sexual fantasies about. More recently, he had had lunch with her. Afterwards he rushed back to tell his sister Ellen, 'I'm in love.' Ellen responded dryly, 'Well, she's the right age.'

Romance did not develop. Nor did Fonda and Travolta's plan for a movie co-venture, a reported remake of '*Mr Deeds Goes to Washington*' (either a *Variety* misprint or a cavalier conflation of Frank Capra's two best-known comedies). However, John avidly compared notes with Jane on the culture and methodology of the physical workout. For in the wake of her smash-hit health videos he was planning his very own John Travolta Dance and Workout Center.

It happened like this. In 1982 Travolta's film career was dawdling. There were long uncommitted months between *Blow Out* and his next movie, which the world was told would be a musical. Brian De Palma's *Fire*, with Travolta playing Doors singer Jim Morrison, was contending with the *Saturday Night Fever* sequel being urged by Paramount and Robert Stigwood. *Fire* flickered hopefully for a year before dying out. 'We gave the project to Paramount initially but couldn't agree on a budget,' says George Litto. 'Everyone was into "financial diligence" at the time. Then it became academic because the Doors wouldn't give us the music rights. They were worried about how they'd be portrayed.'

Fever fever, though, was still a marketable disease. Witness the excitement surrounding the auction of Travolta's white suit from the film; or one of them, since the other had been earmarked for the Smithsonian, where it resides today. The auctioned suit went for $2000 to critic Gene Siskel who beat off a loyally bidding Jane Fonda.

In the summer of 1982, with the *Fever* sequel still not firmed up, Travolta appeared on stage in the Rocky Mountains. 'I was getting antsy. I hadn't worked in a year and a half, so I accepted a play in Aspen.' This was *Mass Appeal* by Bill C. Davis, a Catholic drama in which Travolta played a young priest. It was staged in a

300-seat converted movie theatre in Snowmass Village, just outside Aspen, and earned Travolta $350 a week to co-star with veteran Hollywood character actor Charles Durning. It also gave him time on his hands during the day to work with local gym trainer Dan Isaacson.

Weeks later, having brushed the Colorado snow off his boots, Travolta allowed the Hollywood-transplanted Isaacson to pump and pummel the superstar frame while ensuring that its stomach was fed with a low-calorie, high-vitamin diet. Even in health-freakish California this might have seemed excessive, but Travolta kept it up for week after week.

So stern a body-beautiful regime was not primarily Isaacson's idea, nor his. It was the brainstorm of an actor-filmmaker with large clout in the industry who had been elected to make Travolta's next film. The director of *Staying Alive*, the sequel to *Saturday Night Fever*, would be Sylvester Stallone.

10

NARCISSUS AND PSYCHE

Before the Italian stallion entered the picture, the sequel to *Saturday Night Fever* was in the creative hands of Norman Wexler. The screenwriter was entrusted with remodelling Tony Manero, the Brooklyn paintseller with glitterball dreams whom he had designed so skilfully in the first film that John Travolta had taken him all the way to stardom.

Producer Robert Stigwood and Paramount Pictures wanted more of the same, but also more *than* the same. The *Fever* Tony was fine: he danced and swore, he fretted, sweated and heavy-petted through what passed for a sex life in Catholic Brooklyn. Then he stubbed his toe – his best dancing toe – against the limits of his wish fulfilment world. Though he won the dance contest, he knew he wasn't as good as the two Latinos who lost. So, instead of a true-to-form Hollywood ending in which he crossed the Brooklyn Bridge to fame and glory on Broadway, he returned to being a human being in Bay Ridge. It was the perfect ending to a lumpenprole tragicomedy. Everyone was allowed to dream. Everyone made final landfall in reality.

It wasn't to be the same this time. The evolution of the sequel became one of the great gaga stories of misplaced zeal in modern Hollywood history. Wexler, fifteen years later on a dark and stormy night in Connecticut, passing a frequent hand over hair that seemed to be greying by the minute, recalled for me, 'I wrote a version straight after *Saturday Night Fever*. How would this kid without a lot going for him make his way in New York – without his becoming a showbiz star with a guitar slung over his shoulder

and audiences going crazy in the final reel? I didn't want to write
42nd Street. In my script he got a job in the chorus, I wanted to
take him to that level. He ends up looking out into the future, not
knowing quite what it holds for him.'

So he and Stigwood showed the script to Travolta. 'He had had
two huge hits, his ego was interplanetary and he wasn't gonna do
it: *Moment by Moment* by itself had not been enough to bring
him down, it needed a couple more things,' says Wexler. So it
wasn't until the summer of 1981, after *Blow Out*'s commercial
failure, that the writer claims Travolta was 'punctured enough to
be willing to consider the sequel'.

Even now it was not to be any old sequel.

'Travolta decided it must be about this guy who becomes a
star as a dancer. It was a projection of his own narcissism – it's
not enough to be a star yourself, you have to play a star in the
movie. Then Robert Stigwood told me *he* wanted to do a showbiz
story too.'

Stigwood was wooing Travolta hard. He had entertained him
on his yacht in August 1981 and the two men had agreed on a
united front regarding Wexler's first script. For the actor, it was
'an anti-dance piece, very cynical . . . I felt you needed to put it
in overdrive and send it into space.'

Back at his writing desk Wexler scratched his head and
conscience.

'Did I need the money then? I'd just blown a lot on a spending
spree, so yes, I needed the bucks, I needed the work. I hated the
idea I'd be writing this showbiz story about a kid who becomes
a star. It violated the whole spirit of the original movie, totally
violated it. But I persuaded myself there are a lot of actors out
there who do scrub up and try to get ahead, so maybe there was
a legitimate story, not just a showbiz story. I had Tony and his
buddy removing furniture, struggling along, and saying to each
other, "When we make it we'll remember this." And I had a lot
of other stuff that Sylvester Stallone would call "anti-showbiz".'

For the writer-star of *Rocky*, ambitious for a mainstream
directing career after one previous calling card as metteur-en-scene
(*Paradise Alley*, a sort of Puccini-meets-Steinbeck labour opera),
had signed on for the *Fever* sequel at the behest of Travolta himself.

Holidaying in Hawaii one June, the younger star had seen Sly's latest Balboa boxing saga and immediately red-telephoned his, Travolta's, agent Michael Ovitz. He told Ovitz, 'If I can get the kind of energy and excitement and pacing that Stallone brought to *Rocky III*, that's where I think this movie is going.'

Let us rewind briefly for cast identification, Travolta's career was now filling up with new personalities much like a lifeboat that takes on fresh passengers when, even at its most rickety, it still looks the most seaworthy thing in sight. Mike Ovitz was the Hollywood prodigy who founded the super-agency Creative Artists and would go on to run, albeit briefly, the Disney studio. He replaced Bob Le Mond as the star's right-hand man after Travolta's manager of twelve years had disgraced himself by (first) arguing with his client over *An Officer and a Gentleman* and (then) failing to extract him from the *Fever* sequel imposed by Paramount chief Michael Eisner. Travolta recounted to *Playboy* the pain of parting from Le Mond.

'There came a point where he called me and said, "There's nothing I can do. He [Eisner] won't let you out of the sequel." And I said, "Well, if you can't fix this, then why am I paying you fifteen percent? This is something I need you to fix." Bob said, "I'm sorry, I can't do it." I got really mad, didn't think and let him go. It wasn't fair, because I had made every move to get myself in that predicament.'

Exit one wounded manager.

Back in the new world order, Ovitz responded enthusiastically to Travolta's Stallone suggestion, and so did Robert Stigwood.

'Absolutely,' Stigwood tells me. 'It became a great pleasure working with Sly. And I don't think Norman [Wexler] was too bitter at all.'

Norman was bitter however, though soon in no position for it to make any difference. He was appalled by the decision to go with Stallone, as rubberstamped by the Paramount boss ('I've always despised Michael Eisner for it'). And he swiftly saw his script taken away and hewn into new, showbizzy shape. Anyone peering into the abyss of movie karma might have believed that Stallone's appointment was some bizarre payback, organised by the Hollywood chapter of the Furies, for director John *Rocky*

Avildsen's sacking from *Saturday Night Fever*, a dismissal for which Wexler was obliquely responsible. 'It does seem as if *Rocky* is following me around,' says the writer with a sigh.

Stallone carried other baggage with him into *Staying Alive*. As Rocky and Rambo, he was the cinema's two-in-one muscle star: an actor so determined to present macho triumphalism as the American way of life that he liked to interfere with scripts when he could not write them from scratch.

Wexler's ego could not begin to match that of Stallone, fresh from making *Rocky III* and *First Blood*, the Rambo pilot feature. And this time the writer did not have Stigwood or Travolta championing him. All else apart, Stigwood was not attracted to the expense of uniting east-coast Wexler and west-coast Travolta for constant script pow-wows. Recalls the writer, 'Stigwood said to me one day, "It's very expensive having John come in for meetings." I said, "Why?" He said, "I can't tell you." Finally he says, "To get John to come in, he has to fly his own plane and he makes me pay for the fuel." '

Travolta and Stallone saw eye to eye on almost everything. Even when they disagreed, for instance when the new director insisted on cleaning up Wexler's four-letter language (part of the enlivening honesty of the earlier film), harmony won through, mainly because Stallone got his way.

'When you're not a teenager any more,' Travolta was persuaded to announce to the press, 'you stop punctuating your sentences with profanity.' (A lesson he would conveniently forget when rebounding from oblivion in *Pulp Fiction*.)

Stallone was determined to Rocky-ise *Staying Alive*, as the sequel would be called in honour of the Bee Gees' hit song. The film would be upbeat, affirmative, virile. While realising that Tony Manero was not a boxer and could not end up fighting Apollo Creed for the world middleweight title, Stallone did want his star to have a new and better body. '[Sly] showed me a small statue of a discus thrower and said, "How would you like to look like that?" ' recalls Travolta. 'I said, "Terrific!" '

So off he went for four months' work with the aforementioned Isaacson. While Stallone chipped and chiselled at Wexler's script, film star and trainer performed sculptural marvels on the film's

body elective. They erected a tent lined with mirrors in the garden of Rancho Tajiguas, so that Travolta could watch himself dancing and weight-pumping for five hours a day, transforming the slumped shoulders and expanded girth.

'I had a big, thick roll of fat around my waist and I was bloated,' he recalls. 'My hair was dry and flaky. My skin was bad. I was feeling so bad that I thought to myself, "I'm going to be like Muhammad Ali and get my act together!" ' Stallone, he says, 'wanted to see this fat boy get into great shape and then feature it as a highlight of the film.'

For the ebullient director, Tony Manero was more than a cissy dancer, he was off-Broadway's answer to a bullfighter. 'El Cordobes,' intoned Stallone to an awed press. 'He [Tony] is a street animal who has this generic sense of survival.'

'Survival.' He had only to pronounce these syllables to Travolta – the word is very big in Scientology – to pull all the right levers. The star responded like a fruit machine, cascading pertinent thoughts to the media. 'No one could have gotten to the place I am and survived it so long without being strong,' he told reporters, discoursing on what he called Hollywood's 'counter-survival' obsession with fame and success. The actor also returned the word with interest at his new guru. 'Sly has so much unique survival energy in him that he makes everything matter.'

He mimicked Stallone's style of encouragement: ' "This is going to be a *great* movie." "This is going to be a *great* dance number." "We're going to get you in *great* shape." '

And this director who was part drill sergeant, part demonic Pygmalion, *was* getting Travolta in great shape. 'If John keeps it up I'll have to fight him in *Rocky IV*,' Sly cracked. The star's weight changed from 185 pounds of flab to 168 pounds of muscle-tone. His measurements mutated as follows: chest 38½ inches to 40, upper arms 12½ inches to 14, upper legs 21 inches to 22, waist 33½ to 30. He was also told to wax the hair off his body and highlight his muscles with a tanning machine. His friend Nancy Allen, on a visit, remembers him proudly lifting his shirt to show off washboard abdominals.

Every two weeks Travolta jetted across the States to be inspected by Stallone, who was scouting locations in New York in between

sessions of tearing up the Norman Wexler script. The actor confirmed that he was keeping to his diet of chicken, broccoli, fresh fruit, Perrier, Emegen-C vitamin drink, zinc tablets and wheatgerm capsules. Finally the director was satisfied. 'He's purified his system,' announced Stallone. 'At twenty-nine he looks like a Greek god.'

No one, except possibly the silenced Wexler, thought to ask: 'What does a Greek god have to do with a struggling ex-paintstore assistant who can barely get into a chorus line?' But the screenwriter was absorbed by his own purgatorial preoccupations: namely whether to take his name off the picture. He finally rejected the move on the grounds that, with a two-man credit title honouring both Norman and Sly, 'people would figure Wexler wrote the original script and Stallone wrote the piece of shit'.

Scepticism about Greek gods would have been dismissed by Stallone as *lèse-mythologie*, and certainly as anti-showbiz. For it disprized *Staying Alive*'s upbeat mythic leanings. Stallone planned to climax the movie with a big musical rendition of 'The Odyssey' (as in Homer, not Bay Ridge discotheques). The only reason he later settled for 'Heaven and Hell' was because 'more people know about it'.

There were personal myths to be incorporated too, reverberant character tensions plucked from Sly's own life and legend. For instance, the role of Tony's father would be expanded to reflect the troubled relationship the director had had with his father, a domineering hairdresser. But this role was scrapped before shooting when the actor cast as Manero senior, Val Bisoglio, demanded better billing.

The dynastic reverb denied here asserted itself elsewhere. Stallone wanted a composer who would match the high-impact tunefulness of the first film's songtrack by the Bee Gees, who had not yet been asked by a cost-watching Stigwood to contribute to the sequel. Finally, after an exhaustive search, Stallone found the ideal tunesmith: his brother Frank, a little-known actor-singer who penned nine songs for the film, four of which ended up in the album.

'Sure, some people said, "Nepotism, nepotism",' says Stallone (Sylvester). But he relates that before Frank was signed he, Sly,

personally took the new songs to Stigwood and played them to the producer without telling him who they were by. 'Great,' said Stigwood, though with unrecorded inflection. 'It's my brother,' revealed Stallone. And the brother went on not just to write the songs but to sing most of them. When Travolta was asked why he himself, an experienced chart-topping vocalist, hadn't sung in the film, he said, 'Sly didn't think it was appropriate.'

(Travolta, through his character, has a kind of revenge in the film. When he first sights Frank Stallone, playing the minor role of a rock musician who becomes his love rival, he casts an eye over the chunky figure wearing trendy street-fatigues and says to the disputed girl, 'He looks like a demented paratrooper.')

Stigwood's response to Frank Stallone's music may be indicated by the speed with which he put in that overdue call to the Bee Gees. The band's Maurice Gibb still regards the commission as an afterthought, 'which we found a little insulting, but what the hell.' The album went on to become a strong seller, helped by Paramount's promotion campaign for both film and record. Frank Stallone commented, 'There's nothing like $8 million of publicity backing your music.'

On the soundstages *Staying Alive* powered remorselessly towards completion. As in *Saturday Night Fever* there was a romantic subplot involving one nice girl who is rejected and one snobbish girl who catches our hero's heart. However this time, typifying the difference between the two films, the nice girl (Cynthia Rhodes) is a no more than a vapidly sweetfaced appendage to the hero's backstage life – unlike the subtly pitiful figure of Donna Pescow's Annette – and the snob (Finola Hughes) comes on more like a rent-by-the-hour Joan Collins than the poignant, conflicted scatterbain played by Karen Lynn Gorney.

The British Hughes was flown specially across the Atlantic because, she says, 'Sly thought someone with an English accent could deliver bitchy lines better than an American actress.' She too, once the camera rolled, felt the force of Stallone's zeal. 'The film was hard work because everything had to be done with maximum energy. . . . Before each take [Sly] would say, "Enthusiasm! Energy up!" and off we'd go.'

For Travolta pain and danger as well as hard work added to

the thrill of creation. The final 'Heaven and Hell' number, an extravagant whip-lashing fantasia set in what seems to be a dry ice factory staffed by half-clad Maenads, was especially arduous.

'One of the whips was supposed to go around my neck but it ended up going around my eye. I got sort of a welt right above the eye. . . . . It was much more painful than the damage was, but it did feel like I'd taken an eye out or something.'

Audiences watching the completed *Staying Alive* might be grateful to have an eye taken out, plus both ears. It is hard to believe that a film whose visuals resemble a bad night at a Bacchanalia and whose dialogue ranges from the sanctimonious ('I respect your womanhood') to the kitschy-epigrammatic ('Guys like you aren't relationships, you're exercise') came from the same storytelling start-block as the leaner, lither *Saturday Night Fever*. The sequel's tributes to the first film only make the second more embarrassing: not least the moment when a Tony disillusioned by love and career ill-luck takes out from his clothes closet *that* suit.

One wishes he had worn it in the final number instead of the campy dèshabille flaunted by him and everyone else. As a dance finale the 'Satan's Alley' number almost beggars description: Busby Berkeley out of Hieronymus Bosch. To crown the farrago, the film's rapid editing deprives us of the one spectacle that might compensate us for so much aesthetic pain: a sequence of sustained dance virtuosity by Travolta.

The film was finally laid before the critics, who ignored all proverbs about kicking creatures when they are down. 'Travolta is a major actor, but Stallone treats him like a vapid hunk,' said the *L.A. Herald-Examiner*. The *New York Times* called the movie 'a sequel with no understanding of what made its predecesor work . . . Clumsy, mean-spirited and amazingly unmusical.' For the *Western Mail*, *Staying Alive* was a misnomer: 'It's staying awake that's the problem.'

It was sweet vindicating music to Norman Wexler, who seized a press microphone one day to attack both the star, who 'went along with the obliteration of my script', and his director. 'Vacuous, impoverished, crass and crude,' Wexler called the film. 'Stallone's religion is showbusiness narcissism.'

Even Travolta's most respected champion joined the dissidents. For Pauline Kael here was a travesty, self-willed, of what had seemed, only the movie before, a significant acting career. 'Stallone doesn't bother much with character, scenes or dialogue. He just puts the newly muscle-plated Travolta in front of the camera, covers him with what looks like an oil slick and goes for the whambams. . . . [Travolta] is in danger of turning into a laughing stock if he doesn't put some clothes on and stop posing for magazine covers as though it were Hiawatha Night at the O.K. Corral.'

This last referred to a special cover issue of *Rolling Stone* in August 1983, in which the Avedon-photographed actor bared all, or almost, both literally and figuratively. The sexually enhanced star, who had sold his bodily birthright for a mess of muscles, flaunted his loinclothed physique at newsstand-passers while inside the counterculture pages, interviewer Nancy Collins led him through a marathon questionnaire on sex.

Travolta participated in this catechism with his special blend of boyish frankness and addled circumlocution. Is he aware that he appeals to gay men, asks Collins? 'My characters have always been very masculine. If I am androgynous I'd say I lean towards the macho androgynous.' He must know, she ventures, that Hollywood loves to think all leading men are secretly gay? 'Oh yes, that's a notorious rumour. . . . They say that about me, Marlon Brando, every male, especially the first year you become a star.' Are you gay? 'No.'

Then, on to the non-gay specifics. What does he like in women? A good mind, he says. 'Bottom line, a woman's got to be stimulating, which would then provoke a continuous sexual appeal.' Does he have a strong sex drive? 'Yes. But it needs to be unleashed by someone who likes it. Otherwise I tend to inhibit it. I like being with women who have the same sexual appetite. I get frustrated if they don't because it's very difficult for me to be with someone I have to coach. You know, "Okay, honey, I'm the sex master here, and I'll get you through your paces, and together we will solve your psychological blocks." '

Collins finally comments that people would be hard-pressed to name a single girl that Travolta had actually, provably dated. 'Many of them are famous,' he answers. 'But I just don't go

places where we're photographed. Besides, I don't stay in one place very long.'

The interview is not exactly a scalding confessional. But it gained notoriety as an example of how far a publicity-seeking star will go in selling himself to the press. Travolta was pilloried by the very hacks who had sought out – who spend their lives seeking out – this kind of pillow talk. And the hapless blabbermouth was later forced to give other interviews explaining why he had given this one.

'Why did I go that far to make an impression?', he asks rhetorically of *Playboy*. 'I'll tell you what, I was running out of things to say and do at the time. I was suffering from something that I won't fall into again, and that was, how do I entertain the press? I had something like a thousand interviews – covers of every magazine. So I said to [the writer], "What's your angle?" I was hip, you know. It was like, "What's your fucking angle and I'll join you on it." '

Only in Showbizland can men and women become lost in such a maze of beleaguered self-regard. The tent full of mirrors at Rancho Tajiguas is a mere Platonic shadow of the Orson Welles-worthy hall of glass a star may eventually find himself in. Dazed with the reflective surfaces into which he is forced to gaze to perfect his image for the world's worship – numbed by so much regimented vanity – he can end up saying to the mirror-wielding cupids, 'Tell me what you want to see and I'll pretend I'm it.' (It is a Cuckooland extension of the logic Travolta improvised in *Saturday Night Fever*: 'I saw it on TV, then I made it up.')

For how can the truth alone be interesting for the media? Inside every showbiz Superman is a Clark Kent bewildered by the attention accorded his alter ego. A star may not be a star to himself, as Travolta himself once explained with unassuming acuity to a reporter, 'We're sitting here talking about this mystical "image" of the movie star and the problem is, I'm not the perfect person to discuss the effect that I've made . . . The point is I've made an effect on the public; I haven't made an effect on me.'

That is only half-true, though. An actor has to make an effect on himself initially; he has to be a little dazzled by his own image to believe that he can use it to dazzle others. He has to start with a pinch of Narcissus, as Travolta once admitted he did,

though it took a French magazine to coax this more *recherché* confession.

'*Etes-vous narcissistique?*' quizzed *Paris Match* in a mid-1986 interface with the idol. '*Vous aimez-vous physiquement?*'

'I think I have an actor's face,' Travolta answers (re-translated into English). 'I can be handsome, ugly, wicked, romantic. It depends on the angles. When I was fifteen or sixteen I liked my body and often spent time gazing in mirrors.'

To love oneself is the beginning of a lifetime of exposure by movie iconographers, who cry 'Ah-ha!' at each giveaway sign. David Thomson's sketch of Travolta in his influential *Biographical Dictionary of Film* seizes on the semiography of self-infatuation detected in the young actor's features. 'It's a mother's boy's face, a gaunt, narcissistic horse's head flabby with self-pity and butterfly lips . . . It's the face of heavy, swollen passion brought on by mirror-gazing. Travolta was an odalisque of sorrowful self; his dynamic was inward and stroking.'

Against this Travolta did once declare, albeit in another example of his bemused mental syntax, 'I like sex too much not to share it.' And by 1983, according to Marilu Henner's autobiography, he was sharing it again with her. Having ditched Frederic Forrest after three years of quarrelling from Bel-Air to Paris to Hong Kong, she re-contacted 'Johnny', who still had her skis from the pre-Mammoth walkout.

He had missed her, he told the press, from the moment she vanished into wedlock. 'I was upset, very upset for her, because I thought it was too quick. And upset for myself as time went on, because we didn't, during the period of her marriage, connect as friends.'

So they went back to the old romantic arrangement, whatever exactly that was. 'Sure we live together, the way some people do in Hollywood,' said Travolta. 'I leave some of my clothes at her place and she leaves some of hers at mine.'

Henner was soon so impressed by the new-look Travolta *without* clothes – sleek and Stallone-tooled – that she began working out with Dan Isaacson herself. She followed in other Travolta footsteps. She accompanied him on his European tour with *Staying Alive*. And around Christmas 1983, when 'Johnny and I were getting

into a very comfortable, almost ideal, groove' she joined him on a chartered sailing ship for a week-long cruise for family and friends around the French West Indies.

'My bonds to Johnny were unlike anything either of us had had,' she writes. 'Our relationship had lasted well over a decade, had been through a half-dozen incarnations, had survived my two-year marriage to Freddie and several girlfriends of his; it had swung between a bedrock brother-sister friendship and, on trips like the one to the Caribbean, charged-up sexual passion.'

Travolta himself, asked about marriage plans, said, 'In a lot of ways I feel married now. I live with her down at her place in Los Angeles when I'm there and she lives with me when she's in Santa Barbara.'

Yet as Henner also relates, the affair kept hitting the buffers of Travolta's refusal to make a permanent commitment. So that after weeks of swapping weekends, he would finally say to her, 'I can't do this any more.' She would say, 'What are you talking about?' And he would say, 'Everybody sees us as a couple, and I'm just not good at relationships. I can't make it work. It's just too hard for me.'

So life with Marilu never turned into Life With Marilu. And the press went back to scratching its collective head and asking, 'What *does* make John Travolta tick romantically?'

At least there were signs that he wanted to bin the narcissistic theme and all life-from-art extrapolations. The crash course in idiot self-adoration provided by Stallone must have come close to purging Travolta of all mirror-gazing instincts. 'By the end of that movie I had had it,' he says. 'I was finished with the body trip. Stallone's view of the human body is different from mine. I'm basically a spiritualist. I feel that we're spirits who use the body to function – to eat, to sleep, to have sex and to perform various duties. He thinks of the body as art. He puts more significance on it than I do.'

But since he was a film star he was trapped. And since *Staying Alive*, for all its preening stupidity, outgrossed *Blow Out*, for all its tenebrous intelligence, audiences were decreeing that Travolta stay in iconic – that is, narcissised – mode. He was called on not to be an actor, except incidentally, but to be a star. And he

was entering a movie age when the grandstanding populist fable, manned by heroes who glistened with the beauty of male pride and strength, was pushing aside tales about artists, intellectuals, truth-seekers, introverts and other wimps and cissies.

He was entering, in short, the Interregnum.

11

THE INTERREGNUM

Ronald Reagan had been sworn in as America's 40th President in January 1981. This was too late for him or his political climate to put a curse on production of the unAmerican *Blow Out*, with its left-of-centre disquisitions on political corruption and conspiracy; a film whose very colour scheme was a spoof of the American flag. (Then again perhaps the disappearance of the Liberty Day footage, followed by that of the movie's audience, was a piece of dark Republican sorcery.)

But an American ready for Reagan and quick to give a box office thumbs-down to De Palma was more than ready for *Staying Alive*. Here was proud-nation populism, a film that said: An American from nowhere, given talent, energy and mindless optimism, can go anywhere. If the Tony Manero of *Saturday Night Fever* was a Democratic creation, a gifted youth stopped in his tracks by the crabbed inadequacies of his environment, the Tony of *Staying Alive* was a goer, an achiever, a superman. And he was pushed to that eminence by Sylvester Stallone, no less, a man who in his other guise as the Reagan-admired Rambo was virtually Hollywood's foreign policy Muse to the White House.

But the redeeming charm of Travolta's talent to that date was its discomfort with any role that hinted at gung-ho. He was a cowboy who looked as if the cow would chase him in *Urban Cowboy*. In *Staying Alive* his pumped and oily-pectoral'd machismo is about as convincing as seeing Hamlet compete in a Mr Denmark contest.

It is not just a matter of association: of our knowing Travolta from his rainbow gallery of lovably downtrodden or demotic

roles in the Carter era, from *The Boy in the Plastic Bubble* to *Blow Out* via Badham-Wexler's Brooklyn frustration opera and the fallible, Brylcreem-deep machismo of *Grease*. Vulnerability is built into his voice, manner, body language. A Jerry Lewis gangliness underlies and undermines the Travolta cool. And the larynx is a lazy, likable, line-of-least-resistance instrument. 'I cou' watch you watch f'r hours, 't's like watchin' smoke moofe,' he says to Finola Hughes in *Staying Alive*. The mushy consonants and the vowels that lie somewhere in the croak channel – that bedroomy register between sleeping and waking – give the lie to any role requiring fanfares of self-assertion. Only much later, by the time of *Get Shorty* and *Broken Arrow*, will Travolta learn how to make a skilled postmodern feint at macho characters even if they don't lie within his natural tessitura.

What is a man to do, though, when the epoch says, 'Come on in, the triumphalism is lovely' ? He cannot sit on the beach allowing Stallone to kick sand in his face. He must pretend to play. He may even persuade himself, since he is an actor, that he has slipped into the zeitgeisty embrace of the new Cro-magnon masculism, mimicking its tics almost without realising. A friend remembers a restaurant conversation he had with Travolta during the filming of *Staying Alive*. Noticing an arriving customer who gave him a disdainful look, the actor said, 'If that guy keeps looking at me, I'm going to deck him.'

Friend: 'You're going to what?'

Travolta: 'I'm going to deck him.'

Friend: 'John, you're not going to deck him. You're not going to deck anybody. The word "deck" isn't even in your vocabulary.'

Travolta then realised (says the friend) that he had turned into Sly Stallone.

Travolta decides to run for cover, or what he thinks is cover. He re-teams with Olivia Newton-John, his good luck charm from *Grease*, in a film whose plot combines a low-life Bohemianism we could describe as vaguely pre-Reaganite with a safely Republican line in moralistic religious fantasising.

Two of a Kind is a metaphysical romantic comedy written and directed by John Herzfeld. Travolta is a smalltime inventor who robs a bank and Newton-John is a crime-prone aspiring actress

who gets caught in the mêlée. Their souls can be saved only if they fall in love, thereby enabling the angel Gabriel and three winged friends to intercede with God (Gene Hackman), who has decreed that the world must end unless two good people can be found. Oliver Reed plays the Devil, who uses a cosmic version of video-age trickery – fast-forwarding or rewinding reality – to upset the angle's plans.

'The film has elements of *It's a Wonderful Life* and *Stairway to Heaven* (U.S. title for Michael Powell's *A Matter of Life and Death*),' said Travolta, stretching optimism to breaking point. It is about 'bad people who turn good. I think that's much more interesting than good people who turn bad.'

He goes on, 'I really chose it more for Olivia than myself . . . we're both playing against type. For half of the movie we're quite obnoxious.'

Newton-John had asked Travolta to co-star in her earlier *Xanadu*, which he wisely rejected. She failed to show the same wisdom here when he insisted, 'If you don't do this one, I'll quit looking for a picture for us.'

There are some bright spots in this fresco of doom. Any film that begins with Travolta donning a blonde wig to hold up a bank must go into some collector's book. ('I like myself as a blonde,' he said to the press). And Herzfeld's technical tricks with time and motion deserve an interested respect. Finally, though, the archness is overwhelming. We try in vain to surf the whimsicalities – the edible sunglasses, the barking-dog doorbell, the 'daring' love scene ('I wouldn't do it with anyone but John,' said Olivia), the folksy-conversational voice of God sequences and the dandyish deviltry of Reed, dressed like a cross between Jack the Ripper and Toulouse-Lautrec. We finally heave a sigh of relief and agreement at Travolta's last line: 'God, this has been a crazy week,' he says as he and Olivia walk off together into the night.

The reviews showed no mercy. 'A stupefying shambles' pronounced *Time*. 'An embarrassment of the first order,' volunteered *Variety*. 'The fate of all mankind rests on whether or not John Travolta and Olivia Newton-John fall in love – and I still didn't care,' said the *Village Voice*. The response can have offered little surprise to Twentieth Century-Fox, who had been in panic mode

since post-production began. The press shows were postponed and the publicity slogans changed. The poster finally read, 'It took a twist of fate to make them two of kind,' simply to chime in with a closing-credits song 'Twist of Fate', sung by Newton-John, which had become a hit. Fox had also gone for broke by replacing the original score by Bill *Rocky* Conti with music by Paul Williams. The singer-composer, who had provided the climactic treacle for *The Boy in the Plastic Bubble*, was given two weeks to bring in new tunes. 'This kind of thing happens all the time,' spin-doctored Fox's music chief Newman. 'It's like the reporter changing a lead on a story.' A prophetic analogy in the light of Travolta's next film.

Travolta tiptoed away from the shambles, leaving for posterity only some loose-change reflections on his acting craft. These show why, at least in this first phase of his career, he is so good with a judicious director and so bad with a bad one. He invents, and inventors need intelligent feedback.

'Some of my biggest arguments have been when I've told a director, "Let me hesitate here, or stammer here," let me not finish that sentence. That way it'll sound more natural,' he said.

He likes to change lines too. 'It's rather like the way I speak when I'm talking with my friend Gérard Depardieu. He lets me speak French the way the French usually speak English – "I go now", that sort of thing. He doesn't constantly *correct* me.'

A good director, however, does correct. He may do it in a way that doesn't ruffle the star's vanity, but he knows when to say 'Keep this, lose that.' Travolta's acting in *Two of a Kind* suggests that no one was guiding him. No one was telling him to be less 'cute' or discouraging him from strutting around showing off his *Staying Alive* musculature. He even wears a denim shirt whose high-cut short sleeves allow him to flaunt his Sylvestered biceps. The audience cannot help wondering, When did this inventor and part-time bank thief do all this heavy gymwork?

But this was madness time for the human body in the US. If Stallone in *Rocky* hadn't been enough to send everyone to the weight machines, Schwarzenegger had now appeared in *Conan the Barbarian* to dispatch the message of hulkdom from 10,000 BC Hyboria to eighties California. Women too, in the wake of Jane Fonda's workout tapes and actress Linda Hamilton's Amazonian

self-improvements in and after *The Terminator*, flocked to the gyms. Here was Reaganite self-improvement made manifest: muscular Republicanism. A boy or girl with a barbell in each hand and a leotard in the sports bag.

What more perfect time for the team of James Bridges and Aaron Latham, purveyors of *Urban Cowboy* to the gentry, to swing into topical action again? After taking a previous era's pulse by dealing with dude rodeos, they would now address dude athleticism. Latham had written a piece for *Rolling Stone* called *Looking for Mr Goodbody*, which pointed a finger at the way fitness gymnasiums were becoming 'the new singles bars'. People came to train, stayed to flirt, and went away with the finely tooled sex-engine of their choice.

A cynical perspective on modern America? Perhaps. But Latham also had idealistic things to say, through his own mouth in the article and that of the same-initialled reporter hero ('Adam Lawrence') in his movie script, about the return to Emersonian values. Ralph Waldo Emerson, that is, not tennis ace Roy Emerson as some fitness freaks thought. R.W.E. was the man who told 19th-century America essentially – or as essentially as Latham thought fit to present – to go out into the fresh air and get a life.

'James and I had always wanted to make a second picture,' Latham says today. 'I wrote the *Rolling Stone* article with half a mind on it becoming a movie, though not with John Travolta in mind. The original character in my story was out of shape, more like me, and doing a story about people who were in fabulous shape. That was part of the original tension of the story.'

So for Bridges and Latham that new body beautiful called John Travolta was not initially in the reckoning. Nor was the film that would become *Perfect* in *his* reckoning. Travolta was still in that seesawing period of his life when he balanced a downward-tending movie career with an upward-tending mindset. He sought fresh challenges, even non-Hollywood or non-acting ones.

He was drawn to the prospect of working with Truffaut or Louis Malle. And he considered directing a film himself. His favourite early project had been an Altmanesque-sounding movie about the sixties. This would be seen, he said, 'from the perspective of people who were on the other side of the Vietnam experience, to

whom Vietnam wasn't real. There was this other life going on
that involved Andy Warhol, *Vogue* magazine, sex and drugs and
music, and great superficial stuff as juxtaposed to the significance
and heaviness of the Vietnam war.'

It would have reflected the teenaged Travolta's own view-from-
the-sidelines: 'I can't say I was an activist. I was an observer of
the activists.'

But this movie notion never progressed beyond a mental
smoke-ring. By the mid eighties Travolta had replaced it with a
firmer pipe dream, a family drama by writer Ken Griswold called
Greenwich. Based on Griswold's own life, it was in Travolta's
words, 'a riches-to-rags-to-riches story that ends with emotional
riches instead of material ones.' The title later mutated to *Lake
Forest*, after the tale's small-town setting near Chicago, and was
said to be shaping up as an *Ordinary People*-style movie about,
said Travolta, 'the consequences of wrong financial moves by
the father that lead to bankruptcy. It's an American tragedy that
involves replacing our excessive materialism.'

Travolta himself had just waved away the excessive materialism
of a multi-million-dollar offer to star in *A Chorus Line*, in the
director role later taken by Michael Douglas. 'It's an ensemble
piece,' he said of the hit Broadway musical, 'I would stand out in
an ensemble situation for the obvious reason that I'm better known.'
There was no role for him in *Lake Forest* either, but, 'The story just
floored me. I felt that this was something I just had to be involved
with.' He buttonholed Columbia president Guy McElwaine; he
worked with Griswold on the script, he brushed aside questions
about his inexperience behind the camera – 'It's not a technical
film anyway, but a film of the heart. Not cut-and-dry [sic] as
a Spielberg film.' He even contacted his old friend, casting tsar
Lynn Stalmaster, to begin picking faces out of agents' books.

Stalmaster says, 'It was when things weren't blossoming in his
own films and I was thrilled that he brought me this project. I
thought with his sensitivity he'd make a good director. We sat
and went over ideas for leading roles, but then the whole project
seemed to disappear.'

Either plans for *Greenwich* were shelved while he made *Perfect*
– after which Travolta's whole mainstream career was shelved –

or the project's disappearance showed how quickly a plan could vaporise in this man's head. Take the case of the thirtieth birthday party. In February 1984 Travolta planned to fly his friends and family on a big, barnstorming, cross-country junket.

'I was going to get into my plane and fly to different cities and celebrate,' he says. Instead he had a change of heart. He sent for his sister Margaret and her family in Chicago and threw a small party on his ranch. 'I have it on videotape. It's so weird. If you've seen photographs or film of those old-age homes when they have kids' birthday parties with hats and things – that's what this looked like. It's really sort of pathetic, you know.'

But endearing too. Even though Travolta was now a licenced multi-engine and jet pilot, and had hired TransWorld Airways to help him restore his Constellation to its former glory and original TWA decor, home and paper hats could suddenly seem more fun. And even though in his other plane, the Lockheed JetStar 731, he frequently hosted mile-high dinners of poached artichoke hearts, salad of radicchio and sweetcorn, and mille feuille of king salmon with mousseline de mer – these would arrive together with a printed menu at the pre-departure plane in a silver stretch limo – he could suddenly see that pizzas and Coca-Cola at Rancho Tajiguas were less of a sweat. And even though Travolta enjoyed descending at night in a far-off city, with nought but the landing lights stretched before him like terrestrial stars and a song on his lips ('The Heart of Rock and Roll' was a favourite), there were times when it was nice to have nothing to come down *to* or *from*.

Also, when flying a plane, there was no time for his impressions, which as everyone in Hollywood testifies, are a Travolta passion. Instead of running around on the ground doing Barbra Streisand, James Stewart, Cyndi Lauper or Stevie Wonder, at 30,000 feet he had to impersonate a Captain. This would allow time only for short chats with the passengers in his swivel chair, while his black-tied steward prepared drinks and hors d'oeuvres, then it would be back to the cockpit.

On the ground the impersonations he loved had free play. (They were a sort of instant acting: the mummer's answer to fast food.) Warren Beatty was a favourite, centred around the breathy inflections and squint: 'Warren has a little trouble with his eyes that

borders on the Hasidic.' And before exiting a room Travolta could suddenly throw off a Faye Dunaway as Joan Crawford: 'Take a letter. Tell my fans that I'm going to change my shirt.'

It seemed cruel to force this man, whose mind and talent could pinball in so many inventive, flibbertigibbet directions, to play one-note heroes for the new America. A performer secretly yearning to be a character actor – Olivia Newton-John remembers hearing an after-dinner speech full of mimicry that prompted her to whisper to him, 'You should do character roles!' – was asked to press himself into the bland mould of Superstud (*Urban Cowboy*), Supergypsy (*Staying Alive*) and now, in *Perfect*, Superhack. And if the freshly sculpted star was blatantly unsuited to playing a physically out-of-condition reporter, never mind. The film would change to suit him.

Says Aaron Latham, with a trace of sheepish irony, 'Our reporter got to be in better shape when Travolta was cast. I always missed that out-of-shape element, but there's a trade-off. You get Travolta with all that's good about him as well as all that might not be good for the role.'

But doesn't this mess up the whole point of the story (I asked Latham)? Without the satirical abrasiveness provided by the sight of an ill-honed journalist rubbing up against the Adonis demi-monde, where is the tension, the bite?

Latham says that he and Bridges compensated, or tried to, by going for an all-through realism. What *Perfect* lost in contrasty satire it would gain in docudrama authenticity. So co-star Jamie Lee Curtis, cast as the gym's aerobics trainer who falls in love with the newshound hero after a few scenes of quarrelsome distrust, *became* an aerobics trainer: she went out and put herself through all the stations of exhaustion and officiousness. (According to Travolta, Curtis landed the role after some impassioned lobbying for it by his friend Debra Winger – 'Debra was climbing all over me, as if to say: "This is my territory." ') 'James wanted to make things as real as possible,' Latham says, 'even to Curtis doing aerobics teaching, even to the point of casting real people in supporting parts. So just as we'd had real Gilleys cowboys in *Urban Cowboy*, in *Perfect* we had real fitness instructors for the Sports Connection gym. And Jann Wenner playing himself was an extension of that.'

Wenner, the editor of *Rolling Stone*, was cast as himself – the film's second male lead – after a brief audition. He fought shy at first, suggesting actor Peter Riegert or Jeff Bridges: somewhat idealised stand-ins for the tubby editor. But after the test, 'I knew I wanted the part.' He asked only that his character be rechristened Mark Roth, and from professional amour-propre he refused to let the Travolta character smash up Roth's office with a baseball bat as in the screenplay, when the hero is peeved at having his cover article on gyms-as-singles-bars changed by the editor.

Wenner claimed that *Rolling Stone* and peer periodicals did *not* rewrite stories. 'That's the movie,' he said; whereupon Aaron Latham riposted, 'I can cite chapter and verse. I was an editor at *Esquire* myself, and I rewrote several stories, totally turned them around.' Wenner came back, this time tucking more small print into his response: 'We've never rewritten a writer's piece while he was out of the country, without telling him. That was all dramatic licence.'

Deaf to this squall of shop talk, Travolta got busy pondering the life and character of a reporter. 'I've had ten years of being interviewed throughout the world, so I had all sorts of lessons, tricks of the trade, that I've learned.'

He also tapped away excitedly on the new TRS-80 word-processor that Bridges had given him as a pre-production gift. 'I could write with the computer at the same rate that I could think and I found that my thoughts are much clearer on paper than they are when I think.' He wrote profiles on colleagues, beginning with a Sylvester Stallone piece – 'a big success among my friends' – and going on to include James Bridges, Jamie Lee Curtis and Debra Winger; Winger's comment on reading her portrait in print was, 'I'm going to tell people to stay away while you're writing.'

His magnum opus, though, was a production diary written during the making of *Perfect*. This was specially commissioned by *Rolling Stone*, whose editor must have loved the description of his own screen test. 'Jann was overacting,' Travolta records. 'Mugging. Rolling his eyes. It was really funny, and would have been more appropriate for a comedy. So we had to unrehearse him from the previous night.'

Elsewhere in the diary, Travolta hints at his production nerves

and vulnerable ego. 'At the end of one scene I used an improv about being sore, and [Bridges] said it seemed to fall apart at that point. I hope that comment doesn't ruin my weekend . . . I'm curious what my cinematographer will do with my looks. Some trust must come into play here. After all, Gordon Willis [cameraman on *The Godfather* and *Manhattan*] is the best there is.' He muses on the pros and cons of romancing one's leading lady: 'Should we do it because it's good for our roles, or are attracted to each other anyway, so why not? . . . With Jamie I get the feeling that she would want it to be genuine but that she gets confused as to when the time would be right. I'm more comfortable being seduced by a woman the first time, and she doesn't know that. Maybe she is waiting for me to take over. I don't know. Maybe I should ask.'

Maybe so. Maybe not. Or maybe Curtis saw in her co-star not so much a potential lover, more a man poignantly lost in self-obsession. His diary includes a description of a trip Travolta took in his own plane to the mountain location of Mammoth in northern California with Curtis and Aaron Latham on board.

'During our final approach, the air became turbulent and, because of the altitude, I had to use extra power. My dark glasses impaired my vision, so I threw them off my face, brushed the hair off my forehead and gripped the throttles in preparation for landing. . . . When my passengers deplaned. I learned that they had loved the flight, except when they saw me whip off the sunglasses and brush my hair back. To them it looked like I meant business. I did, but then I always do. I just didn't know that they were watching so closely. Next time, I'll close the curtains or change my technique.'

Technique? For removing sunglasses and brushing back hair?

The moment is as insanely cosmetic – yet meta-cosmetic – as Mom's vision of young John piloting her up to heaven in a white turtleneck sweater. But Travolta's gestural self-awareness also shows how much a star, or this star, exteriorises himself. In the diary's most wonderfully madcap, solemn section, Travolta gazes upon his essence with the rapt concentration of a scientist in a genetics lab.

'There has to be a lesson in objectivity. So I tried to write about myself:

'At first glance, you might perceive John Travolta to be, as a well-known critic said, "Warren Beatty's Neanderthal brother." To those who don't know him, he may appear a not particularly smart, somewhat dimwitted person.

'Better look again. He is really a chameleon, to the frightening degree that his empathy for people makes him become them even when he is not conscious of doing so. Even if the roles he plays call upon him to have an ability that is incongruous with his education and upbringing, he still comes up with the goods.

'Is he just a man without a soul who should not be buried in sacred ground? . . . Or is he just smarter than the roles he plays? He seems always to surprise people, while at the same time surprising himself.'

So what is he? A noble savage fallen among film-makers? Or a kind of palpitating tabula rasa, open to the world's automatic writing – a human word-processor?

Sometimes, of course, a word-processor can find nothing worth processing and a tabula rasa can be just that. Blank. The career crisis through which Travolta was passing was caused by the world's failure to write the right patterns on him. So more power, perhaps, to the vestigial pride in him that said, 'No, I will not give myself or my expressive instrumentation to this dude cowboy, this brainless Broadway gypsy or this idiot reporter who chases a non-story through the empty corridors of a non-movie.'

Perfect is as perfect does, and *Perfect* doesn't. The film, like its star, ends up as two hours of grinning blandness centred around a non-issue. Gymnasiums are the new singles bars – so what? For a movie born in the brain of a journalistic sharpshooter who had pumped bullets into the phony frontier spirit of cowboy bars, *Perfect* requires a strangely stuffy Republican response if audiences are to get het up about people picking other people up at health clubs. *Perfect* is a Reaganite movie with tabloid trimmings. Gaining thrills from ogling bodies in gymnastic motion, it also features neck-cricking glances towards a bygone, virtuous golden age in its ruminations about sports clubs being 'little pockets of Emersonian America scattered from sea to shining sea'.

Small wonder that none of the makers could satisfactorily answer the question, 'What is the film about?'

'It's about how the First Amendment should protect all the media,' Bridges told the press. 'I think that a free society and a free press should go hand in hand.' But though he and Latham tried to wrestle some extra 'issue' tension into the film with a subplot in which Adam Lawrence goes on a cross-country investigation into a John DeLorean-type businessman, a story based on Latham's own interview dealings with DeLorean (which almost landed him in jail), this secondary story is thinly developed and embarrassedly adrift from the main plot.

The greatest mystery of all about *Perfect* is why the makers didn't pick up a thematic hint almost yelling at them from Latham's original article. Near the beginning he writes: 'Co-ed health clubs, the new singles bars of the eighties, have usurped the sounds and the energy of the discotheques. They have also usurped the discotheques' raison d'etre. They have become part of the mating ritual.' Later Latham quotes a girl who works out at the gym and who says, 'It's an alternative to the disco era . . . Now it's not fashionable to go to a disco, but it is fashionable to go to a health club.'

Latham and Bridges had the disco king in their very midst! – a man whose past reputation could surely have been cashed in for a little publicity change. Or is it possible that Travolta himself vetoed the disco theme, determined not to backpedal to past glories?

As opening date neared, Paramount's publicity department did its best for the film. There were PR stunts to persuade potential audiences that the movie was more about the beauty of the body than the beast of journalistic corruption. These included a 'Search for the Perfect Man' contest at Chippendales nightclub ('We're looking for bulging biceps and thighs that bring sighs' fanfared the owner). There were fitness supplements fattening up L.A. newspapers and magazines. And Jann Wenner unblenchingly ran a *Rolling Stone* cover article in the summer of the film's release: 'I'm always using the magazine to promote somebody else's movie, so why not promote this one?'

When *Perfect* hit the screen, though, the bad publicity quickly outswelled the good. Critics were running out of pejoratives for Travolta films. 'Embarrassment' once more did the rounds. 'Crude' and 'travesty' came back from the cleaners after *Staying Alive*. And

Stanley Kauffman proffered 'dialogue of ostentatious vulgarity.' San Francisco's famed Joe Bob Briggs wrote, '[The hero's] dream is to write up a big story on a guy that looks like John De Lorean, or to hang around the aerobics class and watch women's garbonzas bounce up and down . . . The best horror film of 1985.'

The newspapers went on to print tales of unhappiness among the real gym-hangers on whom the film was based, such as the girl whose promiscuity inspired the Laraine Newman character and who received obscene phone calls as a result. Another girl, played in the film by Marilu Henner, first complained that Latham had crudely misrepresented her in his article and then protested that she didn't get the decent role in the movie he had promised: 'I only had one line.'

It was Babel time all round. At press conferences there was an almost pentecostal variety of hype strategies. Jamie Lee Curtis talked loftily of the film's 'aerobic love scenes' and read a poem she had written called 'I Felt my Body go Today.' James Bridges, asked what all his films had in common, replied, 'Lack of style.' And when a reporter asked Travolta about his 'new life', the actor replied, 'What new life?' The hack said it was in the press notes, whereupon Travolta shuffled through the Columbia biog to find out what it said about the recent changes in his outlook and interests. 'Oh, I've grown up, that's all. . . . I've joined the Me generation a decade too late, even though I started it. I had to vamp between the ages of twenty-one and thirty-one because I became famous at such a young age. I think I'm a spiritualist by nature.'

It was a circus. And the only thing that could make Travolta run away from this circus was another, more pressing one. A spiritual circus.

12

BURNOUT

In May 1985 the streets of downtown Portland, Oregon, surged and seethed with protesters. Thousands of them, from America, Europe and Australia. They marched through three city blocks around the state capital's courthouse. They carried banners and chanted 'Religious freedom now'. They were joined in outrage against the slur on their religion made by a court verdict on Friday May 17th: a $39 million fraud judgment awarded in favour of twenty-seven-year-old Julie Christofferson Tichbourne against the Church of Scientology. The Church stood accused of defrauding the plaintiff of thousands of dollars after enrolling her, some ten years before, in a 'Communications course'.

The judgment against L. Ron Hubbard's cult brought a wrathful response from Kathleen Gorgon, head of Scientology in California. 'This is part of a bizarre plot to destroy the church. At the trial we demonstrated beyond question that the plaintiff's witnesses were government agents involved in a conspiracy against us.'

(Tichbourne's victory was later challenged by the Scientologists in a series of actions for mis-trial based on religious prejudice. The saga ended with a reportedly small out-of-court settlement in December 1989.)

In that torrid early summer of 1985 John Travolta broke away from the *Perfect* promotional tour to lend support. 'I feel it's time to stand up for what I believe in and I certainly believe in Scientology,' he told the press. He agreed with those who considered the judgment 'an affront to First Amendment rights of freedom of religion'. And he made clear that he was at one with the other showbiz celebrities

in speaking up, or in some cases singing up, for liberty in open-air get togethers. These included Karen Black who sang 'I Shall be Released', and Frank Stallone who led a tearful rendition of 'God Bless America'. Singer Chick Corea also cancelled a Japanese tour to join what he called 'this crusade for religious freedom'.

Travolta's loyalty to Scientology was imperturbable. Dianetics disciples worldwide must have thought him a gift from heaven, or wherever gifts come from in their cosmology. Before and after his Oregon visit the actor lost few chances to scatter Scientological lore through his interviews.

His mystical tendencies were bursting out in other places. Perhaps he was suffering from a backlash after making two body-obsessed movies, *Staying Alive* and *Perfect*, in which there had been scant room to choreograph *any* spiritual impulses. 'The body, the body!' (he might have said to himself) – 'how does one escape it?'

He escaped it almost literally, he says, on the night of the Grammy awards, that annual Hollywood beanfeast in honour of the record companies. 'I was exterior most of that night.' And he had other out-of-body experiences, or visions. One night at home he dreamed he saw a man in a football jersey numbered nineteen running across his courtyard. He woke up and ran into the kitchen area, where he claims there *was* a man, an intruder, wearing a green-black jersey with the number nineteen. He chased him away.

Is he not worried, someone asks, that people will think him a bit of a flake, a mystical nutcase, like Shirley MacLaine? 'With me – God! – my image has been all over the place. Fat in one movie, great body in the next, sort of intellectual in one, and stupid in another. Who knows what people think of me?'

Of course the material side of mysticism is that people run around doing good works. While taking his time to ponder new movie possibilities – including a remake of *Zorba the Greek* with Anthony Quinn and a police thriller called *Crack* that he spent months developing with Whoopi Goldberg – Travolta became involved with a police campaign to deter drunk-driving among youngsters in Santa Barbara. 'I talked to the student bodies, telling them how I got stopped once after having only one beer. They listened to what I had to say about staying sober on graduation night.'

And – heed the power of the right star in the right place! – there was not a single drunk-drive arrest the following graduation night.

What can be done locally can be done nationally, Travolta announced, some time in 1986, 'I'm meeting soon with Nancy Reagan to do what I can for SADD [Students Against Drunk Driving].' And he put in work for another acronymed charity, SAGE, or 'Set A Good Example', a nationwide contest to exemplify good character by saying no to drugs and exhibiting leadership.

Mixed in with these government-sponsored initiatives was his work for Narconon, a movement with a more controversial background. 'It's the only really successful rehabilitation programme for recovering from drug abuse,' said Travolta. 'It involves sweat-boxes, diet control and mineral intake under authorised medical supervision.' And it was initiated by one L. Ron Hubbard, giving Travolta a chance to deliver another message on behalf of his mentor. 'All of these things lead to a book I very much believe in, *Dianetics*. It's enjoying a fantastic comeback . . . It was published first back in 1950 and is a terrific blueprint for getting off drugs.'

Meanwhile, as the public puzzled over why this movie star was active in every area but acting, Travolta explained why he hadn't signed for another film. 'I needed the time off. I was burnt out from three pictures in a row. I wanted to ease some of the stress.'

He could have played safe by making *Saturday Night Fever 3*, but it would be the safety of artistic atrophy. Although Robert Stigwood was in favour, and although Norman Wexler hauled himself once more towards his Remington, there was a weariness on the land. 'Whore that I am, I hated the idea, but once again I had money problems,' sighs Wexler. 'Stigwood said John Travolta would do the story but that he wanted it to mirror his own career. Big star crashes, goes a little wild, loses his friends, no one hires him. But again I didn't have a free hand. This time John, who'd caught the writing bug on *Perfect*, began turning out script pages himself.'

The project went as far as registering a title, *Far From Home*, and announcing a $4 million fee for Travolta. But despite brief newsflashes in the Hollywood trades, including a rumour that

Mel Gibson would co-star, *SNF3* fizzled out through a lack of conviction.

Travolta by this time was barely *reading* the trades. He sent shockwaves through movieland by cancelling his subscription to *Variety*, the Hollywood equivalent of going on a hunger strike. He was disillusioned with the industry and its obsessionalism and burned out by publicity fatigue. 'I must have done some 1400 interviews,' he says, though he had learned by now to handle the negative press with equanimity. 'It wasn't anything new. After *Saturday Night Fever* and *Grease*, two of the biggest pictures ever, I made *Moment by Moment* and it was the worst press attack that I had ever experienced. Whatever else I encountered later was mild by comparison.'

Still, his filmography was reaching a dangerous point. In a grand count of all his movies to date, the flops were threatening to outnumber the hits. So he changed his management team. His agent Michael Ovitz had exasperated Travolta, first by attempting to co-package him for movie projects with other clients, a practise pioneered by Ovitz's Creative Artists Agency, secondly by discouraging him from making *Splash*, a little Disney comedy that became a large hit, launching the star career of Tom Hanks.

Perhaps Travolta had read the thumbnail analysis of his own career offered by critic Stanley Kauffman in the *New Republic*. In the course of his review of *Perfect* Kauffman wrote: 'What happens to [Travolta] in the post-studio film world? Dubiously blessed with freedom of choice – dubious for him, anyway – he is the key element in separate packages sold to various independent producers, without the supervising care of a studio chief.' Result? 'Eight years after *Saturday Night Fever* he is still groping and hoping.'

Travolta turned to Jonathan Krane, an ex-Yale law school student who after co-founding and managing Blake Edwards Entertainment with the director of '*10*' and the *Pink Panther* films, now ran MCEG (Management Consultancy and Entertainment Group). The actor first met him in 1983 through Marilu Henner. Krane had signed Henner after her Blake Edwards' comedy *The Man Who Loved Women*, adding her to a talent

roster that included Sandra Bernhard, Drew Barrymore and Carol Kane.

Tall, rangy and young-looking, with a hint of the Travolta features, Krane treats the world as a power breakfast. He can talk you into the ground, then exhume you to talk some more. On the day I met him he had a slight catarrh, a common Hollywood affliction. But he spoke with a relaxed, forward-thrusting urgency, fuelled by superlatives about John, and only became impatient when I corrected him once or twice about his client's film chronology. Krane tends to forget Travolta's bad films in the course of eulogising the good ones.

Travolta's divorce from Ovitz, Krane recalls, was far from amicable. 'CAA blamed me and Mike Ovitz was very angry. But he and John had disagreed over a number of things, the biggest of which was the packaging. Ovitz was upset with me because he thought I was competing with him. I said, "Are you kidding?" What I and MCEG was trying to do was put together something like a small, old-fashioned, thirties-style studio. I had $200 million to make movies, I had a home video distribution company, plus a stable of a 150 clients.'

Krane looked at Travolta and Travolta looked at Krane. Travolta must have seen a whiz kid who would either go far with him or crash on take-off. (The second began to seem more likely when MCEG went into financial crisis in the late eighties after trying to swallow the Virgin Vision video company). And Krane must have seen an actor whose golden age was past but who still had charisma and brand recognition if they could be properly exploited.

Just look at the facts. On whom did Britain's Princess Diana bestow her favours when she was offered a celebrity guest of her own choice for a White House party in November 1985? The summons went out to Rancho Tajiguas. Travolta donned his black tie, gulfstreamed to Washington and submitted to the glare of the chandeliers. In mid-evening he was taken aside by Nancy Reagan who indicated that the Princess would enjoy a 'turn around the floor'. To approach Her Highness was the work of an instant; so was the docking procedure as the band struck up. Recalls Travolta, 'I just brought her arm down and put my hand back of her back and led her away.'

Themes from *Fever* broke out across the ballroom. The jewelled and splendoured guests looked on as the couple offered what the the *New York Times* described as 'a whirling, syncopated display of charming touch-dancing'.

'I found her refreshing and down to earth. She has style and rhythm,' approved Travolta. At the next day's royal press conference the Princess herself reportedly 'remained silent, eyes down, fighting a smile that blossomed on her lips'. But the Prince of Wales, asked if his wife had enjoyed the dance, first said, 'I am not a glove puppet,' then ventured, 'She would be an idiot if she didn't enjoy dancing with John Travolta, wouldn't she?'

The night became a poignant marker in the Travolta myth, and the frontispiece to an almost unimaginable tale of fortune's reversals. Diana was a fairytale heroine who seemed destined to grow old beautifully, shedding her radiance on all she met and strewing her children around the throne of England. John Travolta was a waning member of the Hollywood 'royalty' whose last two films were jokes and whose reputation was speeding towards oblivion. By September 1997, fate or chance had rewritten everything. Diana was a divorced princess slain in a senseless, appalling accident. John Travolta was one of the half-dozen highest-paid stars in the world.

That was now, this was then. Travolta in 1985 was secure in his achieved fame but insecure in his future, full of life while preoccupied with death. That subject comes up again and again. It's as if the career death whose approach he senses has pushed him towards contemplating that other, bigger quietus, and into auditing mortality to find out if it includes – surely it must? – a beyond.

'Unlike most Americans who wish to deny death or ignore it I envisage it calmly,' he told *Paris Match*. He believes in life, or even lives, after death. 'That's why I'm not afraid of dying. I'm just very curious to see what lies on the other side. The way I look at it there's the "genes" cycle and the "spirit" cycle. The one simply enters the other for a lifetime and then departs.

'I don't believe a spirit is capable of dying. There's like a dance of the spirit that we don't see.'

To balance these 'Death, where is thy sting?' musings, there

were two happier 'Life, where is the sting?' episodes. Sting the singer, to be exact. The pop star's tenderly off-wall ballads sung in that skyscraping treble appealed to Travolta. Sting was not just a secret soulmate but someone whose chance reachability reassured the actor at just the right time. 'I called Sting the other day just because I wanted to meet him,' said Travolta. 'That's one thing about being known, you can do that sort of thing.' He also exercised his healing skills on Sting one evening, a showbiz messiah reaching out to his fellow. Attending a Sting concert in Canada, he went backstage to cure a bad throat the singer had by performing a Scientological 'contact assist'.

In the new year a new movie, the first under Krane's management finally began, forcing Travolta to face a camera. *The Experts* was a $13 million Paramount comedy to be made by television director Dave Thomas. Travolta and co-star Arye Gross would play a pair of hip nightclub owners who are persuaded to open a club in a small town that is in reality a training ground for Soviet spies.

It makes startling watching today, if only in showing how Travolta had occupied much of his non-filming sabbatical: in eating. The body is swathed in suspiciously loose-fitting, cossack-style black leather. The face is a pudgy moon with bluish five o'clock shadow. The long black hair is skimmed back behind the ears, as if in readiness for the rat-tail look in *Pulp Fiction*. Gone is the demigod of *Staying Alive* and even the semi-demigod of *Perfect*. Newly arrived, eight years before Tarantino, is the Mark-2 Travolta, the slob pin-up who spreads in all directions.

Rumours of Travolta's weight fluctuations circulated around the Hollywood trade papers (which happily he no longer bought). It was even reported that after filming he gained forty pounds, so that planned pick-up shots for *The Experts* had to be cancelled. Jonathan Krane, who was on hand as the film's executive producer, insists to me that the reshoots went ahead, though without specifying whether Travolta was involved.

'The original ending to *The Experts* had the townies lined up blocking the Russians from stopping the plane leaving, it was kind of a corny ending. So it was re-shot for more of an adventure-type ending. John was the same weight as he was later for *Look Who's*

Talking, which was thin, which was thin! [very emphatic] I have pictures I could show you.'

I saw once again why Travolta had taken on Krane. He is one of those 'There is no such rumour and if there is I deny it' operators. But not even Krane could will *The Experts* towards triumph. Though there are incidental charms – mainly provided by Travolta's funky comic timing and inventive body language, which now stretches to spoof dance numbers, including a Michael Jackson-style moonwalk and an erotic cod-Russian tango in which he sweeps up attractive co-star Kelly Preston – the plot and script could have been devised by a team of Soviet comedians shut up in a sputnik.

Travolta first met Preston at her screen test. She was a bright-eyed Australian-raised actress with fair-to-blonde hair, a smart smile and the permanently teenaged looks that come from growing up on Antipodean beaches. Her early film career did not inspire – *Metalstorm: The Destruction of Jared-Syn, Amazon Women on the Moon*, a role as a nude model in *52 Pick-up*. But she had just played Arnold Schwarzenegger's love interest in *Twins*, proving she could mix it with a megastar.

When shooting began on *The Experts*, she and he, says Travolta, 'got intimate right away because we had to do this erotic dance.' This number makes Travolta's previous stabs at sexy choreography on screen, including the *paso doble* passages in *Saturday Night Fever* and the pelvic-thrust aerobics in *Perfect*, seem like *Come Dancing*. Finger-biting, hip-waggling and bottom-groping abound as Travolta and Preston devour the dance floor and each other, before adjourning to Preston's place to make passionate love. She drags his trousers off, climbs on bed, kneels over him and tears open his shirt: at which point Travolta, whose face is upside down to the camera, tilts it towards us and breathes, 'Isn't this girl terrific, or what?'

Soon actor and actress were rumoured to be as compatible off-screen as on. Travolta later recalled the moment when he believed there might be warmth and durability, not just sudden heat, in their attraction.

'At the wrap party [for *The Experts*] she sat next to me. I'm not a big party person – I don't do that roaming thing well. I'd rather

sit in one place and have people come to me. So I sat there and for four hours Kelly never left my side. I thought, Gee, I've been with other people whose attention was focused on who else they could talk to. All she cared about was being next to me. I know it sounds weird for a star to say that was such a big deal, but for me it was. There was nothing upstaging her commitment. I thought, That's the sort of person I'd love to have in my life all the time.'

Sweet and sweetly put, but isn't there a hint of the old mirror-gazing? On whom is his concern actually focused here? Not on her, but on himself. Not on her, but on her attention to him. Narcissus is still somewhere inside the Travolta psyche, waited on by the defiant vanity of a falling star ('I'd rather sit in one place and have people come to me'). At the same time there is something touching about this hunger for an attentive presence that stays at his side, that doesn't go on musical-chairs trips seeking other, younger stardust.

Few reporters would have bothered to check out the subtleties of this incipient romance, since few bothered to visit the filming. This star had made one bad movie too many – why trek to Vancouver to look at *The Experts*? A collective Hollywood sigh of 'We told you so' greeted news that the completed film was deemed unreleasable by Paramount. It would go straight to video, apart from far-flung showings in places like Louisiana, Oklahoma and Texas, where Travolta still had a following after *Urban Cowboy*. Not that this stopped one Houston critic from writing, 'If *The Experts* were a horse, you'd avert your face, close your eyes and shoot it.' Jerry Wurms, Travolta's old friend from the Englewood and early Hollywood days, looked on and said, 'John is snatching at B-movie scripts he would once have shredded.'

The actor was hurt by the studio's decision not to release the movie in major cities: 'I called over there and said, "I don't get it." But in many ways the film was another instance of a star out of sync with his time. America's new rapprochement with Russia, as Reagan segued into Bush and Strategic Defence Initiative sabre-rattling turned into political handshakes and economic handouts, made the old cliches of Cold War incompatibility – even comically or affectionately presented as in *The Experts* – seem as stale as yesterday's *blinis*. The film's brightest moment

comes when Preston reveals to Travolta that their love-making has been caught on Russian surveillance video. 'Can we get the tapes?' he says with a lustful glint, obliterating for one second the film's cumbrous political 'satire' with the flash of a new Travolta lubriciousness.

It was ironic – or perhaps inevitable – that this man should become a freer, looser, even better actor as soon as he stepped down from the pedestal on which he had been placed. Losing the pleasures and privileges of fame can mean shrugging off the pressures and responsibilities too. Interesting roles that would have been thought too lowly or recherché are suddenly there for the taking – with no Mr Ten-Percent to hiss in your ear, 'Think how it will lower your fee or shrink your audience!' So Travolta would describe his next project as 'like being off-Broadway again. No stakes, no $20 million breathing down your neck again.'

When ABC Television executive Gary Pudney, who had helped arrange Travolta's first date with stardom in *Welcome Back Kotter*, rang the actor to offer him a role in one of two one-act plays to be filmed back-to-back, he said yes. The simple part of the proposition was that he would play a thug preparing to make a 'hit'. More challengingly, the plays were by Harold Pinter and Travolta would need a cockney accent. The actor agreed to meet *The Dumb Waiter*'s proposed director, another prodigy fallen on hard times, Robert (pre-*The Player*) Altman.

'I arranged for the three of us to meet in New York at the Russian Tea Room,' says Gary Pudney. 'It was the first meeting between the two of them. Bob and I got there first and then John came in, right on time as always. And he *was* the character. He came in with the cockney voice, knowing his lines: he'd memorised most of the play. It's stupefying how good he was and Altman was dutifully impressed.'

Dutifully? Does Pudney mean 'duly'? Or does one sense an adverb Freudianly picked to suggest a man hanging back from the party? Altman later said, 'I would never have cast [Travolta] based on what I'd seen him do before . . . [but] when we talked about it I was impressed with his confidence. He said he could do it and I believed him.'

If Altman had any doubts about this notional ratings coup for

ABC, they were soon too late. In February 1987 he and Travolta were in coldest Quebec, where they were joined by British actor Tom Conti.

Travolta's co-star in the two-handed play to be shot in a Canadian studio over eleven days remembers being taken aback by the speed of the enterprise. 'When I was in London, Altman rang me and asked me to choose either role, saying that John would play the other,' Conti recalls. 'So I said, "Oh I don't know, I'll play Gus." And five minutes later Bob rang back and said, "That's okay, John'll play the other." I've never known anything done so quickly.'

Or, soon, so coldly. 'We were in Montreal in winter and I don't think John or I had ever been so cold in our lives. It must have been about 300 degrees below the liquefying point of nitrogen. John kept saying, 'Jet engines love this kind of weather, they love cold air.' We hardly went out: at best we might rush to a restaurant and then rush back. Mostly we were in the hotel for a week before shooting began, learning and rehearsing our lines. Pinter's dialogue is fiendish. But it's also so funny that we'd keep going into paroxysms of laughter.'

Conti claims that Travolta quickly mastered cockney, the only word he could not pronounce correctly being 'lorry', which came out 'law-wy'. Seeing the film today, though, makes clear that a lot more than this exercised the actor's skills. He is erratic with glottal stops, those defining tropes of the cockney brogue, so that he says 'priddy quick' instead of 'pri'y quick', though he can somehow manage 'ke'le' for 'kettle'. 'Comes' is pronounced 'cowms.' 'Crawled' comes out 'crooled', as in 'he crooled under a law-wy'. And so on.

As if to lend moral support. Tom Conti offered his own dog's dinner accent, a straight-from-the-tin stage Irish. Conti also increases ethnic/cultural confusion by sporting a funny moustache and greasy forelock of black hair, as if playing an Italian barber in a Chaplin film. There is a connoisseur moment when the more conservatively presented Travolta – cleanly shaven, smartly waistcoated – goes face to face with Conti, scrutinising him all over in a moment of appraising silence, like a man who has suddenly realised that his best friend is a freakshow.

Altman's direction provides few moments approaching even this

modest high point, though Travolta credits him with one brainwave that helped his performance. 'I had a scene where I was reading a newspaper aloud. I was rattling away. Altman didn't say much at first. Then he came over and whispered in my ear, "What if your character is illiterate and can't read a word on the page, is making it all up as he goes along?" Wow. That changed everything, permeated the whole scenario.'

One is not clear how, except by providing one more layer of redundant obliquity. Altman favours shooting the play at a 'menacing' tempo, often through mesh patterns provided by the basement set's metal-frame service lift that provides the play's title. The off-kilter angles are underscored with off-kilter music: plinks, twings and twangles as if from a group of Japanese busker percussionists.

'What really killed the film,' says Conti, who is no apologist, 'was this dreadful "spooky" music. It signalled the sombre ending right at the beginning. I remember a journalist at the press screening said to me, "Wasn't the music wonderful?" I thought you stupid cow.'

Others who attended the preview of this ABC TV Pinter double-bill at the New York Museum of Television and Radio were no less pointed, including Harold Pinter. 'He was a little bit sharp, he hated the movie,' Conti says. And the playwright buttonholed the actor some weeks later in London.

'Harold took me aside at some book function,' Conti says. 'He said, "Can I have a word with you? I just wanted you to know I was really very deeply disappointed in the film." I said, "Oh really?" And he said, "The principal cause of my disappointment was you." "Oh, why?" "Because you said forty-seven of my lines and 357 of your own.'

'He was exaggerating. I went back and counted the inaccuracies and found about forty. But Harold doesn't realise that movies are different from plays. You've got eleven days to shoot the thing, and you're working in Canada with an American director and a script girl whose first language is French and who doesn't know that Pinter will go ballistic if you change "and" to "er". '

Of Travolta himself, Conti says, 'The most difficult thing about acting is to make it look easy, as I've been accused of doing. But people don't know the thousands of tiny decisions made in a

two-minute take to make it look like that. John is a pure actor, with a very considered craft.'

John was also an actor whose relief at this newfound, careless sovereignty over choice of roles – nothing to lose, no reason to play safe – might be more theoretical than actual. Yes, he had shrugged off the burden of popularity. Yes, he would claim in one interview that he was 'happier now in my work than I've been in a long time . . . Right now, the thing for me is the film's story – not just my character. I want to be part of the film. I don't want to be the film. Do you know?' (He speaks as if he has been imbibing the all-the-world's-an-ensemble philosophy of Robert Altman.)

But had it occurred to this actor, while he was shooting a modest filmed play in the permafrost reaches of North America, that ten years before to the very month, he had been lording it on the streets of Bay Ridge filming *Saturday Night Fever* and pacing out the lines of his own legend? In one decade a man whose mythic leasehold had been compared with that of Dean, Brando or Presley was on celebrity's equivalent of Skid Row.

There must have been a quiet desperation shared by Krane and Travolta. 'It got to the point when I thought I'm just going to have to accept anything that comes along,' the actor admitted years later. 'I was very vulnerable to people and very easily invalidated and made less of and I would take it to heart.' He told one reporter that he was offered 'maybe three movies a year, but not really things I wanted to do.' For a star who could have built a house from the scripts offered in one year during the late seventies, it was a tragic diet. And who could be proud of *The Experts* or *The Dumb Waiter*?

Mysteriously – or not – none of the filmmakers responsible for the mid-period Travolta disasters, between *Perfect* and *Pulp Fiction*, ageed to talk to me for this book. Since one or two responded to my request by saying they would refer to John, or Jonathan, or some greenlighting Travolta eminence, and then never contacted me again, the conclusion is inevitable. The Travolta office would prefer to keep these films from the prying eyes of biographers. (One of these directors, with a surreal touch, said he couldn't talk to me without asking a London friend about me first, the writer Lynda La Plante of *Prime Suspect*. I assured him that Miss La Plante wouldn't know me, nor I her, from the man in the moon.)

The Travolta claiming to be 'happy in his work' impressed no one with his happiness at the Cannes Film Festival, where he went to promote *The Dumb Waiter*. A journalist described him as 'pale and ill-at-ease' and reported a Travolta aide as saying, 'He's nervous because he doesn't appear much in public these days.'

'I am not obsessed with having that life again,' he told Cannes, quizzed about the glitter years. 'If you had told me two years ago that I would never have to work again, I would have said "Great".'

Jonathan Krane insists that Travolta was never troubled by the loss of fame, because he was never hooked on it in the first place. 'He never got into the Hollywood lifestyle. And even later, there were always offers. He regards the years when he wasn't getting big parts as a vacation, a time when he could fly and travel. When he couldn't find any role he liked at his price, which was $3 million, he would go off on his trips.'

These included a visit to London to see the stage musical *Time*. The rumour mill was busy saying that Travolta would replace Cliff Richard in the hit West End show created by Dave Clark and Tim Rice. (The mill had been busy earlier saying he would star in the Broadway staging of *Cats*.) After the performance, however, the American star did not go backstage to see the British star. 'We can't seem to get them together,' lamented a theatre spokesman. So the casting coup never happened. The only explanation Travolta later provided was that there were scheduling problems: 'The gap just closed up.'

But in this land of royalty, this England, John Travolta was still seen as a kind of royalty himself. Eighteen months after cutting a White House caper with Princess Diana, he was invited to tourney mediaevally with Prince Andrew, Fergie and other House of Windsor blue-bloods at the Alton Towers theme park.

It was latterday knight fever. For this royal edition of TV's *It's a Knockout*, also graced by Christopher Reeve of *Superman* and Margot 'Lois Lane' Kidder, Travolta wore a doublet, hose and gold lamé knickerbockers, topped off with a floppy ducal crown. He danced with Fergie, participated in a 'damsel in distress' contest and rode a horse on castors, coming last in the jousting competition.

He was also there when Fergie hit Andrew over the head with a rubber chicken.

There was more social high-flying on the romantic front. At Cannes Travolta had fallen into friendship or more with French screen *déesse* Catherine Deneueve. After the festival they spent time in Paris, followed by a brief idyll at Santa Barbara. Travolta wanted to make a movie with Catherine and their mutual friend Gérard (Depardieu). And he was still drawn to the challenge of making a European film with one of the great French directors. But the man who believed he could shrug off Hollywood stardom also still hankered for it.

'I'm rebuilding my career from the ground up,' he told the Cannes reporters. If he was going to restart from scratch, though, he would have sell off some of the Travolta assets: including a plane or two, a car or two, perhaps even the multi-million-dollar Rancho Tajiguas. He looked east towards Florida. There the climate was clearer and the houses were cheaper. And he would not wake up every day to look out on the cruel coast of Movieland.

'I knew I had to get out to survive. The seriousness with which everyone took their careers robbed me of the fun and playfulness of making films. I just could not get things done when the stakes became so high, and so I moved out.'

PART TWO

PRELUDE

LOST IN FLORIDA

The geography of the United States is designed to take a gifted showbiz performer in a two-stage zigzag across, then back across the continent. This zigzag can take anything from half a century to a lifespan. Or it can take just twelve years.

Born in or near New York, within sound of the foghorns that may have brought his forefathers to America, the baby trouper will start by coveting a Broadway career. After initiation in the sweatshop capital of live performance, he will be hauled across country by the lure of Hollywood. Then after finding fame on that sunbed of achievement he will slide back across America to Florida. Here all exertion ceases; the sun doesn't; and your money does your work for you.

The third stage is optional, but the first two happened to nearly all of them. Hoffman, De Niro, Pacino, Hackman, Streisand. And John Travolta. Only with him, it happened faster than anyone. Before he was sure he was born, he was acting in New York. Before he was sure he was an actor, he was a TV star. Before he had read the ratings, he was a movie star. Before he had taken in his own stupefying fame, it was over.

He came back from *Moment by Moment*, but like a man climbing a difficult mountain, where each upward grunt is followed by an indeterminate slither, he never recaptured the heights of *Fever* and *Grease*. And after *Perfect* he was back at base camp. A grounded millionaire, he was ready for the retirement coach to Palm Beach.

Not quite retirement, though. Travolta was not quitting acting.

And Florida held out limitless playspace for his two passions, flying (so many private air clubs) and Scientology. One of this creed's main HQs stood on the state's western coast in the town of Clearwater. Here Hubbardites could complete courses in spiritual self-discipline while devouring good food and bathing in voluptuous gulf water.

Many people believe America's centre of monied insanity is Hollywood. But Hollywood is liberated and levelheaded compared to Florida. The sunshine state has a siege mentality: the psychosis of self-protectiveness. It is full of religion, rightwing politics and enviro-fundamentalism. Its gated communities are so gated you'd need a bombardment from sea to pierce them. And its greenness is sometimes that of a jungle, sometimes of a funeral parlour: so many flowers, so much verdure at once luxuriant and manicured.

Something about the state makes you want to muss it up. On my only field trip, to the area near Daytona, I soon found that no amount of strategic ingenuity could get me in for a leisurely look at the fly-in compound where Travolta lived in the late eighties and early nineties. You needed a pass, or invitation, or millionaire credit rating. To console myself I joked to an American friend that within two hours I could find and meet someone who knew or had known John Travolta. This without penetrating the compound and without, at that time, knowing anyone in the state who had actually met him.

He said I couldn't.

I said I could.

(1) Yin

In my modest seafront suite at the Best Western Hotel La Playa on Daytona Beach (TV, air-conditioning, competitive off-season rates) I got out the yellow pages and rummaged under R for restaurants. I searched out the nearest pizzeria to Travolta's fly-in community, telephoned it and made a reservation for a late lunch/early dinner at 4pm. Then I dragged my friend off to it.

As well as probing the state and its VIP defences, I wanted to test a theory. That the easiest way to find a celebrity – or people

who've met him – is to forget he is a celebrity. He isn't, at least to himself. Just like us, he wants to sleep, drink, chat with friends, watch TV, hang out – and eat.

At the Spruce Creek Pizza Restaurant my friend and I consumed a huge *pizze diavole* that neither of us wanted. He had had lunch, I had had brunch. Then I pounced. Had John Travolta ever been there, I asked the waitress.

'Oh, why, sure. He used t'come here. Sure he did. Liked his pizzas. Nick knew him better 'n I. *Nick!!*'

Nick was the young pizza chef, a dark good-looking Italian. Yes, John Travolta had been there and Nick had delivered pizzas to him. Went there once and cleaned out his aircraft hangar. Nice guy. Nick and a friend used to watch his plane fly in and out.

What sort of pizzas did he like?, I asked, giving my friend time to count the bet money with which he would pay the bill.

'Plain. No toppings. But Mark knew him better than I did.'

Mark?

'Yeah. Friend of mine, works at Hooters in Orlando. He knew Ron Zupanic too, who looked after John's place.'

We were out of there in two minutes. A little later I rang Mark at Hooters.

Mark was cagier, much cagier. He suggested I call him at his apartment the following morning, which I did. The phone was answered by a man who went to fetch Mark, who sounded as if he had just woken up. He also sounded like an experienced pest-deterrer. Yes, he had known Travolta. Yes, he had done some work around his house: cleared his hangar, cleaned his pool. He knew Nick and Ron. Had I spoken to Ron, he asked? He'd have to call Ron and see if he wanted to talk. He wasn't sure if he should say any more himself. He'd get back to me.

He didn't. But that was all right. I had achieved my hairline breach in the state's security and proved, more or less, my theory that a star is just a bloke. Since I was in Florida mainly for just-a-bloke reasons myself – a holiday – I wanted to hurry over to vacationland on the gulf.

(ii) Yang

Equal and antithetical theories co-exist: especially in Florida. On its western coast is a shrine to the obverse contention – that a star *isn't* just a bloke. He is an avatar, mouthpiece, figurehead. He can be used. Ambushed at the pizza restaurant, he can be coaxed up to the VIP penthouse. From there, his voice bodied out with the thousand voices of the believers stacked up in the floors below him, he can speak to the multitudes. He is an answer to the prayers of creed-making spiritual ventriloquists.

When I passed Clearwater, I looked up at the Scientology building. Behind each of its windows sat – who could doubt? – a man or woman progressing towards a wondrous self-knowledge. Here too L. Ron Hubbard might have groomed and refined his theory of a star's importance to the faith. In 1955 he inaugurated 'Project Celebrity', a long-term plan to bring in VIPs as Scientology 'trophies'. The wish-list included Marlene Dietrich, Ernest Hemingway, Howard Hughes, Greta Garbo and Walt Disney. 'If you bring one of them home you will get a small plaque as a reward,' he wrote in a Scientology magazine. Twenty years, and again forty years, later, what greater showbiz trophy was there than John Travolta? Even during his forgotten epoch, the Hubbardites could bide their time. It was worth at least a Pascalian wager that he would bounce back.

If he did not he was still a fair-to-middling prize. And from Travolta's own viewpoint, he could spend his troubled years seeking and perhaps finding himself – his true, inner-lighted self, not the one distorted by fame's illumination.

For what do any of us know about the meaning of life? Perhaps Hubbard is right. Perhaps we are all neurotic trace-patterns seeking to be audited back to zero. And where better to do that than Florida? It is all about stopping dead with an option to start again. Here John Travolta could retire or be re-born, whatever the gods of Condo-land in conference with the lords of the E-meter, should decide.

1

IN THE DOGHOUSE

The Spruce Creek estate near Daytona Beach was an exclusive residential compound with a 4000-foot landing strip for private planes. More than 1000 acres in area, the estate boasted thirty-six miles of private streets and taxiways, with shops, restaurants and an eighteen-hole golf course.

The style of the homes was French Provincial with matching aircraft hangars. What Travolta liked about his new $500,000 mansion was its mixture of hideaway privacy and getaway convenience. He could walk round the kitchen naked without being seen by a living being save his two dogs Taboo and Sinner; he also had a houseboy and personal trainer, though not on twenty-four-hour duty. And having put on clothes, he could walk out of his back door and be in New York in four hours, Los Angeles in five.

He felt ready to make three films in a rush of productivity. The first was surely a good box-office bet (Krane and Travolta prayed) since it was being masterminded by actor-producer Michael Douglas and producer Michael Phillips, formerly of *The Sting* and *Close Encounters of the Third Kind*. *The Tender*, said Phillips, was 'a cross between *Taxi Driver* and *Lassie*'. 'It's very primal, very intense,' he emphasised, outlining the story of a smalltime Mafia debt collector fleeing underworld retribution, who to please or appease his daughter adopts a mutt left for dead after being wounded in an illegal organised dog-fight. Man, girl and dog spend the movie crisscrossing Chicago and environs, looking for love, safety and redemption.

Travolta was cast, says Phillips, because the character he plays, a desperate, recovering alcoholic, 'is so hard-edged that we had to have someone in the role who is inherently likable. Or we will turn off the audience from the first frame.'

If Travolta was their good luck talisman, they needed one. The production was designed to flout that primal Hollywood proverb, 'Never work with children or animals'. Here were both, and in one case the curse was multiplied. Eight Doberman Pinschers were used in the principal dog role, none of whom proved capable of hitting a mark.

'The key word that sums up our problems is "dog",' said director Robert Harmon as the two designated weeks of second-unit photography stretched to five. 'When someone watches a scene and says, "Gee, that dog is great," I always feel like saying, "Yes, and it only took 100 takes." '

Travolta suffered with scarcely a complaint up to and including the final night's shooting, when he was required to do thirty-one takes for a scene in sub-zero weather with rain and wind-machines gusting all around. After that life should have been simple. Plans for the film's general release reached poster stage, though the poster's copyline seemed to have been composed by someone chained to a rhyming dictionary: 'A man in over his head. A child hanging by a thread. A dog in the street left for dead. An enemy with a gun full of lead. Love conquers all.' Chased by doggerel, the film was then dogged by controversy over its handling of the animals, a row climaxing in an American Humane Society's advertisement in *Variety* that condemned 'the agitation and worrying of dogs to the point of ferocity'. It claimed that this constituted 'a violation of CPC 597 (Cruelty to Animals)'. Though the American Humane Movie Review awarded a grudging bill of health, producer Phillips said he 'rued the day' he ever became involved with the canines.

Like its predecessors, *The Tender* reached barely a single movie theatre. Jonathan Krane's version of events is that 'the company backing it got into financial trouble, the film got stuck and then it went straight to video.'

It deserved no kinder fate, though there is a mixture of agony and awe in watching Travolta go so far out on a rainy spur of cinematic land in an attempt to find complexity and even tragedy

Scenes from an Englewood childhood:
the scrapbook of Travolta neighbour
Eddie Costenuic.

Winning his wings with the Dwight Morrow High School flying club, aged 14 (Travolta back row in middle).

JOHN TRAVOLTA

John Travolta got his start from Allenberry

Local performers do make good and John Travolta, Academy Award nominee for his starring role and dancing in the movie, "Saturday Night Fever," is Allenberry Playhouse's shining example.

Before he became "Vinnie Barbarino" in the television production of "Welcome Back Kotter," Travolta was hired in the summer of 1971 by the late Richard North Gage to appear in the Boiling Springs playhouse in a singing and dancing role in "The Boyfriend."

He also danced the "Tango Tragique" with Marjorie Honre in Allenberry's production of "She Loves Me."

Travolta was able to receive his actor's equity card by his work at Allenberry, thus launching his professional career.

In the chorus of *The Boyfriend* at Allenberry Playhouse, 1971: the show that won Travolta, kneeling at right, his Equity Card. (Photo courtesy of John Heinze)

Travolta wins nationwide fame as TV heartthrob Vinnie Barbarino in *Welcome Back Kotter*.

Rehearsing *Welcome Back Kotter* with John Sylvester White. (Photo courtesy of Marcia Strassman)

Fans of Travolta in *Kotter* had their first large-screen sighting of him, as another high school hellraiser, in *Carrie*.

Brooklyn, and a disco-dancing hero's dreams of leaving it, in *Saturday Night Fever*.

Persistence of a vision. Travolta plus iconic white suit in the little film that became a

world sensation, *Saturday Night Fever.*

Travolta with parents Helen and Sam in the photo commemorating his mother's death in the *Englewood Press-Journal*, December 1978.

Travolta and Olivia Newton-John set the prom swinging in *Grease*.

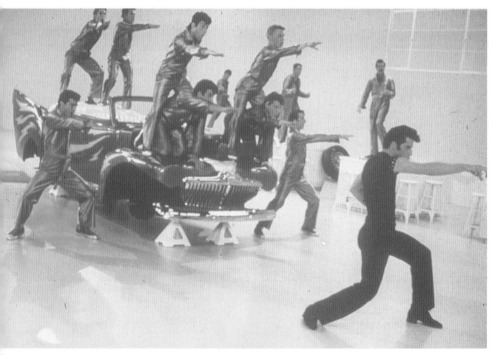

Travolta and cast revving up for *Greased Lightning* from *Grease*.

Movie sound-effects expert stumbles on murder, and Travolta in his best mid-career role, in Brian DePalma's *Blow Out*.

Travolta shows off his body beautiful, sculpted for *Staying Alive* director Sylvester Stallone.

Sex, sweat and aerobics. Intrepid *Rolling Stone* reporter Travolta exposes the new singles scene in *Perfect*.

Travolta meets his wife-to-be Kelly Preston on the set of *The Experts*.

'This is your captain ...' Real-life flying enthusiast Travolta at the controls in *Look Who's Talking Now*.

Travolta and Samuel L. Jackson prepare to clean up in *Pulp Fiction*.

From *Fever* to *Fiction*: Travolta explores new dance sensations as Vincent Vega.

Pulp Fiction director Quentin Tarantino with new protegé.

Angel with dirty wings. Travolta scruffs up to play Nora Ephron's *Michael*.

Major Vic Deakins, unhinged and dangerous, with nuclear bomb in John Woo's *Broken Arrow*.

Salt on ketchup – the pros and cons – in the race drama *White Man's Burden*. With Harry Belafonte.

A star reborn, at the 50th Cannes Film Festival.

'The work is its own reward ...'

Staying alive, despite the critics. Travolta with *Fever* sequel director Sylvester Stallone.

Stepping back into the limelight: Travolta with Kelly Preston.

Mr and Mrs John Travolta, off duty.

Travolta's Clinton-modelled Presidential candidate on the hustings with Emma 'Hillary' Thompson.

in his character. He plays desperation with all nerves whirring: perhaps it is now typecasting. And he can do a crying scene as well as cheapjack material allows. Collapsing in sobs on a roadside, his streaming nose is as grimly authentic as the tears descending the travel-greasy face. And though the plot and script virtually beg him to overplay in the bonding scenes with girl and dog, Travolta consistently chooses the nuance, gestural aside, revelatory flicker of response – the incandescent small change of emotion over the gaudy rhetoric.

Even so, what value will audiences place on a good performance in a god-awful film? The day after watching *The Tender* you try mentally to annotate Travolta's good work. But your head is haunted by the plangent girl and maudlin mutt, the latter endowed in some scenes with luminous eyes, as if the makers had tried out a glamorising keylight only for it to turn into a sci-fi horror effect. Also sinister rather than appealing is the dog's ability to walk all over Illinois without losing its way: along with the orphan girl, it seems possessed of a nightmare ubiquity.

After a whirlwind guest role as a music teacher in a cornball, minibudget song-and-dance film called *Shout* – 'We were sitting in John's house in Florida,' says Krane, 'and Universal called me begging John to do this cameo, ten days' work for $2 million' – Krane and Travolta planned to segue to another medium-ambitious star vehicle, a drugs and crime thriller called *Chains of Gold*. Both these films, though, were to suffer what was becoming the standard fate for Travolta movies: aborted or postponed fruition. While *Shout* would sit around for so long not being shown that recent filmographies vacillate helplessly between 1988 and 1990 as its release date, *Chains of Gold* would wait for months to be made, then more months to be exhibited. All else apart, Krane's company was going through its solvency convulsions. 'My acquisition of Virgin Vision caused huge problems for my company. We were seriously overstretched. I had 200 employees and I had bankers saying, "You can't spend this, can't spend that".'

As an interlude between crises, though, there was a little project involving a talking baby.

'I got my hands on *Look Who's Talking* and thought it the funniest script I'd read,' says Jonathan Krane. 'I was sitting here'

– in his tree-bowered hacienda off L.A.'s Mulholland Drive – 'and I was laughing out loud. My wife Sally Kellerman wondered what was going on. Then I told TriStar, who had budgeted it at $15 million, that I'd make the film for half the price. I'd make it at seven million, as a negative pick-up for them to distribute.'

Krane pushed for Travolta to be cast as the taxi driver who befriends Kirstie Alley after rushing her to hospital to deliver her talking-baby prodigy. Bruce Willis, then in the first flush of fame after leaving TV's *Moonlighting* for the big screen's *Die Hard*, would voice the baby, some of whose wisecracks were scripted by Joan Rivers. And George Segal would play the overgrown yuppie father, who abandons girl and tot with the excuse that he is 'going through a selfish phase'. Director Amy Heckerling, of *Fast Times at Ridgemont High*, co-wrote the script with husband Neal Israel. But once she knew Travolta would play the cabbie she customised the role for him.

'In the early drafts, I felt I knew the story of the woman and baby,' says Heckerling. 'But I was floundering in terms of what they were looking for in a man. When John came in, suddenly the whole character began to emerge.'

As well as curvetting in a yellow cab around New York (played by Vancouver), the baby's stand-in father would have an Englewood background and a sideline as a flying enthusiast. 'I asked John what it would be like if you're learning to be a pilot, how much lessons would cost and so on,' Heckerling says. In addition, a mock-choric scene of massed babies being pushed through Manhattan in strollers would be scored to 'Stayin' Alive'.

On set the process of role-appropriation became even more noticeable. 'John's own speech patterns and mannerisms all bring something,' Heckerling says. 'He's not someone who comes in with ten minutes of improv: the dialogue stayed close to the script. But he's so quick to adapt his responses. When the other actor you've partnered with is an infant, and its reactions might not make any sense with what you're doing in a scene, you have to be focused. Plus, babies related to him too because they sense he's a warm, open person, not nervous around them.'

Travolta kept his head and inventiveness in these scenes, even though a third party often breathed literally down his neck. 'The

baby wrangler stands behind the actor,' he explains. 'Their job is to hold up rattles or pull faces to make the baby laugh, or try to startle him to make him cry.' (Vancouver was chosen as location partly because of Canada's more lenient laws on infant working hours.)

This fun-loving, food-loving guy off the street might plausibly run to a minor paunch, as Travolta now did. Though he had camouflaged his avoirdupois with baggy clothes in *The Experts* and *The Tender*, there was no mistaking the strain on his waistbutton now that he was rolling around on a floor with a baby and on a kingsize bed with the baby's mother.

Heckerling shrugs: 'John loves food, he's a very sensual person. The most fun thing is watching him eat something he enjoys. It's like watching a baby discover candy for the first time. And with *Look Who's Talking* it wasn't like, "Look, you gotta get in shape for this." He's playing a warm-hearted cab driver, not a dancer.'

In one fantasy scene Travolta is allowed to spoof his nascent beer-bellied self. Kirstie Alley has a daydream, or daymare, of a kitchen-sink future with this barrel-paunched prole: Alley's downtrodden slattern bickers through clouds of grease at a fag-smoking Travolta whose vest barely holds in his Silenus stomach.

Though the actor weighed in at 210 pounds and claims he refused to get on a scale, he was co-starring with an actress so *simpatico* and easygoing that she would hardly bawl him out for failing to provide a suitable love object. He and Kirstie Alley became fast friends, as if they had known each other for years. She and her actor husband Parker Stevenson (of TV's *Baywatch*) even insisted John come and stay at their new home in Maine, a visit she never forgot.

'I was setting up the guest wing and I decided I wanted my visitors to be treated as if they were staying at the Pierre Hotel in New York – a big mistake. I said to John, "Come and be my guinea pig and I'll make out a questionnaire. What soaps do you like? What candies do you like? Do you like tea?"

'He was horrible. He took all the shampoos and stuff with him. That was the end of the Pierre Hotel idea.'

Alley was joking, of course. It was actually she who did the stealing: she stole the whole incident and used it as the starting

point for her movie comedy _Madhouse_, in which a guest weekend in a private home becomes a furlough in Hell.

Had Alley and Travolta known each other before? Amy Heckerling claims that the rising _Cheers_ star and fallen _Grease_ idol had never met. But Alley was a Scientologist of long standing. In the early eighties she shared an apartment with actress and fellow Hubbardite Mimi Rogers, who in turn married co-believer Tom Cruise. After admitting to a period of drug difficulties in the late seventies, she became a campaigner and fund-raiser for Narconon, the L. Ron Hubbard-inspired drugs programme with which Travolta had been involved since the mid-eighties. She performed other Scientological good works, such as helping to disseminate a forty-seven-page booklet on environmental preservation called _Cry Out_ (named after a song by L. Ron Hubbard). So it seems surprising that she and her fellow performer/proselytiser had never met.

On the set of _Look Who's Talking_ Alley and Travolta behaved like old-established cronies. They could even joke about pretending to be lovers. 'John told me I was kissing him like his next-door neighbour, so I asked him to sing something romantic to put me in the mood. Instead, every time we started to shoot the scene he started impersonating Barbra Streisand, singing songs from _Yentl_, and I broke out laughing.'

Alley also served as confidante to Travolta's latest heartaches over Kelly Preston. The _Experts_ actress had become engaged to Charlie Sheen, to the chagrin of the wannabe matchmaker Alley. 'I don't know why you and Kelly aren't together,' she blurted to Travolta. 'Frankly, neither do I,' he said, 'but it's too late now.' He had a glimpse of the betrothed couple when they visited him in Florida. 'It seemed she was very much in love with Charlie,' he recalled. 'I wasn't jealous, it was something else, more beautiful. I said to myself simply, "I want a girl like that who is wrapped up in me and gazes at me like she does at her fiance." I had the feeling, looking at her, of bathing in tenderness and joy. I wanted her to be mine.'

(Once again, to split nuances, his interest seems to be less in Kelly than in the promise of her supportive sacrificial radiance, of a girl 'wrapped up in me').

By the time _Look Who's Talking_ itself wrapped, everyone was

convinced they had a winner. This time, surely, nothing would prevent that natural progression Travolta had once taken for granted, whereby a film star would put in so many weeks of honest work and then the film would actually *appear* in front of an audience. Things looked good: sneak previews recorded ninety-percent approval ratings. But the studio made no move towards a summer release.

'It tested like *ET*, but they didn't want to release it because they didn't think it would make money,' says Jonathan Krane in retrospective despair.

'New people had taken over TriStar and they didn't know how to sell it,' says Heckerling. 'John and I were languishing, knowing we had a movie that people responded to. The studio sat on it all summer, then they came up with a new poster and said, "Look how we've saved your movie!" '

The poster's main saving tactic was to push Travolta out of sight. In the afterglow of *Pulp Fiction* one has to rewire one's brain to realise that in the late eighties this actor's box-office value was deemed zero or less. A studio executive interviewed by the *Washington Post* in 1989 said, 'I've just cast a pretty big film. I think the name of every actor in the business between the ages of twenty-two and thirty-five came up. And I never heard a single mention of John. He doesn't even make the casting lists these days.' (That he still commanded up to $2 million a film, down from the $3 million he received on *Blow Out* and *Perfect*, was attributed to his continuing box-office clout outside America.)

'It wouldn't have been fair for the movie to sell it as a John Travolta film,' TriStar said of *Look Who's Talking*. 'When you have an actor whose last few movies didn't do well, you have to stop and think. And we wanted to sell it as a comedy.'

They did. Come October 1989, *Look Who's Talking* was a hit, or more accurately a phenomenon. Ignoring reviews from the baby-resistant trades – 'palpitates with desperation . . . destined for a short life in theatres, wrote a soon red-faced *Variety* – Heckerling's comedy became the highest-earning film ever directed by a woman. It was in gross profit on its first weekend, when the $8-million movie made $12 million. Overseas it became Columbia's second-largest moneyspinner after *Ghostbusters 2*.

In America the man who was persona non grata on the poster was deemed to have restored himself, a little, on the screen. '[Travolta is] every bit as charming and vulnerable as we've all forgotten he could be,' wrote the *Los Angeles Times*.

So why did he still have to wait for good offers to come in? It is one of the dark wonders of Hollywood history that *Look Who's Talking*, a generation-crossing hit, did nothing to turn Travolta's career around. That event would have to wait five more years, for a bloodthirsty essay in post-modernism by a director no one had heard of.

There may be sloughs of schmaltz between the jokes in *Look Who's Talking*, but Travolta sidesteps them nimbly. He even brings a little acerbity to the film, whether double-entendring with Alley over how to use the joystick during a plane trip or wisecracking to the baby about birth and life: 'You spend nine months trying to get out and the rest of your life trying to get back in.' His looseness as an actor is a delight. Next to him everyone else, including Alley and Segal, seems to be reading lines.

Amy Heckerling believes Travolta remained a movie outcast even after her film, because America couldn't forgive him for having held it in thrall before. 'I have this theory that people are embarrassed about anything they liked in the seventies. I think people hold their hatred for discos against John. And for bell-bottoms and the rest of the fads.'

The concept 'John Travolta' did seem stuck in that seventies memory museum. Early during shooting on the forthcoming *Chains of Gold* a teenaged onlooker would ask him to pose for her and her friends in the finger-pointing *Fever* stance. He refuses; they plead; he acquiesces. There are squeals, giggles and the thrusting forward of an autograph book. The girls do not even ask about the new film.

The press showed more interest, marginally, after *Look Who's Talking*: perhaps they wanted to probe the mystery of Travolta's failure to come back from the dead. Perhaps they wanted to prod the corpse. And a further advantage of doing a Travolta interview in the late eighties was that you could sit in on the dazzling food shows.

'A waiter enters, pushing puddings,' describes one reporter.

'Chocolate is the theme: three scoops of chocolate ice-cream; chocolate truffle cake in raspberry sauce; and a large bowl of chocolate mousse-cum-trifle piped with white cream. John offers some to the Press. But the Press declines, and John tucks in. Spoonful after brown spoonful, the actor devours almost all.'

'I don't have very much time for my body,' he explains, 'because I've always had a lot of confidence in my personality.'

This was just public relations. Travolta was giving plenty of time to his body, to maintaining it and not just stuffing it. He had hired a personal trainer called Brad Bigelow. Tired of jokes about 'Fat-urday Night Fever', the actor began lifting weights and running four miles a day. He went on jogs with Tom Cruise, during and after which they discussed the finer points of Dianetics. He exercised even if he didn't enjoy it. 'I can't diet so I have to work out every day. It takes an hour and a half . . . I get depressed just thinking about it.'

On the set of *Chains of Gold*, for which he claims to have lost twenty-five pounds, he and Bigelow played 'suspect and inspector' games. After Travolta left to act in a scene, Bigelow would comb the mobile home looking for illicit confectionery. One day he found unopened packets of Giggles and Pepperidge Farm Nantuckets. He confronted his employer. 'Someone must have snuck them aboard!' protested Travolta. Further investigation proved him correct.

The actor had to look leaner to pass as a Galahadish social worker for *Chains of Gold*. He would be running all over Miami looking for villains to clobber and a drug-racket-endangered boy (Joey Lawrence) to rescue in a script by John Petz that Travolta had spent three months 'improving'. (The actor shares screenplay credit.) Then there were the love scenes with friend Marilu Henner, drafted in to play the lawyer for a local drug lord. These required shirtlessness and even with a new improved torso, and an old, indulgent girlfriend, he was worried.

'I don't know what audiences will think. I mean, do you want to see this?' (pulling up his shirt to reveal to a reporter the industrial-size love handles). 'Feel these,' he insists.

The script was being written from minute to minute. Henner's boyfriend of those years, film director Robert Lieberman (of the Jon Voight weepie *Table for Five*), rewrote one of her big dramatic

speeches. Henner reports that she and Travolta ad-libbed several of their scenes. 'We lifted dialogue from our own history, and it helped make for a very good movie.' And co-star Ramon Franco, who played chief villain, says: 'We never did a scene as originally written. We rewrote it all to make it more believable and to not give away any of the plot surprises, which the original script did.'

One scarcely dares think of the original script. *Chains of Gold* may be the nadir of Travolta's career. Never mind the distribution delays caused by the collapse of Jonathan Krane's company. ('The film was 100 percent funded by foreign pre-sales,' he insists.) *Chains* never opened in theatres at all and never deserved to. Though purporting to be based on actual events, it blends junk-Hispanic dialogue on the level of 'Thees time you really gonna die' with ill-motivated, anything-goes action scenes. The hero suffers torture, a pool of alligators and a climactic flight from the villain's lair that begins with his sliding down the wall-buttress of a giant Aztec-style hotel and climaxes in his leaping from one maw to another of an opening river-bridge. No wonder Travolta needed a physical trainer.

Few scenes lead with logic to any other and the star, when not puffing around town in an artfully loose-fitting shirt, provides what may be the only moments of outright bad acting in his entire career: notably a scene of hammy grief over a dead boy's body. The emotion seems applied and pantomimic. It makes you realise how good Travolta is, how unfussy and inner-directed, at major moments in more major movies.

There was one mercy. *Chains of Gold* took so long to be released that it outlasted critical patience. When it reached TV and video in late 1992, most reviewers had forgotten its existence. *Variety* spoke up for all by calling the film 'Earnest with a capital E'. Travolta was 'tiresome in the stolid goody two-shoes role'.

Taken in tandem with *Shout*, which had also shuffled into video stores nationwide, *Chains of Gold* suggested that all might truly, finally be up with this actor. Though *Shout* features a more assured Travolta – he seems to enjoy his flit-through role as a manic music teacher urging pupils to 'let go' by imitating chickens, playing blues music and opening their hearts and ears to nature – he is cramped by the formulary plot. His almost-first line gives us the

movie's hackneyed narrative peg: 'You need somebody to get the boys ready for the Fourth of July concert, right? I'm your man.' And he is still there, bravely smoking, drinking and acting wild, when he delivers the script's climactic prophecy of a brave new world to come. 'It's called rock 'n' roll, boys. Only a select few people know about this right now. But it's gonna burn through this country like a prairie fire. You think you can handle it?'

They think they can. But the world was no longer sure it could handle Travolta, or his ill-chosen vehicles: least of all a film with *Shout*'s freight of tragic, absurdist irony. Half a generation after being rock music's man of the moment, the star was now relegated to playing John the Baptist to the dimly-imagined glory hour *he* would bestride. Sometimes the time and relativity contortions of popular cinema need an Einstein – or an angel with *Two of a Kind*'s metaphysical speed-wind – to do them justice.

2

LOOK WHO'S MARRYING

Kelly Preston was back in John Travolta's life and we cannot allow their relationship to develop without discovering more about this beautiful, fine-boned twenty-seven-year-old. She has a high forehead and prettily sparkling eyes. Her chin sculpts itself into a petite peninsula, beyond the exact line of jaw, as if to accommodate the dimple that matches, uncannily, her ex-superstar boyfriend's. Her hair is fair, blonde or reddish, according to the requirements of the moment or the movie. And her personality is forthright and effervescent without being pushy.

At the time of Kelly's birth, her mother Linda Carlson was Director of the Hawaii Mental Health Center. She later brought up her daughter in Iran and Australia, where in the late seventies a teenaged Kelly remembers looking at John Travolta's image in a *Grease* poster and saying to herself, 'That's the man I'm going to marry.' Instead, having come to Hollywood to be an actress, she married actor Kevin Gage, with whom she co-starred in the science fiction adventure *Spacecamp*. Her most famous role was in *Twins*, where she romanced Arnold Schwarzenegger, who later directed her in the lead role of an episode of television's *Tales from the Crypt*. Other TV assignments included, by spooky coincidence, a role in *Eight is Enough*, the sitcom that had once starred Diana Hyland.

Travolta knew Preston's marriage to Gage was in trouble and offered Scientological comfort. Though he and Kelly were attracted to each other during filming on *The Experts*, he says, 'Her marriage was a precarious thing, but we were very clean in our interplay with

each other. We were above board. But I knew that was when I first loved her.'

After breaking up with Gage, Kelly moved in with actor George Clooney (pre-*ER* fame). Unfortunately for her, this developed into a *menage à trois* with a pig. In a moment of eccentric affection the dark-haired, macho-voiced star-to-be gave her a black porker for her twenty-sixth birthday. The relationship ended within the year. Clooney kept custody of Max the pig.

Kelly moved on to fast-living, fast-working actor Charlie Sheen, who found the time and resources between gilt-edging his career with films like *Hot Spots* and *Terminal Velocity* to buy her a $200,000 engagement ring. Marriage was thought imminent.

Even now, however, Travolta went on carrying a torch for his Hawaiian-Iranian-Australian-American enchantress. Preston's appetite for romance only demonstrated to him her 'capacity to be devoted'.

'I think she really wanted her husband to work out. She wanted George to work out and she wanted Charlie to work out. . . . She and Charlie had a poetic kind of relationship, like Diana was for me, that will always remain very special to her. And I have to grant her that, because she grants me Diana.'

Finally however, Kelly and Charlie, having reached terminal velocity, stalled and nosedived. The parting was not without incident since Kelly reportedly refused to return the valuable ring. (She later insisted that she and Sheen had sold it and shared the proceeds.) But she was soon willing and able to give herself to John Travolta. The two re-met in Vancouver, where Preston was making a movie called *Run* and Travolta was serving time on *Look Who's Talking Too*.

They were suddenly an item in the gossip pages, or those pages that thought the dwindled *Saturday Night Fever* star worth gossiping about. As ever, he was a prophet more honoured abroad. He and Kelly flew as guests to the Giffoni Film Festival in Italy. Here the good news was a Francois Truffaut Prize, given to arts personalities 'distinguished for their moral involvement with children and their creative achievement in motion pictures', while the bad news was that they had to sit through a gala showing of *The Tender*. Travolta came to treasure the award named after his

favourite French film-maker, a prize previously won by Robert De Niro, Jeremy Irons and other performers valued for their moral involvement with children.

These were carefree, jet-setting years, or came to be chronicled that way. Travolta may not have enjoyed the starry esteem of his *Fever/Grease* epoch, but *Look Who's Talking* was now a box-office goldmine and manager Jonathan Krane made sure the gold did not slip through his client's fingers.

'When I first got involved with John I changed his entire financial structure. I showed him exactly what he had to have to live for the rest of his life, if he didn't want to work again and just wanted to fly around. He had the wherewithal to do that.'

So he did it. Flying gave Travolta the instant apotheoses he no longer received from the cinema. At 30,000 feet he could be a god, a hero or a cloud-borne nonentity. He could be a lover, claiming to have initiated Kelly into the Mile High Club. He could jet off on party dates or foreign trips or mercy missions.

He would think nothing, for example, of zooming off in his Gulfstream to rescue a godson involved in a train crash, as he did when his assistant Ron Zupanic and Ron's ten-month-old son John survived a derailment in South Carolina that killed seven and injured eighty. It was quite normal, too, to fly from Florida to California for the Superbowl, looping back in midflight on one occasion to collect the forgotten tickets.

Aeromania helped to assuage the deepening misery over his acting career. On screen little was working, even if cash, though not kudos, still flowed from *Look Who's Talking*.

'I was flying high as the man everyone wanted to know. I had offers you wouldn't believe and then, just as suddenly, I was yesterday's man. I am a reasonably calm person and I tried not to let things bother me. [But] the failures and criticisms hurt at the time more than I cared to admit. Everything I touched seemed to be criticised . . .

'I was afraid and confused in those days, but I wouldn't admit it. I tried to put on a brave face when really I was having ulcers because of all the pressure to make films that didn't exploit my image.'

Image? What image? Surely Travolta's singularity as a star was

that he *had* no fixed image? Even *Saturday Night Fever* and *Grease*, though both portraits of a dandefied-demotic adolescence, purveyed antithetical heroes: a sombre Bay Ridge misfit and a duck-quiffed, pinbrained pack leader. It was the protean Travolta more than a graven 'image' that would gain him his second, post-*Pulp Fiction* career. He was – he is – a human Rorschach test in whom audiences see their dreams, frailties, hopes or anxieties, see that part of them, perhaps, that never quite grows up.

They weren't seeing it in the early nineties, though. In the yuppyish west vulnerability and retarded maturity were off the menu. In his depths, a Travolta thrown upon video fodder like *Shout* and *Chains of Gold* more than once contemplated changing professions. 'I thought about becoming an airline captain after all. Acting was making me unhappy, whereas flying gave me so much pleasure. . . . I thought, "Wouldn't it be wild to give up acting and then be going, 'Hello, this is your captain, John Travolta'." '

Since flying imagery was built even into the language of his depression – 'Every day you're complimented and insulted, every day there are safe landings and crash landings' – it would have been a logical career swap. That he didn't make it may be due to the satisfaction he got from *private* flying and to his freedom from financial need. While *Look Who's Talking* paid the grocery bills, the continuing income from the *Fever* and *Grease* albums was enough to keep him in French Provincial aircraft hangars. Travolta later mocked the public perception of his oblivion years: 'There I was in, like, Atlanta, in some furnished apartment with a single lightbulb hanging over my head!'

He was more likely to be found – happy or unhappy – in a private lounge a mile above Earth. There he played host and family man, or flew friends off to Gstaad in Switzerland for a spend-all-you-like New Year as he did in 1990/1991.

'He invited thirty of us to the Palace Hotel and rented a big MGM Grand jet to fly us out there for a week,' says Jonathan Krane. Travolta's manager was with him when the actor revealed another reason behind the trip. 'He said, "I think I'm gonna propose to Kelly." I said, "Go for it." ' With Krane, one auspicious day, Travolta walked down a boutique-lined corridor in the hotel and spied a large yellow diamond ring, square-cut, six-carats.

'He bought it right there,' says Krane. 'It was New Year's Eve and I said, "Are you gonna do this tonight?" He said, "Ya, tonight." So at midnight we were sitting in the hotel watching some goofy floor show, the four of us, Kelly, John, me and my wife Sally Kellerman. The clock's striking and everyone's going, "Happy New Year!" And John turns to propose to Kelly and give her the ring. And right at that moment Sally reaches across the table and blurts out, "John, Happy New Year!" and stops him giving the ring. Only my wife could do that, totally stop the proceedings. I said, "Sally! He's *proposing* to her!" She said, "Oh my God," and backed off. And then finally John proposed and Kelly said yes.'

The year rolled happily on, reducing to innocuousness even the reviews for *Look Who's Talking Too*. Nearly everyone winced at this film, including those who made it. 'It was very rushed,' says director Amy Heckerling. 'There was no time to finesse a terrific story. It was "This is the day we're starting, this is the day it's released. Go out and do it." You think, "Eughh!" John was so good because all I could say was, "You wanna do some of *this* shtick or some of this?"'

Much of the shtick, says Heckerling, hit the cutting-room floor. 'There was a take-off on $8\frac{1}{2}$ where Kirstie thinks, "My husband is cute, all these women love him", and she starts to fantasise a Fellini movie with John as Mastroianni, all Italian accent and white suit. Looking back I could say, "Who'd get the reference except film school students?" But he was fabulous in it. There was wonderful footage taken out.'

Enough footage stayed in to showcase Travolta's gift for improvisation, even when prompted by panic shooting conditions. He deals debonair impressions of Popeye, Pee Wee Herman and Arnold Schwarzenegger, and dusts off his dancing pumps for a pastiche musical number to a Presley soundtrack. This scene's very untidiness lends it an idiot glee. 'It had to be planned as best we could, we only had a day and half,' shrugs Heckerling. 'We used a Louma crane, so everyone had to know where they were supposed to be at particular points, the children and toddlers as well as John. That's why it looks looser than it should, it was like doing traffic control.'

When *LWT2* opened, few critics thought the funny stuff coming

through the cracks made up for the collapsing edifice as a whole. A collective brave face was worn at the film's pizza-provisioned opening party at the Twenty/20 disco palace. A reporter asked co-star Roseanne Barr, who voiced Bruce Willis's newborn baby sister, what was the best thing in the movie. 'Me,' she said. Some celebrities hid behind slices of pizza, but Sally Kellerman enunciated her sense of identification with the film's parenting comedy. 'The pee-pee and poo-poo is what Jonathan and I go through twenty-four hours a day with our twins.' And Travolta himself was asked if the film gave *him* a longing for the sound of little feet? 'Yeah,' he smiled, giving Kelly a squeeze. 'We're working on it.'

They were. Conception occurred, Kelly testified, during a weekend at Bruce Willis and Demi Moore's house. 'We thought, "Why don't we just try?" And *boom*, first night, we got pregnant.' (Did some god with a sitcom writer's sense of humour think up the skewy congruity of John's baby being conceived in the home of the star who had voiced the *Look Who's Talking* infant?)

'I knew we'd get pregnant,' says Kelly, 'because we were talking about it and, you know, excited about it. The month before, I bought a little baseball outfit. I thought the baby might be a boy. But I also bought a dress. And a little book, like *365 Fun Things to Do With Your Child*. So we had pretty much planned for him to come.'

Another little book, of course, soon came into play, called *Dianetics*. For Scientology had strict and idiosyncratic ideas about pregnancy and childbirth, and Kelly Preston had now enrolled in the creed herself. 'She became one through knowing me,' says Travolta.

According to L. Ron Hubbard, there were dangerous examples of mother–child communication pre-birth. Silence was often better than sound, however tenderly the sounds were dispensed. Travolta explains, 'Even if the mother were to injure herself during pregnancy, she should keep quiet. She should keep quiet even if she sneezes.'

Just because an infant is in the womb does not mean it is safe from those scarring traumas known as engrams. L. Ron Hubbard himself writes in *Dianetics*, 'Birth can even be in sight and there may

still remain half a hundred severe pre-natal experiences.' Sneezing is only one of them. 'Mama sneezes, baby gets knocked unconscious. Mama runs lightly and blithely into a table and baby gets its head staved in. Mama has constipation and baby, in the anxious effort, gets squashed. Papa becomes passionate and baby has the sensation of being put into a running washing machine. Mama gets hysterical, baby gets an engram. Papa hits Mama, baby gets an engram. Junior bounces on Mama's lap, baby gets an engram. And so it goes.'

This makes it all the more alarming that key sequences of the *Look Who's Talking* films – *faute de mieux*, John Travolta's flagship movie statements at this time – feature him and Kirstie Alley bouncing all over Manhattan, talking nineteen to the dozen, while baby one or baby two sits helpless in the womb. What is the message in this disjunction between faith and fiction? That what is sauce for the gurus is not sauce for propaganda?

Of course the *Look Who's Talking* films, of which a third was already in the birth channel, can be coaxed another way towards the light. They can be seen as amiable, artfully midwived riffs on and *for* Dianetics. They are all about babies carrying on a fully responsive life inside and outside the womb. Scientologists would applaud the moment when an *in utero* Roseanne Barr, within pre-natal earshot of a pop song, complains, 'Oh now I'll never get that tune out of my head.' (Engrams as the stuff of knockabout comedy.) And in both the first two *LWT* movies there is a virtually direct hot-line between the humans 'out there' and the vigilant, articulate foetus inside.

But how seriously does Travolta *really* take this bizarre gospel and the ethical universe that comes with it? This question is prompted by another flurry of press attention preceding the Kelly Preston betrothal/pregnancy. In 1990 an actor and male model called Paul Barressi went public with claims that he and Travolta had enjoyed a homosexual affair in the early eighties. Barressi, who had a small role as a gym stud in *Perfect*, said the star had paid him for sex which they had enjoyed 'dozens of times' over two years.

The story prompted from Travolta a denial issued through his press representatives, though not a libel action. But it seems a good point at which to wonder what the actor's views on

homosexuality are or were. On one hand he has always seemed a hip baby-boom liberal, one of those 'Kennedy's children' who came of age in the sixties and swam in the ether of free love, free opinion and the freedom to swing any way sexually. He certainly did not blench when non-marital heterosexual romances were reported that involved him, even with women old enough to be his mother.

Yet gay love is a different matter, even in that land of millionaire gypsies called Hollywood. And homosexuality receives one of L. Ron Hubbard's most memorable effusions in *Dianetics*, though he orients the psychodramatic meltdown around the mother rather than the victim.

'The best previous explanation for [homosexuality] was something about girls becoming envious of Papa's penis or boys becoming upset about that terrible thing, the vulva, which Mama was incautious enough to show one day. It takes a great deal more than this utter tripe [sic] to make a pervert. It is, rather, something on the order of kicking a baby's head in, running over him with a steamroller, cutting him in half with a rusty knife, boiling him in Lysol, and all the while with crazy people screaming the most horrifying and unprintable things at him.'

By this we infer that Hubbard takes a broadly negative view of homosexuality. So was it by coincidence or design that the printing of the Barressi scuffle but was soon followed by the announcement of Travolta's engagement to Kelly Preston? Was he using the world's perception of propriety to camouflage something both the world and his own religion deemed improper?

Let us put Dianetics on hold and advance to September 1991. The sun is shining over Paris and it is time to allow John and Kelly their solemnisation. Every star enjoys a starry wedding and this one took place at midnight on Thursday September 5th at the Crillon Hotel near the Arc de Triomphe. The bride, two months pregnant, was squeezed inside a pearl-beaded mermaid wedding gown from Renee Strauss of Beverly Hills. An orange-blossom *couronne* graced her head. Travolta wore an elegant morning suit.

The hotel staff, though not told about the coming nuptials until four in the afternoon, prepared a three-tier wedding cake. And a Scientology minister was flown in from Florida to supervise the

ceremony. 'I was determined to marry according to these rites, because it's my religion,' said the groom.

Travolta ordered the small string ensemble to play 'Chabada-bada' from Lelouch's *Un Homme et une Femme* – 'my favourite French film' – and after vows had been exchanged, guests showered the couple with rose petals. By three in the morning, after friends and family had drifted away, John and Kelly felt free to order pizzas from the Champs Elysées.

The night of bliss was conducted in a bed whose headframe was upholstered in red plush set off by a border of gold beading. The next morning the couple breakfasted on the roof of the Plaza-Athenée Hotel, to the delight of *Paris Match* photographers. They snapped them at sea in an ocean of freshly baked croissants, jugs of orange juice, silver galligaskins of coffee, a red-ribboned basket of fruit and walnuts and an opulent flower arrangement. Sitting at the poppy-decorated white-and-red tablecloth, John wore a smile and a slate-grey sweater. Kelly wore a simple black dress.

So much largesse prompted the inevitable question from a country with a then Socialist President. Would John continue to give to charity as he had done while a bachelor?

'Yes. I used to make after-dinner speeches and thus collect money for orphans and alcoholics.'

Voilà. John and Kelly could now enjoy a brief honeymoon before addressing the serious business of finding work, escorting their baby through the hazards of seven more months in the womb, and buying and furnishing a new home.

John had a problem with the Spruce Creek, Florida, residence. Other home-owners disliked the noise from his Gulfstream G-2, which took off and landed almost as regularly as they started and stopped their cars. They wanted to sue him. Their lawyer Stephen Ponder said, 'It's a big, big plane. It looks like a commercial jet that seats thirty to forty people.'

The now married Travolta could snap back, 'When I was single a Lear Jet was fine, but now we have three times as much stuff.' And his wife saw the plane as a life-enhancement accessory. 'One evening at home in Florida John and I felt like dancing. We upped and decided to hop on the jet and fly to New York. In a few hours

we were boogeying in the Rainbow Room. Life just doesn't get any better than that.'

Unmoved, the residents' association began drafting retrospective legislation which would restrict aeroplanes to 12,500 pounds in weight: 'a question of safety and welfare for the community,' said Ponder. Travolta in response would hire a lawyer called Kermit Coble, who would argue that restrictions could not be introduced without a ninety percent approval vote by the home-owners.

But who *needed* all this? Surely it was better to move to a mansion on the sea in Penobscot Bay, Maine. Standing there already, all but giftwrapped for the Florida refugees and near the home of John's friend Kirstie Alley, was a fifteen-bedroomed pile with thirty-five acres of land. The small island town of Dark Harbor had a population of 700 and a store that opened only in summer. The price paid by Travolta for the house was $995,000.

As they pondered houses, Kelly approached the full term of her pregnancy. Finally delivered on April 13th 1992, weighing eight pounds twelve ounces, the baby boy was christened Jett. (It was John's choice; Kelly agreed to it only if there were two Ts.) But in picking that name, did the father build a curse, even an engram, into his family's immediate destiny? In a mere seven months Jett, John and Kelly would be involved, high above America's capital, in one of the most frightening incidents in the history of east-coast private aviation.

3

CLOUDS OF UNKNOWING

It was black and white and read all over. The story of John Travolta's night of fear in his Gulfstream 2 turbo-jet came to be recounted in every headline-hungry newspaper. Two miles above Washington on November 24th 1992, an aeroplane flying through bad weather at over 400 miles per hour, and containing one film star, one film star's wife, one baby, one co-pilot and four passengers, suffered an electrical emergency. The lights and instruments failed. So did several flight controls. So, finally, did the radio, though not before Travolta had put out a Mayday call to all three airports in the region.

Though the sky was thick with traffic during Thanksgiving week, Washington Dulles, Washington National and Baltimore all closed their runways to other planes. The Gulfstream, flying blind with only a flashlight and compass to aid the pilot, began to descend through dense cloud, aiming for National Airport. Travolta takes up the story.

'I was near Washington. There was intermittent light coming through the layer of weather, so you could see there was a big city below. But when we lost electric, we lost every system. We had a series of seven consecutive failures that were contagious.'

Ground control had learned already that the plane was in trouble. 'We reported it before the radio went out. We had three minutes left on back-up, which is the battery basically. It drained everything.'

The Gulfstream had to descend from 39,000 feet to 10,000 before finding a hole in the cloud. Then –

'I noticed the Washington Monument on my second turn around the area and I knew National Airport was near.'

Later reports suggested that Travolta emerged from the cloud at about 1,000 feet, the height of a tall skyscraper. Though he began his approach and prepared his passengers for an emergency landing, he had to adopt a greater than normal speed of 170 miles per hour to compensate for his inability to lower the flaps. When the plane hit the ground, four tyres burst immediately. The passengers, in brace position, had no idea if the Gulfstream would stop safely even now that it had landed. Finally, with Travolta using a nitrogen-charged emergency brake, the aircraft ground to a halt with no human injury.

He recalls, 'People came down from the offices at National to congratulate the pilot who brought that plane in safely, they had no idea it was John Travolta.'

Indeed not. Airport official Frank Walton commented, 'I spoke to the man who said he was the pilot of the plane several hours after the landing and he definitely wasn't John Travolta.' And a Federal Aviation Administration spokesman was later quoted as saying, 'We have no record of John Travolta being anywhere near Washington that night. Beyond that, I can't comment.'

Assuming that Travolta was on the plane – of which there seems no doubt since friends confirm he was flying his family from Florida to Maine to celebrate his seven-month-old son's first Thanksgiving – what are the mystery and identity confusions about?

Though the near-disaster came to be widely reported, this was despite rather than because of Travolta. Wreathed in reticence initially, the story was picked up only by reporters who noticed it in an American aviation newsletter sent to private subscribers. The fact that tower officials at National Airport were unaware that Travolta was on board the imperilled plane suggests that another name, possibly that of co-pilot John Messina, was used in air-to-ground communication.

Although Travolta had owned the twenty-two-year-old Gulf-stream for only nine months, having bought it in February 1992 from the International Brotherhood of Teamsters, there is no indication that inexperience or human error rather than mechanical failure caused the incident. Travolta held seven jet

licences at the time and had racked up an estimated 3,000 hours' flying time.

In a newspaper inquest conducted by the *Washington Post*, the source of the breakdown was said to be 'a small bearing in the turbo-jet's left electrical generator'. When this failed, the plane 'switched to a second generator on the right engine, but a resulting power surge tripped the circuit breaker, and the generator shut down.' Travolta and Messina then had to rely on two nickel cadmium batteries which would allow little more than five minutes' operational power. When one last energy source malfunctioned – the transformer rectifier – the two-man crew was left with its flashlight and compass, massaging the controls as the plane dipped towards the American capital.

Surely this is the stuff of heroism? It is Dean Martin in the cockpit in *Airport* or Karen Black, a Travolta friend and fellow Scientologist, squinting her way to salvation in *Airport 1975*. Yet the actor seemed determined to follow his flying blackout with a media blackout. All he would say when the tale first broke was that there had been an electrical problem and 'everyone was fine'. Only years later in a *Playboy* interview published in 1996, and the same year in a documentary for TV's Learning Channel, did he seem disposed to enjoy and exploit the incident's Boy's Own heroism.

Perhaps by then people would have forgotten, if they had ever known, another detail of the crisis: indeed an entire subplot.

On that November night a USAir passenger plane was directed by Washington air traffic control to help find Travolta's Gulfstream. 'I know it will be hard to see him,' radioed the controller to USAir Captain Jeff Hightower. 'He has no electrical system, so he won't be lit up.' Hightower later said, 'I remember thinking, "This is kinda stupid." I remember getting this uncomfortable feeling that I shouldn't be here. You want to help other people out, but he didn't have any lights . . . It's like driving into a head-on collision. It didn't make sense, you know? What were we going to do – lead these guys down through the clouds?'

In the event the two planes – or at least the USAir plane and one thought to be Travolta's – passed close by each other, narrowly averting disaster. Said an official safety report, 'The [two] aircraft

could have been at the same altitude, and consequently the threat of a mid-air collision was very real.' The controller who had sent USAir 1729 on its potential suicide mission was later reprimanded and reassigned.

Travolta's unwillingness to dwell on the incident may have reflected his embarrassment at it happening at all, although he could hardly be blamed for the expanded danger of involving a commercial passenger plane. Or perhaps there was another reason nearer home. Travolta was locked in legal combat at the time with the Spruce Creek residents. One of the home-owners' contentions was that Travolta's plane 'presented a safety hazard', and opposition to his aircraft intensified when they learned of his air-miss.

In the end he won the case, plus $60,000 in reimbursed legal fees. The attorney who opposed him, Stephen Ponder, admits today that it was fair and square, 'One of the restrictions when the Spruce Creek community was built was that you couldn't put any limitations on the use of the airport. So when the owners said, "Mr Travolta, your plane's too big," he and his lawyers simply said, "Wait a minute" and went back to the conditions recorded at the beginning of the [land] subdivision. The court ruled in his favour, and rather than spend eighteen years litigating we accepted the decision.'

The Spruce Creek set-to may or may not have influenced the actor's reticence about the Washington emergency. But for the Travolta portraitist, concerned with the myth as well as minutiae, there is a larger, more alluring speculation about the incident as a whole.

What if the Gulfstream 2 had gone down with all hands?

What if John Travolta had joined those stars who leave us in a blaze of tragedy, whether in the air like Carole Lombard and Leslie Howard or on the ground like James Dean and Jayne Mansfield?

While they died at the peak of their legend, Travolta would have been remembered as the man who wrote a fiery streak across the popculture sky with two musical movies, then vanished into night. Comeback biographies would not have been written; the history of Hollywood would not have been *re*written. And the

former superstar's death would have been an inside-page story in newspapers, with the obituarists girding up their solemnity for a brief farewell.

'Mr Travolta was once adjudged a gifted actor, a charismatic screen presence and one of popular music's most idolised solo performers since Mr Buddy Holly. He was nominated for an Oscar after his first leading film role. But he never quite fulfilled his early promise, becoming, many thought, a victim of fashion as he had once been its leader. At the time of Mr Travolta's death he was due to commence work on *Look Who's Talking 3*.'

Amy Heckerling, who had inserted a few pieces of wit into the earlier films' schmaltz and would vindicate her career entirely with *Clueless*, stayed out of the director's chair for the trequel, although she had penned a first script.

'I developed it with [writer-comedian] Paul Reiser. It's not that the studio didn't like it, but Kirstie Alley went for another screenplay they developed with Leslie Dixon. So I thought fine. I had nothing more to say about talking babies really. I was tired with the subject.'

The new writer, also feeling that infants were exhausted, went for lower but still loquacious life forms. She was encouraged by Jonathan Krane, again acting as producer.

'We thought a talking dog would work,' he says. 'Look at the pig in *Babe*. We didn't have the technology back in 1992, maybe. But the concept of a talking animal movie was still valid.'

Travolta once again dragged himself towards Vancouver. This film was directed by Tom Ropelewski and, seen today, combines an animal plot of maudlin imbecility with odd shards of referential Travolta mythology. While the two dogs adopted by Kirstie Alley's Mollie and Travolta's James perform their variants on *Lady and the Tramp*, and the human plot involves James in a near-amorous tangle with British actress Lysette Anthony (another player from the Joan Collins substitutes bench), the film throws forth like gleaming shrapnel little hints, invocations and premonitions of Travolta's own life.

The male dog is voiced by Danny DeVito who would soon play a starring role in his fellow Italian-American's career. The same

dog tells James's little son, 'You smell good, like cookies,' just as Travolta's angel will smell in *Michael*. The same little son is shown watching Mary Martin as Peter Pan on TV, in the very flying scene that inspired the young Travolta to leap off the third stair at 135 Morse Place. And Olympia Dukakis, playing Mollie's mother, says threateningly of the infatuated James, 'I know people who could have him audited.' (See Scientologyspeak.)

None of this subtext saved or helped the movie. *Look Who's Talking Now* was another descending line in the graph of Travolta's downfall. Much more of this and the line would be off the graph altogether.

He was reassured spiritually by two support systems. One was his extended metaphysical family, the brotherhood and sisterhood of Scientology, to which he devoted increasing time and energy. The other was his immediate family, now grown to three. He was a parent, with that delight at once universal and unique in discovering a new area of struggle and crisis. No reporter could enter the Travolta home without finding the couple eye-deep in child-care books.

' "Sometimes the plastic diapers have tape that's hard or rough, and the edges can scrape the baby's leg," ' the actor reads aloud one day for an interview. 'We found a little red mark on Jett,' he says, looking up, 'near where the tape was. So we had to cover that tape with some surgical tape. And we thought, "How many other babies are being hurt by this?" '

The reporter composes a look of interested concern. Kelly chimes in, 'They didn't think of the consumer – you know, the baby who's actually wearing it!'

Travolta jumps up and disappears into another room. He returns carrying a demonstration nappy. He stands and delivers a speech, with gestures, on the dangers of the disposable diaper. The reporter sits attentively.

Travolta then shares his thoughts for a book of rules about parenting.

'Number one. Try to stay in hospital for at least two days or more to recover and prepare for the new experience . . . We left hospital too soon. We should have stayed a second day, but we were anxious to get home.'

'We thought, "Oh, we've got our family now," ' interjects Kelly.

'We'll start our new life. Just be peaceful in a cosy home by our-selves. And the first couple of days were blissful, I admit. We were like, "Oh, three hours of sleep, isn't it wonderful? I can live on this." And then, by the fourth day, it was like delirium had set in.'

'Yeah,' says Travolta. 'I wasn't working. And we thought, "Why didn't anyone tell us, we could have afforded a nurse." '

The fatherly wisdoms wing on. (It is not talking babies the world should be wary of, the reporter reflects, it is talking parents.) 'I would love to have four or five children, the only problem is the multiplication of baggage . . . I called him Jett because I was crazy about aeroplanes since I was fifteen. If later he doesn't like it, he could always choose Jackson, his second name . . . Kelly breast-fed him without a precise timetable . . . We eventually got an English nurse called Diana.'

At this name the reporter, lost in dazed contemplation of the baby-blue upholstery and white metalwork of Jett's pram with matching blue-and-white wheel hubs, suddenly clicks back to attention. 'Diana.' 'Diana.' That name again.

Would it forever cross John Travolta's path? As if those earlier, contrasting encounters with Diana Hyland and Diana Princess of Wales did not suffice, here was a third trisyllabic muse. The reporter ponders the possible cross-reverberations between Lotusland stardom and Latin mythology. Then again – he notices a copy of L. Ron Hubbard's best-known work in the Travolta bookcase – it is a small step for lexical man from Diana to Dianetics. Was fate weaving these two kismets into one?

Travolta was now embarking on the advanced Hubbard Key to Life course at Celebrity Center International in Clearwater, Florida. He had also become a 'Clear' and an Operating Thetan III. Explains a Center newsletter: 'An Operating Thetan is knowing and willing cause over life, thought, matter, energy, space and time. Operating Thetan III designates one of the grades achieved on the route to full Operating Thetan.'

But Travolta was no longer just a student of Scientology, he was an evangelist. Soon after *Look Who's Talking Now* he went on a propagandist trip to England. Its purpose and parameters were explained in a question-and-answer feature in the Church of Scientology's *Celebrity* newsletter.

Q: You promoted Dianetics in radio programs, an *OK* magazine cover interview, visits to hospitals and schools and a speech to the United Publishers Association, correct?
A: That's correct.

Journalists, Travolta expanded, knew that his 'main intention and communication would be Dianetics.' He believes the mission was a success, he tells *Celebrity*, because 'simple and honest stories from the heart got the publishing industry excited about Dianetics.'

What, the actor is asked as the piece winds to its decorous close, are his ambitions?

'I guess my personal goal would be to affect as many creative people as I can and enlighten them on Dianetics.'

The main professional gain for him, he says, has been 'the ability to use the Scientology communication skills and really be there for a scene. I can become the character and deliver a product with less uncertainties and effort.'

Maybe too Scientology had found, through its own strange routes, a way to address the problem of Travolta's career crisis. In one of L. Ron Hubbard's more sustained flights of salvation-salesmanship he addresses the syndrome of the burnt-out performer, though his example is a child pianist rather than a post-adolescent movie star.

'The "child wonder" who early "burns out" is actually, via therapy, about as burned out as a banked furnace,' he writes in *Dianetics*. 'Any "child wonder" is a forced affair: think of the dreams Mama must have poured through his engrams.'

Early in his precocious career, 'The child is a great success – musical ear, practice and great "purpose". He gets this engram restimulated constantly by his mother. But then, one day, he loses a contest, he knows suddenly he is no longer a child, that he has failed. His purpose wavers. He ... is at last "neurotic" and "burned out".

'Cleared, he went back to being a pianist' – Hubbard suddenly and typically switches from speculation to supposed case history – 'not as an "adjusted" person but one of the

best-paid concert pianists in Hollywood [sic]. Music aligned with basic purpose.'

Travolta must have seen the resonances with his own life here: not least the ambitious mother forever stoking his engrams. Scientology may have helped him see that the obsession with success can be as damaging as the corrosive effects of failure.

Whether Dianetics aided him or not, there is a degree of truth in Krane and Travolta's protestations. The actor never really behaved like a burned-out star, even when he no longer blazed. He could seem happy even when everything good about his film career was in the past tense: illustrated by the weekend-long *Grease* reunion – dinners, cocktail parties – at Hollywood's Sheraton Universal at the end of 1992. John and Kelly were present along with Olivia Newton-John, Randal Kleiser, Jim Jacobs and others. The nostalgia industry had worked overtime: at each place-setting there was a brown lunchbag containing two plastic combs, one piece of Bazooka bubble-gum, a pack of candy cigarettes, one condom and a pair of paper sunglasses adorned with palm trees. The guests talked on every *Grease*-related topic, though on some more enthusiastically than others. *Grease 2*, noted an eavesdropper, 'was spoken of only in the hushed tones usually reserved for an axe murderer in the family'.

When not spreading cheer at commemoration parties, making rare films, or promoting the gospel according to St Ron, Travolta lived the placid life of a man whose agent barely if ever rang but whose bank account is hardly empty. One can almost hear the flip-flop of the retirement slippers, the crackle of the Sunday papers.

'I sleep until noon. Usually I go to bed around four or five in the morning, because that's the way I've always been, since I was five years old. It's the theatre background which I never quite got over. I'm better than I used to be – I used to get up at three. Then I spend two hours with Jett, and then I usually have some appointment to go to. When I come back, I see him off to sleep, and that's kind of how it goes. The truth is, I'm not lazy. I work as hard as anyone else. I do like free

time, but I think it's always a balance of things. I go to jet school, once a year, and I go to Scientology classes almost every night.'

He had narrowly lost what might have been his last lifeline to movie stardom: the lead role in Robert Altman's *The Player*. 'Robert called me and said, "John, you know you can do this part easily. I just don't want you to tip it." When I saw the movie, I knew what he meant.' Having told Travolta that the part was between him and Tim Robbins, the director gave it to Robbins. The younger star, presumably, wouldn't 'tip' the leading role of a murdering movie executive towards something too charismatic and sympathetic. *The Player* went on to give Altman, another fallen idol of the seventies, his nineties comeback. Travolta would have to wait a little longer.

He couldn't help a twinge of despair, with or without Scientology's moral support. 'I started to lose confidence in my career. Not in my *talents* but in my career. I was thinking, maybe it's all over. Maybe I have to face the fact that for whatever reasons, this doesn't work as far as film is concerned any more.'

The ghosts of a busier past swirled around him like Richard III's haunting crew before the Battle of Bosworth. 'There was a moment when I was working on the third *Look Who's Talking* – I was lucky to get that job and it paid well. But I thought, "Uh-oh. Altman isn't bailing me out yet. Truffaut is dead. Pauline Kael is not reviewing anymore. Okay, what do we do here, guys?" '

We read another inauspicious script that arrives at our trailer.

We open the big brown envelope with weary hands.

We look at a two-word title above an unheard-of director's name. It seems to spell out, once again, straight-to-video.

Pulp Fiction

by Quentin Tarantino

PART THREE

PRELUDE

LOST AND FOUND IN HOLLYWOOD

The visitor to Hollywood has a wide choice of maps, none of which tells him anything.

It is true that he can locate famous epicenters like 'Hollywood and Vine' or Paramount Studios or the intersection of Sunset and Gower, where the cowboy extras used to hang out waiting for work, or the Directors Guild of America, a brick-and-dark-glass building shaped like Darth Vader's helmet, where every evening in December and January the glittering are swallowed up by Oscar previews.

But how does he find his way, especially if he is a biographer, around those tortured hills and valleys called the Hollywood mind?

Researching a book about a living star is a combination of jungle exploration and guerrilla warfare. You communicate with friends or enemies – impossible to tell the difference early on – either by fax, the electronic equivalent of a flare shot into the sky, or by tapping out hopeful sound-messages on your hotel phone, the biographer's answer to Mau-mau drums.

Hollywood helps the movie writer in this respect: nearly all the stars' personal publicists have unforgettable names. The A-to-Z of contact folk, mostly women, goes straight into your head and stays there. From Spooky Stevens to Desirée Jelleratte to Bumble Ward (all real), they have emerged from some lost Lewis Carroll novella. And like drones around the queen bee their more simply named male assistants – Chris, Steve or Bob – listen to your overtures

and then turn to the offstage silence to see if Spooky, Desirée or Bumble is available. She isn't. Or not until your fourth or fifth call, at which point she might be 'conferenced in'. Then she will say like an old friend, 'Hi, Nigel! How you doing? How long are you in Hollywood?' And after my answer: 'Oh that's a shame. Because, do you know, Randal or Olivia or Quentin has *just* left town?'

No friends could believe, when I told them, that I spent my entire first morning in Hollywood making telephone calls – four hours, non-stop – and ended up with one appointment, with someone I did not want to interview.

Slowly, over days, the picture improves. You return to your room from pacing the hotel courtyard and the red message light is flashing. The poet's delight at a rainbow holds no measure to your leaping heart. Might there be two, four, half a dozen call-backs? Excitedly you press the message button.

'Hello. Welcome to the Hyatt Regency message service. You have one unplayed call. "Hi, Nigel, this is Sparky Van Windmill returning your call regarding Debra Winger/Jamie Lee Curtis/Nicolas Cage. They say they would love to talk to you for your book but won't be back in Hollywood/California/America until after you have gone. Do give me a call to let me know when you are going. Bye." '

Then comes a day when lightning strikes from a clear sky, twice. Having fluked a connection with Karen Lynn Gorney, the *Saturday Night Fever* actress, I was in mid-phone conversation with her when my incoming-call light flashed. I asked Miss Gorney to hold and pressed line two.

'Hello,' said a strong, urgent male voice. 'Is this Nigel Andrews? This is Jonathan Krane, John Travolta's manager . . .'

In mental disarray, I asked Travolta's manager to wait for my return call. I finished with the lively, acerbic Miss Gorney and then re-contacted Krane.

He sounded aggrieved that I hadn't tried to call him before while in LA. I said that my best efforts had failed to locate a number for him, which was true. He asked with an audible frown what kind of book I was writing: 'It's not an exposé, is it?' I mentally scanned the possible responses to this, before choosing calm-and-reassuring. 'No,' I said, as if implying 'What is there to expose?' Then I explained in words put together at the moment,

words I barely understood myself, my aim in the book. I spoke of sociological undercurrents and cultural flashpoints and may even have mentioned zeitgeists. I added that to me John Travolta was the best actor in Hollywood, possibly the universe, and that a serious, enthusiast's book, not another paste-and-scissors exercise of which there were already far too many (for my comfort), was what was now needed.

By the end of the call I believe that Krane believed me. More unnervingly, I began to believe myself. As many modern authors and novelists have claimed, from Bellow to Vonnegut, we become what we pretend. And as actors know, you must plug yourself into the self-persuasion power supply in order to persuade the audience. You must think you *are* Richard III or Hamlet or Tony Manero or Vincent Vega, at least for the duration of the scene or take.

So when I was with interviewees in LA, through those topsy-turvy weeks I 'was' the uncritical Travolta devotee. I laughed to hear of his impersonations, tutted over his troubles, gasped at tales of his inventiveness as an actor.

It went further than moments, or hours, of self-convinced imposture. As I found two years ago when researching my last subject, Arnold Schwarzenegger, an *amour fou* comes over the biographer. It is not that the subject can do no wrong. It is that both his wrongs and rights become absorbing, resonant, fabular, representative of humanity at large. It is as if one knows him as well as oneself. The John Travolta biographer gets up each morning, looks in the shaving mirror and sees – John Travolta.

Against the danger of infatuation or identification, one tries to erect a battlement of cold strategy. I said to myself that on this first research visit I would be Mr Nice Guy and ask no questions about Scientology, while keeping some serious queries on hold for a second visit. If a comment on the cult was volunteered during a conversation, my expression would say, 'Scientology? What is that?'

I did, though, allow myself a visit to the Hubbard Museum of Life on Hollywood Boulevard. I knew nothing about this repository of wisdom except that it was there, since I had driven past it almost every day on the way to some inquisition victim. It was a big imposing building with a big imposing sign.

On that Sunday afternoon I entered the lobby, its far wall adorned with plaques memorialising the words of the famous including Tom Cruise, singer Chick Corea, soprano Julia Migenes-Johnson and yes, John Travolta. And I paid my $5 admission to a woman I had not seen when I entered, since her honey-beige suit melted into the honey-beige desk she sat behind.

I first smelled danger when I was asked my name. Only a fellow Hollywood biographer could understand the mental alarm bell this set off. The delicate knitwork of early contacts I had created could be unravelled in a moment, so sensitive is Hollywood to bad-news biographers. For all I knew – and paranoia thrives on ignorance – there was a daily e-mail service between the Scientology Foundation and the John Travolta offices, tipping the wink about snoopy writers, especially with suspicious foreign accents.

'I'm just a tourist from London, England,' I said, 'here to see your exhibition.' It was like a line from a bad film.

A door opened silently and disgorged a small, spidery woman with silver hair and a black dress. 'I'm Millie,' she said (not actual name), smiling graciously and extending a hand. Pause. 'And you are?'

I smiled nervously. 'I'm just a tourist from London, England, here to see your exhibition.'

A quick, silent look was exchanged between Miss Black and Miss Beige. Then a third woman, dressed in scarlet, came out of another door, passed by the reception desk and exchanged either a look or an inaudible word with Miss Beige. Then she passed out of the building.

'Would you like to leave your jacket?' asked Miss Black.

'No,' I said hastily. (It contained vital identification documents.) She paused, turned around, indicating imminent return, and left the lobby.

Miss Beige said, 'If you are from the media, perhaps you would like the two-hour tour?'

'I'm not from the media,' I said, wondering if I was technically lying.

By now I was into the early stages of panic. I imagined concealed surveillance cameras recording my every move – not so improbable, given the litigious vigilance of the Hubbard empire – and that the

pictures would be APB'd across Hollywood. By sundown Jonathan Krane, whom I was due to see the next day, would have my likeness on his desk and would know that this Englishman who rattled on about zeitgeists was actually a dirt-digger like all the rest.

'I think I'd better feed my traffic meter,' I said to Miss Beige, who gave a look of polite surprise.

'If you are in a hurry, you could have the twenty-minute tour.'

'No, I'll just put a coin in and come back.'

I fled. Driving back to my hotel, I realised I had done two irrecoverable things. Looking down at my T-shirt, I discovered I had put on that morning a garment emblazoned with the Venice Film Festival logo: so much for 'I'm not from the media'. Secondly, I realised that I had contributed five dollars, never to be retrieved, to the cause of Scientology.

The next day I sat in Jonathan Krane's rambling, tree-girt bungalow off Mulholland Drive, reaching a mutual accord about the greatness of John Travolta as human being and actor. I liked Krane. He seemed capable of being a scoundrel, as all managers should be, but he had taken a leap of courage in seeing me at all, let alone in talking to me for over an hour about John's life, career, marriage, dreams.

How did he know I would not traduce him and all his words? Why, before and after we met, did he allow – for he had the power to disallow – so many directors and actors who had worked with his client to talk to me? Was he overwhelmed, in Anglophile America, by the Englishness of my credentials?

Perhaps he took my air of foreign incredulity – one I always wear in Hollywood since it is genuine – for wonderment at his client. And he was partly right. Travolta is fascinating not just as Travolta but as a representative, one of the greatest living representatives, of a phenomenon that no one can ever quite plumb.

Superstardom.

Being a superstar is the art of the impossible. No human being is special enough to be that famous and adored, let alone to generate that much wealth merely by walking from one chalkmark to the next. Wealth for himself, for his movies, for his casts and crews, for his agent, for his manager, for his support system, for his family, even perhaps (it will go to charity) for his biographer.

As Krane said, Travolta today is '$60 million dollar a year industry.'

So what is the marvellous force that turns a humbly born New Jerseyite with a mind no better, possibly worse, than most of us, into something supernormal, supernoval? And by what access to miraculous powers does a man who loses that hotline to the impossible, during a blackout in his career, then rediscover it: thus making the impossible doubly impossible?

Time to ponder the marvel of *Pulp Fiction*.

1

F FOR FLAKE

Actor-director-producer Danny DeVito is sitting in London's Dorchester Hotel. While his feet barely touch the ground, his brain and voice are approaching lift-off. He is telling me how in the early to middle nineties a new page was turned in modern cinema and his own company did the turning.

'My partner in the production company we set up, Jersey Films, said one day, read this screenplay. I read this script which was called *Reservoir Dogs*. It was terrific, fresh, bizarre. And I said, "Who is this guy?" "Someone called Quentin Tarantino and he's making the film already, a real low-budget movie." I said, "Lemme meet the guy."

'He walks in. I say, "Quentin, hey, what's going on! This is a great script!" He starts rattling on, he talks faster than I do, he leaves Marty Scorsese in the dust. I say, "Look, I wanna be in business with you, 'cos I really think you got a passion for what you do, so what you got next?" He says, "I got this movie in my head about intertwining tales." I said, "Let's make a deal. I wanna make your next movie at Jersey Films." Bingo! He says, "Okay." And I do a deal with TriStar for the script.'

Then, for a while, Tarantino dropped off the atlas. He vanished from Hollywood, from America, from the known English-speaking world. His movements could be charted only as a small red blip on the world's film festival map. 'He goes to every goddam festival on Earth,' says DeVito. For at this time *Reservoir Dogs* was becoming the toast of Europe, Asia, the Far East, moving in on

Fiji and Yucatan. And Tarantino made sure he was always there to answer the toast.

The film-maker was that dangerous form of gypsy, someone who spoke and moved at the same time and did both at mach-2. Tarantino was born, like Travolta and DeVito, into an Italian-American family, with no prospects or talents save his own giddy chutzpah. Leaving school, he worked in a video store, where he watched a lot of bad movies made in English and good ones made in foreign languages. (Godard was a favourite.) By an accident of nature, even Tarantino's looks labelled him 'video geek'. The large expanse of forehead and chin framed closely packed features, as if their owner spent every sleepless night staring at tiny rectangles.

Tarantino met a producer at a party with enough money to finance a violent, colourfully scripted heist thriller, loosely based on a Hong Kong film called *City on Fire* known only to video geeks. *Reservoir Dogs*, full of spendthrift wit, structural ingenuity and Jacobean bloodletting, was born. So were Tarantino's credo and signature: 'I don't make movies that bring people together. I make movies that split people apart.' Demand for the film outstripped expectation; prints multiplied; the litter of infamy spread across the world.

Tarantino used the free travel pass of fame to find quiet spots, from Amsterdam to Cannes, to work on *Pulp Fiction*. ('We kept calling him in places I didn't even know the name of,' DeVito raps.) This new film would take structural ideas from Mario Bava's 1963 Gothic-horror compendium *Black Sabbath*, applying them to a gangster idiom and milieu inspired by writers like Elmore Leonard and Charles Willeford. Tarantino also bought, and blended in, a script by his friend Roger Avary for a shorter film called *Pandemonium Reigns*.

'It was the chance to do three movies for the price of one,' the director says. 'The idea was to take the oldest situations in the book: the boxer who's supposed to throw a fight and doesn't, the mob guy who's supposed to take the boss's wife out for the evening. The third story, *The Wolf* [called *The Bonnie Situation* in the script] is basically the first five minutes of every Joel Silver movie: two men come in and kill these guys and then they cut to

Arnold Schwarzenegger a hundred miles away and eventually the two stories converge.

'I really liked the idea that all these characters would be the stars of their own movie, and as far as I'm concerned they are.'

Back in Hollywood, Danny DeVito waited for the manuscript.

'Finally, about a year later,' he says, 'we had a 158 page screenplay. I get the script. I'm at my house with my wife Rhea [Perlman, the actress/barmaid from TV's *Cheers*]. And there's no cover note, it just says, "*Pulp Fiction* by Quentin Tarantino. Final draft." That's the guy!

'I sit down, read the script. I'm laughing my head off. It's the most bizarre thing I've read. I say to Rhea, "Either I'm the sickest guy around or this is really funny stuff." '

There remained the formality of taking it to TriStar for the final lick of wax. But DeVito received a surprise.

'They say they won't make it.' [Pause to convey incredulity.] 'I say, "What? It's gonna cost just $9 million and you're not gonna make it? What am I doin' here?"

'I stood on the guy's desk at TriStar and said, "You *gotta* make this movie!" I was ballistic. I was like a pitbull I was so upset. They said they'd just got back from some meeting in Washington and all the senators were talking about violence. I said, "You're a studio that's got *Cliffhanger* out now! Whaddaya talkin' to me about violence??" '

DeVito stamped out, crossed the country to New York and did a deal with Miramax. This was the mini-major that by 1997 would be awash with Oscars for *The English Patient*. Then he and Tarantino set about casting their multi-character gangster opera. Early names for the plum role of Vincent Vega, drug dealer, heroin addict and hired assassin, included Daniel Day-Lewis and Michael Madsen, whose ear-slicing prowess had been a highlight of *Reservoir Dogs* (in which he played a character called Victor Vega). When those two options fell away Tarantino suggested an old screen favourite of his, John Travolta. DeVito blanched, then bit the bullet. 'I told Quentin I was gonna do the film, so I had to put my money where my mouth was. You gotta protect your director. When someone says they want John Travolta, who's cold as a fish at the box office, whaddaya do?'

Tarantino knew that Travolta was cold at the box office.

'The whole teenybopper-slash-disco stigma weighed John's career down tremendously,' he says. 'Even if you did like him, at a certain point in the eighties you couldn't admit to it. Because you weren't just talking about an actor, you were talking about a figurehead for something that was despised, disco.

'Miramax would do these little office polls where they would ask the secretaries, "What do you think of John Travolta?" And they'd say, "Him? Oohh, YUCK!!" I was just holding onto my Pauline Kael reviews and saying, "Fuck all you guys! Did you read the reviews for *Blow Out*?" '

Tarantino had already wooed Travolta with a lunch invitation, transmitted through Jonathan Krane. Says Krane, 'I didn't know about Quentin's love for John until he contacted me about working together and told me about it. But he was *passionate* about John. It was really overwhelming.'

Tarantino hadn't made up his mind to offer the *Pulp Fiction* role when he lunched the actor. At the time he was weighing him as a possible co-lead in a smaller project, the horror western *From Dusk Till Dawn*.

When the actor went along to the director's home on One Hundred South Doheny Drive, the address rang a bell before he did. Travolta realised that the man of destiny proposed for his career lived in his own former building.

'I thought, "Wouldn't it be amazing if he were in the same *apartment*. When I got up there, I knocked on his door and said to him, "Before you say anything, let me tell you something about the apartment you live in. You have a maroon and pink tile in your bathroom. Your refrigerator is on the north wall. You have an oddly designed window in the bedroom." I named about a half-dozen things. He went nuts! He said, "How do you know that?" I said, "I used to live here. I was cast in *Carrie* and *Welcome Back Kotter* in this very apartment!" '

After a short drink they crossed the road for lunch at the Four Seasons Hotel. Here they were interrupted by a table-surfing Emma Thompson. She introduced herself to John as a fan and told Quentin, 'Put this man in one of your movies. He needs a good movie.' The two men returned to spend the rest of the day playing

fifteen-year-old John Travolta board games, including 'Welcome Back Kotter', 'Saturday Night Fever' and 'Grease'.

'I said to Quentin, "Let's complete the fantasy. Do you want to compete with Barbarino or Danny Zuko or Tony Manero? I can do that for you." He said, "No, no. I'd like you to play as John Travolta. But if at any time you want to drop into character and say a *line*, that would be really cool." '

The day was not all nostalgia. Tarantino thought Travolta was overdue for a career lecture. The director loved the fallen star's old movies, except the *Look Who's Talking* series which he couldn't watch. But he told Travolta that there was no point in his just sitting around being 'fallen'.

'What did you *do*?' Tarantino expostulated. 'Don't you remember what Pauline Kael said about you, what *Truffaut* said about you? Don't you know what you *mean* to the American cinema? John, what did you do?'

Travolta took it in and took his leave. 'I went out of there with my tail between my legs. I was devastated.' The man who had survived eight years of pariah status was still the boy who never quite understood why he was a star in the first place. So managers and movie-makers – those who could make or unmake the miracle – were like father figures or schoolteachers. They had only to hand him a formulation and he accepted it. Tarantino, like Bob Le Mond ('old silver tongue') or Jonathan Krane, was one of life's hustlers. If you weren't persuaded by what he said, you could still be overpowered by the way he said it.

Soon the new movie offer reached the star's manager. 'I had no idea at that point that *Pulp Fiction* would be a commercial success,' says Krane, 'but I knew from *Reservoir Dogs* it would be artistically interesting. My thinking was that John's *own* thinking would be that it was too violent. Playing a heroin-addicted hit man was not something he'd normally jump at. But I remember saying, "You've played all the good guys. This is like a bad guy with a heart of gold. You're a *sweet* bad guy. It's a unique role." '

Travolta took several looks at the *Pulp Fiction* script, including some despairing ones. 'I was saying to Quentin, "No, I'll do *Look Who's Talking Four* instead. In which the *chairs* talk." '

He finally decided in favour. 'I wanted to show I can do more

than play safe, pretty-boy roles. This movie had it all . . . I realised the only way for me to have a second chance as an actor was to do something shocking, something that people wouldn't expect from me. No one expects to see me killing someone and getting covered with blood. The public still thinks I'm somewhere out there on the disco floor.'

He signed on for a pocket-money fee of $145,000 of which he would spend on paying for his family to be with him during filming.

This was a chance to star in a cutting-edge movie that might cut him free from the trussed state of his own acting career. Meanwhile he used the sharp edge of his intellect to re-hew the perspective in which this violent low-life character might be seen – this man who kills, takes drugs and dies in a bathroom after being blasted by a machine-gun.

'I said, either this is going to be the best move of my career or the worst, because I have never seen an actor filmed on a toilet, especially someone who's supposedly a superstar.' Vincent also has 'the unfortunate quality of being a charming criminal. Personally I want to see a criminal coming. I don't want to be charmed by him. I think the most dangerous criminals in the world were charming.' He cited Dillinger and might also have cited Bonnie and Clyde, the folk-heroes of his early fancy-dress photograph.

Then, too, what about his own church's response to Travolta's role choice? All those Hubbardites were not going to jump up and down saying, 'Yes, John, you *must* work for the violent Tarantino, with his foul-mouthed dialogue, post-modern punch-ups and torture scenes.'

The actor pulled out all sophistical stops.

'The particular character I am playing,' he told *Celebrity*, the Scientology newsletter, 'is a hitman and a heroin addict. He is stuck in a moral code that he thinks is a survival way of life and that's just where he's at. It is a very anti-drug, anti-crime story. You see the demise of all the characters, it doesn't glamorise drugs and it doesn't glamorise crime. It shows the brutality and crudeness of it all.'

Does it? Surely the profane spell of *Pulp Fiction* is that it enjoys the brutality and crudeness: that it makes them playful and hilarious

even in their monstrosity. This may be a form of ironic distancing, but hardly of high moral disapproval.

Tarantino's casting of Travolta underscores the ludic quality. To play the movie's most delinquent character, who better than the toyboy actor who strutted like a consumer icon through the seventies before slamming, with all clockwork whirring, into the unfriendly wall of the eighties. 'We were sitting here talking,' the film-maker remembers of that Doheny Drive day, 'and I thought, "God, this is a really good idea – casting him as Vincent. What a way to go." '

Sensitivity, even innocence, to play brutishness. Tarantino believed that as an actor Travolta was 'right up there with Montgomery Clift . . . With John, you absolutely don't know what you're gonna get. By putting him close to the centre of *Pulp*, his weird persona throws a whole other colour on to the movie.'

At the same time, a sensitive actor at a sensitive career point needed careful handling.

'I love directors who are actors, especially if they can actually act,' Travolta said. 'If there was ever a line that I didn't agree with, or didn't like, I could say, "You do it." . . . Everyone else treated that script like it was the Bible. I didn't feel that way. I added a line here and there, or even a word or two, which changed the whole tone of my character.

'The reason Quentin and I get along so well together is that he says to me, "I didn't hire you for the Al Pacino speeches. You're about the moments that surprise me, like the way you say 'pork-chop steaks'." '

Sometimes, though, Travolta was too finicky, too volatile, even for a patient Tarantino. The film-maker recalls one difficult day.

'It was a really, really long take, a ton of dialogue, a big camera move, and I was only shooting it in one take. And a couple of different times, right towards the end of the take, John would skip a word and then he'd cut it, say, "Stop, I screwed up." And I would go: "John, don't cut it, man, you know we've done the whole scene and I might like the stumble but I can't use it if you just stop it." We were getting a little tense.

'And then he did one take that was absolutely terrific and I was

like, "John! Great! Wonderful! Excellent! Let's do a few more like that!" So he goes and does another one and it's even better than the last. And then he turned to me and said, "You see what effect love has on me?" He couldn't even function when he thought I was mad at him.'

Samuel L. Jackson, cast as fellow hitman Jules, remembers Tarantino's fondness for long, long takes. 'We rehearsed every day for two and a half weeks before shooting, on a big soundstage at Danny DeVito's production company. Quentin had mapped out that hallway walk that John and I take going to the killing room. He taped the floor so we'd hit exact marks when we have that conversation about the foot massage and Marcellus's wife. Then we'd sit in two chairs in the middle of the floor to do the car conversation, the "Royale with Cheese".'

This scene virtually defined Tarantino-ism: the elevation of trivia to life-and-death resonance, often accompanied by the relegation of life and death to trivia or serendipity. Tarantino movies blur the point at which a consumer society merges with a self-consuming one. They say: There is no demarcation point between a car where people shoot the breeze about junk food and a car where people shoot the brains out of junk dealers – except in the mind of the privileged beholder with time and space to moralise. (Note too the rhyme between hamburger meat as conversation topic and human brain matter as interior decor.) Where *Reservoir Dogs* shocked audiences with its casual horror, *Pulp Fiction* shocks them, or rearranges *their* brains, through casual comedy.

Travolta used his acting instincts to make it more casual still. In the scene of the accidental shooting he invented the character's quick self-excuse and look of covered-up panic.

'As it was written, there was more of a dramatic reaction to [the death] . . . If I had to do something that gross and not expect the audience to get grossed out and leave the theatre, I had to put a twist on it. So I thought, the nature of man is to lessen the bad things he does. He shoots this guy's head off and it's like, "I shot Marvin in the face," like it was nothing. And add to it, "You must have hit a bump or something." It was so clear there was no bump! Sam Jackson says, "I didn't hit no bump." '

Jackson says Tarantino approved the idea of making the scene funnier. 'I've talked to more and more people about that scene and they were disturbed by the fact they laughed at it. This kid's head gets blown off and all of a sudden they realise, "Oh my god, I'm laughing."

'But Quentin knew what he was doing. I think he did it because of what happened when the guy's ear is cut off in *Reservoir Dogs*. I was at the first screening of that at the Sundance Festival and there were all these auteurs running up the aisles saying, "Oh this is sick!" and I was going, "This is pretty amazing stuff this guy is doing." Quentin wrote the *Pulp Fiction* scene to show how complex our response to violence is. You can enjoy it in a real and funny way, then realise what you're laughing at, and *still* not be able to stop laughing.'

The moment is also true to the Laurel-and-Hardy relationship between Travolta's Vincent and Jackson's Jules: one a bubblebrain with a gift for mishap, the other a long-suffering mentor trying to be businesslike. The relationship was echoed off-screen. Though Jackson didn't subscribe to has-been assessments of Travolta – 'He was working all the time: *Look Who's Talking*, *Look Who's Talkin' Now*, *Look Who's Talkin' S'More*; you don't make three of something that's not making money' – he saw his own role in the production as that of a friendly encourager: the new star shepherding the out-of-practice one, just as the tightly packed Jules watches over the unwrapped Vincent.

'Vincent's a flake,' Jackson says. 'That's why he dies. He drifts. And it's Jules's job to keep him focused. Vincent's been gone for a while, though they were partners before. And Jules knows you've got to keep him on a tight rein and yank his chain sometimes.'

Travolta's most endearing scene of mental and physical *déshabille* is the one he shares with Jackson and Tarantino. The corpse-splashed car fetches up at the home of a minor mobster played by the director. While Jackson takes the older brother role, shielding Travolta as best he can from Tarantino's sarcastic stream of political incorrectness – 'Did you see a sign that said "Dead nigger storage"?' – Travolta plays along with every demand, up to and including stripping down to clean the car. The actor's naked bulk is a frightening sight for any filmgoer who hadn't tuned in to a Travolta disrobing since *Staying*

Alive. It was obvious, at last and at length, that this Adonis had been spending much of his away-decade at the doughnuts.

Travolta's other major scenes were with Uma Thurman, playing the gangster's moll he squires to a movie-themed dinner before taking her home, where she passes out from a heroin overdose. What follows is queasily uproarious: a frightmare for anyone who has ever trembled at a hypodermic needle, which means most of us. The adrenaline-filled instrument is plunged into the heroine's breastbone after enough tension-building anxiety to dampen the palms of everyone in the cinema.

It is high gothic as low comedy, with Travolta's gangland escort resembling a walking-dead Richard III: a look perfectly complemented by Uma Thurman, all junior-Mata Hari hair and dazed, ethereal prettiness. This Sleeping Beauty is aroused from her drug coma by a beast who thinks he's the Prince. Travolta's greasy black rat-tails frame a face of deathmask pallor, while the single gold earring completes the vision of a figure from some poignant *age d'or* of debauchery. At the same time, the actor pumps innocence into the role as if Vincent Vega is redeemed by his stupidity, which to a degree he is.

This is a man bathed in idiot self-congratulation. In Jack Rabbit Slim's Diner he accompanies his threadbare small talk with little shoulder-jiggers of mirth, as if Thurman should be *so* lucky to have a companion of his easy wit. And when she tells him how comfortable she is being silent when she is with the right man – a remark any normal beau-for-the-night would take as a hint to shut up – he construes it as a seduction move and convulses himself with giggly suavity: 'Don't think we're quite there yet, but don't feel bad about it, we've only just met each other!'

When they take to the dance floor, it is *Saturday Night Fever* with drug aggravation. 'That scene gave me a new opportunity,' says Travolta. 'I was on heroin. I had a little gut. I was like in another zone . . .' He pillaged his memory for forgotten dances. 'Quentin only wanted the Twist at first. And I said: "Quentin, I grew up with some dances you're not familiar with. I'm forty and Vincent's forty. When I was a kid in the sixties we did the Swim, we did the Batman . . . We did the Hitchhiker and the Mashed Potato." And I said, "Vincent would have grown up on those dances." '

The scene becomes a medley of bygone novelty jigs, performed by two underworlders who give more the impression of being underwater. Just before the dance, Thurman has been to powder her nose – an old politeness restored to new-age literalness – and Travolta has been on a week-long heroin jag. They gyrate with a goofy, aquarian grace in an idyll of forbidden romance, a caricature of courtly love between a knight seriously errant and an unattainable lady. It is *Pulp Fiction*'s love scene and Travolta's tenderest, funniest hour.

Pulp Fiction premiered at the Cannes Film Festival in May 1995, where the crowded press preview began with a bruising cattle-rush up the Palais des Festival's steps. On the night of the official showing, emotion was high. In America Tarantino had already set the tone for the movie by addressing test-preview audiences with, 'Give me a show of hands who liked *The Remains of the Day*? Get the fuck out of this theatre.'

Samuel L. Jackson remembers, 'I was sitting there watching the film in Cannes, and I didn't realise it had subtitles till about half way through, 'cos I was watching the pictures. Then I looked down and saw, oh they're doing this in French. But the audience was reacting to the whole film, and that's when I realised this is gonna work, 'cos these people are "reading" this film and still getting it. That's when I knew it was something special. By the time it was over, I was so proud I was literally brought to tears. I was crying.'

It was infectious. At the Cannes press conference, when Travolta was lavished with flattering remarks about his comeback, he disappeared for a moment behind a room-divider. 'I went behind this screen, and I lost it. Somebody was giving me back this credit that I once thought would always be there, but that most people had forgotten. It made me cry.'

As well as crying, everyone was laughing. 'My Dad's eighty-two,' said Travolta, 'and he thought the scene blowing that guy's head off was the funniest thing he's ever seen.'

Down there on the Cote d'Azur, surrounded by giggling former executioner-critics who in a previous age had escorted to the block honourable movies about violence like *The Wild Bunch*, *Straw Dogs* and *A Clockwork Orange*, and who now cooed in unison at

every frame of *Pulp Fiction*, this critic wondered – he worried over – he still worries over – how much the film was a kind of narcotic itself. In a moment of excess contrariness, I took on the role of the negligent ex-Jeremiahs myself, posting a hostile review from Cannes and then expanding it when the film opened in London.

I overreacted to the film's violence and felt I had overreacted. I later performed the *mea culpa* of mopping up, in essays and interviews, those more venturesome aspects of the film which I had left unattended.

I still believe, though, that there are questions to be asked and answered about Tarantino's use of violence. (Is it really more salutary and enlightened to giggle at death and brutality than to gasp at it?) And I'd argue that the durable originality of *Pulp Fiction* lies not in its offhand carnage but in the film's screwball-existential vision of its characters: one that may not need violence at all to catalyse it. With or without bloodbaths, Tarantino's human beings are cherishable, funny loners. They are dream-seekers who stub their toes on reality, but keep on walking or even dancing. They are trivia merchants who look to the stars, while the stars look down with bemused compassion on them. They are monomaniacs who spy openings into freedom and fulfilment, only to realise they are openings into more monomania.

Eternal energy and eternal regeneration, even in the cause of an eternal absurdism. It could be a vision of John Travolta's own life, at least during that momentous arc from 1985 to 1995, from the torments of *Perfect* to the triumphs of *Pulp Fiction*.

2

A TOUCH OF ZEN

The $250,000 Tudor-style Beverly Hills home Travolta rented, with four bedrooms and seven bathrooms, was the outward and visible sign of a new industry kudos. *Pulp Fiction* was soaring up the box-office charts, thanks in part to the actor's own marketing savvy.

'I told Weinstein [Harvey, head of Miramax], "You can't fuck around with this movie. You do *not* release this in the summer. The hardest group to get is the intellectual group. Give them the respect of loving this movie as an art film, and you'll get a big commercial success out of it." '

So it opened in the fall of 1994. When it did, word of mouth was good, critical word was better and people fainted at the violence, which is the best publicity of all. Tarantino personally rushed to the projection booth to stop the film when a man passed out at the New York premiere.

The reviews could have been written by the director. 'A spectacularly entertaining piece of pop culture,' said *Variety*. '*Die Hard* with a brain' (*Time*). 'Tarantino is a masterful cinematic storyteller,' (*Playboy*). 'Rubbish about scum,' said the *Phoenix New Times*, but went on, 'It's also very funny and entertaining.'

Tarantino was becoming the best-known personality director since Hitchcock. On TV he guested in chat shows, cooking programmes and comedy spots, including a turn as a chef viciously stabbing a turkey with a thermometer, parodying *Pulp Fiction*'s needle episode.

This scene in the movie became a fashionable *cause célèbre*.

Swoonings and vomitings were noted and one Manhattan cinema reported 'two seizures a week'. The usual doctors were rounded up, first by theatre managers, then by interviewers. One medic broke rank to reproach the film. 'The scene was ridiculous, especially the way Travolta held up the needle, like Macbeth with the dagger . . . He would have snapped the needle off, trying to go through bone.' The expert went on to explain that the correct drug would have been intra-cardiac epinephrine inserted slowly between the ribs. Adrenaline wouldn't have done it. 'There is only one Lazarus I know of,' he scoffed, 'and he didn't come from Hollywood.'

But someone else once deemed deader than dead was throwing off the winding-sheet. And who had supervised the Travolta miracle? 'It was like I was at the back of the line and Quentin leans out and beckons me over. "You! Over there! I remember you! You can do this!" '

Now, he said, Quentin was going around the world behaving like his personal PR machine. The director even rang him from Sweden with news of his latest coup on John's behalf.

'This is quintessential Quentin,' burbles Travolta. 'He calls me from Stockholm. *Pulp Fiction* is at the height of its success, and he's talking to me about how he arranged a screening for 200 people to see *Blow Out* the way it should be seen, on an eighty-foot screen. He went into depth about every scene that he liked – for thirty minutes he went on about a performance of mine that was fifteen years old. Not about our mutual success with *Pulp Fiction*, but about a screening of *Blow Out*.

'He loves me in the true sense of the word. It's the coolest thing anyone has ever done in my life. I've never seen such selflessness.'

Tarantino guided his protégé in post-*Pulp* career choices. Travolta, a stranger to success in the nineties, was nervous about picking a snake not a ladder. Though he had raced away from square one with *Pulp Fiction*, one bad choice would slither him back to *Look Who's Talking Four*. Even in his dreams Tarantino's film took the shape of an unrepeatable, or inescapable, phenomenon. A final glowing shrine, a Madame Tussaud's of the soul.

'You know that scene with me and Uma? That restaurant? That purgatory, like the limbo where all the icons go? I woke up crying

because I had a nightmare that Quentin left me there. You know, Uma goes and Quentin goes and I'm left with Marilyn and James Dean and Buddy Holly and all these people that died. I thought did Quentin just write this movie so I had a place to go?'

With the spotlight on him again, Travolta was determined to enjoy and exploit it. He would not show panic, though he might show manic. A reporter lunching with him noted the combative eating style. Forward leaning, elbows cocked – 'His jaw did not receive the mouthfuls passively, but pounced, took prisoners, so that ingestion became an exercise in Seek and Destroy.'

Fame restored meant this: he would eat in top restaurants, talk to top interviewers and refuse to travel steerage to foreign movie premieres. His *Pulp Fiction* paycheck may have been a laughable $150,000. But almost the same sum, gargantuan in a different context, would soon be paid at auction for the white suit he made famous in *Saturday Night Fever*. In the early summer of 1995 film critic and original buyer Gene Siskel pocketed $145,000 – 'certainly a record for polyester,' cracked the auctioneer – for the fabled three-piece, which over the years so many Siskel friends had tried on at the Chicago scribe's home, jutting a hip and striking a high-finger pose.

Restored to legend, Travolta refused even first-class air tickets to London, later to Japan, to attend *Pulp Fiction* galas. He wanted $100,000 to fuel his private jet or nothing. He wanted a pilot, three co-pilots and an entourage of friends and family. The plane's loo must be stocked with its usual supply of fancy lotions, soaps and perfumes, plus the seasonal flower bouquets which went on display at each take-off. It was a hundred grand or nothing: miramax made a polite show of agonising and then decided. Nothing.

But one could see Travolta's point. Why expose himself to even first-class pawing or gawping when on the Gulfstream 2 he had privacy and control, even of the in-flight movies? The plane's video library, which fed the two televisions and two VCRs, contained no Travolta films. He didn't want the three-year-old Jett confused by Dad's image. He and the boy had enough of that at home, where Jett enjoyed the boppy musical numbers from *Grease*, like 'Greased Lightning' and 'You're the One That I Want', but started caterwauling when his father kissed Kirstie Alley in *Look Who's*

Talking. This was particularly confusing to the child since he knew Alley as the near neighbour in Maine who left her pets with the Travoltas when she went away.

Fame, like an aeroplane, must be maintained, fuelled and serviced. So in the summer of 1994 Travolta signed for the comedy gangster movie *Get Shorty*. This promised $3.5 million plus a brace of sweeteners: an extra $750,000 if he was nominated for an Oscar for *Pulp Fiction* (which he was) and another $750,000 if he won (which he didn't).

Before that he would make – was already making – a little fable about racism whose script had intrigued Tarantino enough for him to pass it to Travolta, without planning to direct it himself. *White Man's Burden* was being processed by QT's own production company Band Apart, named after the Jean-Luc Godard movie *Bande à Part*, which featured a dinky little dance number that helped to inspire the Thurman–Travolta two-step. Tarantino thrust the script at Travolta in Cannes, when the prospect of a $500,000 acting fee for this new project must have seemed like a purse of gold. 'I wanted to go back to work,' Travolta says, 'because it had been a year and I was a little bored. Quentin hadn't wanted me to do anything after *Pulp*.'

Travolta read Desmond Nakano's screenplay at a single sitting, or standing. His feet were rooted to his kitchen floor (though in another telling it was the bathroom) as he paged through the tale of a white man struggling for dignity and survival in an imaginary state where apartheid had been reversed. Blacks run banks, industries and government. White men run debts, errands, or gauntlets of humiliation like the hero's dismissal from his job after a misunderstanding with boss Harry Belafonte. He is sacked after innocently catching sight of Belafonte's wife half-naked while delivering a package to the mansion.

'When I read it, without exaggeration, I couldn't put it down. I knew it wasn't commercial, but I thought I know how to play this guy to the hilt. I should do this ... The racial flip, wear-the-other-shoe concept fascinated me.' His character goes on to kidnap the boss and embark on an odyssey of flight, fear and mistrust that ends in one man's death.

Jonathan Krane knew the film was a time-marker: 'John did *White*

Man's Burden as an art film, as a favour to Quentin Tarantino.' And Nakano, best-known previously as the screenwriter of *Last Exit to Brooklyn*, knew he had been lucky to snare Travolta.

'When I first went to a Hollywood studio, they didn't want to touch it because of the subject matter,' Nakano says. Then Band Apart made a deal with the French company UGC, after *Pulp Fiction*'s Golden Palm victory at Cannes. The French stipulated that *Burden* must have a budget of under $7 million and, as box-office insurance, one name star.

'Travolta was not in my mind when I wrote the script,' Nakano says, who wasn't convinced he was suitable even after seeing *Pulp Fiction*. But 'you have to adapt the role to the actor and I was very happy with what he brought to it'.

One puzzles at first over why a film-maker living in Hollywood would want to root through the ashes of the apartheid system in a grim allegorical two-hander set in an unnamed land. Though shot in Los Angeles, the film's setting is not specified as American; nor as African, nor as belonging to any other continent. Then one learns that Nakano is a Japanese-American whose parents were interned, with thousands of Oriental immigrants, in Californian camps during World War Two.

Travolta came from the other side of America and might have come from the other side of the moon for all his experience of race prejudice. For Nakano this was an advantage. The actor had to traverse that distance *imaginatively*.

'I saw him shaping it. He had the clothes, the walk, the gestures, the accent' – southern trash shading to African-American – 'and he wanted them to go together. If you watch his hands, he uses them differently from other films.' (More cumbrously, bunchily.) 'And there's one shot where he drops his son off the last time he sees him and walks back to his truck, where I love the way he moves. It told so much about the character. The shoulders are hunched over, yet there's an almost shuffling gait. You *feel* the weight on him.'

Sometimes Nakano thought Travolta pushed the ethnicity too far. 'Once I started shooting, we had a discussion about the degree of the accent. I wanted to cut it back and he pushed it to an extreme he was comfortable with. He'd say "axed" instead of "asked", which is really a black idiom, and it stuck out. I

re-looped a couple of words that I thought overplayed the role reversal.'

Travolta had his own agenda against hyperbole. It was he who proposed Harry Belafonte for the black boss, to temper prejudicial caricature with proven charisma. 'Without Harry and his persona and his elegance and grace, I just didn't feel that it would work,' Travolta said.

Belafonte initially turned the script down. 'I thought it was terribly naive. I just felt that Hollywood's history on movies about race relations is so black, why flirt with it. If it doesn't work it can be really horrible.'

Belafonte relented when Travolta pressed him: 'He is asking me to work with him, a black actor who hasn't been on the screen in twenty years.' The older actor was tickled by the young man's new career euphoria. 'He was giddy about the success of *Pulp Fiction*, which he had not quite fathomed.'

Tarantino's movie opened in the States during the filming of *White Man's Burden*. 'You could just see it rocketing,' remembers Desmond Nakano. 'It was very fortunate for our shoot because John was in a great mood. You could see him just "fill up". More and more offers were coming in.'

Just as well. *White Man's Burden* began to seem not just a coterie project but a cackhanded one. The two actors struggled unevenly. Where Belafonte tried to see off the beamers and daisycutters of a tendentious script with a straight bat, Travolta more effectively improvised and counter-stroked.

He focused on the one emotional truth he could instantly engage with. 'I've never played a man with such a rage before. But I think he has a justifiable rage. The survival of his family is at stake and I can identify with that.' And he did some of his best acting with no dialogue at all. His dumbshow reaction to being turned down at a job exchange – head hidden in hands, then lifted to pan the room in a dazed, raking gaze of emotional stocktaking – has the mute power of a Brando. A proletarian-tragic weightiness, allied to a childlike transparency.

Travolta also knew that heavy drama needs the foil of an occasional comic scene. I tell Nakano that my favourite scene, partly because it is the film's only funny one, is the diner duologue

with Travolta and Belafonte debating the virtues of putting salt on ketchup (very Tarantino).

'I was going to cut that out of the script,' the director says, 'because in terms of plot it makes no difference and we were trimming for budget and time. But when the draft came back, John said, "What happened to that ketchup thing?" "The scene ran long," I said. "Oh, I *like* that scene," he said. So we shot it and I realised it's important because of the humanity, it lightens the film up.'

Travolta won all battles except the one over his hair. When I ask Nakano why the actor wears an unspeakable shade of distressed russet-orange, riveting the viewer's eye like a road accident, he gives a good-humoured groan. 'My idea was to divorce his image from previous movies, to take away the film-star glamour. But I had no idea about the complexity of dyeing hair. The first time John came back he looked like Billy Idol, late seventies: bright platinum blond hair sticking straight up. We almost had to postpone the shoot because he looked so terrible. We brought someone else in to redo it. But John was obviously nervous, and I was horrified when I saw the result. It was supposed to be dirty blondish, to push you away from the old John Travolta.'

Instead it looks as if the character has fallen into a vat of henna. 'What you're seeing is a series of corrections,' Travolta explained to a visiting reporter. 'In the hundreds of years people have been colouring their hair, they still don't have it right.'

The release of *White Man's Burden* was delayed by months, partly so that Travolta could open first in a more likely box-office winner (*Get Shorty*). Nakano's film, which had added yet another production company to its masthead with Savoy Pictures, finally reached American screens just before Christmas, when it was hit by another squall of ill luck. 'Savoy went bust on the day of release and fired all employees,' says Nakano. 'The movie didn't open that badly. But Savoy couldn't bribe the cinemas to keep it running with the promise of another picture.'

Critics damned the film, ignored it or praised it wearily for good intentions. The most intriguing fallout concerned the racially divided public response. Polls and auditorium stakeouts showed that whites regarded the film as a heavy race melodrama while

blacks thought it was a comedy. They roared with laughter at the dinner scene where Harry Belafonte's family and their guests – including Attallah Shabazz, Malcolm X's daughter, in a cameo role – are served by a white maid. They guffawed too at the scene where Travolta drives past plush Beverly Hills mansions, all owned by blacks.

The whites in the audience just sat there silently, taking their punishment.

It was fantasyland, of course. The houses of Beverly Hills are actually owned by people like John Travolta, Gene Hackman, director Barry Sonnenfeld and actor-producer Danny DeVito, all involved in the next film on the Travolta slate.

DeVito and Sonnenfeld had been friends since *Throw Momma From the Train*, which the first directed and starred in and the second photographed. Sonnenfeld then graduated to shouting 'Action!' himself, notably on *The Addams Family* and the humungously successful *Men in Black*. Back then he was looking for a film to direct for DeVito's company Jersey Films.

Recalls DeVito, 'I was in a car in the middle of some business stuff and Barry calls me from vacation – "I think I've found it!" He said, "I read this book by Elmore Leonard, *Get Shorty*. I think it's one I wanna do." "Okay," I says, "so I'll buy it." So I get on the phone right away and find out who has the rights and buy it, even though I hadn't read it.'

Who had the rights, I ask DeVito? Hadn't I read in the trades that Tarantino had bought all the Elmore Leonards?

Never a man to be halted in mid-speech, DeVito gives a menacing snort like an annoyed rhinoceros. 'I think he bought them all up after *Pulp Fiction*, this was before,' he mutters. Then back to the one-man stampede. 'I rang Barry back, I said look I bought the book, he said hey what d'you think of it, I said I dunno I haven't read it, he said well sit down and read it, I said I gotta go get the book, he said, whaddayou mean I thought you said you *bought* the book, I said I "bought" the "book"!! I said, becos' people're after it, I hadda "buy" the "book"! People were bidding on it!'

Collapse of stout party on Dorchester chair, helpless with incredulity at life's linguistic jokes.

In another part of space-time, Barry Sonnenfeld was on a cruise ship in 1994, failing to convalesce from Hollywood pressures.

'At that time I saw Danny DeVito as Chili Palmer,' he says. 'Danny is the single most confident person I ever met in my life. And this book is not about Hollywood, it's about self-confidence – if you're self-confident you'll prevail in any situation, because everyone else isn't. So for the first two years of development Danny was going to be the lead.'

Chili Palmer is the truth-based Mafia hit man who bestrides Leonard's fish-out-of-water tale of a Cosa Nostra go-getter in Hollywood. Chili goes west from Miami to do a 'job', but instead finds a job. Falling in love with movies, he acquires some hot-money projects and becomes an Italian-American power in filmland, just like Danny DeVito.

'I didn't see myself playing Chili,' DeVito says. 'I said to Barry, there are half a dozen other parts I could play.' His interest definitively faded after a big read-through of the script with, Sonnenfeld recalls, 'Danny as Chili, and Gene Hackman , and Samuel L. Jackson (in the role later played by Delroy Lindo).' Calls went out to other potential Chilis, including Warren Beatty who declined, saying, 'How could a guy who looks like me not be further up the Mafia chain? People won't believe it.' Finally, says DeVito, 'it worked out good because [our company] did *Pulp Fiction* and, bingo!, John Travolta was on the comeback trail.'

But Travolta turned the role down too. 'It was maybe too close to *Pulp Fiction*,' says DeVito. Sonnenfeld won the actor over during a power dinner. 'I explained that Chili was quite different from Vincent Vega and we discussed putting more stuff in the picture. John wanted more about the guy loving movies. The original script didn't have the scene where Chili goes to watch *Touch of Evil* and mouths along with the dialogue.'

'I liked the idea that Chili Palmer was gifted, but in the wrong profession,' explains Travolta. 'Here was a loan shark who loved films. I thought it was really funny that he had this vulnerability and turns into a little boy when he goes into a cinema. It's the only time you see Chili not being cool.'

This brand of trainspotting cinephilia, though, sounds suspiciously like Quentin Tarantino. 'What really did it for John,'

Sonnenfeld reveals on cue, 'was that Tarantino, who's a huge Elmore Leonard fan, called him up and said, "John, this is not [the film] you turn down." ' 'Quentin said to me that I should go ahead and make the movie and make them change the script for me,' says Travolta.

So he went to screenwriter Scott Frank and told him Leonard's dialogue was 'so fabulous, but in the script it's been paraphrased. You've taken off the edge. Then I gave them an example by reading a whole scene from the book, then from the script.' This was the opening restaurant scene where Chili asks for his coat, which has been taken away by another client.

'In the original script it said something like, "Where's my coat? You better find it. It cost $400." But in the book it was, "You see a black leather jacket fingertip length, has lapels like a suitcoat? You don't, you owe me $379 . . . . You get the coat back or you give me the $379 my wife paid for it at Alexander's." It was the detail. I said I'd do the movie, but they had to put back everything they paraphrased.' It took three weeks, Travolta says, but, 'They put every goodie back.'

Sonnenfeld supplies an ironic postscript. Once shooting began, Travolta asked for much of the Leonard material to be thrown out again. 'He felt he was asked to learn too much and asked us to shorten speeches or change words. The challenge was to shorten and still keep the rhythm.'

The re-scripting episode prompts questions about how much Travolta works by intellect and how much by instinct – or indeed by virtual passivity. Here was a man being puppeteered turn-and-turn-about by those classic Hollywood opposing forces, the personal guru (Tarantino) and the project mastermind (Sonnenfeld). That these forces pulled in different directions artistically hardly mattered when both pulled, more or less, upwards. With the whole of Hollywood now turning into a support system – an uplift system – for the recently unemployable actor, who could blame him if he surrendered his will and ego to his well-wishers?

After *Pulp Fiction* Travolta was a-blush with gratitude, to the world, to Hollywood, above all to Tarantino. 'He doesn't want anything back other than my well-being and every time I think about that it makes me want to cry or something.'

Almost everything did at this point in his life, from art and music – 'Violins and the French horn make me cry . . . I wouldn't know what to do if there weren't a Picasso or music or a favourite actor – because my life has been filled with the joy of these creations' – to his awareness of a world raining down praise and grace. 'I've been touched to tears many times over the last year. I feel like I matter to people again. It's like people love me and want to see me survive, which was more stellar this time. I almost can't move when I think about it.'

Fame has a hundred ways to immobilise its victims, some more antic than others. Travolta recalls an outing in his 1964 red Jaguar. 'I'm driving down Sunset Boulevard like the cool movie star that I am, right? I have the top down and I light up a cigar. I've got the theme music from *A Man and a Woman* on my tape deck.' (Francis Lai's 'Chabadabada,' as played at John and Kelly's wedding.) 'I've got the sunglasses on.'

Then his car sputtered to a halt. 'I hear people honking their horns. I'm thinking, "Why did I try to be cool?" People are screaming at me. Finally, a guy comes down out of one of the mansions and helps me push my car into his driveway. I asked him if he wanted an autograph or a picture with me or something. He wanted a dance lesson.'

The actor tells this story more than once. He likes it as a fable of the powerlessness of power, or of self-discovery as the moment when you stop to look back self-mockingly at your own legend. For this is the man who has been through the fire and emerged alive: a sort of one-man Shadrach, Meshach and Abednego, with a sense of humour about his own survival. 'I've had other famous people come up to me and say, "John, we've learned from your mistake." And I say, "Which one?" '

After *Perfect*, 'I'd gone knee-deep into a cynical black hole, and it put me on a spiral where I could hardly function. All this false information about how art works, how art comes out of depression and suffering – that the darker you are, the more depth you have – I finally learned that it isn't true.'

But isn't it? Travolta's new bearing and behaviour suggest it might well be. 'He has a Zen steadiness about him, as if a collection of childhood masks has dropped away,' writes one interviewer.

Another is astonished to see Travolta shed a tear at a story of personal loss the reporter tells. 'I became you,' the actor explains. 'I didn't expect to become you so quickly, but I couldn't listen to your story without becoming you. If I didn't respond I would be, to that degree, dead. And I don't want to be dead.' Yet a third interviewer, from MTV, is given a hug when Travolta notices he is shaking with nervousness.

'I can walk into a room and, like a magnet, I'll find the person who is bummed out,' he says. 'Now, I can actually help someone. But before I would have empathised and felt like there was no hope.'

This begins to seem like the gospel according to Mills and Boon. Coming through his Passion to know compassion, the cinema's ex-discomaniac is remade as a beautiful soul.

1994 is a tough year for the biographer. We warned at the outset that unguarded chroniclers can end up joining the 'Everyone loves John Travolta' club. Even Martin Amis, not one of nature's soft touches, ended a long Travolta interview feature for the *Sunday Times* in February 1995 with the words, 'For two decades, on and off, I have been interviewing famous people. And I have to confess that I have never interviewed anyone as generous as Travolta: generous with his time, his trouble, his attentiveness.' But from the moment he came through the door Amis was probably a goner: 'It was like bumping into Jim Morrison, or Jimi Hendrix [he writes]. You feel that John Travolta is so iconic that he ought to be dead.'

That he wasn't dead sent the Amis prose into orbit. 'In the firmament, the brightest stars have the shortest lives: blue giant to black hole. But the universe isn't old enough to encompass the degeneration which T managed. It will take 20 billion years for our sun to reach its ultimate state, frozen in crystalline indetectability. Travolta did it in ten.'

Now he is back and wreathed in beatitude. Nice guy. Icon. Hugger. Man of Zen serenity. The Lazarus everyone loves.

Only on the screen is Travolta going against the grain. After the heroin-addicted hit man of *Pulp Fiction* he was now impersonating a mob killer turned movie mogul. Next, he would play a psychotic military man threatening nuclear Armageddon.

Maybe fiction was the one place where John Travolta could rest from being the sweet soul of America; where he could stop staying 'Thank you' and shedding tears of public gratitude. Instead he could incarnate, in a series of alter ego-maniacs streaked with ambition and self-conceit, the heretical thought: 'I *don't* owe it all to Quentin, Barry, Danny and Jonathan. I owe it to myself. I was the one who survived. *I* made it possible for me to say, "I am John Travolta still." '

3

HOODLUMS

The best way to prove you are a living icon is to spoof yourself. That way, you establish your mythic status even as you mock it; for caricature highlights the lines and contours of that myth. On October 15th 1994, John Travolta was the VIP host on the popular, long-running NBC comedy show *Saturday Night Live*. His appearance may be Hollywood's most bizarre instance – or *only* instance – of a born-again legend deconstructing each of his two careers.

First up on the screen: a *Fever*-style walking sequence down the studio corridor, Travolta's legs all but kicking into the camera, accompanied by boppy Bee Gees music that cuts out each time the star stops to ask – in a diffident gentlemanly voice – the way to the men's room.

Next up: Travolta introduces himself to the audience with a warm-up speech in which he tub-thumps for his new movie career. He insists he has no need to dig up past hits (he absentmindedly slicks a giant *Grease* comb through his hair) or remember old comeback movies (he tries on an *Urban Cowboy* stetson passed by a stagehand), or resurrect the memory of old disco smashes. 'What is that, a light?' he asks, pointing with a one-fingered high sign at the ceiling while jutting a *Fever*-ish hip.

It is not exactly the Marx Brothers, but the studio audience guffaws. It feels good just to see a star subject himself to such *lèse majesté*.

What follows is the best and worst of Travolta the funny man. Dragged up in chestnut-blond hair, frock and full make-up as

Barbra Streisand, he submits to a spoof interview with Mike Myers of *Wayne's World*, also in drag as Barbara Walters. On this evidence, though, and that of his later Marlon Brando turn, grilled by a mock Larry King of CNN, Travolta is no Rich Little or Rory Bremner. The Streisand is all tinkly adenoids and overworked moue. The Brando is all paunch, nasality and room-raking pauses. Assembly-kit impersonations almost any of us could do.

Give Travolta more plot and playspace, though, and he shows the magic. He does a hilarious Mafia capo, all clockwork Italian gestures, *Godfather* cadence and cupped-ear attentiveness, in a sketch making fun of the old 'Did I hear you correctly?' gangster trope. As two Dons constantly misconstrue each other's smalltalk, we realise it is less out of tactical or menacing incredulity than authentic deafness. And in a longer vampire skit he is a toothy English-accented Dracula, voiced as if by Boris Karloff in harness with Alfred Hitchcock.

Travolta has the insouciance here, through a sketch to which he obviously gave blessing, to mock all those interviewers who have pestered him, over the years, about his sexuality. To the insinuations of his visitors concerning their host's bachelor existence with live-in male valet and secretary – 'The guy is definitely gay,' they hiss to each other – Count Travolta toothily affirms, 'I am secure in my masculinity!' He opens a drawer in his gaming table to convince them – 'Look, playing cards with naked women!' And when he turns at twilight into a bat, flying out of the window to be audibly ravished off-screen by another bat, he still comes back protesting that it was accident not preference.

The sketch derides the gossip merchants but also pokes sympathetic fun at their victim. The precious, high-strung VIP sits in his all-too-public private sanctum, making every new protestation seem a confession. At the same time, the high carelessness of the sketch disarms tittle-tattle more effectively than any of Travolta's earnest interview demurrals.

If *Saturday Night Live* seemed a mildly risky way of exposing his reputation, what of it? Risks were a way to wake people up: risks such as specialising in a whole new species of character on the large screen.

After *Pulp Fiction*'s Vincent Vega, here was *Get Shorty*'s Chili

Palmer: another low-life greaseball, only better dressed, better spoken and better prepared for gangland emergencies. The new film was wrapped and all but released by the time Travolta strutted his *Saturday Night Live* stuff. But Barry Sonnenfeld says the actor's rehearsal methods might have been a dry run for the TV show.

'You could run the camera and not know if he was going to do the take in English, Japanese or German, as Elvis Presley or James Bond. I have outtakes of a scene where he and Rene Russo are in bed and get a phone call saying Gene Hackman's been beaten up, and John did that in four or five different languages. He's a clown, joking with the crew. You never see him sweat or be nervous.'

He was no stickler for research either. In a Hollywood where, if we believe the PR blurbs, every actor playing a pianist attains Carnegie Hall standard and every actress playing a waitress does a month's hard labour in McDonald's, every star playing a gangster ought presumably to mix in at Mob socials or attend learn-on-the-job muggings. 'As far as I know,' says Sonnenfeld, 'John didn't prepare for the role at all in terms of research.'

He barely even met his real-life model. Says Sonnenfeld, 'In the last two days we shot what is actually the opening scene, where the rival gangster played by Dennis Farina comes up to John in a restaurant accompanied by two other guys. One of these was played by the actual Chili Palmer. They'd never met before. John said to me, "You know, we are just so unbelievably lucky that I didn't know there really *was* a Chili Palmer. Otherwise I'd have insisted on going to Miami for two weeks to watch him, and for the whole performance I'd be saying, 'No, no. Chili walks like this and he has a tic.' "

'We laughed about this at the time, because the real Chili Palmer is a very slight, unassuming, undynamic type of guy, and it would have totally screwed up the whole movie.'

(Sonnenfeld's memory may be massaging the facts a little. A reporter who visited the set and saw other scenes being shot, remembers Chili being on hand and available for consultation the entire day. 'After one particularly menacing take, [Travolta] turned to him and said, "How was that, Chili? Was that like you would have done it?" ')

The main thing Travolta worked on was his walk. It's a hip,

lissom swagger, like Frank Sinatra strutting onto a stage, mixed with Bugsy Siegel jaunting off to a kill. The torso swings from the pelvis, the legs all-but-swing from the shiny-loafered feet, the head more purposefully swings – eyes raking the terrain – from the Travolta neck. 'Chili's got confidence,' explains the actor. 'He walks like a man who gets what he wants . . . I study the character in as many details as I can. I physicalise him until the thinkingness [sic] comes together. There's a moment when everything you say comes out exactly like [Chili] would say it. The way you dress, the way you smoke, the way you speak, the way you walk. When it's all automatic, at that moment you know it's happened.'

Despite their common Travolta-ness, no two movie walks of his are the same. 'Give me a thought and I'll give you a walk,' he quick-snapped to a reporter one day. 'You have to think it before you can do it.' And he demonstrated *Pulp Fiction*'s Vincent Vega, dropping his arms to his side, slinking down and slithering – 'He shuffles because he's high.' Then he grew fresh inches to become (his) Chili Palmer.

This is like a mad mating of Travolta the *Saturday Night Live* mimic with a new Travolta, the Method actor: with the caveat that his flair doesn't come from theories – impossible to imagine him curled up with the works of Strasberg or Stanislavski – but from his own delight in hijacking and ritualising people's mannerisms. The costume trunk mentality he developed as a child is translated into playful echopractic gesture, then into serio-comic art.

Both come with a shrugging-off of vanity. The physical self-concern which undid him in *Staying Alive* and *Perfect* is now relegated to off-screen comedy. Travolta claims his only moments of discomfiture during *Get Shorty* were when he had bad hair mornings. 'I'll usually take a shower the night before shooting so I can get up and go right to the set. But when I get up, my hair is in a thousand different cowlicks and I look puffy. One morning, I walked into the make-up trailer and Gene Hackman was in there, and he was just shocked by how bad I looked. He said, "Oh God, make-up and hair do wonders for you." '

Get Shorty is a comedy about imposture and Travolta picks up the vibes and carries them deftly through the film. He carries virtually everything. A miscast Hackman – too gritty and intense

to play an oafish, medallion-wearing B-picture producer – throws the movie off-kilter early on and Rene Russo's leading lady is lost in uncharted spaces between hauteur and ditziness.

The best moments are those Travolta shares with supporting players, notably Danny DeVito as a vainglorious actor. One scene is a mock masterclass with the gangster teaching the actor how to act: it's almost an allegory for the superiority of Travolta's unschooled flair over regimented theory. The other scene is lifted from fact and dropped into fiction. The 'ordering off the menu' vignette, with Travolta watching in polite incredulity as DeVito co-opts a waitress to give design specifications for his omelette, is a little classic. Every journalist who has met a Hollywood star knows the pests they can make of themselves in restaurants. Used to an *à la carte* world where the wish is father to the dish, they rant on about just what they want the chef to do, just for them.

'It's true,' DeVito admits. 'You go, "I don't want any salt, could you please use olive oil not butter, can you take the yolk out, use just the white?" When I go to an Italian restaurant it's very hard not to say, "Could you take some garlic and fry it up and cook me some pasta *al dente*, throw a little hot pepper on it and then bring it out. I'll toss it up." Mmm, my mouth is watering, it must be lunchtime.'

'I've eaten with Danny a lot and we didn't have to invent anything,' comments Sonnenfeld. He invented little in adapting the novel either. 'The only restructuring was to give it a movie-ish ending. Novels don't need endings but movies do. The last scene of the book just has Chili and the producer character getting in a car after they've pitched an idea to a studio and saying, "Endings are a bitch." That works on the page, but on film you need something stronger and more visual.'

So they came up with a felicitous pay-off to a story about the interchangeability of the real and unreal. The camera tracks out from the hero's perilous climactic raid on an airport luggage locker to reveal that we are watching a movie being shot. Chili Palmer's life story has become a screen fiction, with Harvey Keitel (fresh from *Pulp Fiction*) playing Travolta playing Chili. Wheels within wheels, turning slyly and sweetly.

*   *   *

When not being Chili Palmer, Travolta could take the best relaxation and be himself. That self was still one of the odder organisms in the showbiz world. It was part man, part boy; part Hollywood grandee, part unreconstructed Englewood faddist. In 1994 he published privately a fantasy memoir about flying he had written called *Propeller One-Way Night Coach*. Wistful going on winsome, it may be Travolta's greatest masterpiece of uncool. It combines the confessions of an aeromaniac – a young boy taking his first flight – with passages of vertical-takeoff daydreaming. And in the author's enraptured identification with his pre-teen hero it adds substance to what we had always suspected: that part of Travolta is a child in a man's body, and a child who empathises with the child in everyone else.

In the real world, who could fail to note that his devotion to Jett is more fulsomely articulated – at every interview opportunity – than his devotion to Kelly? This father-son passion smacks almost of mirror-gazing. Travolta seems to have designed the whole of his Maine mansion around its main man, this three-year-old reflection of himself who carries the Travolta name, the Travolta genes, the Travolta innocence.

Up there in Penobscot the sea and sky enclose an enchanted compound. In the bay, waves crash and sailboats frolic. Outside the Travolta mansion's window, deer browse on the blueberries in the garden. And in Jett's bedroom a giant *papier maché* beanstalk climbs from floor to ceiling.

Mixing themes, this room is shaped like the hull of a plane. Jett also has access, elsewhere in the house, to an ice-cream parlour, a seesaw, a make-believe school and a Peter Pan-themed room with glow-in-the-dark stars. 'This is Wonderland,' intones Kelly Preston. 'John and I got together and figured out what all our fantasies were as kids.'

'I work to keep traditional family values together, that's what matters to me now,' declares John, who in 1995 could move his family round two other homes, in Beverly Hills and Carmel, where they rent a house down the road from Clint Eastwood. 'I never believed in my own happiness before. It's like I accepted that I would always have a side to myself that was lonely and desperate.

Even when I was at the height of my celebrity, I always hated the life I was leading.'

Now, as well as feeling better adjusted himself, he can look at a time-warped version of John Travolta – pre-fame, pre-*Fever*, pre-*Pulp Fiction* – in Jett. 'That little boy . . . overwhelms me,' gushes the father. 'I've never felt that level of love for another person. We watch *Barney* together.' And when not watching the cuddly dinosaur show, Jett and his dad dance around the room to the music of 'Baby Bop'. And when not doing that, Jett, the incarnation of privileged innocence, is allowed to treat the Penobscot home as Liberty Castle. Ex-servants tempted into chequebook gossip allege that the boy is permitted to draw on walls or tear up fifty-year-old copies of valuable magazines. An insect-free garden has even been created for him and for Kelly, who hates bugs.

'I love the selflessness, the idea that you can enjoy someone else's survival and development more than you do your own,' chants Travolta. 'I love the joy I have about Jett's joy, seeing him happy. I love the concept that you didn't know you could be so generous.

'I didn't expect to fall so deeply in love. I thought I'd love my son like I love my nephews and nieces – family in general. But the depth of love is kind of scary.'

Travolta had only to march out the door, though, and the world saw another version of him. Not doting father but wheeling, dealing actor-careerist: the Travolta who may have caught or learned some of Chili Palmer's savvy and sang froid. British film-maker Mike Newell met this Travolta while visiting him in Florida. Newell was sounding him out about starring in a movie that would later – much later and without Newell – become *Phenomenon*.

'It was in Clearwater. He was staying in a hotel owned by the Scientologists and there was, as I recall, somebody around who was from that outfit. But we didn't discuss Scientology. We merely talked about the film and I was very struck by how smart he was. He's very acute and astute. He's got a good "nose" for deals.

'We spent a long time talking about his aeroplanes and I remember thinking how bizarre it was that I was sitting in front of this icon – *Saturday Night Fever* and so on – and yet this guy

was also certificated to fly mid-fifties British jet fighters. In fact he *owned* a fighter called a Vampire.

'I remember he had a lively sense of the business possibilities in a movie. I came away thinking, Boy, this guy is shrewd. I think he knew he'd been given another chance. And though he wouldn't have believed then that he'd turn into a $20 million actor who could open a movie, he'd done a rough calculation of how many films he'd do and how much they'd add up to. I thought this is a man who hangs onto his money and makes it work for him.'

Or, between them, he and Jonathan Krane do. The Travolta career was becoming a series of shrewd quantum leaps. $150,000 for *Pulp*; $500,000 for *Burden*; $3.5 million (plus Oscar nomination bonus) for *Get Shorty*. Next – before going phenomenal with *Phenomenon* – the actor-manager team would sign on for $8 million to do *Broken Arrow*.

This was an inspired career choice. Never mind the quality of the movie, or the size of the money, feel the width of Travolta's chutzpah. A high-style psychotic villain was at the far end of his supposed range, if not right off it. A renegade Air Force Major who steals two nuclear missiles from a plane during a training trip, and then points them at Washington with some colourful proposals about ransom money, would seem to require at best a Jack Nicholson, at second best a Dennis Hopper.

Director John Woo had brought to Hollywood a made-in-Hong-Kong reputation for balletic violence (*The Killer*, *One More Time*). He fills movie theatres by emptying gun chambers. One film by Woo uses more bullets than a year's movie output by Scorsese, John Milius or Walter Hill. In addition, characters crash through windows, hurtle from high buildings, knock each other senseless and generally behave like Kamikaze warriors on overtime.

Woo saw in Travolta a chance to cast against type: to hire not an action star but an ex-dancer whose locomotion now largely confined itself to wry eyebrow-work and hip-magisterial walks.

'I wanted a normal person, charming, elegant and very smart,' says Woo, who wears a blindingly clean open-neck shirt and greets you like the most honoured guest in the history of East–West relations. He also talks like a man to whom the English language is an intricate, puzzling toy, sometimes pausing for up to thirty

seconds to find the right word or phrase. 'I wanted someone who looks friendly but you never know what he's thinking, what his next move is. That's much more dangerous. John Travolta – he's got the eyes of an angel! But when he stares without saying anything, he looks so cool like the devil.'

And who, speaking of the devil, should turn out to have brokered this casting coup? 'Quentin Tarantino is a good friend of mine,' says Woo. 'He helped put me and John together and showed him all my movies. John fell in love with them and had the confidence in me to make him look good.'

Woo sent Travolta the script without specifying which of the two main roles he wanted him to play, villain or hero: the nutty Major or his Air Force comrade who bales out before the Montana crash landing, to spend the rest of the film trying to run his demented crony to ground.

'I didn't dare tell John I wanted him to be the bad guy,' says Woo, 'because there's a saying in Hollywood: All big stars wanna play hero. So I let him make the decision.'

Travolta duly picked the scene-stealer. He saw Vic Deakins as 'a smart, sinewy, almost *elegant* bad guy. At first you think he's probably just a jerk, and then you see that underneath it is true psychotic behaviour.'

After Vincent Vega and Chili Palmer this was geometrical progression in baddie-playing. After the sleazoid, the self-raising gangster. After that, the stratospheric fruitcake.

By the time the hacks had hacked their way to Montana, Travolta was in a whirl. 'Oh man, am I bad,' he exulted. 'Despicable, just psychotic to no end. But it's very funny. When you're that bad, you can go all the way. For example, I kill a guy with the back of a flashlight. I then blow smoke in his mouth, for fun, then I kick him out of a Humvee and then I pontificate about the subject of death. That's just one little thing – besides setting off a nuclear weapon.'

It was hog heaven, with the proviso that Travolta stay out of the trough. It was easy to shed weight, though, and to keep it shed in the heat of the semi-desert. Travolta claims he lost seven pounds between *Pulp Fiction* and *White Man's Burden*, another ten before *Get Shorty* and ten more to fine down to 190 for *Broken Arrow*.

He ordered what food he wanted, he says, but took only one or two bites.

Again he crafted a special walk, a military strut as cocky and formalised as his bristlecut hair. 'I went to some bases and watched how they moved. It wasn't hard. I got to pontificate and order people around and smoke cigarettes a lot . . . I observed how the guys walked in their big black boots.'

For co-star Christian Slater, acting with John Travolta was like being translated to movie heaven while still alive. The younger star lost no chance to tell the world that his first date had been at age thirteen when he took a girl to *Staying Alive*, and that before that his casting-director mother had smuggled him onto the set of *Grease*. He had bought the records, slicked his hair, danced to the music.

Now here was this older dancer/singer/icon who instead of being a cadaver preserved in chemical, with one arm and finger permanently pointing up through the formaldehyde, was a friend and fellow horseplayer. 'He is the first actor of his calibre who ever knocked on my trailer door,' Slater said. 'Usually, I'm the one who has to make the first move with a more-established actor. But he stopped by just to chat. I was stunned when I opened the door. He really is warm and embracing as a human being.'

Sitting in the fighter-plane cockpit between takes, Travolta taught Slater to hand-jive. And if Slater didn't think *that* was cool enough, Travolta picked one of his own non-working days to barnstorm over the Montana set in his private plane. This amused everyone except the insurers, who thought they had made it clear they didn't want Travolta flying during production.

'The crew became unglued,' giggled the actor, 'it was fun to be bad.' Kirstie Alley, asked to comment from her experienced position on the actor's Maine flightpath, remarked enigmatically, 'John inhabits a different universe.'

For director Woo the barnstorming was scarcely a distraction. How do you distract – or even gain the attention of – a man masterminding one explosion, gun battle, plane crash and jeep chase after another? Though all the Stealth bomber sequences, and some of the helicopter and train scenes, were simulated with models or trick photography, the armaments were real and noisy. Weapons

specialist Robert Galotti of *The Rock* gave Travolta a wooden-grip Beretta machine-gun that fired 1,200 rounds a minute. Even this was minor-league by Woo's standards and ambitions. At the end of one scene, estimated a visiting Hollywood trade, the director had fired off 'at least 60,000 rounds of ammunition'.

Yet Travolta knew when hokum shaded into bunkum. It was all right for Major Vic Deakins to career across deserts and mountains, blowing smoke in cronies' faces, shooting defectors and riffing debonair one-liners ('Do you mind *not* firing at the thermonuclear missiles'). This was the logic of hyperthyroid action cinema. But it was not all right for him, Woo remembers, that two buddies-turned-antagonists should have a dialogue scene in an abandoned mine where dramatic tension rather than physical plausibility required them to be separated.

'John wasn't comfortable with the scene in the tunnel,' Woo says. 'In the film, after the grenade blows up, John is separated from Christian Slater and they talk to each other through a wall of debris. In the script there had been no explosion, it was pretty open. John said, "It's too much like a Hollywood film." He wanted there to be a good reason why they were in different worlds. So we changed the script and built another set, when Christian tosses the grenade to him it blows up and brings down the wall. It was his idea. He wanted everything natural. If they're separated psychologically, why not separate them for real?'

Lulls in explosions allowed Woo and Travolta to sit and discuss favourite films. 'He loves old-time movies,' Woo says. 'Roman Polanski's *Knife in the Water*, Fellini's films, Bogart. We both love *Lawrence of Arabia*. We are both old-fashioned, we like the great art movies of the sixties and seventies. We both like the true value of morality, that people care about each other, help each other; loyalty to family, country, friends.'

Woo has an Oriental tendency to commute between parallel thought-universes. Before I can stop him, he has jumped all the way from European movie pantheons to the beauty of Travolta's soul. 'He's a man with a kind heart. Whenever you give him help, or even a cup of water, he remembers it for life. He told me in this business he has not got too many friends. The day before shooting ended, he brought Tom Hanks to see me. He talked a lot about

me to Tom Hanks. He and Tom Hanks have been friends for over twenty years.'

This would have to mean ever since Hanks won stardom in *Splash*, the film whose loss caused Travolta to sack his agent. If you can forgive an actor that, you can forgive him anything. A few months after *Broken Arrow* wrapped, John and Tom and their wives made a social foursome just before Oscar night in 1995: the night Travolta was up for Best Actor in *Pulp Fiction* and Hanks in *Philadelphia*.

'I had a four-hour dinner with Tom and his wonderful wife Rita last week,' declaimed Travolta to an army of reporters, 'and that totally dissipated all this kind of competitive feeling, and I found a new friend. I can't wait to have this friendship with Tom.'

Travolta had obviously forgotten, in the media heat of the moment, that he had already had the friendship for many years, at least according to Woo. But the older actor had plenty on his mind. That he did not go on to win the Oscar that night – Hanks won – was the least of the setbacks or stresses. More disturbingly, there was an echo of the last and first time he had attended the ceremony as a contender in 1978. He remembered his mother in pain that March night eight weeks before she died of cancer. She had sat there in the Dorothy Chandler Pavilion among the stars, rubbing her knees as her son wondered whether to soothe her or to urge her to leave the show.

This time John's father, Sal, long afflicted with heart trouble, gave him concern, though from different signs and symptoms.

'On Oscar night I could see he had decided that was his last night. Because he ate what he wanted, he drank, he smoked – and he hadn't in a few years. And I said, "He's making this his last hurrah, isn't he?" '

The next day, his eighty-two-year-old father went into hospital.

4

ONLY CONNECT

John Travolta's father died in hospital in Santa Barbara on May 29th 1995, after a long struggle with heart disease.

His mother's death had drawn from John the tributes and remembrances of a felt, particular grief for the human being he had loved first and longest. His response to Sal's passing was more muted and generalised. He mourned his father, for the world's hearing, in the context of broad philosophical musings dutifully edged with sadness. He linked his death to his forthcoming movie *Phenomenon*, where John was cast as a dying man. And he sought refuge in the plenitude of human bereavements to camouflage his diminished response to this specific loss.

'I've learned that death is part of life,' he said. 'I think I've worked around those tragic moments like everyone has. As you get older you lose people, but I think that I had a source of experience to identify with. I don't like losing people. It's painful, frustrating to feel that you can't keep Mom and Dad. When I read the script [of *Phenomenon*] I cried very hard. I threw it across the room because I was so moved by it.'

An odd gesture to express grief; it more suggests anger or frustration. Was John's mourning for Sal complicated by the sense of an unresolved relationship? The son had barely spoken about the father in recent years. In a history of public soliloquy that included regular references to his mother, and not a few to his siblings, Sal Travolta was a missing page in the family album. Back in 1990 he had spared a few fraught but grudging words in an interview: 'My mother is dead now, but my dad is still well.

He's seventy-seven and I reckon he's getting his own back now and it serves me right. He gives me a really hard time.'

Even in the months after Sal's death, the long-gone mother seemed a more vivid presence than the late-departed father. Perhaps his son had never forgiven, or at least forgotten, the older man's re-marriage: in 1979, just seven months after his wife's death, Sal Travolta married the nurse who had looked after her in her final illness.

On the set of *Phenomenon* in 1995 John Travolta would rhapsodise again about Helen Travolta's teachings, with their wisdom about the interconnectedness of moral outlook and actor's vision.

'It was never about how people looked,' he says. 'Mom was a big stickler for that. She always thought people were attractive even if they weren't and we all kind of inherited that – to see the beauty in people. Appearance was interpretative, so this whole sex appeal thing happened via character. Look at the difference between Chili Palmer [in *Get Shorty*] and my part in *White Man's Burden*. Chili is beautiful and the guy in *White Man's Burden* is hard to look at.'

Mom had moulded his mind and encouraged his talent. Perhaps the only lasting gift Sal Travolta handed down to his son was a patient, dazed attentiveness to the thoughts and teachings of Helen Travolta.

Patient because John could recite her acting decalogues at enraptured length. Dazed because he could also misconstrue them. Surely, in the two roles he cites, the man with the beautiful soul is the protagonist of *White Man's Burden* – near-martyred by racism but struggling on to save his life, family and dignity – rather than the Miami hoodlum who wheels and deals through Hollywood, glamorous as *Get Shorty*'s Chili Palmer may be on the outside.

But Travolta's gift as an actor is that he thinks in curves and contradictions and sometimes downright nonsense. In the off-camera campaign ground of daily survival he is a great organiser of essentials like food, aeroplanes and money: the fuel of existence and tools of necessary transport, emotional and geographical. You couldn't knock him off course on any of these. But clothe Travolta in philosopher's garb and he is

all ill-coordination and multi-directional gesture, an intellectual Laocoon.

It suits, one could argue, the profession. The good actor is in a great American tradition of licensed self-multiplication. Along with Walt 'Very well then, I contradict myself' Whitman, we could subpoena Ralph Waldo Emerson. The man who achieved posthumous fame as the patron philosopher of *Perfect* also famously said, 'Consistency is the hobglobin of little minds . . . With consistency a great mind has almost nothing to do.'

The more contrariness an actor offers, the better: at least a Travolta-style actor, specialising in a quizzical plurality rather than a Wayne/Eastwood iconic steadfastness. 'I get very entertained by the illusions that are created about me,' he said. 'I'm as complex as the next guy and may give various impressions of who I am at different times. If you went to dinner with my best friend and myself, that would be one impression. Then my wife and myself, another impression. Me at a table with the Rothschilds in Maine at a formal dinner, another impression.'

And we remember Pauline Kael being charmed by Travolta's educated manner at a Hollywood formal dinner, while Marcia Strassman later laughed, 'Oh, that was John doing his posh voice.'

An actor who carries his morphic talents into off-duty life is not a deceiver, just a natural mutant. A reporter who contacted Travolta after listening to the tapes of his recent interview with him told him he was startled to note that at a certain point Travolta had started speaking in his, the reporter's, voice. The actor serenely replied, 'I do not deny the chameleon in me.'

In February 1995 the several Travoltas all named John visited the Berlin Film Festival to promote *Get Shorty*. His genius for flaky behaviour was on display when he threw a tantrum about his food: 'Everything I've had here since yesterday morning has been unacceptable,' he was heard snapping to an aide. Yet exposed to the media lions at press conferences, he showed his smiling self-confidence and adaptability.

'You once made *Saturday Night Fever*, Herr Travolta,' piped up a facetious German newsman. 'Are you in a *Fever* of excitement now that your new film is being shown here this *Saturday*?'

Travolta's voice rose above the groans and catcalls: 'Ich bin ein

Berliner.' It made no sense as an answer. But then the question had made little sense as a question.

Travolta's free-range mutability meant that, with the right conjunction of stars and portents, whatever he said, did or played could turn magical. Such as embracing low-life and psychotic roles after a pre-existence as the golden boy of *Grease*, *Urban Cowboy* and *Staying Alive*.

World acclaim for *Get Shorty* was followed by American acclaim for *Broken Arrow*. A few critics demurred at the B-movie action excesses in a film where sense was battered by stuntwork and spectacle. (Director John Woo later admitted, 'I learned a lesson on *Broken Arrow*. We spent too much time and money on those big effects and on the computer graphics. We did not give enough room to the drama.') But the barbs were outnumbered by the bouquets hurled at Travolta.

The actor 'hits all the right insolent notes and opens up a whole new world of villainy-minded career choices,' said the *New York Times*. 'Travolta succeeds in being genuinely alarming without relying on either oily menace or wild-eyed hysteria,' wrote *Modern Screen*.

This was Toytown villainy, but done with childlike delight – 'Look at me, aren't I bad?' And his line-readings had a connoisseur self-confidence. 'You're out of your mind!' Christian Slater rants at him in one scene. 'Yeah, ain't it cool,' ripostes Travolta with a mile-wide smile.

'He moves, he stands, he poses, he actualises like no one else on the screen,' wrote critic David Thomson. The old self-regard is noted again – 'He has always seemed to carry his own intellectual or spiritual mirror with him' – but more indulgently than in Thomson's prior pen portrait in his *Biographical Dictionary of Film*. And he sees Travolta's *Broken Arrow* villain as a thing of ludic grace-notes and actor/audience conspiracy. 'Travolta doesn't have evil in him – but he has found a terrific gesture, brushing the underside of his chin with the backs of his fingers. Don't be surprised if you see Americans doing this all the time. It's a ten-year-old's idea of evil, in a mastermind who is as smart and attractive as an action figure who talks trash.'

Only a biographer cumbrous with research would point out

that Travolta had used this gesture before, in the forgotten films of his doldrum years, and would use it again shortly, in the far-from-villainous context of *Phenomenon*.

The oddest film of Travolta's career was one he would soon cite as his favourite. George Malley, the owner of a small-town repair garage, is struck by a bolt of light from the sky on the night of his birthday. He develops miraculous mental powers and no less marvellous gifts of love and selflessness, before succumbing to a mysterious, fatal illness.

The script by Gerald DiPego, a TV writer whose only previous feature was the Burt Reynolds shoot-'em-up *Sharky's Machine*, found its way to Disney. The Disney bosses located British director Mike Newell, glowing with recent success from *Four Weddings and a Funeral*. And Newell then tracked his way at Disney's suggestion to a Scientology hotel in Florida containing John Travolta. His mission was to persuade him to play George Malley.

'I thought Travolta was an inspired casting idea,' says Newell. 'When we met he very strongly liked what the film had to say. He liked this notion of the power from above intervening, this uplift of the human spirit by outside means, and this heroic dealing with difficulty and death. He felt it was a very positive, life-affirming story.'

With a Scientological subtext?

'The word Scientology was never mentioned between me and Travolta,' says Newell, who knows it has been mentioned a hundred times since by commentators battening on *Phenomenon*'s themes of self-help, mental advance and mysterious psychic forces. 'Everyone knows Travolta is a Scientologist. But neither with him nor with Gerald DiPego in script discussions did it ever come up. It was never, "What does L. Ron Hubbard say on this subject?" '

Travolta sent Newell away with a message of enthusiasm, but Newell himself was more equivocal. 'I wasn't going to tell him I was sceptical, but I was aware that I might be at variance with the approach Disney wanted to take, which was more [pause] "inspirational" than I wanted.' The Newell–DiPego script discussions lasted only a month. Wrestling with rival projects, Newell finally plumped for the Mafia drama *Donnie Brasco*.

'I just fell in love with it. It was a movie whose uplifting

qualities came from the spirit of absolutely real, ordinary people, whereas in *Phenomenon* there's another quality that's more than realism. There's a "power at work". The two films have different philosophies.'

The name John Travolta, coincidentally, was also bandied for the title role in *Donnie Brasco*. This finally went to Johnny Depp, an actor fast becoming the Richard Gere *de ses jours*. He had already stepped into the lead of John Badham's assassination thriller *Nick of Time* after Travolta refused to gratify his old *Saturday Night Fever* director by accepting the $4 million role.

In for Mike Newell came director Jon Turteltaub. The man who had minted millions for Disney with the Sandra Bullock romantic comedy *While You Were Sleeping* first knew of the job when Disney boss Joe Roth 'kidnapped' him in the studio grounds and drove him to a trailer meeting with Travolta on the set of *Broken Arrow*.

'I walked in and we started talking about the *Phenomenon* script,' recalls Turteltaub, 'and I said, "I can't believe how good my life is! I'm sitting on a movie set with the chairman of Disney and John Travolta. It doesn't get any better than this." And all of a sudden there's a knock on the door and Tom Hanks walks in!'

When Hanks left after a chat, Travolta began monologuing about the character of George Malley. 'He started getting tears in his eyes,' Turteltaub says. 'He was talking about what the role and story meant for him. I thought, this is gonna be good, I might as well jump on the train now. And John looked at me at the end of the meeting with those deep crystal-blue eyes and said, "You're gonna do the movie, aren't you?" I said, "*Yes*." '

Travolta had fallen in love with *Phenomenon*'s main character and theme. 'George is a guy who is never self-serving,' he explained. 'He's always looking for ways to help others. At one point he is even willing to sacrifice his life for the betterment of others, because he sees the bigger picture. He loves in spite of all reasons to hate, and he's generous in spite of all reasons not to be generous.'

'Life was better because he existed,' he sums up. 'If I died tomorrow and I knew that life was better because I existed I could go away feeling better. The secret was being at peace with death.'

So what exactly is this film? A Christ story? A Zen parable?

Or, pressing the point again, a Scientology fable wrapped up in a feelgood Frank Capra fantasy – 'It's A Wonderful Death'.

Writer DiPego says the film is about nature and the interconnectedness of things.

'I had a ranch in California, very remote up in the hills. It was a great retreat and it would pull me into nature. Anyone who goes into the wilderness finds that after a few days everything else wears off and you're living to a different rhythm, the rhythm of the natural world. Combined with that was a great big "What if?" What if there was a human being who could use one hundred percent of his brain? What would that person be like? What would they know? Well, if you're the writer dreaming it up, you can say what lies at the far reaches of human intelligence.'

So DiPego, who was dipping into the New Physics at the time, dreamed up a story in which a man was struck by the mysterious harmonies linking human life to everything large and small, from the interstellar to the sub-atomic. 'We're not separated from the world or each other when we look at the larger picture. I thought, this is what George is going to see and understand.'

So no Scientology?

'It was never in my mind. I know nothing about Scientology. It only came up later through the media because the world knows that certain Hollywood stars are Scientologists.'

Says Jon Turteltaub, 'The irony is, when I read the movie I thought, "Here I am, a Jewish director about to tell a Christ story." Later, all anybody saw was Scientology. They couldn't have been more off-base. How could anyone *not* see it as a Christ story? It's about a lone man who does nothing but give and love and ultimately dies so that other people can experience a better life. Didn't I read that in Sunday School?'

Back at the writing desk, DiPego had already refashioned the script once for Disney before putting it through more drafts for Newell, then Turteltaub. Newell wanted to emphasise exterior forces like the FBI and the military, eager to suppress if they cannot exploit George Malley's hyper-sensory powers. For Turteltaub, recalls DiPego, the secret was to keep the initial idea of a spiritual apocalypse 'while emphasising more the humour and the small-town feel'.

Travolta then threw out all these later revisions.

'The studio and Turteltaub had both given me notes expressing the view that the picture's third act was not rousing enough,' DiPego says. 'It made them nervous that there was a long denouement after George comes out of hospital, in which not very much happens. So we put in a plot about George defending the town against evil outsiders. Travolta read the changes and said, "Wait a minute, this process is getting out of hand. I signed up to a certain draft [DiPego's earliest revised script] and unless you go back to it I'm walking." '

They went back to it. Turteltaub's direction, though, would continue to reflect his interest in small-town atmospherics and gentle human comedy.

'John and I would talk about the character's home. What kind of furniture would he have? What size house, what wardrobe? It's the backdoor technique. By talking about these externals, rather than abstractly saying, "What does he like or dislike?", you find your way into the character.'

Cast and crew soon found their way to the tiny town of Auburn, California, standing in for DiPego's fictional, fabular Harmon (add a 'y'). Here the movie's symbolic topography was laid out stone by stone, brick by brick. George, a mechanic, runs a body repair shop – his pre-enlightenment career before that flash in the night sky turns him to spiritual repairwork. He is also, Christ at one remove, a proxy carpenter: he woos his mother-of-two lady love Kyra Sedgwick by buying, and pretending to sell for her, the rickety rustic chairs she makes. Elsewhere *Phenomenon* fills up with trunkfuls of take-it-or-leave-it mysticism about natural forces (wind sculpting the trees into everchanging shapes), the miracle of growth (George's cottage garden grows ever larger turnips), eternal recurrence (George lectures Sedgwick's kid on the never-ending life of the apple he is eating) and making contact with infinity and ultimate meaning (George catches messages no one else can from a friend's ham radio).

One has an inkling of why Newell fled. It could have been overarchingly schematic, like a church sermon reinforced with fan-vaulted fable. The main reason it isn't is Travolta. Piety isn't in his repertoire, nor humourlessness; and for any filmgoer so

young as to have been suckled only on *Pulp Fiction*, *Get Shorty* and *Broken Arrow*, he isn't even, here, the hip salesman of contrary creeds dressed to murder or menace.

'What you see on screen is the closest you'll get in any movie to what John really is,' claims Turteltaub. 'When I met him I was expecting this very slick, urban, dark cynical guy who'd help me get dates. Instead I found a goofy, gentle big kid, with no desire to help me get dates. He's fun, silly, unpretentious.'

Silly on set, if not on screen. 'Robert Duvall [playing the town doctor] started at the end of our second week of shooting and I was dreading his arrival,' says Turteltaub. 'I'm thinking, "Oh my goodness, Travolta is doing imitations of Barbara Stanwyck and Barbra Streisand and dancing with everybody on the set, and when Mr Duvall turns up, Mr Serious Actor, we're dead." I prayed John would shape up. So when Duvall came on set the first day I was literally walking on eggshells. By three o'clock Duvall was doing imitations and dancing round the set and John hadn't shaped up.'

Travolta's other co-star, though, Kyra Sedgwick, was a little unnerved by the split-personality work style. 'During one of the very, very emotional scenes he started going into Bette Davis imitations and Barbara Stanwyck, and I said, "What are you doing? I'm tearing myself apart here." But that's the way John works.' He also held up filming one day, with a Jeremiad about ice-cream. 'Butter pecan, chocolate chip mint, those were valid flavours!' he cried. 'I mean, you younger guys, whaddya got now??'

Travolta defends an approach that can make him seem like the Lee Trevino of screen acting: talk to the crowds, joke with the commentators, then hole out in one. 'On the set of a movie I'm playful, giddy and fun-loving, because I can create from that better than from a grave solidity. If I had to cry in a scene, or die, I could more easily do it from a playful perspective than I could from spending all day in a cemetery. It gives me more of a neutral position, and then I can go into any gear.'

Turteltaub calls it an Old Hollywood view of acting.

'He understands the concept of "performance". John knows what an exit line is and how to sell a joke. He doesn't have to search

deep in his soul to find a funny way to leave a room. He understands that we're making a fake story to entertain an audience. I don't every time have to give him some bullshit motivational garbage about "As you leave the room it's really your search for your mother's love." I can just say to John, "Can you do it quicker/slower?" and he'll say yes.'

Real in movies is what *seems* real. So as well as making it appear that George is every blue-collar thing the drama requires – even to Travolta insisting that the right amount of dirt be pushed under his fingernails, so that as Turteltaub recalls, 'Every day he'd ask, "Is that enough? Does the pinky need a little more? How about some engine oil under there?" ' – actor and director sought to create moments of ordinary human reaction, whose realism would combat the movie's sermonising.

One such moment came in a scene that would soon be used as the film's standard publicity clip. George Malley moves a pencil by mental will power to the amazement not just of Dr Robert Duvall but also of himself.

'There's a line in that scene that was an ad-libbed mistake,' says Turteltaub. 'When Robert Duvall says, "That's telekinesis," John in the script was supposed to say, "I know. I read four books on it this morning." But he was so "into" the scene that what came out of his mouth was this childlike "Is that okay?" Everyone just broke up. It was so much better, and funny, and he looked so boyish, so sweet.'

Travolta also riffed through different readings to find the best way to enact the death scene. Deaths in Hollywood movies can be occasions for overload sanctimony. A hush gathers round the genteelly-lit death bed as half a dozen actors, radiating suppressed emotion, try to make up the shortfall in wattage. The death scene in *Phenomenon* doesn't quite vanquish the feeling of power-surge piety, but Travolta and Turteltaub tried to find a way through.

'We shot the scene several different ways,' the director says. 'With him laughing and smiling through it, calm and peaceful through it and sobbing uncontrollably. He went through all of them and then we picked.'

Calm and peaceful won, with the scene lent a little roughening idiosyncrasy by Duvall's cranky-stoical reaction as the doctor. You

sense him choking back his grief, but without any sense of the solemn or sacramental. 'I just sat on the emotion. Sometimes you get more truth by going against the feeling, by pushing it down. More shows in your face,' says Duvall.

Phenomenon opened to mixed reviews, though the worst were so toxic they didn't encourage you to read the others. One motif was prevalent. 'Is it the barely concealed Scientology agenda that makes *Phenomenon* so creepy?' wrote the *Village Voice*'s Amy Taubin.

'[The film is] like a brain-dead *bildungsroman* for the Scientology set,' echoed Claudia Ise in *L.A. View*, going on to list four key Dianetic tenets which she accused the film of parroting or promoting. One: that humans use only a tiny fraction of their brain's potential. Two: that from the right 'teaching' you can acquire a new zest for life. Three: that with a little (Hubbard) help you can make major contributions to society. Four: that through such means you will learn the meaning of love.

During shooting, it didn't help the makers' cries of 'Look, no Scientology' that Travolta was busy performing cures. When a young boy injured his leg climbing a tree house and a crew member was hurt in an accident, the actor says he 'used about four different processes to help them heal . . . And when anyone has a cold I use certain processes to help them.'

Though Turteltaub still insists that Travolta's casting was the main or only reason that commentators kept invoking the cult – 'If Richard Gere was in it, they would have said it was a film about Buddhism' – *Phenomenon* no sooner started its march across the world than it caused uproar in Scientology-sensitive countries like Holland and Germany. Turteltaub was in the eye of each storm.

'If there weren't so much intolerance and hate in the world I'd just laugh it off. In Germany it became a big deal, and it bothered me because people weren't watching the movie but their own politics. When people condemn the film because of Scientology, what they're condemning is notions such as love, tolerance and the human spirit.'

But let us not go to the other extreme and Disneyfy *Phenomenon*, even though Disney produced it. If it has any merit – and for many critics it didn't – the movie rises above the abstractions

Turteltaub invokes here with the featherlight charm and honesty of the small-town genre-painting he brought to it. Also helping to outsmart gloppy mysticism is Travolta's ease in the main role.

Pauline Kael thinks *Phenomenon*, which she hates, didn't deserve its star. When we talk about the film, she cannot even bring herself to pronounce the title. 'That terrible movie where he plays a simpleton who gains enlightenment. He was wonderful in it. He's such a sincere actor that there are times when you want to say, "It would be better if you were more cynical." He gave the film more than was its due.'

Phenomenon improves on a second viewing. Even on a first its bemused if sometimes ponderous pantheism is at least on a par with models like *Friendly Persuasion* and *Field of Dreams*; which may explain how the film sidestepped grim-reaper critics to reap, itself, a $100 million at the American box office.

'While I was making the film, I thought it might bomb commercially but that critics would like it,' says Turteltaub. 'I couldn't have been more wrong. Audiences loved it and the critics didn't. They all liked John Travolta, they just didn't love the movie.'

They all liked John Travolta. Why?

Gerald DiPego: 'He's someone who walks out on screen and the audience gives him the benefit of the doubt by liking him right off the bat. Certain actors have to earn that during the course of a role, but with Travolta there's an instant likability and a feeling of Everyman about him. It hit all of us that he was right for the film as soon as his name was mentioned.'

Even Mike Newell, who had wanted to streak *Phenomenon* with darker hues, looks on Travolta fondly as a kind of semipaternal movie folk-hero. 'I have a teenage daughter and when John Travolta's career was in the depths she was watching movies like *Look Who's Talking* and *Look Who's Talking Too*. I used to sit through endless Saturday mornings in front of the telly, and I got to have a huge affection for that tub-of-guts character he played and I thought he played it really well. It's a daft quality to mention, but he's "cheerful". He's an optimist. He has this little shine that comes out of him, this twinkle. There's something about life in his hands that makes you feel cheerful. You can't help liking him.'

5

ANGELS AND
MINISTERS OF GRACE

'Give us a fucking break,' said John Travolta. 'Being the bold personalities we are, do you honestly think we'd let ourselves be controlled?'

He was telling a pressman where to get off after a question about him, Tom Cruise and – yes, again – Scientology. Sometimes it wasn't enough to be patient: you had to counter-attack. Like mosquitoes these hacks went straight for the celebrity's ankles, the nearest they could get to his Achilles heel, and a good slap could feel better than gracious restraint. Couldn't they shut up about Scientology?

Yet at the same time Travolta seemed to invite the bites. He kept hosting interviews in his luxury fourth-floor apartment in the Scientology Celebrity Center. So what was the newshound supposed to do – *not* ask about Dianetics, Ron Hubbard and Tom fellow-mystic Cruise?

Usually Travolta was the soul of perfect PR. He let it be known that, inspired by Hubbardism, he gave to charities promoting drug rehabilitation, the rain forest, the clean-up of radioactive food in Russia, cancer, Aids research and programmes for the learning-disabled. He told reporters that his co-religionists were in like Flynn at any major national crisis. 'Take the Oklahoma City bombing. Scientologists were all over that place, trying to help people out of the building, trying to help people recover from their injuries.' And so far as he, Travolta, was concerned, far from feeling any sinister pressure to stay inside the organisation, 'It's

more like it works so good and you feel so much better that you want to stick around.'

And on the subject of Tom Cruise (if the reporter insists), 'We're at the same level, but he did his courses over a two-year period full-time. And I did mine over a longer period of time.' One minute for photos. Gentlemen and ladies, thank you for coming.'

Few can resist the charms of Travolta the man, even when they quail at Travolta the missionary. One visitor to the star's Celebrity Center eyrie was the author who helped to make him famous. British writer Nik Cohn, who penned the source story for *Saturday Night Fever*, recalls the day he spent *chez* Travolta as an interviewer for *Vogue*. It happened soon after *Pulp Fiction* had placed the actor on the show business map again.

'He was a very sweet man,' Cohn recalls. 'Extraordinarily, almost preternaturally gentle, nurturing – to use all those Hollywood words. You know, "How *are* you?" Not insincere, he wasn't at all fake. But he takes care of everyone around him. I liked him a lot.'

Cohn even takes an indulgent view of Scientology. It goes, he says, with the territory.

'It's the old blues line, isn't it? Whatever helps you through the night. The movie world is very rootless, one lives in an unreal climate where the only reality is box-office figures and your popularity rating. This produces a spiritual hunger, and Scientology is well slanted towards celebrity because, one, it's new and intriguing – it's not a religion any of them grew up with, so it has a certain mystique and glamour – and two, you don't have to mingle with the hoi polloi as you would in a normal congregation. You can retain the full measure of your stardom, and have beautiful meals brought to you. They have a fully-fledged gourmet restaurant. There's no giving up on luxuries. Hairshirts are in small demand.'

But how can Scientology's showbiz converts and beneficiaries not look on this manifest elitism and be cynical?

'Cynicism is not a part of Hollywood thinking,' Cohn says. 'Not among stars and actors. Look at John Travolta. His mother gave him a cosseted, "you-are-special" life and by the time he was nineteen the world agreed with her. The closest to a

reality check he ever had was when his box-office rating went down.'

Jon Turteltaub believes that the mid-career fall helped Travolta to grow up. 'During those down years when things weren't happening he was able to make the transition from young man to man.' But it can't have been painless, even with the Hubbardites for spiritual support. At the worst, his fall from fame must have seemed a betrayal of faith by the public. ['I've often put my heart on the table and misjudged who would treat it correctly.'] At best it was a bad accident. No one's *fault* exactly, and no one's responsiblity to do repairwork except the victim; just one of those learning tragedies that leave scars while strengthening the skin, hopefully, against further wounding.

Actor Richard Dreyfuss, who had a similar tumble from fame after *Jaws* and *Close Encounters of the Third Kind*, and after pipping John Travolta to the 1978 Best Actor Oscar with *The Goodbye Girl*, sees his fellow actor's story as a kind of romance.

'It was an interrupted love affair,' he says. 'This great love affair began and then he missed the train, or everyone else missed the train. They went in opposite directions. And although John never really thought he was gone – he has the greatest attitude on earth about his life and career – he just waited for people to wake up and say, "Oh, John!" And they did.'

By the late eighties, early nineties Dreyfuss had made his own pact with the comeback gods; after a burnout interlude caused by drugs and drink, he was on screen again as a character star. But others who had fallen in the seventies or early eighties began looking at Travolta as a great Stakhanovite paradigm. If he could do it, surely they could. And what had been his method? Taking a glorified bit role in a low-budget independent movie.

So casting agents, including Ronnie Yeskel who had cast Tarantino's film, were suddenly besieged with calls from ex-stars seeking their own *Pulp Fiction*s. They were soon seen everywhere. Michael J. Fox and Lily Tomlin did cameos in Wayne Wang's *Blue in the Face*. Burt Reynolds signed for a bit in *Bean*, then a larger bit in *Boogie Nights*. Elliott Gould, a quarter-century after being the darling of the counter-culture (*M*a*s*h*, *The Long Goodbye*),

could be seen mugging earnestly in a micro-budget movie about gay life called *Johns*.

But there was only one John. And being him was not all smooth ascension. He wasn't just a successful middle-aged film star reborn: he was a revenant heart-throb who had once created havoc among the world's hormones. That world wanted a chance to strip him bare all over again. In 1995 the L.A. rock band Extra Fancy flyposted the city's bus stops with nude posters of Travolta to publicise their new single, 'You look like a movie star, honey'. The posters, based on an explicit drawing that had first appeared in the seventies counter-culture rag *Skin*, were torn down and appropriated by fans as soon as they appeared.

Record companies rushed out the ex-crooner's old songs. CDs appeared whose cover designs depicted the teenage Travolta in an explosion of hair and a kitschy meltingness of blue eyes and cupid lips. A request from Warner for John to record a new album produced a surprising 'I have no objection to doing it'. Probably he thought a new record would take the spotlight off the old ones.

For there was still a vestigial anxiety about being yesterday's man all over again, of being an adoration victim for all the wrong or most passive reasons. 'Just a pretty face', 'just a nice voice', 'just a pair of dancing legs', or even, 'just a natural screen presence'. He wanted to be in charge of his destiny, not destiny's passive darling.

So he began to *act* as if he was in charge. By the mid nineties, he was learning courtliness and *grandezza*, two of the higher manifestations of middle-life movie star charisma and two ways to make the world know – or think – that he is no longer a child but a grown-up large enough to fill his own legend.

'Oh, he's such a big being!' Kelly Preston helpfully effused. 'We're all just these beings, you know, and to change the world the way John did – well, you have to be a very big being.'

'I'm a big man, and I need the room,' John concurred, in a verbal sweep that took in his mansions, his planes, his charcoal-grey Rolls Royce and his tendency to travel about the world with a retinue that would flatter Genghis Khan. (In 1997 he would come top of a magazine poll seeking to identify the most waited-upon superstar.)

He had another fount of strength and majesty. In the precise operational space of his two favoured pastimes – and never mind the planning, dealing and thinking around them – he had no insecurity. 'There are two areas in my life where I am fearless, and that's in acting and aviation.' They complemented each other. 'Flying is very extroverted and focused and A-to-B-ish. Whereas there's a kind of euphoria about acting, when you're in a zone that's very creative and you become another character.'

His acting, furthermore, seemed to be *imitating* his flying. From a heroin-dependent gangster he had risen to a mental genius, striving to understand life on earth before being dispatched to heaven. Now, soaring further to a role as an angel could be no surprise, least of all to a man who lived in a house bursting with them.

Kelly, to her husband's bemusement, had a weakness for fey statuary. 'I don't mind an *occasional* angel, but . . .' he affectionately protested, gesturing at the winged guardians in stone or clay who clogged up the living space. (There were also a dozen lifesize cherubs.) Now he would play the archangel Michael in a whimsical comedy shaped by Nora and Delia Ephron from an original darker screenplay by Pete Dexter with Jim Quinlan.

Film-maker Nora Ephron, who wrote *Heartburn* and *When Harry Met Sally* before launching a thousand kleenexes by directing *Sleepless in Seattle*, explains. 'For me it became a romantic comedy about cynicism versus love. That wasn't there in the first script, but it seemed to me what it should be about.'

So she and sister Delia stressed the humanisation of the two hardboiled journalists and their female 'angel expert', played in the film by William Hurt, Robert Pastorelli and Andie MacDowell. On learning that the blessed Michael is enjoying an earthly vacation in Iowa, they track down this scoop of scoops, with the final twist that Hurt and MacDowell end up scooping each other romantically.

'These people who'd given up, who believed in nothing, had to believe in something,' Ephron says. 'So naturally it seemed they had to believe in what *I* believe in, which is love.'

In a phrase, the new writers softened the story up. Did the original writers approve? 'I sent the shooting script to Dexter and Quinlan and I assumed that Pete, certainly, was not particularly happy,' Ephron says. 'But he came to the opening in L.A. and was very

pleased with the film. I didn't want him to hate us for kidnapping his movie, which no question we did.'

Who to play Michael? Who to enact this terrestrialised angel who stuffs himself so devoutly with earthly pleasures – food, sex, drink, cigarettes – that he resembles more a winged Falstaff than the celebrated swashbuckler who routed Lucifer?

'He has to be innocent and sexy at the same time, which is a very tricky combination for an actor,' says Ephron. 'I thought Gérard Depardieu would be almost ideal, but it worried me that I couldn't think of anyone else. Then when *Pulp Fiction* came out Delia said to me, "Well, that's Michael!"

'It was clear to us but not to Universal. They had an "A" list of actors in their heads and would have been happy to pay Jack Nicholson $15 million to do it, but not the half that sum which John wanted. His price was going up by the minute and it was shocking to everyone that this actor who couldn't get arrested two years earlier was suddenly asking $8 million for a movie. By the time Delia and I had found another studio, Turner Pictures, his price has gone up to $11 million and only a week or two had passed.'

Travolta received a thirty-minute recruiting call from Steven Spielberg. The *Jurassic Park* director telephoned to say he had wanted to direct the picture himself, that it was a great story, that he was a friend of Nora's, and that John *must* do it. 'I told him, "I'm there",' says Travolta, ' "the speech is not even necessary, but I'm glad you feel that way." '

Turner Pictures gave over the cash and Travolta was expected to give himself over to the business of getting into – or rather out of – shape. 'I'd like to say I put on weight . . . but they just caught me at a good time.'

Travolta was hitting the larder again. Guests at his Brentwood hacienda were awed at what appeared on the dining table on an average evening in the mid-nineties. After the maidservant lit the coloured glass centrepiece and arranged each place-setting – a mat, a bottle of Evian, a frosted glass with a slice of lemon impaled on the side – chef Dara Crouch would announce the culinary order of play. A mushroom-and-goat's-cheese timbale with toast points and fried leeks in a mushroom demiglaze; a main course of groaning

flesh or fowl; then for dessert a slab of chocolate surmounted with a scoop of vanilla ice cream, a cluster of berries, a poached pear and a crinkly golden caramel cage.

So Travolta would clump into his first scene in *Michael* and take the crew's breath away, and later the audience's, with his hungover grossness, the hairy spread of his unshirted torso. 'In the tradition of great comedians John has no vanity,' understates Ephron. 'He's got enormous confidence in his own charm, so he knew he could look like a total slob. He's willing to let his gut hang out knowing you'll still want to jump him.'

Travolta saw contradictoriness as the character's main appeal: 'He's a warrior, yes, but he has been through so many historical events that he's just thrashed. Even his wings are dirty.' So he presented a fuddled, outsized bear of an archangel, clothed in a crumpled raincoat that would do Colombo proud and sporting a tumble of long hair, an illshaven face and those shopsoiled feathery appendages. ('It's like some great big bird made love to that man's mother,' comments Hurt on first sighting.)

Ephron wanted her hero's actions too to seem gauche, diselemented. 'I suggested to John he eat left-handed to seem clumsier.' She also encouraged him to improvise gestures and dialogue. 'He's very good at it. The scene where they're in the car playing "car bingo", that was all improvised in rehearsals, with John and the others driving round and round while I sat inside and took notes.

'He did a lot of interesting, bizarre, contradictory things that somehow hung together,' Ephron says. They included manic guffaws, crotch-scratchings, picking his teeth with a wing-feather, becoming teary-melancholic on a bench (shades of the Verrazano Bridge in *Saturday Night Fever*) and alternating moments of genial hamming – like his "surprised" expression each time he is punched during the bar brawl – with a touching inwardness in quieter scenes. Even at his profanest, this Michael persuades you he has a soul tucked inside the roly-poly physique. Travolta was the perfect star to mollify the moral majority, if the film needed to.

'There's a slight risk of religious offence in any comedy where the archangel Michael smokes and flirts with women,' says Ephron. 'But John protected us because he can do almost anything and not

seem awful. Look at *Pulp Fiction*. He's like a mass murderer in that, but you still think he's completely adorable.'

In for one good-humoured heresy, in for a dozen. *Michael*'s title hero claims to have done a lot of middle-management creation in his time. He invented queuing: 'Before that, everybody milled around.' And he wrote Psalm 85. So his character lends itself to a romantic comedy cum road movie whose itinerary celebrates the art of the brainstorm. The main characters motor across America visiting weird landmarks. A giant milk bottle. The world's largest ball of twine and non-stick frying pan. All the things this archangel might have come up with after psalm-writing and queue-inventing.

'It was an excuse for them to stay on the roads,' Ephron says. 'Excuses for road movies are usually so pathetic. "Flying's not safe." We've seen all that. But this was a way to keep them driving and also to convey an idea of Americana.'

Which pinpoints *Michael*'s charm. It's about a prelapsarian country where the chthonic innocence of a backwoods culture meets the heaven-hewn 'innocence' of an angel who acknowledges no sin: not at least among the petty vices classed as sins by earthly Pharisees. Smoking, drinking, eating, fornicating: all so minor-league. Aren't the greater sins those of cold-heartedness, exploitation, deception, hypocrisy – the newspaper-world vices of which Hurt and Pastorelli are cured by an angel, a journey and a love match struck on the tinder of a scoop epiphany?

This could have been, yet again, a sub-Capra comedy-fable complete with folksy redemption. *Michael* is at once an advertisement for the next world and its lovable guardians – 'It's A Wonderful Afterlife' – and a mind-how-you-go message for this life. But as in *Phenomenon*, Travolta syphons away the mawkishness and Ephron has the sense to let the film be as loose and funky as its star.

Indeed *Michael*'s only major flaw is that it is sometimes *too* loose, especially around the middle. One wishes it would draw in its gut and tighten its structure. Instead scenes amble in and out, like an overweight busker who has lost the drift of his act but hopes everyone will throw a penny in the hat anyway. There is even the all-but-inevitable Travolta dance scene, this time a splay-legged saloon-bar hoof to the sound of 'Chain of Fools'.

When *Michael* went into PR warp, much was made of the fact that the star had behaved like an angel off camera as well as on. When a dazed Andie MacDowell appeared with Travolta on TV's *Oprah*, she told the world how he had spoiled everyone with gifts.

'Chocolates,' rhapsodised MacDowell. 'He gave me the best chocolates. I mean, it was amazing chocolate. You know those chocolates – ?'

Winfrey clucked in sympathetic wonder. She asked MacDowell if Travolta had given her anything else.

'He gave me a tea set. He's a very generous man. He is a *very* generous man. He gave me a beautiful, beautiful tea set.'

Winfrey turned to Travolta to ask him why he had done this. He explained, 'Well, I saw this beautiful woman in the middle of the Texas desert, and I thought, she's got to have something proper to put her tea in.'

'And you brought her a tea set?' says Winfrey.

('It was a beautiful tea set,' interjects a still dazed MacDowell.)

'Well, sort of,' says Travolta. 'I also bought one for Robert Pastorelli and William Hurt. They all had to have them.'

Even Nora Ephron. I asked the director what she made of it. Was Travolta 'living the role' – being an earthly angel off-camera? 'He's just a very generous, nice guy,' she says. 'I don't think he was living the role. I can't imagine that on the set of *Pulp Fiction* he walked around threatening people. He probably gave away chocolates there too. He's a sweet man, one of the nicest people anybody knows.'

Et tu, Ephron. Like the rest of Planet Showbiz, the astringent creator of *Heartburn* and *Harry/Sally* joins the ranks of the Travolta charm victims, nine-pinned by the actor's niceness as his career rolls on through devilry and angelry to this second Nirvana of adoration.

Something has to go wrong, surely. Or the whole world will fall to its knees in fan worship. From the land of sunset to the land of sunrise, the atlas will become as pink as the bygone British empire, only this time with the candy-floss heraldry of the John Travolta Fan Club.

So something does go wrong. By some dark prompting Travolta signs a deal to star in a European film to be directed by that

imp of the surreal, Roman Polanski. Hollywood's Mr Nice Guy will dance a career two-step with the man who made *Repulsion*, *Cul-de-Sac* and *Rosemary's Baby*. The new film, *The Double*, is about a meek accountant who falls under the sway of his more roguish *doppelgänger*. Travolta would play both roles and, after signing for the $18-million fee, plans to fly to Paris to do so.

First though, he will have a brief nastiness workout in Hollywood: a cameo role in *She's De Lovely* for actor-turned-filmmaker Nick Cassavetes. Re-tooling an unrealised project by his father John, Cassavetes and actor Sean Penn had worked to shape the tale of a disturbed working-class husband (played by Penn) who goes to jail for killing two policemen in a blaze of irrationality after a neighbour has raped his wife (Robin Wright, newly Mrs Sean Penn). He emerges ten years later to find that Wright has married John Travolta. She and this retired construction boss with gangland connections live in a chintzy suburbia where Travolta puts the frighteners on anyone threatening his domestic serenity. This includes Penn when he finally visits with a present, a gun and crony Harry Dean Stanton. Like many an archetypal Cassavetes movie, *She's De Lovely* ends with a lot of shouting and running around, as human life levels up to its natural state of tragi-comic farce.

Travolta does a princely turn as the husband. But the turn will stay on the shelf for many months before this odd, unclassifiable film finally reveals itself at the 1997 Cannes Film Festival.

Before that the actor has his other rendezvous in France. The start date for *The Double* is mid-June 1996: the place, Billancourt Studios in Paris. Travolta has a $200,000 trailer shipped out from the States and follows soon after in his Gulfstream II. Since one of his two characters speaks perfect French, he must have language coaching – none of that 'I like to parler with Gerard' stuff. And since bubble-blowing is a prerequisite for the meek accountant a bubble coach must be in attendance.

Travolta settled into his $15,000-a-month hotel suite before sallying forth to survey the state of pre-production. $13 million dollars had been spent, partly in doing scenic justice to the Dostoevskian atmospherics of the script by Jeremy (*Don Juan De Marcos*) Leven. Leven had taken the Russian writer's novella *The Double* and transformed it into a boulevard comedy. Travolta

was attracted by the screenplay's gentle humour: '[It was] a *Being There* type of subtle comedy'; referring to the 1979 Peter Sellers comedy about a gardener raised to social and political heights by being mistaken for a sage.

The actor joked in happy anticipation of filming this dual-identity caprice. 'I negotiated to get paid twice as much. I get twice as many meal breaks, and I'm asking for two trailers.'

The trouble began when he was handed the second of two scripts. Roman Polanski gave him a newly revised draft in which the tone of *The Double* seemed to have changed beyond recognition. And there was something about a nude scene.

6

COMEBACK IN CRISIS

(i) Double Trouble

After one week in Paris, John Travolta caught a commercial night flight back to America. He never returned to Polanski's film. Initially the trip was explained as a medical emergency. Kelly had telephoned him in mid-rehearsal to reveal that Jett had seen a doctor and been diagnosed with 'water behind the eardrums': a non-critical childhood affliction which required the ear to be drained using two small tubes.

The operation 'was all scheduled', Travolta later said, but he saw it as his mission to travel to America and postpone it. '[Jett] didn't have to have it ultimately. When I was in Paris I said [to Kelly], "Would you mind just holding off until I come home, because I want to check with some other doctors." Then we went to a highly respected doctor in Beverly Hills, who said he shouldn't have the surgery. It turned out he didn't have that fluid behind the eardrum. So surgery was unnecessary.'

So, it seemed, was the red-eye from France to California. But it soon became clear that the journey had been made for other or additional reasons; that *The Double* had lost a star and gained a black hole full of impending litigation. Travolta stayed in America to oversee the war of words between a director who had been professionally jilted and an actor who claimed that the concept of the movie he had signed for had changed. The working atmosphere in Paris hadn't helped.

'From the beginning, at the first reading, Roman didn't like my

acting. He told me I was bad and showed me what I should do
. . . Our views on the film were completely different. I wanted to
do a dramatic comedy, he wanted a cartoon.'

'Sure, there were changes in the script, but they were not that
dramatic,' responds Polanski today. The problem, he says, was that
Travolta 'resented any kind of comment. He seemed to have some
kind of inferiority complex, perhaps from some period of his life
when he was not justly dealt with. During the third read-through,
about a week before we were supposed to start shooting, there was
a heated conversation between us. I made some comment about his
line-readings in a scene – I said something like, "That's not how I
heard it in my mind" – and he said, "Well, that's how I heard it."
I said, "Well, there may be as many ideas of how this scene should
be dealt with as there are people in the world. Who takes the final
decision? I'm here to direct." And we started arguing. It was not
a fight but it was quite uneasy, as when people don't say exactly
what's on their mind. He is more a passive-aggressive person, he
does not come right out and say, "You asshole!" '

Then there was the supposed nude scene.

'There were no naked scenes in the original script,' Travolta
stated from his American exile. 'Roman added it for no reason
. . . I have never acted naked in my whole career, and it's not now
that I'm fat that I'm going to start.'

'Total bullshit,' Polanski responds. 'Can you possibly imagine
I would want to show him with his dick dangling or something?
It's crazy. This was a comedy destined for a wide audience.'

He admits when pressed, however, that there *was* a brief scene
in which Travolta's character pads about with nothing on. 'The
character's in his bathtub when his intercom rings and he gets out
and goes naked to the intercom dripping water. But it's a question
of how you film it. I wanted to go on his feet splashing water
across the apartment, then maybe a close-up where he picks up
the phone; then he reaches for a trenchcoat hanging on the door
and puts it on. It's a funny scene, but "nudity"! – Christ, it's so
preposterous I should not even dignify it with a comment.'

But maybe he should have dignified it with a clearer explanation
to Travolta, specifying what would or wouldn't be seen on screen.
This actor had revealed all or nearly all, goodness knows, in *Pulp*

Fiction. And as an angel of Falstaffian girth in *Michael* he hadn't been afraid of stripping down to the jockey shorts.

Polanski admits he might have been more tactful in his whole handling of Travolta.

'Maybe in the readings I should have just sat there and listened without reacting, just to get him acclimatised. But from what I had seen of him, I thought he was a real pro, and with pros, you know, you work without thinking of all this sensitivity. You just give direction and sometimes you show what you want that's different.'

Back in the US, while there were still hopes of keeping the film alive, Travolta put out his conditions for returning. He wanted Polanski banned from script meetings and barred from directing the actor's 'personal appearances'. The film-maker was also required to submit his 'creative vision' in writing for the actor's approval, who would also control the number of camera takes involving him.

Polanski and Mandalay rejected the conditions and published their counter-charges. Travolta had 'wanted to co-opt the function of the director and required a level of creative control that is not normally delegated to actors for hire.' Travolta took that on the chin and then attempted his own knockout. He would make the film but not with Polanski. He called for him to be replaced with the movie's producer Lili Fini Zanuck, daughter-in-law of the legendary mogul Darryl and director of the modestly greeted drugs thriller *Rush*. He even offered to buy Polanski out at a personal cost of $3.2 million.

Mandalay responded with a multi-million dollar lawsuit filed in a Los Angeles court. The suit cited that 'Travolta began a concerted and deliberate course of conduct designed to disrupt the progress . . . of the picture.' It further claimed that 'Polanski and Liteoffer [his production company] were prepared to accede to outrageous requests. To mollify Travolta, the parties had scheduled the creative meetings Travolta insisted upon, to take place from June 2nd through June 4th in Paris with rehearsals to recommence June 5th.' But Travolta and manager Jonathan Krane 'suddenly and with no notice . . . left Paris on June 2nd, later denying any agreement to make the film'.

Bert Fields, Travolta's lawyer, claimed, 'John never reached an

agreement with the Guber company [Mandalay].' A fee and script approval had been negotiated, said Fields, but Mandalay made 'significant changes' to the screenplay. 'It [had] spread more into slapstick and I didn't know how to do it the way it was presented to me,' stated Travolta. The later script, reworked from Leven's original by Dennis Keith, the writer-creator of TV's *Larry Sanders Show*, contained an alleged twenty-five changed pages out of 110. The actor summed up, 'If you were presented with a Rolex, and now you're being given a Timex, you'd say, "Wait a minute! Where's the Rolex you presented me?" . . . With this new wave of success, I'm getting braver in my old age to say, "I can't perform that." '

Brave or impulsive: it depends on the beholder.

Is there is something of the eternal child about Travolta here? Is that what Polanski reckoned lay behind all of this?

'Yes, and of course that's part of his charm,' says the director. 'These things have their shortcomings and also their advantages.'

But childlikeness doesn't make up, he feels, for the final games of hide-and-seek in France. 'The last I saw of him was that third reading when we had the argument. Several of us were supposed to have dinner later, but John didn't turn up. Jonathan Krane told Lili Zanuck that he'd gone to the airport but there was no plane or something. The next day there was panic among us. Krane said Travolta just wanted a pat on the shoulder, because he looked on the director as a father figure, he just needed to be talked to. So I rang his hotel, but my call was never returned. It went on like that and a couple of days later Travolta left.

'I've never known any instance of an actor walking out like this so close to filming. They tried to blame me and my behaviour, suggesting I don't know how films are made now, that I'm history. But the fact is, if you are an actor and people depend on you, you cannot just bolt like that.'

The Double finally went down in a chaos of salvage attempts. Mandalay and Polanski tried to keep it afloat with a new star, settling for Steve Martin, bargain-priced at $4 million, after Sean Penn, Robert De Niro and Al Pacino had all declined. Then co-star Isabelle Adjani jumped ship when she wasn't consulted over the change to Martin. And when Polanski replaced her with Carole Bouquet, Peter Guber of Mandalay threw a tantrum because *he*

hadn't been consulted over Bouquet. The ship went down, or by a general vote was scuttled.

When Polanski sought peace and quiet as jury president at the Venice Film Festival in late August, *he* encountered what many celebrities might consider the worst punishment of all. A John Travolta biographer, keen for an update on the then continuing court action.

(ii) The Medium is the Messenger

Biographers are supposed to be invisible. We are not expected to step into our books except in the Introduction – 'Why I am writing this' – and in the Acknowledgements – 'I would like to thank the world, the flesh and the devil, plus my agent and editor.'

But sometimes it is against nature for an author to hide behind his subject. A star is defined by the world's response to the star and the author is ambassador for that response. Armed with the questions others might like to ask, as well as his own, he criss-crosses the terrain between idol and idolators. He is part of the action, if only as the man trying to turn a stand-off into an entente.

In the process – in the very negotiating madness of telephones, fax machines, secretaries, more secretaries and occasional personal encounters (though not with the person) – he discovers the drama and arcana of the world of stardom. He learns that 'Frustrate the ambassador' is moviedom's gentler version of 'Shoot the messenger'. And he learns that information is not just power, but the entire currency of the biographical process. The way stars or directors parcel out that information, or don't, is integral to the story he is telling.

So the eighteen months of globe-trotting that began for me at the 1996 Venice Film Festival was part assault course, part strategising exam and part sheer hard labour as I quarried into the two contrasting mineral contents of celebrity: paranoia and the urge to self-publicity.

The first I quickly struck, though persecution mania in this case was partly legitimised by *sub judice* discretion. More than a year before he unburdened himself to me from Paris, Roman Polanski begged out of an interview when I ambushed him by

house telephone at Venice's Excelsior Hotel. 'It's in the hands of my lawyers,' he said. 'I hope it is resolved soon. Thank you, but I can't speak. No, no, I can't have you turn this into an interview.'

Biographers quickly become imperturbable. Rejection is like a loss at the gaming table for an addicted gambler. The player instantly wants to hazard more, as much for the adventure of playing as for the hope of winning. And Venice 1996 was laid out like a John Travolta casino cum theme park. Wherever you looked, there was someone or something connected to the main man.

Stalled by Polanski, and realising *The Double* would have to be spiked until its legal course had run, my thoughts turned to Dustin Hoffman. He was in Venice, scheduled to give a press conference after a screening of *American Buffalo*. Hoffman's new film in production was *Mad City*, which had recently co-signed John Travolta on the very rebound from his Parisian debacle.

Directed by Costa-Gavras, the issue-movie specialist of *Z* and *Missing*, *Mad City* tells of a museum security guard, played by Travolta, who when fired from his job takes a group of museum visitors hostage. The crisis is exploited by an ambitious TV reporter played by Hoffman. Venice seemed the perfect opportunity to get an early Hoffman soundbite, coaxed by some tortuous connection I would have to dream up between the Mamet movie he was promoting and the film I wanted to know about.

At the screen end of the Sala Perla, a gambling casino that doubles as viewing theatre, the actor was a weaving, short-statured blur in sneakers and grey sweatshirt. He stood smiling for the bulb-popping photographers. When the lightstorm calmed there were three regulation questions and answers about *American Buffalo*. Then I heard my voice speaking up.

'Mr Hoffman, I wonder if any of the moral questions you've discussed in relation to your film of David Mamet's play are also raised in your new film *Mad City*, co-starring John Travolta?'

Hoffman took it like a born self-publicist.

'I think that Costa-Gavras is a great director and this is his oeuvre, his genre,' he waxed. 'It's almost documentary, it involves the media and the basic fundamental question of a journalist, which is "Do you get in the way of a story or

do you let the story take, as you guys call it, its organic growth?" '

Hoffman had caught the wave of his own eloquence. 'As the reporter said who took the famous photograph of the Vietnamese monk who immolated himself during the Vietnam war, "During all the years since," he said, "people've asked me why I didn't try to put the fire out. Number one, I couldn't have done it because there was a circle of monks around him preventing people from disturbing the symbolic act. Number two, even if they weren't there I wouldn't have done it, because a reporter never puts the fire out. You take the picture." Now from my point of view that's a kind of interesting dilemma. It's an interesting idea, and from Costa-Gavras's point of view that's something we want to play with in terms of the ethos you guys have to operate within.'

Grand themes; the template for a screen morality play. But *Mad City* was about to enter a troubled history, which while not of *Double*-style trouble, began to form an alarming sequence with Polanski's aborted comedy and the ominously long shelf life of the earlier-made *She's De Lovely*.

(iii) Production Pile-up

Movies, one can forget, come in stages. They drag their articulated histories – script, preproduction, production, editing, publicity, release – across time's landscape like Pharaonic slaves dragging the component fragments of a temple. In 1996/97 life was more like that than ever for John Travolta. The start date of each production, assuming that unlike *The Double* it started at all, could have peered at its finishing or release date across a vast desert strewn with bits of other projects – beginnings, middles, ends – hauling their bulks across the waste.

Before *Double* (unmade) there was *De Lovely* (unshown). And before *De Lovely* (shown) there was *City* (made and delayed). And as if this scenario were not bewildering enough, we must add *Face/Off*. This was the action thriller Travolta began making after *Mad City*, but whose release would *precede* the Costa-Gavras drama, destined to be delayed by teething troubles. *Mad City* had been planned for unveiling at the 1997 Cannes Film Festival, but

Travoltaphiles were consoled instead with his guest spot in *She's De Lovely*, now called *She's So Lovely*.

Mad City and *Face/Off*, a John Woo romp on the possibly timely subjects of career breakdown and identity confusion, were being pulled by rival slave armies towards a mid 1997 release. Though *Face/Off* would win the race, *Mad City* qualified for some special grand prize as the most bizarrely procrastinated project of Travolta's comeback.

Who better to pitch this film's story to me than the producer? In a hotel lobby one summer's day Arnold Kopelson (*Platoon, Falling Down, Seven*) did so, punctuating his recital with cigar puffs. Kopelson is a chunkily built mogul with a healthy-to-rosy complexion, large confidence and a brisk but deceptively mild-spoken manner: you don't realise he is barnstorming you until it is too late. Now, as if I was a studio executive being talked into a deal rather than a biographer scavenging for crumbs, he rat-a-tatted through every early scene right up to the gunshot that Travolta's sacked and angry museum guard accidentally discharges, wounding a colleague and sparking a crisis.

'At this very moment a bunch of children comes in who are on a museum tour with their teacher, and Travolta freaks and takes everyone hostage. The phone rings, it's the police, and this poor guy doesn't know what to do. And Dustin as the visiting journalist, instead of reporting, takes over and tells him what to do.'

He thereby risks his own job, Kopelson explains, by leaping that delicate divide between reportorial detachment and human solidarity.

The movie should have been a cinch for Cannes, surely, I said. It even boasts a French director.

'John wanted it to go to the festival, but the music wasn't ready,' Kopelson answers. 'John said, "Can't we show it with a temp track?" I said, "The press'll review it as a finished movie and we'll never get another review." '

The producer may have been overcautious; or there may have been more wrong with the film than he suggests. It wouldn't have been the first time a 'work in progress' had been shown at Cannes – historically it was almost an advantage. *Apocalypse Now* and

The Mission were both unfinished when they won the Palme d'Or for best film.

Costa-Gavras later told me by phone, 'The festival wanted the movie, but Warners decided not to go. With a November opening it would be too long a delay between Cannes and the release. Also there was a little work to be done on the music.'

But *Mad City* didn't have a November opening originally. It was due out the previous spring. And what was all this about undesirable time lags between festival showings and public release? *Pulp Fiction* waited a similar long summer between Cannes and US opening and look what happened to that.

So did all this spin-doctoring disguise a crisis?

In early summer I was faxed by a Hollywood friend who saw a test preview of *Mad City*. She was confused by the film, which seemed a misbegotten take on *Network* with Dustin Hoffman doing the Peter Finch histrionics. 'Weird,' she summed up.

Maybe there were unresolved tensions on the production team. Maybe Costa-Gravas and Kopelson were enacting that old dance of warring sensibilities, Europe versus Hollywood. The Greek-born Parisian who made his reputation with a series of streamlined agitprop thrillers starring Yves Montand had always seemed a risky match with the producer who thundered out *sturm und drang* blockbusters like *The Fugitive* and *Eraser*.

Each man, when prodded, weakened into admission.

Kopelson didn't think that Costa-Gavras, an 'intellectual', was bringing forward enough emotions. 'You have to have resolution. You must give the audience its orgasms,' he declaimed. Costa-Gavras counters tactfully, 'My approach was the European approach versus the American one. Kopelson is a big professional, he knows the American public much more than, than . . .' [he decides not to say 'me'] 'For instance, he said we should have a big orchestra with violins and I said, "No, no. It is not that kind of film. It's a film with modern music; or less music; maybe guitar." '

The one thing both agreed on was the casting of Travolta. Yet this too went through tribulations.

'I needed someone who starts off cynical and becomes more sensitive,' says Costa-Gavras. 'I thought John was the right person

for the reporter. But when we had a reading at his house I saw him little by little changing. A couple of hours later he called to say, "What if I play the other role?" ' The director said fine: 'I had already decided I wanted the museum guard to be less violent, kinder and more human than in the script.'

Events then happened so fast that they became milled together in the maelstrom. First Dustin Hoffman agreed to play the reporter. Then Travolta decamped to *The Double* (from one French-based eastern European director's arms to another's). Then, almost before Kopelson and Costa-Garvas could begin rehearsing their new actor – 'I can't tell you his name,' says the director, 'he was British' – there was another turnaround.

'A week after I learned he was doing the Polanski movie I learn he is dropping it!' Costa-Garvas says. 'John and I had a meeting and he said he liked our script and the film's whole message about the press.' Since several commentators had castigated his exit from *The Double* as a star tantrum – notably *Variety* editor Peter Bart, whose long open letter to Travolta talked of 'symptoms of self-destructiveness' and the 'tyranny of stardom' – the actor looked fondly on any script criticising the press: especially one co-written by a journalist who had honourably defected from the trade (Tom Matthews, formerly of *Box Office* magazine) and a master of aggressive paranoia in a world of failing communications (Ebbe Roe Smith of *Falling Down*).

Kopelson and Costa-Gavras blessed their guardian angels for delivering an actor who seemed to raise the movie's passion and compassion levels at a stroke.

'In the first test we did for make-up and costumes I put him next to Dustin,' says the director. 'I said to John, "You come from the background and sit next to him, you say a few words, see how you feel." John said, could he do one of the big important scenes in the movie? It's where the FBI have just shot at the two men through the window and they run into a room where the television is on. And when Travolta's character is mentioned by name on TV because it's already a news story, he is so surprised and amazed that he begins talking about himself and that begins his relationship with Dustin.

'And John was so moving, and also so funny, and he was going

from one to the other. I saw Dustin was surprised at what John was doing, and after the take I turned to Kopelson who was almost in tears.'

Kopelson confirms. 'John was talking about his family and how he'd lost his job and how he didn't want his little babies to be living in boxes in the street and I had tears in my eyes. Everyone on the set did.'

Before the cameras swung into official action, though, there was a warning Travolta tremor: an *Urban Cowboy*-style rumpus about facial foliage. Costa-Gavras decided to take the actor's side.

'John likes to play an ordinary guy. He's got a bigger belly than usual in this film, he let himself get fatter and we costumed him so you would see it. One day he said, "What do you think if I wear sideburns too?" It was the day of the tests, and the important people from Warners were there and they said to me, "You accept that? That is not John Travolta." I said, "Precisely. We do not *need* 'Travolta'." '

Nor, Costa-Gavras believes, does the actor. 'I don't think he has ever had a personal vision of himself as "Travolta". It's like what the Brechtian theatre used to be: the actors are at the service of the story, not the story at the service of the actors.'

Even as *Mad City* laboured through its troubled post-production and preview history, Costa-Gavras was ready to champion Travolta's instinct and immediacy as an actor. 'With Dustin often I would have to say, "Okay, we stop filming for half an hour to have this discussion." With John he would just get up and do it.' The director thinks the star's openness communicates itself to the spectator. 'It's amazing to see the sympathy he gets from an audience from the start. They trust him; they like him; they go with him completely.'

Emphasising his point with a Parnassian cloud of cigar smoke, Arnold Kopelson opined that *Mad City* audiences too would go with him (assuming they ever got to see the film). 'The guy is on the way to greatness. I think we may be talking Oscars.'

(iv) A Glimpse of Madness

While *Mad City* struggled on, a fleeter production was in progress, masterminded by another Hollywood 'foreigner'. This film-maker

was determined to put skates under a plot so complex it makes *Mad City* seem like 'The Cat in the Hat'.

Broken Arrow taught us that John Woo is an action prodigy. He can make sense of anything, including the senseless. Since he was also the first director I interviewed for this book while Costa-Gavras was almost the last – more topsy-turviness in the Sahara of movie chronicling – he became the work's unofficial mood mascot. When, on the eve of principal shooting (and principal biography-writing), in cadences of broken English with many a torturing pause, Woo explained Face/Off's loopy plot about two men literally swapping faces, I got an inkling of the perfect madness that would punctuate this book's tale of a star risen, fallen, re-risen in the identity-pixilating cosmos of Hollywood.

'John and I both wanted to do a second film together: after *Broken Arrow* we became good friends. We both wanted to do a musical, but Face/Off is an action thriller where we both liked the plot and that it was about characters, not just special effects. John Travolta is a cop chasing Nick Cage who's a terrorist who's set a bomb somewhere and falls into a coma. To find the bomb John goes undercover and takes Nick's face. So the cop and criminal swap roles. It's a little futuristic, set a couple of years from now. It's also a metaphor about all mankind, the bad side and good side, who are always in conflict fighting against each other.'

In short it sounded totally insane, while also seeming a stunt-cinema answer to *The Double*. Could it possibly work?

I pictured the actor in this strange year that followed the angelic ascension of *Michael*, pinballed from point to point on a mazy surface that ensured him repetition, concussion, confusion and the pinging noises of a perpetual spiritual tinnitus. John Travolta would keep meeting his own image, on the simple principle that if you rebound fast enough from one buffer you are sure to meet your earlier self, who has not yet had time to *reach* it.

Was he making too many films? Was he replicating himself in too many guises? Were the films and roles too bitty and those bits beginning not to add up? In sum, was the comeback in crisis?

7

CORE VALUES

(i) The Travoltas at Home

Home must have seemed bliss. Here a man could hang his hat and his identity, and his life partner was there to offer real, not just chequebook, adoration.

'You need to have someone in your life who you can just hug for a minute and make you feel needed,' John Travolta said of Kelly Preston.

You need it because you spend the rest of your life ricocheting around lives and wives and homes that you have no personal business in: those of your characters. So you cling to the sense of self that greets you whenever you cross your doormat.

When visitors dropped by, they noted the tender way the couple sat on the living-room couch, touching and playing with each other's hands. 'Though they have been married for five years, they behaved like people who had just fallen in love,' observed *Good Housekeeping*. 'And in every other breath, they seemed to have something to say about their four-year-old son Jett, who was spending the afternoon at an amusement park with his nanny.' And his bodyguard.

The spacy, sweet-natured Travolta of early years was still evident, and in these middle years his wife was his comfort, his homes were his castles and Jett was the heir – or endearing airhead – apparent. Jett had no idea what to make of a world where security guards shadowed his every outdoor move, even to fun parks. He was also puzzled by the fact that his father appeared

in shiny two-dimensional moving images as well as in the full, live flesh. When Kelly took five-year-old Jett to see *Look Who's Talking Too*, she recalls that he 'looked at me and said, "Noooo!" He was frightened. I said, "My baby, it's just a movie. It's okay, Daddy's *pretending*!" But he didn't get it. Two frames later (in the film) John picked up one of the kids and played with him and kissed him all over . . . And Jett started crying again. I had to take him out of the theatre.'

Jett returned home to the reassuring normalcy of a castle in Maine containing one insect-free garden, one private airstrip, several antique bathrooms and three fantasy bedrooms for his personal use; a Wild West room, a *faux* DC 10 and a Princess room. The ex-servant supergrasses now queueing outside newsrooms claimed that Jett was encouraged to perform skits, playing male or female roles. These included a Princess in a frothy pink gown and high heels (his mother's). At these shows the front row of the audience was always strictly reserved for John, Kelly and Barney the Dinosaur.

Jett was also being introduced to some basic practices of Dianetics. 'If my son were to fall or bump his head, he knows how to give himself a contact assist,' Travolta says. 'He's been doing them since he was about thirteen months old. If he bumps his head, I'd say, "Hey, Jett, you want to do a contact?" He touches it back a few times and just brightens right up.'

Though Jett likes home life, he is a willing traveller. 'He loves it,' Kelly says. 'He travelled so much in utero, I think he was totally ready by the time he was born.' So the whole family flies to the new beach house in Hawaii, where Kelly loves to cook and clean and be near her parents. Or they triangulate between Dark Harbor, Carmel and greater Los Angeles. Here they have bought the Brentford house, with its tennis court, city-to-ocean view, six bedrooms, nine and a half bathrooms, six fireplaces, gym, library–study and bar. They gave up their rented Beverly Hills house after a tiresome legal case brought against them by their former landlord Bob Cohen. In a $500,000 lawsuit he accused the couple who had rented his home between September 1994 and June 1995 of damaging furniture, antiques and artworks. John's lawyer called the charges 'absurd'.

Kelly, a soft touch for any ceramic angel, wouldn't smash an antique if her life depended on it. ('Antiques are my weakness,' she admitted.) And it is hard to imagine John Travolta damaging good fixtures and fittings except with the aim of building something better: a make-believe aircraft cockpit or giant beanstalk. For him, and by genetic bequest for Jett, life is about people keeping trust, exercising love and building Utopias. He will make sure his son grows up as strong and emotionally armed as he was, or preferably more so.

'My parents really adored me, and I wasn't aware that people outside my family might have bad intentions towards me. I wasn't aware that it was a wicked world. And I suffered because I trusted everyone, and I was disappointed at times.'

Now, thanks to Jett, he has got back in touch with innocence. 'I feel more comfortable with children than with adults. I suppose you know there will be no judgment made of you.'

Almost the only tensions in the family come from the difficulty of keeping two unequal acting careers going. While John is an established star, Kelly is groping towards that status with his help. 'I've seen her work *hours* before even a simple audition,' he says, 'where I've drilled her and we've worked on characters.'

More than this, they hope some day to act together.

'We have been offered movies,' Travolta says. 'But this is the trick, we want to be able to do *several* movies together. What happens in Hollywood is that if you do one movie together and it doesn't work, you never get a chance to do another one. I said to her, "You know what? Let your career sizzle." She's on a roll now. "Get hotter than hell, *then* we'll get the right project." Like Kate Hepburn and Spencer Tracy. I'd rather wait for that and have it sizzle than frizzle.'

In other words, he'll let her know.

Travolta is appalled, though, when his altruistic labours on Kelly's behalf, after landing her a key role in the hit film *Jerry Maguire*, are repaid with a graphic sex scene between her and Tom Cruise. She is seen feeding him strawberries, then bonking him against a bookcase. 'Look, I know it's acting,' says John. 'But it's really hard to watch your wife in that situation. I couldn't watch it.'

At least it was a mating of Scientologists. This must have soothed John, although Kelly's fondness for the creed had been momentarily clouded in early 1996 when her husband made a gaffe at the Golden Globe ceremony. Winning the Best Actor in a Comedy or Musical award for *Get Shorty*, he thanked L. Ron Hubbard but forgot to thank or acknowledge his wife.

'I felt so bad for Johnny,' she told a reporter. 'I knew he was going to die when he realised what had happened. When he was walking off the stage, I saw it hit him.' He had carefully rehearsed his speech at home, Kelly says, 'and it was so cute, so loving to me and to Jett.'

The reporter points out that a lot of people feel Travolta missed out the Oscar nomination because of that speech.

'Because he didn't mention me?' Kelly says.

No, because he mentioned L. Ron Hubbard.

'That's fucked up,' she retorts. 'Do you think so? I doubt that people really care one way or the other about Scientology. If they do, it's because they're naive or they've heard all the bullshit. Have you read *Dianetics*? . . . Like I really give a shit what people say, anyway. Why should I have to explain my spiritual side to anyone? You should read *Dianetics*. And call me when you're done. We'll talk.'

Miss Filigree turns feral. Kelly Preston, of course, is right and wrong. Most everyday punters, from Brentwood to Englewood, care not a gram about engrams, nor an iota about Scientology's rules and credos. But on the larger political stage in the mid 1990s the creed is gaining alarming ground as a headline topic.

(ii) Cult Friction

In Europe the movie-oriented Scientology uproar rumbled on through 1996. A spokesman for Nicole Kidman, a.k.a. Mrs Tom Cruise, revealed that the rising actress now taped all her interviews, 'motivated by the unprofessional methods her husband had to face while promoting *Mission: Impossible* in Germany.' The youth movement of the German Christian Democrats had called for a boycott of that film in August whereupon Scientologists launched advertisements featuring pictures of the Nuremberg rallies and

concentration camps, hoping to persuade Westerners that the Germans were guilty of the old sin of religious intolerance. (Cruise himself had sued a top German magazine for $40 million after being misquoted, though he dropped his claims out of sympathy after the death of a publishing-house board member.)

Phenomenon provoked Renata Rennebach, an opposition Social Democrat spokesperson on sects, to call for the banning of the Scientology Church in Germany, claiming (questionably) that the film made references to Scientology and L. Ron Hubbard.

The flak flying between Tinseltown and Teutonland matched charge with counter-charge. Even anti-Scientology acts not directly related to Cruise or Travolta movies were taken personally by Hollywood, as when the south German state of Bavaria banned the employment of Scientologists in local government service, or when Ursula Caberta, a former Social Democrat politician appointed to head an official working party to combat the cult, declared, 'There was once a guy in Germany who wrote a book, and we all said he was a bit crazy. That guy was Adolf Hitler, and I take Hubbard very seriously. Scientology is a state within a state, and it has to be combated. The aim is to take over the planet. That's no joke.'

Hollywood agreed: it was an insult. In the new year of 1997, an advertisement was taken out in the *International Herald Tribune* in the form of an open letter to German Chancellor Helmut Kohl signed by thirty-four celebrities, none of them Scientologists, including Dustin Hoffman, Goldie Hawn, Oliver Stone and Gore Vidal. These scarce-imaginable bedfellows chose to turn the Third Reich invocations on their head, charging that the German authorities were persecuting Scientologists in the same way that a certain previous regime had persecuted other minorities. 'In the thirties it was the Jews. Today it is the Scientologists.'

This, in turn, produced a counterblast. Disgusted commentators accused the signatories of trivialising the Holocaust. The man who conceived, crafted and paid for the letter was none other than lawyer Bert Fields, who had acted for Travolta over *The Double* and who also represented Tom Cruise. He answered that the text specified Jewish persecution in the thirties, before the death camps. This was a masterpiece of disingenuousness; like invoking Attila the Hun and then pointing out that your

timeframe referred to his childhood when he was only *limbering up* to be a tyrant.

Columnist Frank Rich in the *New York Times* took to task another aspect of the letter. 'At least half of the thirty-four signatories have past or professional ties to Tom Cruise or John Travolta, Scientology's most famous recruits. Others may be along just for the ride (what other document has been signed by both Tina Sinatra and Gore Vidal?), but still others, as one producer put it, "would like to be making a movie with Tom Cruise or John Travolta as soon as possible".'

There are sensible folk in Hollywood, though, who think the cult *has* provoked an overreaction. John Landis, once American cinema's busiest lampoonist (*Animal House*, *The Blues Brothers*, *An American Werewolf in London*), spoke to me on the subject during a down-the-phone career interview even as his costume designer wife was hurrying off to upholster Travolta in *Mad City*. Landis admitted to finding many of the cult's activities repugnant, not least its fundraising. 'Only Pat Robertson is more shameless about raising money – "Send me money for Christ and I'll run for President." He should be behind bars.'

But he also thinks you should pause before lambasting Scientology as a creed. 'Let's talk about Mormons, let's talk about Black Muslims, let's talk about Christianity. As soon as you start talking about religion, you can't call other people's faiths silly. If you look at the premises, they're all equally far out. If David Koresh [Seventh Day Adventist leader of the Waco siege victims] had prospered, he'd now be Brigham Young. People forget that the US government actually declared war on the Mormons and sent the Cavalry to kill Brigham Young. As loathsome as I find Scientology, what's the difference between that and the Reverend Moon or that and the Pope?

'The process of being a movie star is crazy-making, they're treated so differently from mere mortals. Think of all those Country and Western drunks who become born-again Christians. It's whatever feeds your ego and vanity and sense of mortality and self-worth.'

John Travolta's ego and vanity were about to have a workout at the 1997 Cannes Film Festival. Mortality was nowhere in sight here,

while self-worth took its bow at the top of the Palais des Festivals' steps, strobed by flashbulbs as in the disco frenzies of yore.

It was twenty years almost to the month since Travolta had finished making *Saturday Night Fever*. And still excited girls, from Europe and beyond, lined the sidewalks. They yelped at his limousine, pointed ecstatic fingers and clutched enraptured faces. They cried:

'John! *John! J-o-h-n!!!*'

8

THROUGH THE LOOKING-GLASS

At the press conference for *She's So Lovely* John Travolta was wearing a suntan, a smile and a tweed jacket over a black T-shirt. He was asked if it felt special to be part of the Cannes 50th Film Festival, three years after the French junket had crowned him as comeback king in *Pulp Fiction*. His smile widened.

'Cannes is responsible for my fourth, or fifth career.' (Laughter.) 'It means a lot to me, because I wouldn't be here today. It enabled me to have a new career. I'm eternally grateful to recognise what Cannes gave to *Pulp Fiction* and Quentin gave to me.'

To his left sat co-stars Sean Penn and his actress wife Robin Wright. Wright, a high-boned beauty with an almost frightening resemblance to Jamie Lee Curtis (of the distant and unmentionable *Perfect*), grinned sportingly. Penn waited for the press to stop talking to Travolta and talk to him. He *was* the film's leading man. He had co-instigated the project with director Nick Cassavetes and before that had confabulated about the script with Nick's father, the legendary John. Now the print-hounds only wanted to talk to the actor playing the small role of his ex-wife's second husband.

How had Travolta got that role in the first place? Penn took a chance to win attention: 'I wrote a footnote to the script. I said, "Dear Nick. Get the kid in the white suit!"' Laughter and applause in the conference room. It was another one-line homage to the god of *Saturday Night Fever*, who had chosen to bless Cannes and who would that night ascend the Palais des Festivals' grand stairway wearing a white tuxedo and wraparound smile. He would turn to

wave to the crowds: possibly on the very step where, 1,100 days before, the world's most poignant remaindered star began the process of being re-pulped.

'What nobody knows' – a new voice is speaking at the press conference – 'is that John did so much for the promotion and marketing of *Pulp Fiction*.' The voice is that of Miramax president Harvey Weinstein, the man who greenlit both that film and the new one, and who is sitting in almost Siamese-twin proximity to Travolta. 'He's not just a student of movies, but a student of movie history. He knows everything there is to know about the business. It hasn't been publicised, but John sacrificed a tremendous payday with a major studio, over $20 million for the same time period, to work for almost nothing on this film [*She's So Lovely*], which had a total budget of $16 million.'

John makes a mock violin-playing gesture. More laughter from the press.

When the conference ends, Mr and Mrs Penn move briskly from the room, followed by every other conferee except Travolta. He stays behind to sign autographs and chat with besotted fans.

Not everyone liked the movie, but everyone liked Travolta in it. For the first time he plays a creep. While he was a villain in *Broken Arrow*, a sociopath in *Pulp Fiction* and a delinquent in *Carrie*, he had never played a graceless smarmball before. On screen for barely twenty minutes, he is as memorably oleaginous as Jerry Lewis in *The King of Comedy*. Playing a retired construction boss with Cosa Nostra links, his gestures have the impudent seigneury of a man used to people saying yes-sir, no-sir. The lordly fist-and-crooked-elbow piston movement with which he ushers Penn inside his house won a roar of laughter at Cannes – it's a mobster's Meccano version of a welcoming gesture. And there's a flourish even to the way Travolta lights a cigarette. In one scene with Penn he recites a list of the husbandly good deeds he has performed for Robin Wright, including keeping her out of jail, saving her from drugs and helping her to give up smoking. At which point he ignites a cigarette and takes a baroque expansive lungful.

The next film out of the gate in Travolta's career, *Face/Off*, which opened in America in July 1977, develops this majestic creepiness.

The script could be *Dr Jekyll and Mr Hyde* seen through the eyes of a mad plastic surgeon. (It was partly inspired by the macabre French film *Eyes Without a Face*, directed by Georges Franju.) A terrorist and FBI agent literally exchange faces. The G-man wants revenge for the death of his little son, slain during a previous showdown with the baddie. The terrorist wants to clear the way for an explosive party piece – the ultimate big bang – at a Los Angeles museum. With a little surgical help, Travolta's lawman 'becomes' Nicolas Cage's urban guerrilla, wearing Cage's face into the jail where the terrorist's brother sits harbouring vital information. Then Cage wakes from the coma *he* is in (from another day, another showdown) and slaps on Travolta's face. It is conveniently lying near his hospital room in a bath of formaldehyde, resembling a jellyfish with one previous careful owner.

Hollywood in 1996 was full of dazed studio executives who had listened to John Woo pitch this story. I had listened to him do it myself (see earlier chapter). I could not imagine how the film was to be done. Would special effects be used? Morphing? Computer graphics?

'There will be only a little bit of special effects or make-up,' said Woo. 'I don't want to use computer technology. The movie's about characters. I don't want them overcome by the effects.'

He had already begun work on the processes by which Cage and Travolta would 'become' each other. 'I had John and Nick work together to practise each other's walk, manner, gestures. Both guys were very serious. They were in the same room with me and I had them watch each other and imitate each other, how they'd smile and cry and express anger; all the different expressions on their faces. It was very funny!'

So is the film: funny in a style of controlled dementia even Woo has not achieved before. The script by Mike Werb and Michael Colleary had first been earmarked as a vehicle for Schwarzenegger and Stallone: more sci-fi, more New Neanderthal. It featured trolley-cars driven by orang-utans and chimpanzee volunteers at the city hospital. When Woo came in he envisaged something more poetic, philosophical: 'My theory is there are no really good guys or bad guys in the world, so good and bad is always like a mirror.' He imposed this existential volatility on the actors. 'I would mess

up their names and call Nick "John" and John "Nick". Even the crew messed up their names.'

Cage saw the acting partnership as fated. Ten years before, during the shooting of *Moonstruck*, his co-star Julie Bovasso, who had played Travolta's mother in *Saturday Night Fever*, told him, 'You're the dark side of John:' Cage became mystical too about working with the other John: 'The first time I saw a couple of John Woo movies it was like an epiphany went off in my mind.' This was not just any old project, nor was Castor Troy, his character, any old villain. 'I see him as the Liberace of crime.'

Travolta took longer to be bewitched by his role as Sean Archer. He was bothered by rude remarks in the script on his looks, which had to be spoken by himself playing Troy-as-Archer. The writers assured him they were a joke: 'You're John Travolta, looking in the mirror saying, "I can't believe I'm stuck with this ugly face," when you're one of the most famously handsome movie stars in the world!' Travolta waived his objections and sportingly ad-libbed more insults, including the reference to 'this ridiculous chin'.

Woo bombarded each actor with the other's mannerisms. 'Most of their scenes were separate, so whenever I finished shooting with one of them, I'd cut his scene together fast and show it to the other one so he could see how he was playing the character.' He also discouraged actorly restraint. 'At first they were playing the emotional scenes a little more subtly, the traditional American way. So after the first day I said, "Let's try it another way – my way. You want to cry, just cry! You want to laugh, just laugh. You want to hit the wall, do it. You want to smash the table, smash the table. Just do it exactly how you feel!" '

So Cage improvised his finest moment, the mimed yanking gesture with his hand accompanied by the maniacally repeated mantra, 'I'm going to take his face – *off*!' ('No more drugs for that man,' murmurs his cocaine-soiree host played by *She's So Lovely* director Nick Cassavetes.) And Travolta's camp overreachings in Woo's *Broken Arrow* here reach further to infect an entire movie. The virtue of *Face/Off* is that there is no Christian Slater-style straight man: there are just these two crazed products of psychic interbreeding.

Though scored for Woo's usual shootouts, explosions and fist fights, the film is an inspired theme-and-variations on movie stardom; or, trading metaphors, a game of catch involving two limber box-office athletes. Travolta throws at Cage the mannerisms that made the older actor a star and extended his *Grease* lease into a new age of louche inventiveness: the disco-cool smile that can now crack open to something parodic, feral; the street-lazy voice toughened to swell or bark; and the enhanced Travolta gesture-language – knuckles fanning underside of chin, or splayed fingers jabbing airy hex signs – that suggests a dandy enjoying a whole new body vocabulary. Cage throws at Travolta *his* trademarks: the spooked eyes, lowslung gestures, foghorn voice, and the sighs that punctuate his sentences with quirky, guerrilla caesurae. 'Slowing things down a bit, with a grandiose flair to certain deliveries' was Cage's self-description. 'When Nick speaks, he extennnds his worrrrds,' onomatapoeised Travolta.

The film could be seen as a curtainraiser for cinema's promised – or threatened – age of the 'synthespian', when actors are supplied by computer and star mannerisms become loose storage in the Hollywood memory bank. What computer, though, could file away a gracenote as casual as Travolta's wittiest in *Face/Off?* When we first see him playing his second role – terrorist with cop's face – he is leaning against a prison doorframe enjoying the horrified understanding on Cage's face; that his antagonist is alive and well and cutting off his retreat to a resumed identity. The little, sly, downward-curved movement of Travolta's head here is perfect. It's a mischief-maker's semaphore for 'Got you!' It won a roar of laughter at the screening I saw.

As in *She's So Lovely*, the actor makes sleaziness magnetic. The plot requires the evil Travolta to take over the good Travolta's life and lifestyle: the virtuous dowdy wife (Joan Allen), the pretty daughter, the neat suburban home. Travolta's face and body are the same, only the Cage-ventriloquised cynicism is new. 'I'll never get a hard-on again,' he murmurs as he drives down the dinky streets for the first time, and he is soon making half-passes at the daughter and summing up, to cop colleagues, the aggravation of life with a wife who acts as if she doesn't quite know him. 'Lies,

distrust, mixed messages,' Travolta declaims, 'this is turning into a real marriage.'

Many critics, especially European, went wild for the film's identity games. For them the climactic scene of Cage and Travolta shooting at each through a double-sided looking-glass – each shooting *through* his own reflection (with the irony that it isn't his own) – was *The Lady From Shanghai* on steroids. It was Orson Welles's hall of mirrors jazzed up for nineties action cinema. '*Dans ce duel,*' breathed *Cahiers du Cinemma*, '*la mise en scène se conjugue parfaitement avec l'angoisse des personnages; l'angoisse de tenir en joue son propre corps, de blesser l'autre, qui est aussie, de fait soi-même.*'

In America, where *Face/Off* became one of the ten top-earning films of 1997, there were less cerebral celebrations in plain English. *Newsweek*: 'Imaginative, crazily funny and, even more surprisingly, oddly moving.' *Village Voice*: 'The first of Woo's movies to suggest the nuttiness of his best Hong Kong films.' *Rolling Stone*: 'This you gotta see.'

An on-screen Travolta who could look in the mirror, or through it, at his own parodied essence, soon showed he could do the same in a roomful of real people. In the month of *Face/Off*'s opening he was guest of honour at the annual Friars Club 'roast'. At these black-tie shindigs, famous film folk, made affectionately rude speeches about other famous film folk, to wit the guest or guests of the evening.

On June 13th 1997 John and Kelly Travolta were put in the pillory while Sylvester Stallone, Shirley MacLaine, the Bee Gees and others threw the Fabergé equivalent of rotten eggs. No eggs actually struck or were allowed to do damage. When comedian Alan King wondered why there weren't more blacks on the celebrity platform – 'John, couldn't you have rented a few?' – Harry Belafonte quickly stepped in with a speech: 'John does in fact have a large number of black friends. They don't come from the economic circles to be here, they are poor and desperate and John Travolta has made it his business to help the people of colour . . .

'The minute I saw John Travolta walk down the street in *Saturday Night Fever*,' Belafonte climaxed, 'I knew a black boy had made good!'

When you are successful every constituency, racial or social, claims you. So does every quango, craft guild and awards committee. John and Kelly had scarcely wrapped the Friars roast with their thank-you badinage – 'Hey, Kelly, did you hear what they said about us? Don't you just love us?' 'I think we should spend more time with ourselves,' agreed Kelly – than John received an invitation to the American Cinematheque's 12th Moving Picture Ball. Here he would be given the Cinematheque's very own annual Award, previously won by such as Steven Spielberg, Mel Gibson, Robin Williams and Tom Cruise.

Another group of people wanted him. Publishers. His story, *Propeller One-Way Night Coach*, written in 1992 for his son Jett, illustrated by the author and samizdated among seventy-five friends and family members, caught the attention of Warners. They told Travolta they wanted to print 250,000 copies in October.

More good news. The legal clouds were clearing around *The Double*. The walkout suit against the actor lasted until midsummer, reaching high drama – or high bizarrerie – with Travolta calling Dustin Hoffman as a witness. The *Mad City* co-star was chauffeured to an attorney's office to make a ringing deposition about his colleague's professionalism. In late July, however, a multi-million-dollar out-of-court settlement was reached between Sony Columbia on Travolta's behalf and Mandalay Productions in the latter's favour. The actor bound himself to make a new film for Sony 'suitable to both parties'.

But what *of Mad City*? Months after completion, it was still suitable to no parties. It had not opened and there were continued rumours of bad feedback from test previews.

Two months before its final, actual release date in November 1997, this movie about press and media responsibility at a scene of crisis had the thunder of its theme stolen – or amplified – by a real-life tragedy. The death of Princess Diana in a Paris road tunnel brought a chorus of vilification against predatory newsmen, though as well as the pursuing paparazzi there were question marks over the fitness-to-drive of the car's chauffeur.

Travolta, the Princess's one-time dance partner, who had clasped the waist of the very dress worn that White House night that had just

sold for $222,500 at a Christie's auction (surpassing the previous record for a costume, established by John Travolta), hastened to condole Britain's royal family. He offered his unstinting support. He would rename one of his planes 'The English Rose' in Diana's memory. He would also christen his daughter, if he begat one, Diana. And he poured out his thoughts and feelings on American TV.

'When I first heard the news, I did cry a lot and for different reasons. The first was because I didn't like the idea of meaningful lives being cut short, and the second was for her children. That was hard for me to imagine what it would do to them.

'What I really want to say to Charles and the boys, that I'm very sorry that this happened and that I want to be there for them if they need me. And I mean that literally, twenty-four hours a day. I'm very dependable when it comes to this kind of thing. I've lost people in my life and I know how to help people through it.'

Asked about the press harassment issue, he spoke from twenty years' experience. 'Laws do have to be made for this kind of thing that's happening with the paparazzi, whether it's pursuit or whether it's invasion. And I also think that celebrities have to always keep in mind their safety. So it's like a two-way street here that's happening and I think now is a good time to pay attention to that.'

With *Mad City* bound to open *some day* soon, now was a doubly good time. For its director Costa-Gavras, the Diana case bore directly on the movie's theme.

'The written press has tried to catch up by becoming more and more aggressive and trying more and more to simplify stories,' he told me. 'The tragedy of Diana happened partly because the press wanted the most scandalous or intrusive pictures and had to go to those lengths. For years I have felt there's a degeneration of a certain kind of press, with even important newspapers running after scoops. It's dangerous because the press is a kind of "third power" in politics and can be very significant in a country with weak or unstable rule.'

By a coincidental prearrangement I met *Mad City*'s producer Arnold Kopelson at the Ritz Hotel, Paris, one week after Diana's death. He sat nimbused by cigar smoke in a corner of the lobby where everyone walked on eggshells as if in shock at the blight

on the hotel's recent history. He gave me a refresher course in the film's themes – 'The film raises very interesting issues, particularly in the light of the tragedy of Diana' – and then became unstoppable on the subject of Travolta's caringness, as instanced in his response to the royal tragedy.

'To meet John is to love him. He cares about everybody. I had a situation of someone on set in *Mad City* who was being abusive to some of the crew and John said, "Can I see you?" And we went into his trailer and he said, "Can you do something about this? I hate the way he's treating people." I already have, I said. It's taken care of. But that's typical John. He sees everyone. Cares about everyone.'

He sums up, 'People ask me, "Why is Travolta a star?" I say, because he's like the guy next door. He has instant credibility, whatever he plays. You feel like you know him.'

Unfortunately, audiences didn't feel like they knew him or wanted to in *Mad City*. When it finally opened in November 1997, *Variety* wrote the first review, which was so implacable it might as well have been the last. 'A simplistic and obvious exposé about the manipulative power of the media . . . script is not only *déjà vu*, it's also terribly schematic . . . even a resourceful thesp like Travolta has a hard time finding the right balance in his characterisation. Like the film itself, the tone of his erratic performance changes from scene to scene, from sweet innocence to monstrous craziness, from cynicism to romanticism and back again.'

As Sam Baily, Travolta acts like a man who has spied an Oscar in this showy role, then has panicked, wondering *which* role. Playing a multi-personality character who can barely keep up with his transformations, he compensates – or tries to – with an ostinato of querulous bewilderment. But from the moment he blabs,'I don't have any demands 'cos I didn't plan on any of this to happen,' it is as if the actor's eternal inner kid has escaped to hold *him* hostage. Travolta's flabby-lipped delivery and brink-of-tears babyishness could have been effective if we felt there was, or had once been, a free-willed adult called Sam Baily. But even this is doubtful (the fault of the script as well as the actor). We learn that Sam was lovable and helpless at home too, that he liked to be called his wife's 'third kid'.

Meanwhile the controversial sideburns tend to make Travolta look like a spent sixties rocker, and the hoped-for star chemistry with Dustin Hoffman, it fizzles in the test-tube. (All the more sadly since Hoffman himself is in shrewd, commanding, funny form.)

Though the movie itself is better than reviews suggest, there are too many echoes of old films that treated this theme more freshly, from Billy Wilder's *Ace in the Hole* (the growth of a media circus outside a freak news event) to Hoffman's own *Accidental Hero*, another disquisition on the blunderbuss effects of headline fame.

Spurned by critics, *Mad City* expired in record time at the box office. It gave even *Moment by Moment* a run for its misery. In four weeks it failed to reach $10 million. It was soon off the chart altogether.

It was enough to prompt an actor to climb into his plane again and escape the world. Instead Travolta invited the world into his plane. With a recklessness scarce-equalled even in the age of celebrity authors – when Duchesses purvey cuddly helicopters and *Dynasty* divas weep to defend their prose in court – he placed *Propeller One-Way Night Coach* in the public's hands. He must have known that critics, pundits and other celebrity-baiters might murder the book's feyness, as well as its dubious grammar and syntax; not to mention – but everyone would – Travolta's illustrations, which suggest a four-year-old mind trapped inside a forty-four-year-old body.

This essay in the childlike, though, unlike *Mad City*, has a real charm. When good, it is entrancing. When bad, it is fearless. It begins with a spendthrift misuse of predicates – 'Any resemblance or likeness to the characters in this book is loosely based on people I have known or met in my life' – and goes onward to mangled cases ('every airline insignia'), dangling participles and long sentences that shed sense like an imperilled balloon jettisoning excess navigation equipment.

Soon you don't care. Set in 1962 when Travolta himself would have been eight, the book has the texture of a dream. For the boy narrator embarking on his first flight, accompanied by an actress mom off to play in summer stock (a conflation of Helen and Ellen Travolta), it is as if the prose world he has known before turns to poetry around him. Not through fancy writing, though there are

beguiling turns of phrase ('Through the window I could see the jetway start to glide over to meet our plane'); but through the airborne quirkiness of the author's mind which mingles surreal characterisation – from an air stewardess who has been in a concentration camp to an escaped mental patient – with a child's almost metaphysical delight in useless information.

'I loved dates and trivia,' the boy relates during a stopover, 'so I asked the man behind the counter when the hotel was built. "In 1951, I believe," he said. "Oh thank you," I responded. Now I could fantasise about all the people that had to do the same thing we were doing in the middle of the night for the last eleven years. Wow!'

All he and Mom are doing is resting between planes. But intensified by this new experience, the boy's every moment becomes special. His curiosity is promiscuous, unformed, uncritical (just like that of Travolta the actor). He sees the poignancy and comedy in routine human behaviour: 'The turbulence got worse and some of the passengers started to look around as if maybe something they could look at would solve this problem.' And he sees the comedy, or Travolta sees it for him, in his own behaviour. When the boy bursts into tears after breaking a toy plane, he is comforted by the stewardess saying, 'Even real planes break', a remark that to anyone but a flying-besotted child passenger (as the author must know) would have made matters even worse.

There are funny running subplots. One involves the boy's attempt to find his mother an interesting, eligible beau ('Mom, you're not gonna believe, I found a new best friend and his dad is rich, sad and doesn't have an accent'). Another is an airline food gag, with a variety of fancy names on different flights flattering the same recurring dish of fried chicken.

The illustrations tell a story too: about Travolta's mind as much as about his characters and their tale. His rickety buildings would be condemned on sight. His human beings are rudimentary, though with a quaint spark of comic-book life. But his aeroplanes are sleek, full-bodied, good enough to fly in. Their line and symmetry are the product of a lifetime of hobbyist passion, in turn projected by the author onto his hero. 'Five years after,' records the boy, 'no matter what negative experience I might have, from the time I would leave

for the airport until the time I would arrive at my destination, life would seem safe and I would be happy.'

Now the real boy who fell in love with altitude has a re-airborne movie career. His next film will allow him to spend hours in planes or studio mock-ups of them. He will be flying from stump to stump on an American adventure. John Travolta will be running for the U.S. Presidency.

9

MR PRESIDENT

John Travolta was signed to play the Bill Clinton lookalike/ soundalike/actalike who strides through the novel *Primary Colors*. Jack Stanton is a Presidential contender sketched with caustic pen by an author who had originally put the book out anonymously. This boosted sales by encouraging worldwide, or at least hemispheric, puzzlement. Who could the writer be? Gore Vidal? Hillary Clinton? George Stephanopoulos (the White House advisor thinly disguised as black campaign aide Henry Burton, who narrates the book)?

The book was a *roman à clef* with a key to every character's identity except the author's. Finally the secret door opened, as if of its own accord, and the novelist took his bow. If anyone knew about electioneering shenanigans, it had to be columnist Joe Klein. He had covered the 1992 Presidential campaign for both *New York* magazine and *Newsweek*.

Tom Hanks was approached to play the scandal-stalked Governor Stanton, alias Clinton, but turned it down out of loyalty to his friend and leader. So did Harrison Ford. When Travolta was asked, he barely hesitated. He read the book, then the script by writer and sometime film-maker Elaine May (*A New Life*, *Ishtar*). Then he met the director, who was May's old comedy partner Mike Nichols, who in the sixties graduated from satirical duologues in New York cabarets to directing *The Graduate*, *Catch-22* and *Who's Afraid of Virginia Woolf*.

Having shown no interest in the novel when he first read it, Nichols paid $1.5 million for the rights from his own pocket when it started to become a bestseller. His only regret was that the

author revealed his identity. 'I'd rather Anonymous had remained mysterious . . . I always regarded *Primary Colors* as a work of the imagination. The story has more power that way.'

This makes it odd that one of the first things the star received from the director was some reality-based homework.

'Mike Nichols has sent me some tapes I'm going to study,' Travolta said, after unpacking the clips of Bill Clinton. 'I'm *very* excited about the project because it's a *killer* script; it's exactly like the book. Emma Thompson is the Hillary-type character. Kathy Bates is [White House adviser] Libby. I'm just challenged and excited about the whole idea because Clinton is very entertaining for me. Just give me a character I can entertain you with and I'm happy. I think his Southern charm and emotion – he's so filled with his emotion, it's just delicious.'

Everybody except Travolta, as if following the higher Nichols plan, was at pains to distance him/herself from the role models. 'I absolutely didn't want to do an impersonation,' said Emma Thompson; 'my character isn't Hillary, it's a composite of various people.' 'I'm not imitating anyone,' echoed actor-writer Billy Bob Thornton, freshly translated from winning the Best Original Screenplay Oscar for *Sling Blade* into playing the book's version of snake-faced campaign manager James Carville. And black British actor Adrian Lester, cast as the Stephanopoulos/Ron Brown clone Henry Burton, said he'd only done 'just a little reading on Ron Brown'.

For John Travolta, though, a role was a role: he would copy everything. The style and colour of Clinton's hair, his body language (down to the hands draped with demotic languor over the speech lectern), his light, fluting Arkansas voice. 'I'm really playing him. It's false PR for me to do it any other way . . . Unless there are some legal issues I don't know about.'

No one thought Clinton would sue Columbia Pictures for portraying him, albeit pseudonymously, as a womaniser and wheeler-dealer with a slick line in populist electioneering. In any case Travolta was bound to make him lovable. He gave reporters tasty bits of Clintonism: 'Ah feel yer pain, son.' And wasn't the casting of this notoriously apolitical star, who as a schoolboy had yawned in the face of the radical sixties, a jape in itself? Here he

was – this non-Robert Redford, non-Jane Fonda, non-Charlton Heston even – translated to the heights of Washington. For extra irony, he was partnered by a non-American First Lady, an actress whose most significant contribution to US culture and society was to have told Quentin Tarantino, all those years ago, to give John Travolta a movie.

Nichols emphasised, in case people were worried, that the film would be faithful to the book. 'We haven't changed any central events of the story in any way. But there are mysterious things being written about how we've handled things. I've read reports that we've taken the lesbian past of Mrs Stanton out of the story. Well, I've read the book five times and we didn't take it out – it's simply not there.'

The budget was trimmed from a frightening $75 million dollars to a merely alarming $65 million, with Travolta deferring a portion of his own $20-million salary. His fee still made up a quarter of the total budget. But how could you pay too much money to a man who virtually guaranteed – give or take *Mad City* – a film's ability to excite interest?

In July 1997 *Variety* printed a list, albeit playful, of the hottest concepts in contemporary movieland.

'Sci-fi Westerns. Clones of *The Rock*. Romantic comedies. Character-driven comedies. Real-life stories gleaned from books and magazine articles. Anything with aliens. Anything with John Travolta. Musicals, especially if John Travolta is attached.'

The score in actor-citations: John Travolta 2, everyone else 0. He was already wading thigh-deep through screenplays as 1997 yielded to 1998. They included a villain in the fifth *Batman* – the Scarecrow to Clint Eastwood's caped crusader in director Tim Burton's return to the franchise – and a hero in *The Shipping News*, Hollywood's bid to grapple with E. Annie Proulx's Pulitzer Prize-winning novel. They included *Dark Horse*, a political thriller, *Have Gun, Will Travel*, an old TV western series being saddled up for the large screen, and *Phantom of the Opera*, which would surely be the dream combination of star and show. Only imagine 'The Music of the Night' issuing from a crooner already so used to screams at his appearance that removing the Phantom's mask

would merely precipitate Travolta business as usual. And was it possible – or just a film buff's reverie turned media rumour – that John Woo would direct?

Reversing the stage-to-screen process, April 1998 saw the opening of a stage version of *Saturday Night Fever*, with Robert Stigwood overseeing the twentieth-anniversary tribute. Premiering in London, the show had Australia's Adam Garcia stepping into the Travolta dancing pumps.

There was also *Battlefield Earth*, a megabuck epic based on a thousand-page L. Ron Hubbard spacebuster. This, insisted Jonathan Krane, 'has nothing to do with Scientology', a curious statement in light of a telephone call I conducted with a senior figure in the Scientology establishment, one Susie Watson-Taylor. She is a Briton, a 'child of the sixties', as a former acquaintance dubbed her, who came to America in the hippie dawn to succumb to conversion. I told her I was winding up research on my book and wanted to find out from an insider about John's relationship with the 'church'.

She: John and I deal with movie business stuff together, so it's probably better if you went to someone else in the church to deal with that. Presumably you've spoken to John himself?

Me: Well, I've spoken to his manager Jonathan Krane and many film-makers who've worked with him . . . (usual speech of flannelling evasion).

She: Well, let me talk to John and see how he wants to tackle this particular side of it. By 'tackle' I mean who you should speak to. I'm not really the right person, although of course I love working with him. I have a professional relationship with him rather than a Scientological one, although of course we're both Scientologists.

Me: Oh, so you have a movie relationship with him?

She: Yes, I have a movie relationship with him on a property called *Battlefield Earth*, for which we have a deal with Fox.

Me: Ah, I've read reports about that in *Variety*. Is this a project that's going to happen? Within the next year or so?

She: Oh definitely, yes, definitely. It's absolutely, absolutely going to happen. Or is in progress happening. But that's with Fox 2000, so if you've been speaking with anyone at Fox they'd be better positioned to give you the information you

need. Look, why don't I take your fax and phone number . . . ?

This woman was the perfect Scientologist. She was able to say nothing while making it seem something. Clearly, she couldn't or wouldn't talk about anything except *Battlefield Earth*, and even that hovered around in a unique zone of qualified absoluteness. (I never did get a phone call or fax from a Scientologist.)

In September 1997 Travolta spent two days on Capitol Hill testifying before Congress about political persecution. Responding to the German attack on the cult, he and musicians Chick Corea and Isaac Hayes spoke up for Scientology. Travolta urged legislators to complain about a country whose ruling party had abetted the attempted boycott of *Mission: Impossible*. He said, 'The mere attempt by politicians to censor art because of the artist's religious affiliations sends chills down my spine.'

'Are the thought police far behind?' he asked rhetorically: a question which struck some Britons as rich in light of the opposition shown by the church, late in 1997, to an hour-long British TV documentary about L. Ron Hubbard. Travolta himself tried to stop the programme by writing a letter to the Channel 4 chief Michael Jackson.

According to one witness, it wouldn't be the first time he had intervened, or tried to, in the processes of broadcasting. Early during my research Travolta's old ABC TV employer Gary Pudney vouchsafed to me, in a voice susurrant with discretion but straight into a tape-recorder: 'John and I have talked about his religion over the years and I've done him a couple of favours with that [pause] "organisation", which he's been very grateful for. In one instance, there was gonna be some TV appearance by someone who was anti this Scientology [pause] "situation". John called me about it and he was very upset. I was able to make an adjustment in that situation – we'll put it that way – wherein I was able to give the other, opposing point of view, make sure it was covered.'

Pudney says this as if tipping the wink to a sympathiser. I feel like a spy being handed unsolicited secrets by the enemy.

Biographers are luckier than broadcasters: no one is likely to write an entire counter-biography to cover the 'opposing point of view'. But with these chroniclers, too, Scientologists can get difficult, as

British author Wensley Clarkson found when researching his book on Tom Cruise. 'They came over from America and doorstepped me,' he told me. 'They got quite nasty.'

With Travolta, whom he also wrote about, what intrigued Clarkson was the origin of the actor's involvement. 'Scientologists usually pull people in like Cruise or Travolta because something unhappy has happened to them. In Travolta's case, apart from having a domineering mother who decided to mould him into what he became – which is not exactly unusual in America – there's nothing disturbing about his childhood or adolescence, unless he was just lonely in L.A. and got sucked in that way. Or unless they put some kind of pressure on him.'

Yet sinister theories of coercion do not square with the convinced and radiantly evangelising Travolta we know. What made him a Scientologist is surely the same as what made him a star: his easily bedazzled naivety. In his middle years he has added craft to sensitivity, perhaps even craftiness. But the reason he grew and still grows as an actor is the same as the reason he has spent twenty-five years offering himself up for self-improvement as a company mystic. He leaves the windows open in his head and heart.

Unlike many stars, secure and lazy in the mansion of their iconhood, Travolta knows that that mansion is never impregnable. The bailiffs invaded his Fortress Stardom in 1985 and didn't leave till 1994 – so why even bother with bolts and burglar alarms?

Also, the breeze through the windows, if left open, will play him like an instrument. For an actor is a kind of Aeolian harp. The less defined his own identity, the more he can respond to being tuned and orchestrated by those of others. The life story of this mimic and eternal kid, this faddist and fly-by-day-and-night, suggests that an anchored identity is the one thing John Travolta rejoices in *not* having. His whole life has been a kind of out-of-body experience. Ever since his youngest years of fame, when an early interviewer noted that 'He has an odd way of regarding himself as separate from his body', a free-range mind and flibbertigibbet spirit have seemed to float above that (increasingly) weighty screen presence.

His solo outing as a novella writer, *Propeller One Way Night Coach*, is also about an imagination bumming a ride to

heaven while reality sprawls 30,000 feet below. And that book's dedication suggests that even a Travolta *marriage* has its special value system and hierarchy. The child – mirror-image of wonder and susceptibility – takes priority over the grown-up spouse. 'This book is dedicated to my son Jett, whom I love more than life itself, and my wife Kelly, who magically holds the key to Jett's first chapter and my second.' Kelly's main or only role is to cue a second apostrophe to the boy loved 'more than life itself' and to the rhyming miracle of John's rebirth as a movie star.

But what a rebirth. No one – not even such love/hate screen idols as Katharine Hepburn, Joan Crawford or Bette Davis (one goes to women to find anything like the kitsch intensity of response Travolta has inspired over twenty years) – ever vanished so completely to be remade for a new age. After *Pulp Fiction* he was given a fresh career, a fresh community of fans, everything but a new identity and personality. It was a witness protection programme without the pain or name-change.

Since then, the on-screen transformations have come fast enough to confound industry minds and infect industry personnel. Today's moguls can hardly believe that a movie-star age has arrived in which the brats actually *work* for a living. Hoffman, De Niro, Stallone, Cage, Demi Moore, all are jumping from project to project – the new lingo even *calls* it 'Travolta-ing' – as if to hesitate is to die. The Hollywood chiefs compare this with a previous zeitgeist, the sixties and seventies, when more than one film a year for the likes of Beatty, Redford or Streisand was thought reckless over-exposure.

Travolta himself, more than any, makes workaholism seem fun. He strides up the slopes, or spirals up the thermals, from gangster to intellectual genius to angel to President, with short detours to play sci-fi face-swappers or to give comeback fans a fright with a real-life disaster (*Mad City*). At this point, though, it hardly matters if his comeback goes away again. The legend is already incised. The supposedly impossible – the trip from top to bottom and right back to top – has happened.

Primary Colors opened in America in the spring of 1998, convoying with other big Travolta events including the twentieth anniversary of *Grease* (plus shindigs) and the stage premiere of *Saturday Night Fever*. The film seemed timed to remind everyone

that this was the mark-one Comeback Kid playing the mark-two Comeback Kid. And Kid One looked more durable than Kid Two. In the first months of 1998 President Clinton showed every sign of falling out of the history books with no parachute. Women appeared all over Washington – or so it seemed – claiming intimate knowledge of the President's body. And by wicked foresight Hollywood had prepped not just one White House satire but two. Even before Travolta's Clinton routine, the David Mamet-scripted *Wag the Dog*, starring another *Mad City* refugee in Dustin Hoffman, hit paydirt with its tale of a U.S. leader declaring war to distract the nation from domestic scandal.

With *Primary Colors*, though, early-year prognosticators weren't sure if true-life parallels would help or cripple the film. By the time *it* came out (they speculated) impeachment, resignation or God knows what might have happened. Would people still laugh at a comedy about a pants-down premier? One studio boss said that if he had *Primary Colors* on his release slate he would hang himself. And Nichols and Universal agonised over early-year commercials that had the grey-quiffed western leader saying, 'I'm going to do something really outrageous. I'm going to tell the truth.'

Late changes were made to the movie, including the excision of an affair between Hillary Clinton – whose stand-by-her-man act had won huge popularity in real America – and the black Stephanopoulos/Brown character. And Mike Nichols, while admitting that 'right now I feel about as bad as everyone else in the country', continued to assert that his film was a 'work of the imagination'.

The idea of John Travolta appearing in one politically controversial movie was far-fetched enough. That he should make two in a row seems like surreal comedy. Yet as *Primary Colors* wound up business, Travolta started shooting *A Civil Action*, scripted by Steven *Schindler's List* Zaillian. The film, with Zaillian also directing, is based on a non-fiction bestseller about a Massachusetts toxic waste lawsuit.

Half a decade after being box-office poison, Travolta is the man you call in to make poison good box office. It was soon evident, though, that *A Civil Action* needed all the goodwill it could get. At the turn of the year a small group of East-coast Americans not

busy contributing opinions about Bill Clinton attacked Disney for not consulting the real families – themselves – whose children had died from leukemia allegedly caused by the pollution. They won a legal battle forbidding the studio to use real names in the movie.

Travolta must have started to feel like a time-traveller. He was in the nineties – the calendar said so – but it felt one moment like the politically agitated sixties, another like the dear, lost seventies, with a lookalike White House crisis, an outbreak of hedonist navel-gazing (including a new fascination with porn as consumer iconography) and a retro pop culture. Most of the acclaimed new movies seemed to be set in the seventies: *The Ice Storm, Boogie Nights* ... And even disco was back, not just in actual clubs aping the sound and strobe-lights of yesteryear, but in musical styles. What ever were the Spice Girls but discomania reborn, the Bee Gees in drag?

It was no longer possible to talk of a Travolta comeback. The man's essence had never gone away, except for a holiday. His selfless egotism, mixing as only Travolta can self-absorption and Good Samaritanism; his Me Decade approach to politics (don't approach it at all, except through career-boosting movie roles); his maverick mysticism; above all, his ability to be eternally in the present while being eternally, somehow, somewhere else. Perhaps in some dream above the Englewood stars.

He is the actor who never grew up. Captured by show business too young, he went through every pain while still in the cradle. And when he resumed normal celebrity, he was still too blithe and innocent to reproach the world for its ingratitude. Like any great consumer icon, he has made himself available as and when the consumer requires. And like movies themselves, John Travolta's essence just stays around, waiting to be threaded into the next generation, projected onto the next dreamwall. He is the ideal movie star. He wants to be what we want him to be.

ACKNOWLEDGEMENTS

It takes an army of people to make a celebrity biography possible, while another army is often busy, during research and writing, trying to make it impossible. It would take a second book to list all the people who refused interviews, or promised photographs and then withheld them, or spent weeks running over the known globe in order to avoid me. 'So-and-So is in Europe/Brazil/Afghanistan' I would be told, while I suspected – and once or twice had evidence – that So-and-So was in Beverly Hills having a restful weekend.

Many people, though, did help. Some Hollywood eminences spoke to me about Travolta during career interviews conducted with them for my newspaper or BBC radio. My thanks to my forbearing arts editor Annalena McAfee and to producer Paul Quinn of BBC's *Kaleidoscope*. He accompanied me on a trip to Hollywood to tape eight celebrities for radio and had to listen to those inevitable moments – judiciously cut from the finished programme – when I would pipe up, 'By the way, did you ever work with John Travolta?'

Some quarries refused to be hunted down. I have no hard feelings about Quentin Tarantino declining to talk to me. After my early review of *Pulp Fiction* I wouldn't have talked to me either. I was more disappointed by Brian De Palma. As a key figure in the early Travolta career, he was a valuable witness who just refused to be subpoenaed.

The following people, however, deserve sincere and generous thanks. Between them, they really did make the book possible.

Nancy Allen, John Badham, Patricia Birch, Ralf Bode, Anne Busse,

Allan Carr, Wensley Clarkson, Nik Cohn, Jeff Conaway, Tom Conti, Costa-Gavras, Eddie Costenuic, Father Robert Curtis, Danny DeVito, Gerald DiPego, Richard Dreyfuss, Robert Duvall, Nora Ephron, Karen Lynn Gorney, Amy Heckerling, John Heinze, Samuel L. Jackson, Jim Jacobs, Pauline Kael, Judy Kaye, Randal Kleiser, Arnold Kopelson, Jonathan Krane, John Landis, Aaron Latham, George Litto, Kevin McCormick, Tom Moore, Joe Morgenstern, Donna Mundy, Desmond Nakano, Olivia Newton-John, Mike Newell, Glynis O'Connor, Ron Palillo, Donna Pescow, Roman Polanski, Stephen Ponder, Gary Pudney, Michael Roth, Kenneth Sarfin, Rogene Schmiedel, Paul Schrader, Barry Sonnenfeld, Lynn Stalmaster, Robert Stigwood, Marcia Strassman, Jon Turteltaub, Dick Van Patten, Patrizia Von Brandenstein, Susie Watson-Taylor, Norman Wexler, Gordon Willis, John Woo, Jerry Zaks, Vilmos Zsigmond.

In Hollywood Barbara Paskin helped with contacts while Sandra Archer at the Motion Picture Academy library sent valuable information and cuttings. My thanks too to Ned Comstock at the University of Southern California, Ann Sparanese at the Englewood Public Library and the staff at the British Film Institute and the British Library's newspaper collection in Colindale. I am particularly grateful to Peter Cheek at the *Financial Times* library, who many times sent sackfuls of material downloaded from the *FT* memory banks.

For Bloomsbury Andrew McAllister did what any good editor should do: made pencil-marks that indicated pain at infelicities, suggested invaluable structural changes, and backed off when I wouldn't budge over particular follies or fancies.

I never spoke to John Travolta, nor was it ever a strong aim to do so. My efforts were confined to one casual remark to Jonathan Krane that his client might like to talk when the mood took him, though I was fairly sure the mood never would. All parties were happy with that. Travolta avoided becoming involved with a loose-cannon biographer, I avoided becoming mush in the hands of a man who, if this book reveals nothing else, is shown to be a master at making interviewers melt in his presence.

Nigel Andrews, February 1998

SOURCES

INTRODUCTION. 'The whole teenybopper-slash-disco.' *Variety* 7/3/96 by F.X. Feeney.

PART ONE

CHAPTER 1. Hudson River and Sunshine Sisters, *Current Biography* 10/78; Thornton Wilder, *Village Voice* 19/12/77 and Paramount notes *Saturday Night Fever*; Sam Snr details, Current Biog. 10/78; parents' courtship, *McCalls* 7/78 by Barbara Grizzuti Harrison and others; Englewood social history, Michael Roth to author; house details, *McCalls* 7/78, *Las Vegas Sun* 21/8/78 by Michael Reeves, and Eddie Costenuic to author; Margaret Travolta quote, *Hearst Company Redbook* 2/93; 'I started looking', *Rolling Stone* 18/8/83 by Nancy Collins; 'I'm throwing myself', *Good Housekeeping* 9/78 by Sheila Walker; cross talk, *McCalls* 7/78 and R. Stone 10/7/80 by Timothy White; 'I was a brat', *L.V. Sun* 21/8/78; dressing up, *Daily Mirror* 5/3/96 and others; Sam's theatre, *Hearst Redbook* 2/93; Cagney, *Playboy* 12/78, *R. Stone* 10/7/80; 'Gypsy', *McCalls* 7/78 and G. *H'keeping* 9/78; 4th July Twist, G. *H'keeping* 9/78 and *Allentown Morning Call* 2/12/95; Catholicism, *The Big Question*, BBC TV 25/1/98; 'Bones', *L.V. Sun* 21/8/78; Mars Bars, *Time* 3/4/78; Peter Pan, G. *H'keeping* 9/78 and P'mount notes *Fever*; 'Why is the sky blue?', *Current Biog* 10/78; 'I'd dream', *L.A. Herald-Examiner* 5/12/78; Ellen and Margaret quotes, *Premiere* 8/96 by Holly Millea; Sam's plane, *L.V. Sun* 21/8/78; bedroom, *Playboy* 3/96 by Judson Klinger; Audi, *Photoplay* 12/81; air tickets and 'I think it's the aesthetics', *Premiere* 8/96; birthday flight, *San Antonio Light* 10/7/83 by Jane Ardmore; 'I always had', Playgirl 3/77 by Cameron Crowe; 'I was a bit', *Current Biog* 10-78; 'He was

very goodlooking,' Donna Munday to author; 'telling a neighbour,' *Playboy* 12/78; Sam building things, *Playboy* 3/96; politics, protest, clothes and Mary Jo story, *Playboy* 12/78; drugs, black friends, sex, soul, kiss, *R. Stone* 18/8/83; Denise, *R. Stone* 22/2/96 by Fred Schruers; dance story, *Daily Mirror* 5/3/96; 'Even after they'd', *R. Stone* 18/8/83; waiting up for mum, *L.A. Times* 19/7/81; odd jobs, *McCalls* 7/78 and *Ladies Home Journal* 6/79 by Al Coombes; 'I think we went,' Kenneth Sarfin to author; Actors Studio, *Current Biog* 10/78 and *Grease* playbill; 'How do you go back,' *Time* 24/7/76; Bonnie and Clyde, *McCalls* 7/85 by Barbara Grizzuti Harrison; 'Growing up, if I', *People* 24/6/78; 'When I was,' *R. Stone* 18/8/83; 'He wanted me', *G. H'keeping* 2/97.

CHAPTER 2. Allenberry details, 'He was an honest' and all John Heinze quotes, Heinze to author; 'I was dragged,' *TV Guide* 4/11/78; 'I have a Kabuki,' *Hollywood Reporter* John Travolta issue 6/3/96; 'Don't make an entrance,' *John and Diana* by Mary Ann Norbum; 'He was very shy,' Rogene Schmiedel to author; off-Broadway plays, *Photoplay* 1/79; 'John and I' and all Jeff Conaway quotes to author; commercials and film try-outs, *McCalls* 1/78; 'It was very affecting,' Nik Cohn to author; 'I'd read a number,' Lynn Stalmaster to author; TV roles, *Grease* playbill and others; 'He was all over' and all Tom Moore quotes to author; 'Bob said,' *Playboy* 3/96; *Grease* genesis and all Jim Jacobs quotes to author; 'There was a young' and all Jerry Zaks quotes to author; 'He was like,' Judy Kaye to author; 'I felt we were' and all Patricia Birch quotes to author; Denise breakup, *G. H'keeping* 9/78; 'met on November 28th' and all Marilu Henner quotes from Henner autobiography *By All Means Keep On Moving* co-written by Jim Jerome; Andrews Sisters, *New York Times* 21/12/74; Earheart gift, Kaye to author.

CHAPTER 3. 'a piece of shit,' *Playgirl* 7/85; 'I was on a thin,' *Entertainment* 7/10/84; 'I went outside,' *Playgirl* 7/85; Le Mond conflict, *Photoplay* 7/79; 'I was just,' *Buffalo News* 23/10/94; 'The title alone,' *Ent't'ment* 7/10/84; 'I was so impressed,' *The Big Question*, BBC TV 25/1/98; 'He said, "It's" ' etc, Jeff Conaway to author; 'I had to,' Gary Pudney to author; 'There were other,' Stalmaster to author; 'when we were casting' and all Marcia Strassman quotes, Strassman to author; 'It started off' etc, Ron Palillo to author; fan worship, Englewood, *McCalls* 7/78; 'The public went,' Pudney to author; 'By about December,' *Playgirl*

3/77; 'He's a Fifties,' *Las Vegas Sun* 21/8/78; Bob Reno, *Seventeen* 10/76 and *Voice* 19/12/78; chart hits, *Current Biog* 10/78; 'Within the realm,' *Photoplay* 1/79; mobbed by fans, *Current Biog* 10/78 and *The Time* 24/7/76; 'That's what you,' *G. H'keeping* 9/78; concert tour, *R. Stone* 15/6/78 by Tom Burke and *N.Y. Times* 11/12/77; 'Bus Stop', *The Time* 24/7/67; 'He had two' etc, Nancy Allen to author; 'He used Scientology,' *Chicago Tribune* 30/6/96.

CHAPTER 4. 'It was a boy' etc, Joe Morgenstern to author; 'You don't look,' *Modern Screen* 3/77; 'it sort of grew' and all Glynis O'Connor quotes, O'Connor to author; 'I had no idea' and all Randal Kleiser quotes to author; 'I never said,' *Premiere* 8/96; 'I thought that if,' *Interview* 1/85; 'The relationship with Strassman to author; Diana romance, *Screen Stars* 1/78, *Photoplay* 2/78; R. Stone 22/2/96 and *John and Diana* by Mary Ann Norbum inter al; 'The age thing,' *R. Stone* 18/8/83; 'I never said,' *Premiere* 8/96; 'Sometimes I feel,' *People* 13/6/77; 'His early start,' *Time* 19/12/77; 'I don't know,' *L.V. Sun* 21/8/78; 'was a real', *Cosmopolitan* 9/78 by Tom Burke; 'John is probably' and Diana's decorating, *Motion Picture* 6/77; 'I made note' and all Robert Stigwood quotes to author; Cohn story background, *Daily Mail* 21/3/78 by Anthea Disney; 'It was incompetent,' Nik Cohn to author; Diana and *Fever* script, *Cosmo* 9/78; Deney Terrio, *San Francisco Chronicle* 31/8/78 by Joseph Torchia; 'I wrote *Saturday*' and all Norman Wexler quotes to author; 'Norman lived in,' Kevin McCormick to author; 'We were talking,' *Observer* 19/3/78 by J. J. Buck; disco field trip, *R. Stone* 15/6/78 by Tom Burke; 'On the first occasion' etc, Patrizia Von Brandenstein to author; 'After the third show' and all Dick Van Patten quotes to author; 'I felt my scalp,' *U.S.* 7/95 by L. Van Buskirk; Zinn as decoy, John Badham to author; 'Surely not' etc, Ralf Bode to author; 'They came to me' and all Father Curtis quotes to author; Warhol incident, *R. Stone* 22/2/96 and *Andy Warhol Diaries*.

Dick Van Patten tells a story he insists is true, but which could not be corroborated by available witnesses, about the aftermath of Diana Hyland's death. He claims that since it was legally impossible for anyone to sign a release for Diana's cremation except her estranged husband – not John Travolta nor even Diana's mother – Van Patten had to drive over, with Travolta as passenger and

in convoy with the undertakers' car carrying Diana's body, to the house of Joseph Goodson (the husband). Goodson refused to sign the release, however, on the grounds that he did not know Diana was definitely dead. Van Patten said Goodson could go right outside and look, but Goodson agreed to sign only after a long argument and after receiving a go-ahead by phone from his lawyer. 'Van Patten says Travolta was present during this argument, though mostly silent and looking in shock. Van Patten came out 'with my knees shaking. It was the most horrible experience of my life.'

CHAPTER 5. James Taylor story, *Playboy* 3/96; 'When I woke,' *McCalls* 7/78; 'It was quite unexpected,' and all John Badham quotes, Badham to author; 'I remember' and all Ralf Bode quotes to author; 'When the girl,' *Guardian* 15/10/81 by Brenda Polan; 'Did I look right?', Karen Lynn Gorney to author; 'I remember thinking' and all Donna Pescow quotes to author; 'They drove him,' Kevin McCormick to author; 'Watching Tony,' *San Francisco Chronicle* 5/1/78; glass floor and smoke, Badham to author; rocking trailer, *Time* 19/12/77; 'My response,' *R. Stone* 15/6/78; 'The character's underwater,' *TV Guide* 4/11/78; 'Romance?', Gorney to author; *Fever* party, *Glasgow Herald* 18/5/78; 'Literally that movie,' Strassman to author; 'To this day,' *Chicago Tribune* 10/7/83; 'The look I created,' *Premiere* 112/81 by Judson Klinger; mismatched cuffs, People 21/6/76; fan mail, *Village Voice* 19/12/77; tycoon's daughter, *L.A. Herald-Examiner* 12/11/76; 'Pa, please don't,' *McCalls* 7/78; 'If we had,' *TV Guide* 1/1/77; Sam Snr on JT's clothes, Eddie Costenuic to author; Cameron Crowe interview, *Playgirl* 3/77; 'John was very,' Jeff Conaway to author.

CHAPTER 6. 'It was considered,' and all Allan Carr quotes, Carr to author; 'I wanted to,' and all Patricia Birch quotes to author; 'The writer of the screenplay' and all Randal Kleiser quotes to author; *People* magazine issue, 13/6/77 by Martha Smilgis; 'I put a walk in,' *Premiere* 12/81; 'I said, "Wait" ' etc, Jeff Conaway to author; 'If I was to play' and all Olivia Newton-John quotes to author; 'The growing, glowing,' *Modern Screen* 10/77; Georgeanne La Pierre, *Screen Stars* 1/78; It was a statement,' Donna Pescow to author; Time letters, *Time* 24/4/78; fan club, *TV Guide* 10/6/78; high schools, N.Y. *Times* 29/4/78 by Angela Taylor; Roger Blaha, *People* 24/4/78; 'Is John Travolta', Walter Scott 21/5/78; 'He dropped by,' *Photoplay* 2/78; 'It was

shortly,' Jerry Zaks to author; 'Warren and I' etc, Jim Jacobs to author.

CHAPTER 7. Helen at Oscars, *McCalls* 7/78; Cadillac and wedding, Eddie Costenuic to author; 'She kept looking,' *McCalls* 7/85; Paris and Antibes, *People* 17/4/78 and *San Antonio Light* 10/7/83; Helen's death, *Ladies Home Journal* 6/79; secret funeral, *Variety* 6/12/78; surgeon quarrel, *R. Stone* 1/8/83; 'When my mother', *Photoplay* 9/85; 'Lily was doing' and all Robert Stigwood quotes, Stigwood to author; 'Lily was coming off' and all Kevin McCormick quotes to author; I was so excited,' *L.A. Times* 16/12/77; 'With marriage' and Wagner directing, *L.A. Times* 6/8/78; Wagner directing and 'It was like being,' *Los Angeles* 2/79; 'I saw the dailies' and all Ralf Bode quotes to author; 'has every dichotomy' and 'You have to watch', *Moment by Moment* press release; 'When Warren Casey,' Jim Jacobs to author; *Grease* foreign titles, *Daily Mirror* 14/8/78; 'I was frightened,' *D. Mirror* 10/6/80; 'The fans were going,' Olivia Newton-John to author; 'People were pushing,' Randal Kleiser to author; Hawaii, *Film Comment* 8/95; 'in a pair,' *Good Housekeeping* 9/78; 'He was still,' *People* 14/10/94; Astaire ball, *People* 27/2/78; Williams joke, Danny DeVito to author; White House invitation, *Variety* 10/10/78; 'He's nothing like,' Pauline Kael to author; 'That's John,' Marcia Strassman to author; 'The eyes are,' *Washington Post* 26/12/77; 'There's no way,' *Variety* 13/12/78; 'I wanted this,' *Cosmopolitan* 9/78; 'I was from,' *Observer* 2/10/94 by Miranda Sawyer; 'People laughed,' *D. Mirror* 10/6/80; 'Sometimes I think,' *L.A. Times* 2/12/79; 'Sometimes I feel,' *Playboy* 12/78; 'I bet I could,' *Playboy* 12/78; 'Different people,' *Cosmo* 9/78; 'After Moment,' *Chicago Tribune* 1/6/80; Armani suits, *Variety* 15/9/78 and *Midnight Globe* 24/10/78; Lederer, *people* 23/10/78; 'The dialogue' and 'Kay, I have,' *McCalls* 7/85; Eisner meeting, *Interview* 8/94 by Rosanna Arquette; 'He had had' etc, Paul Schrader to author; photographer beating, *Ladies Home Journal* 6/79; 'It's been said,' *D. Mirror* 10/6/80; 'Only one joy,' *N.Y. Times* 29/6/79; 'I would just be,' *Chi. Trib.* 1/6/80.

CHAPTER 8. 'I was very surprised,' *L.A. Times* 10/7/78; 'Because I'm so,' *Premiere* 12/81; 'You have to play,' *Rolling Stone* 10/7/80; 'In these anxious,' *Esquire* 9/79; 'We have a need,' *N.Y. Times* 8/10/80; mechanical bull, *L.A. Herald-Examiner* 8/6/80; 'I'm making one,' *After Dark* 6/80; 'I cannot make,' *People* 24/6/85; fan mania. Marquee 5/80 by George Anthony; Fonda's visit, *Sun* 10/10/79; 'He was still' and all Aaron Latham quotes, Latham to author; 'I've never seen',

After Dark 6/80; 'The press relations' and dances, *L.A. Times* 9/4/80 by Lee Grant; gun attack, *U.S.* 11/12/79; injured extra, *L.A. Times*; 'I'm a person' etc, *R. Stone*, 10/7/80; 'Everyone wants a piece,' *Good Housekeeping* 2/97; Travolta siblings, *L.A. Times* 13/1/80 by Ellen Farley; Scientology, *R. Stone* 10/7/80; 'It isn't going,' *L.A. Times* 18/3/80; 'With a newspaper,' *People* 13/6/80; 'John's a worrywort,' *Newsweek* 9/6/80; 'I've gotten this,' *Life* 7/80; 'I'm not saying,' *Daily Mirror* 10/6/80; meeting Cagney, *Newsweek* 9/6/80, *R. Stone* 10/7/80 and *Life* 7/80; return visit, *Variety* 9/6/80; 'My favourite time' and 'glamour shots', *Newsweek* 9/6/80; thighs retouched, *Life* 7/80; bull boom, *N.Y. Times* 8/10/80; Bruce Lehrke, *Variety* 6/8/80; 'I created several,' *Interview* 7/94; 'I was starting,' Henner autobiog; falling mansion, *People* 20/5/85; Cessna, *Life* 7/80.

CHAPTER 9. Spruce Goose, *Photoplay* 12/81 by Marianne Gray and *Films and Filming* 12/81 by Carrie Amata; De Palma and Travolta quotes, *Films and Filming* 12/81; Ford and Gere considered, George Litto to author; 'The most amazing,' *Chicago Tribune* 1/2/81; colour palette, Vilmos Zsigmond to author;'The structure never' and all Nancy Allen quotes, Allen to author; chaise longue and 'Now of course', *Photoplay* 12/81; 'The film was committed,' Litto to author; Ellison walkout, *Variety* 2/9/81; 'nudity, violence,' *Variety* 8/7/81; '*Blow Out* is doing,' *Daily Mirror* 14/9/81; 'The highbrow critics,' *Photoplay* 12/81; 'I know I've lived,' *News of the World* 14/12/81; 'I get up there,' *D. Mirror* 14/9/81; 'I just want to,' *N.Y. Times* 10/7/83; 'Friends, Romans,' *D. Mirror* 20/9/83; 'It's almost as if,' *James Stewart* by Donald Dewey; 'You get in,' *Clint Eastwood* by Richard Shickel; violin, *News of the World*, 14/2/81; French lessons and Depardieu, *Photoplay* 12/81; Brooke Shields, *Screen* by K. McMurran; 'We had something,' *R. Stone* 18/8/83; Fonda lunch, *Good Housekeeping* 9/78; Capra remake, *Premiere* 12/81; 'We gave the project,' Litto to author; 'I was getting,' *San Antonio Light* 10/7/83; Aspen play, *L.A. Times* 14/8/82.

CHAPTER 10. 'I wrote a version' and all Norman Wexler quotes, Wexler to author; Travolta and Ovitz, *N.Y. Times* 10/7/83 and *U.S.* 15/8/83; 'There came a point,' *Playboy* 3/96; 'Absolutely. It became,' Robert Stigwood to author; 'When you're not,' *N.Y. Times* 10/7/83; 'How would you like,' *L.A. Times* 11/2/83; mirror-lined tent, *U.S.* 15/8/83; 'I was not in good,' *Photoplay* 9/85; 'El Cordobes,' *Dance* 8/83; 'No one could have' and following, *R. Stone* 18/8/83; weight and diet, *Time* 7/3/83; hair-waxing and 'He's purified,' *McCalls* 7/83; 'more people know,' *U.S.* 15/8/83; Frank Stallone, *Chicago Tribune*

10/7/83; 'Sly didn't think,' *Photoplay* 1/84; 'which we found' and
'There's nothing like,' *Chi. Trib.* 10/7/83; 'The film was hard,' *L.A.
Times* 14/7/83; *Rolling Stone* int'view, 18/8/83; 'We're sitting here,'
Premiere 12/81; 'Etes-vous narcissistique?', *Paris Match* 2/9/83; 'I
was upset,' *San Antonio Light* 10/7/83; 'Sure we live,' *D. Mirror*
20/9/83; 'My bonds to Johnny,' Henner autobiog; 'In a lot of ways,'
Photoplay 9/85; 'So you don't mind,' *Interview* 6/85; 'By the end,'
Playboy 3/96.

CHAPTER 11. 'If that guy,' *GQ* 10/95 by Tom Junod; 'The film has
elements,' *San Francisco Chronicle* 24/12/83; 'I really chose,' *L.A.
Times* 11/2/83; 'If you don't do,' *Variety* 25/7/83; 'I like myself,'
Time 23/5/83; 'I wouldn't do,' *Variety* 25/7/83; poster change, *L.A.
Times* 16/12/83; 'This kind of thing,' *Variety* 9/12/83; 'Some of my
biggest' and 'It's rather like,' *L.A. Times* 11/12/83; 'James and I' and
all Aaron Latham quotes, Latham to author; Truffaut, Malle etc,
Photoplay 1/83; 'a riches-to-rags' and 'The story just flowed,' *S.F.
Chronicle* 30/7/84; 'the consequences,' 'It's an ensemble' and 'It's not
a technical', *Film Comment* 8/95; 'It was when things,' Stalmaster to
author; 'I was going to,' *People* 24/6/85; inflight menu, *Time* 24/6/85;
'The heart of rock' and 'Take a letter', People 24/6/85; 'You should
do,' Olivia Newton-John to author; 'Debra was climbing,' JT's *Rolling
Stone* diary; Jann Wenner casting, *S.F. Chronicle* 30/6/85 and *Chicago
Tribune* 2/6/85; 'I can cite,' *L.A. Herald Examiner* 20/6/85; 'We've
never rewritten,' *L.A. Weekly* 7/6/85; 'I could write with,' Columbia
press notes *Perfect*; 'I'm going to tell,' *R. Stone* 16/8/84; 'It's about
how' and Chippendales contest, *L.A. Weekly Perfect* supplement
30/5/85; 'It's very hard,' *L.A. Weekly* 7/6/85; 'I'm always using,'
Washington Post 6/6/81; real-life role models, *S.F. Chronicle* 11/6/85;
'aerobic love scenes,' Curtis poem, 'Lack of style' and 'Oh I've grown
up,' *L.A. Weekly* 7/6/85.

CHAPTER 12. Christofferson case, *San Francisco Chronicle* 21/5/85,
L.A. Herald-Examiner 21/5/85 and *Observer* 9/6/85; 'I was exterior'
etc, *Playgirl* 7/85; Goldberg film and 'I talked to', *S.F. Chronicle*
27/1/86; drunk driving, *Detroit Free Press* 21/6/87; *Far From Home,
Daily Mail* 25/10/83; 'It wasn't anything,' *N.Y. Times* 10/5/87; 'What
happens to,' *New Republic* 24/6/85; Jonathan Krane background,
Krane to author and *N.Y. Times* 4/22/88; Princess Diana, *N.Y.
Times* 11/11/85, *Washington Post* 26/8/89 and *Oprah Winfrey Show*
27/12/96; 'Unlike most Americans,' *News of the World* 14/2/81; 'I
don't believe,' *Rolling Stone* 10/7/80; healing Sting, *The Big Question*,

BBC TV 25/1/98; weight change, *L.B. Press-Telegram* 30/7/88; 'got intimate,' *Playboy* 3/96; 'At the wrap,' *Good Housekeeping* 2/97; 'John is snatching,' *Evening Standard* 18/4/89; *Experts* to video and 'I called over', *Wash. Post* 26.8.89; 'I arranged,' *N.Y. Times* 10/5/87 and Gary Pudney to author;'I would never,' *Northern New Jersey Record* 4/10/94; 'Altman rang me' and all Tom Conti quotes, Conti to author; 'What if your character,' *Variety* 7/3/96; 'pale and ill-at-ease' and 'I am not obsessed,' *Daily Mail* 26/5/87 by Baz Bamigboye; 'He never got,' Krane to author; Travolta and *Time, D. Mail* 17/1/87; 'It's a Knockout,' *People* 6/7/87 and *Sunday Telegraph* 16/10/94; Catherine Deneuve, *Today* 15/9/87. 'I'm rebuilding,' *D. Mail* 26/5/87.

PART TWO

PRELUDE. 'Project Celebrity', *L.A. Times* 25/6/80 by Joel Sappell and Robert W. Wilkes.

CHAPTER 1. Spruce Creek details, *Time* 13/11/89 and Anne Busse to author; JT's dogs, *Premiere* 3/90; 'a cross between' and eight Dobermans, *L.B. Press-Telegram* 20/2/88; 'is so hard-edged,' *Washington Post* 26/8/89; 'The key word,' *L.A. Times* 19/3/89; final night filming, *L.B. Press-Telegram* 23/4/88; 'A man is over,' Hollywood reporter 23/2/88; dog rumpus, *Variety* 21/6/89 and 11/9/90;'The company backing it' and all Jonathan Krane quotes, Krane to author; Rivers lines, *L.A. Herald-Examiner* 17/10/89; 'in the early drafts' and all Amy Heckerling quotes to author; 'The baby wrangler,' *Daily Mirror* 3/4/90; Canada child laws, *Hollywood Reporter* 25/9/91; 'I'm fairly big,' *Wash. Post* 26/8/89; Kirstie Alley background, *U.S.* 11/3/85, *Good Housekeeping* 3/90, *Today* 16/11/90 and *Walter Scott* 23/12/90; 'John told me,' *L.A. Herald-Examiner* 4/10/89; 'I don't know why' etc, *Playboy* 3/98; 'I've just cast,' *Wash. Post* 26/8/89; 'It wouldn't have been,' *Time* 18/11/89; Columbia hit, *Variety* 27/495; 'I have this theory' and *Fever* fans, *Wash. Post* 26/8/89; 'A waiter enters,' *Independent on Sunday* 8/4/90; 'Fat-urday Night Fever,' *Sun* 2/4/90; Cruise roadwork and fitness, *Scotsman* 5/4/90 and *Evening Standard* 2/4/90; Bigelow and food crackdown, *Premiere* 3/90; 'I don't know,' *Wash. Post* 26/8/89; *Chains* rewrites, *Hollywood Reporter* 24/7/89 and Henner autobiog.

CHAPTER 2. Kelly Preston background, *Playboy* 3//96 and *Screen* by Scott Haller; 'her marriage was,' *Parade* 22/10/95 by Dotson Rader; George Clooney, *People* 21/1/91; 'I think she really,' *Premiere* 8/96;

Giffoni trip, *Hollywood Reporter* 1/8/91; 'When I first got,' Jonathan Krane to author; train crash, *Today* 3/8/91; 'I was flying high' and 'I thought about becoming,' *Times Supplement* 16/3/96 by Garth Pierce; 'I was afraid,' *Time Out* 21/6/96 by Jan Janssen; 'I thought "Wouldn't",' *Mail on Sunday* 'You' magazine 31/7/94; 'Every day,' *Independent on Sunday* 8/4/90 by Simon Garfield; 'He invited thirty' etc, Krane to author; 'It was very rushed' etc, Amy Heckerling to author; LWT2 party, *U.S.* 7/2/91; 'We thought "Why",' *Premiere* 8/96; 'I knew we'd get,' *Hearst Company Redbook* 2/93; Scientology minister, *Today* 7/10/91; wedding night and breakfast, *Paris Match* 19/9/91; Gulfstream dispute, Reuter 8/3/93 and Stephen Ponder to author; Penobscot purchase, *John Travolta: Back in Character* by Wensley Clarkson; baby's birth, *People* 27/4/92.

CHAPTER 3. Gulfstream crisis based extensively on *Washington Post* feature 'Staying Alive' by Mike James 26/3/92; failing controls, *Daily Telegraph* 11/12/92; 'I was never', 'I noticed' and 'People came down', *Playboy* 3/96; burst tyres, *Evening Standard* 3/12/92; 'I spoke to,' *D. Telegraph* 11/12/92; 'One of the restrictions,' Stephen Ponder to author; 'I developed,' Amy Heckerling to author; 'We thought a talking,' Jonathan Krane to author; Travolta baby, *Hearst Company Redbook* 2/93; naming Jett, *Paris Match* 24/9/92; *Grease* reunion, *L.A. Times* 19/12/92; 'I sleep until noon,' *Hearst Co. Redbook* 2/93; Losing *The Player*, 'There was a moment' and 'Robert called me,' *USA Today* 9/2/96; 'I started to lose,' *U.S.* 7/95.

PART THREE

CHAPTER 1. 'My partner in Jersey Films' and all Danny DeVito quotes, DeVito to author. 'I don't make movies' and Tarantino/*Pulp Fiction* background, *Empire* special anniversary issue 1997; 'The whole teenybopper,' *Variety* 7/3/96 by F.X. Feeney; 'I didn't know' and all Jonathan Krane quotes to author; apartment coincidence, *Premiere* 8/96; Four Seasons lunch, *Entertainment* 11/10/94; board games, *Interview* 8/94; 'I said to Quentin,' *Northern New Jersey Record* 4/10/94; 'What did you *do*?' etc, *Cosmopolitan* 1/96 by Michael Segall; PULP fee, *Interview* 8/94; 'I was saying,' *Sunday Times* magazine 26/2/95 by Martin Amis; 'I wanted to show,' *Cosmo* 1/96; 'I said either,' *Empire* 11/94; 'We were sitting,' *Entertainment* 11/10/94; 'right up there,' *Entertainment* 7/10/94; 'I love directors,' *Playboy* 3/96; 'The reason Quentin,' *Hollywood Reporter* special Travolta issue 6/3/96; 'It was a really,' *Observer* 21/10.94; 'We

rehearsed' and all Samuel L. Jackson quotes to author; 'As it was written,' *Playboy* 3/96;"That scene gave me,' *Buffalo News*; 'I went behind,' *U.S.* 12/95; 'My Dad's 82,' *Ottawa Citizen* 12/10/94.

CHAPTER 2. Beverly Hills home, *L.A. Times* 30/10//94; 'I told Weinstein,' *Empire* special issue 1997; Tarantino to projection booth and 'two seizures a week', *Rolling Stone* 26/1/95; chef Tarantino, *N.Y. Times* 13/2/95; 'The scene was ridiculous' etc, *New York* 12/12/95; 'It was like' and 'You know the scene,' *Observer* 2/10/94; 'This is quintessential,' *Playboy* 3/96; 'His jaw did not,' *Guardian Weekend* 17/9/94; Siskel suit, *People* 3/7/94; airplane choosiness, *Time Out* 2/11/94 and *Guardian Weekend* 17/9/94; inflight videos, *L.A. Times* 15/9/94; Jett and *Grease*, *L.A. Daily News* 25/10/94; Alley's pets, *People* 14/10/94; *Get Shorty* sweeteners, *Hollywood Reporter* 12/8/94 and *Buffalo News* 23/10/94; 'I wanted to go back,' *L.A. Times* 19/3/95; standing read, *N.Y. Times* 6/2/95; 'When I read,' *U.S.* 12/95; 'He did *White*,' Jonathan Krane to author; 'When I first' and all Desmond Nakano quotes, Nakano to author; $7m budget, *Variety* 22/11/95; Belafonte and *Burden*, *San Francisco Chronicle* 26/11/95; 'I've never played,' *Allentown Morning Call* 2/12/95; white vs black response, *L.A. Times* 20/11/95; 'I was in a car' and all Danny DeVito quotes to author; 'At that time' and all Barry Sonnenfeld quotes to author; Beatty refusal, *S.F. Chronicle* 15/10/95; 'I liked the idea,' *Playboy* 3/96; 'Quentin said to me,' *USA Today* 9/2/96; 'so fabulous,' *Playboy* 3/96; 'In the original,' *Time* 16/10/95; 'He went down,' *U.S.* 7/95; 'Violins and the French horn,' *Parade* 22/10/95; 'I've been touched,' *Milwaukee Journal* 12/11/95; 'I'm driving down,' *Allentown Morning Call* 2/12/95; 'I'd gone knee-deep,' *Parade* 22/10/95; 'He has a Zen,' *Variety* 7/96; 'I didn't expect,' *GQ* 10/95; MTV hug, *Mail on Sunday* 'You' magazine 19/11/95.

CHAPTER 3. 'You could run' and all Barry Sonnenfeld quotes, Sonnenfeld to author; Palmer on set, *Mail on Sunday* 28/1/96; 'Give me a thought' etc, *Allentown Morning Call* 2/12/95; 'He's a very cool,' *Daily Mail* 23/2/96; 'I'll usually take,' *Playboy* 3/96; deer browsing, *Milwaukee Journal* 12/11/95; Maine mansion rooms and 'This is Wonderland,' *Cosmopolitan* 1/96; 'I work to keep,' *Today* 3/10.94; Carmel house, *Northern New Jersey Record* 4/10/94; 'Baby Bop,' *Milwaukee Journal* 12/11/95; 'It was like I blinked,' *Vogue* 10/94 by Nik Cohn; 'That little boy,' *Allentown Morning Call* 2/12/95; 'I love the selflessness,' *Cosmo* 1/96, 'It was in Clearwater' etc, Mike Newell to author; 'I wanted a normal' and all John Woo quotes to author; 'Oh man, am I bad,' *Ralegh News* 23/10/95; dieting, *Mail on Sunday*

'You' magazine 19/11/95; 'I went to some bases,' *Hollywood Reporter* special JT issue 6/3/96; 'I observed,' *Irish Times* 23/3/96; Slater's past and 'hand jive,' *Entertainment Today* 15/2/96; 'He is the first,' *Orange Co. Register* 9/2/96; barnstorming, *Cosmo* 1/96; weaponry, *Broken Arrow* press notes; Travolta and Tom Hanks, *Evening Standard* 15/3/95; 'On Oscar night,' *USA Weekend* 20/12/96.

CHAPTER 4. Sam Snr's death, *Variety* 12/6/95; 'I've learned that' and 'It was never about', *Rolling Stone* 22/2/96; 'I get very,' *Entertainment* 7/6/96; 'Everything I've had' and 'You once made,' *Irish Times* 23/3/96 by Sheila Johnston; 'I learned a lesson,' John Woo to author; 'He moves, he stands,' *Independent on Sunday* 3/3/96; 'I thought Travolta' and all Mike Newell quotes, Newell to author; *Nick of Time*, John Badham to author; 'I walked in' and all Jon Turteltaub quotes to author; 'George is a guy,' *Scotland on Sunday* 4/8/96 by Richard Mowe; 'Life was better,' *Sunday Mirror* 4/8/96; 'I had a ranch' and all Gerald DiPego quotes to author; 'During one of,' *Chicago Tribune* 30/6/96; ice cream, *R. Stone* 22/2/96; 'On the set,' *Boston Globe* 6/7/96; 'I just sat,' Robert Duvall to author; Scientology cures, *Daily Telegraph* 25/7/96.

CHAPTER 5. 'Give us a fucking break,' *Time* 14/11/95; charities, *Chicago Tribune* 30/6/96; 'Take the Oklahoma,' *Playboy* 3/96; 'It's more like,' *Rolling Stone* 22/2/96; 'Scientology is not,' *Time Out* 21/2/96; 'It's done,' *Entertainment* 26/6/96; 'We're at the same,' *R. Stone* 22/2/96; 'He was a very sweet' etc, Nik Cohn to author; 'During those years,' Jon Turteltaub to author; 'It was an interrupted,' Richard Dreyfuss to author; comeback wannabes, *Wall Street Journal* 30/1/96; flyposting, *U.S.* 6/95; Warner offer, *Entertainment* 28/6/96; 'What if it came here,' *Daily Record* 18/7/96; 'Don't be fooled,' *Milwaukee Journal* 12/11/95; 'Oh he's such a,' *GQ* 10/95 by Tom Junod; 'There are two areas,' *R. Stone* 22/2/96; 'I don't mind,' *U.S.* 7/95; 'For me it became' and all Nora Ephron quotes, Ephron to author; Spielberg call, *U.S.* 7/95; 'I'd like to say,' *People* 23/12/96; Travolta dining, *Entertainment Weekly* 28/6/96; 'He's a warrior,' *Variety* 7/3/96; *Oprah Winfrey Show* 27/12/96; *The Double* details, Reuter 13/6/96, *Entertainment Weekly* 28/6/96, *Mail on Sunday* 30/6/96, *Guardian* 2/7/96 and *Daily Telegraph* 1/7/96; 'A *Being There* type,' *Sunday Mirror* 4/8/96; 'I negotiated,' *People* 3/11/96.

CHAPTER 6. Night flight and Jett illness, *Entertainment Weekly* 28/6/96; 'didn't have to,' *Good Housekeeping* 2/97; 'From the

beginning,' Reuter 25/7/96; 'Sure, there were' and all Roman Polanski quotes, Polanski to author; 'There were no naked,' Reuter 25/7/96; Travolta conditions, lawsuit and 'John never reached,' *Hollywood Reporter* 13/6/96; 'wanted to co-opt' and Lily Zanuck, *Guardian* 2/7/96; 'it had spread,' *Sunday Mirror* 4/8/96; script changes and 'If you were presented,' *Entertainment Weekly* 28/6/96; salvage attempts, *Daily Telegraph* 2/7/96 and *Guardian* 2/7/96; 'At this very moment' and all Arnold Kopelson quotes to author; 'The festival wanted' and all Costa-Gavras quotes to author; 'John and I,' John Woo to author.

CHAPTER 7. 'You need to have,' *Time Out* 21/2/96; 'Though they have' etc, *Good Housekeeping* 2/97; Jett roles, *Daily Mirror* 4/3/96; 'He really loves it,' *Good Housekeeping* 2/97; new beach house, *Orange Co. Register* 16/11/97; Brentwood house, *Vancouver Sun* 22/2/97; lawsuit, *Daily Record* 12/2/96 and *People* 26/12/96; 'My parents really' and I've seen her,' *Good Housekeeping* 2/97; 'We have been offered,' *Empire* 12/97; 'Look, I know,' *Mr Showbiz* 17/1/97; Golden Globe speech etc, *Movieline* 4/97 by Martha Frankel; Scientology furore, *Sunday Times* 15/9/96 and *Moving Pictures* 2/97; open letter, *Evening Standard* 14/1/97 and others; 'At least half,' *N.Y. Times* 25/1/97; 'Only Pat Robertson' etc, John Landis to author.

CHAPTER 8. 'There will be only' etc, John Woo to author; *Face/Off* back history, *Wall Street Journal* 6/8/97, *Empire* 10/97; Cage quotes and 'You're John,' *Neon* 12/97 by Rupert Howe; 'Most of their scenes,' *New Times L.A.* 26/6/97; 'Slowing things down,' *Neon* 12/97; 'When Nick speaks,' *Empire* 10/97; Friars roast, *USA Today* 16/6/97 and *Variety* 19/6/97; Cinematheque honour, Hollywood Reporter 16/7/97; *The Double* settlement, *L.A. Times* 13/7/97 and 24/7/97 and *Variety* 15/7/97; Diana dress, *L.A. Times* 26/6/97; naming child, *Daily Mail* 1/10/97; 'The written press,' Costa-Gravas to author; 'The film raises,' Kopelson to author.

CHAPTER 9. Actors reject role, *Daily Record* 13/6/97; 'Mike Nichols has sent,' *Mr Showbiz* 17/1/97; 'I absolutely didn't' and other cast comments, *Time* 18/8/97; 'Sci-Fi westerns,' *Variety* 22/7/97; Travolta projects, *People* 23/9/96, *Variety* 15/5/97, *Daily Telegraph* 12/6/97 and *Daily Mail* 13/6/97; *Phantom*, *Daily Mail* 15/7/97; *Battlefield Earth*, *Hollywood Reporter* 3/7/96 and others; Travolta testifies, Associated Press 18/9/97 and *Daily Telegraph* 20/9/97; 'John and I,' Gary Pudney to author; 'They came over' etc, Wensley Clarkson to author; 'He has an odd,' *McCalls* 7/85.

INDEX